# THE GOSPEL OF MATTHEW

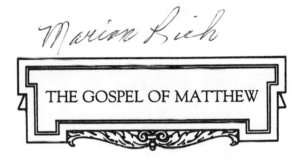

*Marion Lieh*

# THE GOSPEL OF MATTHEW

*William R. Cannon*

The Upper Room
Nashville, Tennessee

THE GOSPEL OF MATTHEW

Copyright © 1982 by The Upper Room

All rights reserved.

All scripture quotations are from the King James Version of the Bible.

Any scripture quotation designated AP is the author's paraphrase.

Book Design: John Robinson
First Printing: January, 1983 (10)
Library of Congress Catalog Card Number: 82-50948

**ISBN 0-8358-0450-X**

Printed in the United States of America

# Contents

Preface . . . . . . . . . . . . . . . . . . . . . . . . . . . . . . . . 7

Introduction . . . . . . . . . . . . . . . . . . . . . . . . . . . 9

1 · The Promised King *Matthew 1-4* . . . . . . . . 13

2 · The Teacher and His Pupils *Matthew 5-10* . . 30

3 · Jesus and the People *Matthew 11-18* . . . . . . 49

4 · Herald of the Kingdom *Matthew 19-20* . . . . 73

5 · King of the Jews *Matthew 21 25* . . . . . . . . . 87

6 · The King of Glory *Matthew 26-28* . . . . . . . . *107*

# Preface

atthew is the most comprehensive of the Gospels. It gives us a broader picture of the life and ministry of Jesus than any of the other three. Matthew is, therefore, the Gospel best designed for general use.

Though I had written earlier on Luke and Mark, I was especially pleased when Maxie Dunnam, then World Editor of The Upper Room, asked me to write on Matthew.

A United Methodist bishop is an itinerant. As chairman of the Executive Committee of the World Methodist Council, much of my itinerancy carries me outside my own episcopal area to various parts of the world. Consequently, much of this book was written while I was in Jerusalem and Galilee. I was in Tiberias when I wrote the section on the Sermon on the Mount. The Jerusalem School of Biblical Studies, in which I was engaged, is situated in the Old City, overlooking "Gordon's Calvary." Indeed, General C. G. Gordon was on the roof of this same building, reading the New Testament, when he associated the site which now bears his name with the place of the Crucifixion.

I hope that much of the inspiration I received in writing these pages in the land where Jesus lived will be conveyed to those who read them.

I am grateful to my gifted secretary, Mrs. Vivian Mitchell, for the care she took in deciphering my handwriting and in typing the manuscript for publication.

WILLIAM R. CANNON
Raleigh, North Carolina

# Introduction

The symbol of Matthew is a man, while the symbols of the other evangelists are animals and a bird: the lion of Mark, the ox of Luke, and the eagle of John. There is a reason why antiquity gave to each of the writers of the Gospels the symbol it did. Each symbol then had reference to a particular wording. But now, when we consider the purpose of the author and the nature of the document he produced, these ancient symbols do not convey the same meaning they conveyed to people of earlier times. We are interested in the impression the evangelist had of Jesus and his motif for the presentation he makes of his Lord. The four symbols are adequate enough collectively since they indicate the fourfold picture of Jesus recorded in the Gospels. Through them we see the same person but from different perspectives. However, in my opinion, they need to be reassigned.

The ox as a beast of burden belongs most appropriately to Mark, who sees Jesus as the servant of the God who sent him, while the man should be given to Luke, who presents Jesus to the Gentiles as the universal man. John's symbol of the eagle is still applicable, for to him Jesus is the divine word made flesh. Many lecterns in our churches carry the Bible on the back of the eagle.

The lion, however, belongs preeminently to Matthew. The lion is the king of beasts. Judah, also, is presented in the Old Testament in the form of a lion.

> Judah, thou art he whom thy brethren shall praise: thy hand shall be in the neck of thine enemies; thy father's children shall bow down before thee. Judah is a lion's whelp: from the prey, my son, thou art gone up: he stooped down, he couched as a lion, and as an old lion; who shall rouse him up? The sceptre shall not depart from Judah, nor a lawgiver from between his feet, until Shiloh come; and unto him shall the gathering of the people be. Binding his foal unto the vine, and his ass's colt unto the choice vine; he washed his garments in wine, and his clothes in the blood of grapes: His eyes shall be red with wine, and his teeth white with milk.
>
> —Genesis 49:8-12

Matthew's purpose is to present Jesus as the long-expected Messiah. He is the king who has been sent to rule his people. There is from start to finish a royal aspect to this Gospel. The nature of the first Gospel is the good news of prophetic fulfillment. That which was foretold long ago by the prophets has at last come about. Matthew's impression of Jesus is that he is of royal lineage, possesses divine authority, and has the prerogatives and powers of God. The Matthean motif in the presentation of Jesus is his inherent relationship to the Old Testament, showing he is not a contradiction to Judaism but rather the climax and completion of Judaic faith.

When Marcion in the second century tried to sever Christianity from its Hebrew origins and to disavow the Old Testament altogether, the Gospel he used was Luke's. After all, Luke had been written for the Gentiles.

But Matthew shows us that we could not have the New Testament if it were not for the Old Testament and that Jesus would not be Jesus if it were not for the God of Abraham, Isaac, and Jacob.

Matthew's is the most Jewish of all the Gospels. We are indebted to this book and its gifted author for maintaining Christianity's continuity with its past. Often, therefore, when Matthew narrates an important event in the life of Jesus, he calls the reader's attention to a prophecy in the Old Testament of which this event is the fulfillment. Indeed, Matthew has devised his own rubric for doing this, and he uses the same pattern each time. "Now," he says, "all this was done, that it might be fulfilled which was spoken of the Lord by the prophet" (Matt. 1:22). There are nine other specific instances of this in his Gospel (Matt. 2:15, 17, 23; 4:14; 8:17; 12:17; 13:35; 21:4; 27:9). But many more times than this Matthew makes allusions to various passages in the Old Testament as he tells his story.

The Gospel was obviously written by a Jew and one who knew his Old Testament well. One British

11

commentator thinks the book is decidedly anti-Jewish, anti-Semitic, as we would say today. I have not been able to detect this in my study of the Gospel. What the British commentator cites as his evidence of anti-Semitism impresses me as being pro-Jewish, an eagerness on the part of a converted Jew to convince his own people of the truth of the message of Jesus and to offer them his savior as their savior, too.

The Gospel of Matthew is probably the fullest and the most well rounded of the four. It is designed especially for use by the growing and expanding church. The early church put Matthew first in the New Testament canon, and it has remained in that position ever since. The early church assumed that it had been written first and by a disciple of Jesus.

There are very close similarities between Matthew and Mark. Most modern scholars, especially among the Protestants, believe that Mark antedates Matthew by twenty or thirty years and that the author of Matthew used Mark as his principal source. Others think that Mark is a condensation of Matthew from a different perspective. Be that as it may, each Gospel has its own special emphasis. Here in Matthew we meet our teacher and savior as King and Lord, before whom in the end every knee shall bow and every tongue shall confess him to be the rightful ruler over all.

## The Promised King
### Matthew 1-4

Chapters, sections, and paragraphs, such as our Bibles display, were unknown in antiquity; so that the divisions we make within the Gospels are artificial. They are ours, not the authors'.

Matthew uses the first few pages of his Gospel, which have been designated as the first four chapters, to introduce Jesus to the readers of his Gospel. Matthew wants us to know at the outset who Jesus is and why he is writing a book about him.

1. *Ancestry (Matt. 1:1-17)*—What better way to introduce a person than to describe that person's ancestry! Matthew, in keeping with the messianic theme of his Gospel, traces the ancestry of Jesus back to King David and also back to Abraham. The Messiah in Old Testament prophecy would come from the line, or lineage, of David. But before David, God had promised that from the seed of Abraham all the nations of the earth would be blessed. So Matthew opens his Gospel with the statement:

13

"The book of the generation of Jesus Christ, the son of David, the son of Abraham" (Matt. 1:1). This is an echo of what God said to David:

> And it shall come to pass, when thy days be expired that thou must go to be with thy fathers, that I will raise up thy seed after thee, which shall be of thy sons; and I will establish his kingdom. He shall build me an house, and I will stablish his throne for ever. I will be his father, and he shall be my son: and I will not take my mercy away from him, as I took it from him that was before thee: But I will settle him in mine house and in my kingdom for ever: and his throne shall be established for evermore.
>
> —1 Chronicles 17:11–14

This refers to Solomon and Solomon's successors. But the proof of its truthfulness had to await the coming of Jesus.

Luke traces the ancestry of Jesus back to Adam. That is because he wrote especially for the Gentiles and presented Jesus to them as the universal man. But Matthew felt it was enough when the genealogy of Jesus reached Abraham, for he sincerely believed that salvation for everybody would come only through the Jews. They were God's chosen people. God did not choose them just to favor them and bestow all benefits upon them. He chose the Jews to prepare and use them for the benefit of all others. "That in blessing I will bless thee, and in multiplying I will multiply thy seed as the stars of the heaven, and as the sand which is upon the sea shore; and thy seed shall possess the gate of his enemies; And in thy seed shall all the nations of the earth be blessed; because thou hast obeyed my voice" (Gen. 22:17-18). The nation faltered and fell. The earthly successors to David and Solomon on the throne of Judah were no more. Nonetheless, the work of God had not been invalidated, nor God's promise forfeited. The Messiah had come. He was of the race of Abraham and of the family of David.

> For unto us a child is born, unto us a son is given: and the government shall be upon his shoulder: and his name shall be called Wonderful, Counsellor, The mighty God, The everlasting Father, The Prince of Peace. Of the increase of his government and peace there shall be no end, upon the throne of David, and upon his kingdom, to order it, and to establish it with judgment and with justice from henceforth even for ever. The zeal of the Lord of hosts will perform this.
>
> —Isaiah 9:6-7

Matthew divides the genealogy of Jesus into three historical eras consisting of fourteen generations apiece. The first era is from Abraham to David, the second from David to the captivity of Judah and the exile of the Jews in Babylon, and the third from the captivity to the birth of Jesus. Each of these three eras has special significance. The first is a period of formation: the development of a small clan into a large society of people; the unification of disparate tribes into a nation; migration in and out of slavery, through the wilderness, and into the land of prom-

15

ise. The second is a period of fulfillment and deterioration: the grandeur of David and the glory of Solomon, followed by deterioration and decline under their successors. The third is a period of patience, long-suffering, and expectancy: the captivity and exile, the return and temporary restoration of the nation, and subjugation by Rome.

Within these periods there are three arresting pieces of information. Matthew does not mention the wife of Abraham, the mother of Isaac. Nor does he include the wife of Jesse, the mother of David, or give the wife of Josiah, the mother of Josiah's son who was king when Jerusalem fell. He omits the names of the women throughout the whole genealogy before Joseph and Mary except for three persons. He says that the mother of Pharez and Zarah was Tamar and their father was Judah, and he calls our attention to the fact that the mother of Boaz was Rahab and that Ruth was the wife of Boaz and the mother of Obed, who was the grandfather of David. Why are these three women included when all the others are not?

Tamar was Judah's daughter-in-law. Her husband had died. The younger brother of her husband failed to honor his obligation to take her as his wife and rear children in honor of the deceased. So Tamar disguised herself as a harlot and tricked her father-in-law into committing adultery with her, and the offspring of this act of adultery were twins, Pharez and Zarah (Gen. 38:6-30). Salmon's wife who bore his son Boaz was Rahab, the harlot of Jericho, who concealed and protected the Israelite spies

16

(Josh. 2; 6:22–27). And Ruth was not Jewish. She was a Moabitess, a foreigner, a woman from a despised enemy of Israel (Ruth 1:4).

There are skeletons in the closet of every family, no matter how respectable. But Matthew insures an accurate record. There was an act of incest and adultery in the ancestry of Jesus. One of the progenitors of the Savior was a prostitute. And the blood of the Messiah was not pure Jewish blood but had mingled with it the blood of an alien people.

This draws our attention to the inclusiveness of the genealogy of Jesus. He belongs to the Gentile as well as the Jew. Even the sinner can identify with the ancestry of Christ. Here at the outset of the career of Jesus we are made to realize the strange and unpredictable providence of God.

But then, after Matthew has gone to such pains to lay out this complicated genealogy, we find it is not that of Jesus after all. It is the genealogy of Joseph, who was only the stepfather of Jesus. The Davidic ancestry is lent to him, because he is the adopted son of Joseph. Mary had conceived her son before her marriage to Joseph took place. To be sure, in the eyes of the general public, he was Joseph's son, and Joseph looked on him and treated him as his own boy. But this in itself would not have been enough to confer Davidic sonship on him, nor would it have thrown on his shoulders the true messianic mantle. Matthew would not have bothered to supply his readers with the family tree unless it had been Jesus' true and authentic lineage.

Matthew knew that Mary, like Joseph, was of the

17

house of David. The two came out of the same family and remained within that large family through marriage. This was not unusual in Jewish society in Bible times. Moses' parents, for example, came from the same family. "And there went a man of the house of Levi, and took to wife a daughter of Levi" (Exod. 2:1). Zechariah realized Mary's Davidic origins when he said: "Blessed be the Lord God of Israel; for he hath visited and redeemed his people, And hath raised up an horn of salvation for us in the house of his servant David; as he spake by the mouth of his holy prophets, which have been since the world began" (Luke 1:68-70). Though it is not explicitly stated in the New Testament that Mary's ancestry is Davidic, this has been the tradition of the church since its inception; and this is the only way satisfactorily to explain the genealogies in Matthew and Luke who both report the virgin birth of Jesus.

2. *Birth and Childhood (Matt. 1:18-2:23)*—Only two persons had to know of the virgin birth of Jesus, the mother who bore him and the alleged father who realized the child was not his. Indeed, Mary alone might have known the exact circumstances surrounding the event, and her husband could have misunderstood what had taken place. As a matter of fact, this was about to happen when God intervened in a dream and told Joseph that his pregnant fiancée was still a virgin and that the embryo in her womb had been miraculously conceived.

Betrothal in those days was different from an engagement today. Back then it gave the man extensive rights over and privileges with the woman he planned to marry but left the woman altogether dependent upon the honor and faithfulness of her affianced. If he decided she was unsuited for him, he could nullify the betrothal simply by telling her in the presence of two witnesses. If his fiancée had illicit relations with another man after her betrothal to him, the Mosaic law was that she should be sentenced to death, together with the guilty male (Deut. 22:23-24). Evidently the betrothed couple could have sexual relations with one another. Therefore, had Joseph broken his engagement to Mary without making a public issue of it, people would have assumed that her child was Joseph's. She would have been disgraced but not physically harmed.

Luke tells the story of the conception of Jesus from Mary's point of view, but we are indebted to Matthew for the same account from the perspective of Joseph.

We think of the name *Jesus* as unique. It was not in that time. Its Hebrew equivalent is Joshua, which is still quite frequently used. The meaning of the word in Hebrew is "God is salvation." Jesus will save his people from their sins. Here in Joseph's dream, Jesus is given his name—a name with a mission to and in behalf of the people. Immediately Matthew attaches the messianic people to their Messiah. In his thinking, the two are inseparable. The uniqueness today of the name *Jesus* is as a result of his mission. We seldom name a person Jesus, be-

19

cause only Jesus of Nazareth is able to save us from our sins.

At this point Matthew uses his rubric to introduce a quotation from the Old Testament, which he amplifies a bit by explaining what the name *Emmanuel* means (Matt. 1:23; Isa. 7:14). In Jesus, God will be with the people, for Emmanuel means "God with us." Oddly enough, the word also means "prosperity." If God is with us, we will always be prosperous, not necessarily in material goods, but rather in the spiritual satisfaction of being with God. Then we will be rich indeed.

Matthew gives us information about the birth of Jesus not given by Luke, just as Luke supplies us with details not found in Matthew's Gospel. The two Gospels complement and supplement one another. Matthew tells of the Wise Men from the East who were led to Judea by the light of a wandering star. They came to Herod in Jerusalem and asked him about the habitation of the newborn king. Herod's Sanhedrin gave them the probable place of birth by consulting the Old Testament and finding a prophecy which designated Bethlehem as the birthplace of the Messiah (Mic. 5:2). Herod pretended to be pleased. He sent them ahead but told them to come back for him when they had found the babe. Herod lied, saying that he, too, wanted to worship the Messiah.

The Wise Men followed a star, which means they were astrologers and had received guidance by divining the heavens. Hebrew thought was divided concerning the value of astrology. Some rabbis accepted it as a gift from God. Others condemned it as necromancy and witchcraft. There are the signs of the zodiac in the mosaic floors of some synagogues, though those are later than the first century. More important than their being astrologers is the fact that the Wise Men were Gentiles. In them, people beyond Jewry paid tribute to Jesus. They were rich and powerful, too, which means that Jesus came not to the poor only but to all people, no matter what their class or station might have been. To delimit the work of Jesus to one class or group is to restrict God's mission of salvation.

Herod was in the last year of his reign, and his life was fast coming to a close. His body was ravaged with disease. Indeed, he was infested with worms which were eating away his flesh. Yet his pride had not waned, and he was maniacally jealous and hungry for power to the end. Herod knew he was hated by the people, so he decreed that members of the Sanhedrin be slain when he died in order to guarantee mourning at his funeral. His sister mercifully lied, saying he had countermanded this order on his deathbed, and so spared the religious leaders of the nation. But there was mourning aplenty anyway, for just before his death Herod had slain all the male children of Bethlehem two years old and younger in an effort to kill the little Messiah whose identity the Wise Men had withheld from him. Fortunately Joseph and Mary had already fled with Jesus into Egypt.

If the Wise Men and shepherds had come to Bethlehem at the same time, there would be a conflict in the accounts of Matthew and Luke. Luke says that Jesus was taken to Jerusalem to be circumcised eight days after he was born. But if we allow time for the Wise Men to get from the East to Bethlehem, there is no conflict. Thus Christmas is the day of the shepherds, and Epiphany is the day of the Wise Men.

The holy family stayed in Egypt until Herod was dead. They did not go back to Judea but returned to Nazareth. Herod's murder of the children in Bethlehem reminds Matthew of a prophecy from Jeremiah when Rachel, who is buried near Bethlehem, weeps for her children (Jer. 31:15). Matthew thinks of Jesus as a second Moses, who will add his new teachings to the Mosaic law, making him a second but greater lawgiver. Therefore, it is appropriate that Jesus should, like Moses, come up out of Egypt. This also is fulfillment of prophecy (Hos. 11:1).

3. *Baptism (Matt. 3:1-17)*—For Matthew, John the Baptist is the equivalent in the New Testament of the prophet Elijah in the Old Testament. Elijah preached the wrath of God. He condemned Ahab and Ahab's subjects in the Northern Kingdom for their apostasy and their sins. They worshiped Baal, a Canaanite god of fertility, caring more for their crops and the yield of their fields than for righteousness and the service of God (1 Kings 16:29-22:38).

The Pharisees and Sadducees cared more for their ancestry and tradition than they did for the people.

They were like vipers to John, who refused to baptize them. He baptized those who were genuinely sorry for their sins and wished to do better. In his appearance, his habits, even his diet, he imitated Elijah. He fulfilled Isaiah's prophecy of a voice crying in the wilderness on behalf of God and God's righteousness (Isa. 40:3). His influence over Judea was considerable, so great in fact that he embarrassed Herod Antipas and his corrupt court.

But John's importance to Matthew was that he heralded the coming of the Messiah and that he was the authentic forerunner of Jesus. John is the first to use the phrase "kingdom of heaven," so frequently on the lips of Jesus, and his assurance that the kingdom is at hand provides Matthew with his first opportunity to use that phrase.

Jesus accepted baptism of John in the River Jordan, not that he needed it as a sign of his own repentance for sin, but only to conform to the providential pattern. The children of Israel had experienced the baptism of deliverance along with adversity when they had come out of slavery in Egypt and crossed the Red Sea into the wilderness. The Apostle Paul says that they "were all baptized unto Moses in the cloud and in the sea" (1 Cor. 10:2). So Jesus was baptized of John and signified thereby his fulfillment of the old dispensation and inauguration of the new, though it meant for him also the experience of alienation and death on the cross.

Matthew says the heavens were opened, the Holy Spirit descended in the form of a dove and lighted on Jesus, and a voice from heaven said, "This is my beloved Son, in whom I am well pleased" (Matt. 3:17). Was this an event observed by John and those with him? Was this a public announcement of Jesus' mission? Such could hardly have been the case, since Matthew is careful to remark that the heavens were opened unto Jesus, who saw the spirit of God descending. What is seen by him is also confirmed by what he heard. What does this mean?

In my opinion it means that the kingdom of God, which Matthew usually calls the kingdom of heaven, can now through Jesus be seen on earth, for this will be the central concern of Jesus' ministry. The spirit of God that moved upon the face of the waters in creation (Gen. 1:2) now lights on Jesus to signify that Jesus will by his life and work effect the new creation. "Therefore," says Paul, "if any man be in Christ, he is a new creature: old things are passed away; behold, all things are become new" (2 Cor. 5:17).

4. *Temptations (Matt. 4:1-11)*—Even the Son of God had to be tempted. Matthew is careful to point out that God himself led his Son into the wilderness to be tempted of the devil. The apprentice is not the master, but neither does anyone ever become a master until as an apprentice he has learned the master's art. Aristotle was a pupil of Plato before he became a teacher with pupils of his own. According to William Wordsworth, "The child is father of the man," which is to say that a grown person has no more at his disposal than what he has acquired in the process of

24

growing up. Like Ulysses, we are a part of all that we have met.

Jesus met the devil, and because he did he knew how to cope with him and how to instruct his disciples to do the same. Goodness is not synonymous with innocence. Goodness, if it is genuine and enduring, comes only after a struggle with evil.

The first temptation had to do with physical and material needs. Jesus had fasted forty days and nights and was depleted and hungry. The devil said, "If you are who people say you are, then your present state should present no problem to you. If you really are the Son of God, then make bread out of these stones" (Matt. 4:3, AP). Jesus answered the devil with a quotation of Moses: "And he humbled thee, and suffered thee to hunger, and fed thee with manna, which thou knewest not, neither did thy fathers know; that he might make thee know that man doth not live by bread only, but by every word that proceedeth out of the mouth of the Lord doth man live" (Deut. 8:3). This shows the inadequacy of material things. The acquisition of goods and the purchase of services, self-indulgence, personal opulence and ease are not consistent with being human. We were created not to please ourselves, but to please God. And knowledge of God and God's will for us is more important than what we can get for ourselves from material things. Jesus would not misuse his divine powers for purely personal ends. He would not employ a miracle to get what he could earn from hard work.

The second temptation had to do with reputation. The devil set Jesus on the pinnacle of the Temple, which is the corner of the wall overlooking the Kidron Valley. "Jump off," he said, "for it is written, 'He shall give his angels charge over thee; to keep thee in all thy ways. They shall bear thee up in their hands, lest thou dash thy foot against a stone,'" (Psalm 91:11-12). The devil shows Jesus that he can quote scripture, too. Jesus refuses to jump, recalling another verse from Deuteronomy, "Ye shall not tempt the Lord your God" (6:16). The quest for fame and notoriety is just as unworthy as the quest for material things.

In the last temptation the devil comes out in the open. He does not flatter Jesus anymore by calling him the Son of God. He shows Jesus all the kingdoms of the world and tells him they will be his if he will forget who he is and fall down and worship him, the devil. Again the second Moses recalls the first, and Jesus answers with still another statement of the great lawgiver in the Book of Deuteronomy, "Thou shalt fear the Lord thy God, and serve him, and shalt swear by his name" (6:13).

The trial is over. The testing period by the devil is at an end. The threefold temptation of wealth, fame, and power, in ascending order, has failed to seduce Jesus. The voice from heaven heard at the baptism of Jesus has been confirmed. He has proved that he deserves the plaudit: "This is my beloved Son, in whom I am well pleased" (Matt. 3:17).

5. *Vocation (Matt. 4:12-25)*—The student has

been graduated. The apprentice has left the master's studio and is now on his own. The new master assumes authority on his own credentials. Just as John the Baptist goes to prison, Jesus goes into Galilee, the Galilee of the Gentiles, where Jews live alongside people of other races and where many of the Jews themselves have been Hellenized.

Jesus establishes himself at Capernaum on the northern shore of the Sea of Galilee, a city with a synagogue built by a Roman centurion and not far from Julias, a thoroughly Hellenized and pagan city. As master, he is now in position to have disciples of his own. He calls Simon and Andrew from their fishing nets on the Sea of Galilee, saying, "Follow me, and I will make you fishers of men" (Matt. 4:19). Later, he sees James and John with their father in a boat. The three men are mending their nets. He calls to them, and they leave their equipment in the boat with their father and follow Jesus. It could be that these four men, the nucleus of the later Twelve, had been disciples of John the Baptist and had been with John when he baptized Jesus. If so, they no longer had a master since John had gone to jail. Also, they would have remembered what John had said about Jesus. This would account for the ease with which Jesus won them. In going to Jesus from John they had exchanged the lesser for the greater.

Shortly it seems the reputation of the new master was established. His fame spread. He healed all manner of sickness and disease among the people, including lunacy and demon possession. Folk came to him in Capernaum from all around: Galilee, the Decapolis (ten Romanized towns), Jerusalem, and even from beyond the Jordan. Jesus had found his vocation, which was to perform in behalf of the people the role of God's messiah and minister on earth. He proclaimed that the kingdom of heaven was at hand. He fulfilled before their eyes the prophecy of Isaiah:

> Nevertheless the dimness shall not be such as was in her vexation, when at the first he lightly afflicted the land of Zebulun and the land of Naphtali, and afterward did more grievously afflict her by the way of the sea, beyond Jordan, in Galilee of the nations. The people that walked in darkness have seen a great light: they that dwell in the land of the shadow of death, upon them hath the light shined.
>
> —Isaiah 9:1-2

Matthew says Jesus is that light, and in Capernaum and the region of Galilee it has begun to shine.

## Personal Reflection

1. Do you think of yourself as having a Jewish faith heritage? Why or why not?
2. John the Baptist was a prophet in the Old Testament mold, dressing oddly and living a separate life. How might a contemporary prophet signal

28

holiness and complete dedication to God?
3. Why is a public act of repentance valuable? Should repentance be a public, one-time act? Why?
4. Consider yourself and your faith. What of the "old you" has disappeared because of your relationship with Christ? What about you is new because of your faith in Christ?
5. The author says that goodness is not synonymous with innocence. What rules of morality seem to equate the two? How did Jesus deal with the sin and evil around him?
6. Do you know anyone who proclaims god's truth uncompromisingly? Is it possible to be a prophet privately? Is private holiness a different kind of devotion than being a prophet in public?

## The Teacher and His Pupils
### Matthew 5–10

irst Matthew uses the testimony of God, through the virgin birth, the baptism, and the temptations, to establish the identity of Jesus.

Now Jesus offers his own testimony to those about him concerning the purpose of his mission and how it is to be accomplished. If he is the true king, then he must possess a kingdom and have subjects over whom to rule. His subjects constitute his kingdom, and they abide by his edicts and live according to his directives. Matthew portrays Jesus as the sublime teacher. Before the multitudes can be brought into the kingdom, however, the Master must teach his own disciples, who later will teach others and give organization to the kingdom of heaven here on earth. Matthew, in this section of his Gospel, portrays Jesus as he trains his disciples. He recounts both the content of Jesus' teaching and the method of its presentation.

1. *The Sermon on the Mount (Matt. 5:1-7:29)*—Just as Moses received the Ten Command-

ments from the top of a high mountain, so Jesus gives his gospel in a discourse on a mountain. Matthew is always eager to relate his account of Jesus to the Old Testament. He constantly draws parallels between the old dispensation and the new. The Jews are the children of the law. The followers of Jesus will be the recipients of the gospel. The Sermon on the Mount was delivered to the disciples. John Wesley says that in this instance the disciples were not just the Twelve but all who desired to learn from him. Wesley's view is dubious. Since Jesus sat down on the mountainside, there must have been only a small group of people gathered around him to hear what he said. Probably it was only the Twelve.

The Sermon on the Mount, from the literary and homiletical point of view, is a perfect document. It is impossible to rearrange it in any way to improve on it. It contains only one hundred nine verses. A little more than half of these verses are peculiar to Matthew's Gospel. They cannot be found anywhere else. The others are in Luke's as well, many in Luke's so-called Sermon on the Plain. Some modern scholars discount the fact that Jesus delivered the message as we have it and attribute the Sermon on the Mount to Matthew's arrangement of Jesus' thoughts gleaned from many different occasions. But it is difficult to conceive of a perfect document such as this apart from an author who is perfection itself. To attribute it to Matthew is almost to make the disciple greater than his Master. No doubt Jesus did repeat his ideas under various circumstances. This is demonstrated in Luke's account where Jesus' many sayings in the Sermon on the Mount are preached in a different setting altogether. But repetitions like these do not preclude a full discourse such as the Sermon on the Mount, where the essence of the Master's teachings is set forth. The Sermon on the Mount is a gorgeous mosaic of the mind of Christ.

The sermon achieves its unity by means of an orderly transition from one section to the next, where each major division carries its special message but needs the others in order for the sermon to make its full impact. The discourse resembles a pyramid with a broad base of specificity. The picture of the two houses is the climax as well as the conclusion of the sermon.

The base of the sermon is the Beatitudes (Matt. 5:3-12), together with their enforcement in terms of Jesus' expectations of his disciples (Matt. 5:13-20). There are eight beatitudes. They have in common the characteristic of the unlikely and unexpected. How can one who is poor in spirit be happy? The opinion of society then, as now, might be that a person who is not motivated to acquire wealth is lazy. Added to this in Jesus' time was the religious interpretation that the good prospered, while the wicked suffered adversity. Not so, Jesus affirms. Those who possess the wealth of heaven cannot be encumbered with the material things of this world. The reward in the first beatitude is the same as that in the last, for those who are persecuted for righteousness' sake as well as the poor in spirit have heaven as their reward.

How do the meek possess the earth? By refusing to contend with others for it, they enjoy their lot in life to the extent that they believe they have everything. Those who moan because of sorrow and pain and untoward circumstances receive divine comfort which more than compensates for anything that distresses them. Likewise, those who are righteous above everything else, who constantly pray for righteousness, will have their prayers answered. We become, Jesus says, what we most desire. The heart was to the Israelites of Jesus' day the center of understanding and the seat of the will. Therefore, if one's mind was clear of wicked thoughts and one's will anchored in the will of God, there would be no obstruction to spiritual vision. A person could not fail to see God. God loves peacemakers more than any other people; therefore, those who promote peace are called God's own children. What God calls anything, that something invariably is, because in God there is no distinction between appearance and reality.

Secular society has a different set of values. Therefore, Jesus tells his disciples that they shall be happy when society persecutes them, for such persecution only increases their rewards from God. He tells them they are like light, and they shine as examples of goodness to humankind. They are a preservative like salt. When people see genuinely good works, good deeds, they respond by acknowledging God whom those doing such good deeds worship and praise.

The Beatitudes are Jesus' transvaluation of all merely human values. They are the hallmarks of his kingdom. They are the basic characteristics of his subjects, of those who become true citizens of the kingdom of heaven, even though they continue to dwell on earth.

There is a decided contrast between the gospel of the kingdom of heaven and the law of the old dispensation (Matt. 5:21-48). The latter regulates behavior and conduct, while the former has to do with the riches of the mind, the feelings of the heart, and the disposition of the will. Consequently Moses forbade murder and manslaughter, while Jesus warns against anger out of which such misdeeds emerge. Moses outlawed adultery. Jesus will not even tolerate lust. He equates the inward craving with the external act. The Old Testament abounds in oaths and swearing, but Jesus says one's whole disposition shall be so oriented to honesty that swearing or taking an oath is unnecessary. A person's character is sufficient bond. Moses taught retaliation and retribution—"An eye for an eye, a tooth for a tooth, a life for a life"—but Jesus teaches his disciples to practice nonresistance by enduring wrongs that others inflict on them rather than defending themselves against evildoers. Love in the kingdom of heaven reaches beyond affection for those who have affection for us. We must love even our enemies. Our standard is not goals we set for ourselves. Our standard is the perfection of God. "Be ye therefore perfect, even as your Father which is in heaven is perfect" (Matt. 5:48).

The only important requirement for a citizen of the kingdom of heaven is that the person please God. One's reward is inward and spiritual with no concern for the recognition and praise of others here

THE TEACHER AND HIS PUPILS

on earth. The outward display of piety is distasteful, as it is also counterproductive. People who engage in such acts are insincere. The purpose of almsgiving is to help the unfortunate. It is not to let the general public know one's worth and generosity. Giving a fifth of one's income to charity instead of the prescribed tenth should bring satisfaction in the greater good it does, not in the reputation it establishes. Both prayer and fasting which accompanies prayer are to be done in secret and not openly to advertise one's piety to the world. Only the treasures accumulated in heaven abide. No matter how extensive one's possessions, nor their guarantee by government, nothing is secure here, not even Social Security. Therefore, it does not pay to worry over gains and losses. It is enough to realize that God loves and cares for us. Trust in God is the only cure for anxiety.

The section of the Sermon on the Mount in which these teachings are set forth (Matt. 6:1-34) is among the noblest passages in all literature. The imagery of Jesus in this passage is exquisite. The Lord's Prayer (Matt. 6:9-13), as Matthew gives it, is the one we repeat collectively in our services of worship. The description of the fowls of the air, the lilies of the field, the grass which today is and tomorrow is cast into the oven, and Solomon in all his glory, has etched itself forever on the memory of humanity in most of the languages of the world.

The last segment of the teachings in the Sermon on the Mount is a collection of admonitions (Matt. 7:1-23). Our Lord admonishes his disciples to refrain from judging others, censuring their deeds and scrutinizing their attitudes and behavior in order to find fault with them. Such people are so busy criticizing others that they do not take time to observe their own faults, which generally are more grievous than the faults of those they condemn. Jesus also cautions his followers against assuming good of everyone and wasting their efforts on those who are too indifferent to appreciate them. Do not throw away the pearls of the gospel on a bunch of hogs who cannot recognize their value.

Jesus promises that what we ask of God is what God will give to us. God rewards in keeping with God's own character and is incapable of giving anything less than the best to us.

Everyone on this earthly pilgrimage is presented, sooner or later, with two ways: the easy way of indifference and self-indulgence which leads inevitably to death and destruction and the more difficult way of hard choices and self-denying experiences, the end of which is life. On the journey we will run into false teachings and dishonest advisors. These people must be tested by the effects of their work. Jesus does not want only verbal assent from his followers but a life of obedience where his disciples actually perform in deeds the will of God.

The sermon concludes with the foolish person who builds his house without foundations, and it collapses. In contrast, the wise man sets his house on a rock foundation which enables it to withstand all calamities.

Here before our eyes in the Sermon on the Mount is the picture of the kingdom of heaven, the means of entering it, the rigorous demands of maintaining one's citizenship in it, and the guarantee of its certain rewards.

2. *Miracles Around the Sea of Galilee (Matt. 8:1-9:38)*—The three chapters in Matthew devoted to the Sermon on the Mount are followed by two chapters describing the miracles of Jesus. These miracles were not, strictly speaking, all performed in Galilee. At least one was done in the Hellenized region of the Decapolis. We do not know precisely where either the centurion's house was or where the ruler lived, so Jesus may have performed a miracle in the Tetrarchy of Philip as well. But we can be certain that all these miracles took place around the Sea of Galilee, a small body of water only seven miles wide and twelve miles long. Unless the weather conditions are unfavorable, one can see all round it from most any vantage point along the shore. So when Jesus was on the mount with his disciples, he had a perspective of all the places where he would perform these miracles.

Matthew, as we will see, alternates his Gospel between teaching and narrative, between the words of Jesus and his deeds. Indeed, Matthew has a little rubric for ending a section of Jesus' teachings and beginning a section of narrative. "And it came to pass, when Jesus had ended these sayings . . . " (Matt 7:28). It would appear, therefore, that Matthew intentionally uses the miracles to illustrate and enforce the teaching, and likewise uses the teaching to explain the miracles.

There are ten specific miracles in the two chapters

37

of Matthew under consideration. These ten miracles are divided into three groups, and the groups are separated from one another by further narrative, but these interspersed bits of narrative present incidents that are not miraculous.

When Jesus first comes down from the mount, he is confronted by a leper who tells him that if he wants to, he can cure him of leprosy. Immediately Jesus replies, "I want to; so you are clean." He touches the leper and tells him to report to the priest and receive from him certification that he is entirely well. Leprosy, a skin disease, during the last stages of which members of the body rot away, was considered a communicable disease in ancient society. Lepers were forbidden to associate with other people. There was a stigma attached to the disease. The person was called "unclean." (Leprosy was looked on then the way our society looks on venereal disease.) It was a disgrace to have it. A leper could not mix again in society until a priest assured the public that the leper was ritually clean (Matt. 8:1-4).

In Capernaum Jesus received an appeal from a centurion to heal his servant. When Jesus volunteered to go with the centurion to see the sick servant, the centurion told him that would not be necessary. This Gentile did not want to contaminate Jesus by taking him into his home. "Just say the word," he said, "and I know my servant will be healed." Jesus was amazed and complimented him by saying that he, a Gentile, had more faith than any Jew Jesus knew (Matt. 8:5-13).

The third miracle in the first group is Jesus' curing

of the mother-in-law of Peter, who had a persistent fever that would not break. He touched her as he had the leper, and she was cured. Indeed, she immediately resumed her household chores and entertained their guests.

Why do these three miracles form one group? They do not seem to have anything in common. They are put together, it seems to me, to show the catholicity of Jesus' work. He heals a Jew, a fellow countryman—the leper. He heals a foreigner, a Roman, one who belonged to the nation which had subjugated and now ruled Jesus' land—the centurion's servant. Finally Jesus heals a close personal friend—the mother-in-law of his disciple, Peter. This was like curing a member of the family. Jesus no doubt stayed in the home of Simon Peter when he was in Capernaum (Matt. 8:14-17).

This first group of miracles is separated from the second group by two unusual incidents (Matt. 8:18-22). One is Jesus' discouragement of the scribe who wanted to follow him. He tells the scribe that he has no place to take him. Animals and birds have habitations, but Jesus has no home of his own, no place to lay his head. The other is the rebuke he administers to one of the disciples who gives what appears to us to be the most primary of all reasons to be excused temporarily from Jesus' company. He wants to go home to bury his father. Our Lord appears heartless. He does not excuse him. The miracles show the Master's dispersal of power in behalf of all types of people in need. He cures the incurable and does not limit his service just to his own. The two incidents show the expectations of discipleship. The catholicity of Jesus' deeds is matched by the exactitude of his demands. A disciple must give up everything if he is to have Jesus for his Master. And anyone less than a fully committed disciple, such as the scribe, has no place in his company. Totality of power carries with it totality of obedience from those who will benefit from that power.

The second group of three miracles consists of the calming of the storm, the only nature miracle in this section; the expulsion of devils from two demented persons; and the healing of the paralytic. The storm was calmed for the disciples who were in the boat with Jesus and thought that he and they were about to drown (Matt. 8:23-27). In the second miracle, Jesus exorcised a company of demons residing in two helpless men. The demons had made the men so ferocious that travelers could not safely pass near them. Jesus destroys the demons. Matthew does not tell us anything more about the two men whom the demons controlled and misused. Presumably they got well (Matt. 8:28-34). Jesus performed the third miracle for the friends of the paralytic who carried him on a pallet into our Lord's presence. At the same time, he did it to display his ability to forgive sins. He tells the paralytic, to the horror of the scribes, "Thy sins be forgiven" (Matt. 9:1-8).

These three miracles are all of a class. What they have in common is the element of demonstration. Jesus, the man, demonstrates his divine power— power to control nature, destroy evil, forgive sins, and relieve the ill effects of sin.

The narrative that follows is in support of these demonstrations (Matt. 9:9-17). Jesus calls a tax collector, a hated and despised publican who raises revenue for the Roman oppressors, and causes him to give up his job in order to be a disciple (Matt. 9:9). He eats with publicans and sinners because they need him. It is his disposition to be merciful. His mission is not to the righteous but to sinners whom he has come to save (Matt. 9:10-13). And finally he answers the disciples of John, saying that there is no need for his disciples to fast for there is nothing for them to fast over (Matt. 9:14-17). What they have fasted for and prayed for has now come about. The Messiah is their Master and Lord. The king resides in the presence of his subjects. God is at home with the people. The old order that John represents has passed away. A new order has taken its place.

The last group of miracles seems almost anticlimactic compared with this middle group. The last group is not followed by any specific incidents from the career of Jesus but only by a general observation. There are in this last group four miracles: the raising of the ruler's daughter from the dead, the healing of the woman with a continuous menstrual hemorrhage, the restoration of sight to two blind men, and the enabling of a dumb man to speak (Matt. 9:18-34). The very order of these miracles is on a descending scale. Matthew starts with the dead daughter to whom Jesus restores life and ends with the casting out of a little devil who had tied a man's tongue so he could not speak until the devil was removed. The last group is made to correspond with the first

41

group, except in the first group each person cured came from a different category: fellow countryman, foreigner, friend. There are not any such categories in the last group. This group just represents all sorts and conditions of people. Therefore, the narrative that follows supports the same by saying that Jesus went about everywhere in the region teaching and preaching and healing all manner of disease. These four cures are typical examples of all the misery that flesh is heir to. But Jesus is capable of meeting any human demand; he can cope with any and all infirmities.

Now Jesus does all this in company with his disciples. He says that the needs of people are so great that there are not enough disciples to cope with these needs. ''The harvest truly is plenteous, but the labourers are few'' (Matt. 9:37).

3. *The Formation of the Apostolate (Matt. 10:1-42)*—Though Jesus has done a lot for many individuals through these ten miracles and though the general public has been greatly impressed by his wonderful works, everything that he has said and done around the Sea of Galilee has been in the presence of his disciples and, from Matthew's viewpoint, principally for their benefit. The Sermon on the Mount was preached to them. They, too, were spectators at all his miracles.

At this juncture Matthew makes clear that Jesus has been preparing his disciples for their mission in the world. By precept and example he has been developing them to do the work he has called them to do. The plenteous harvest, which heretofore has d too few laborers to pluck it, will soon have more than enough to gather its crops. The Master will not have to work alone. There will be other laborers to assist him.

Note carefully the chief characteristic of the newly formed apostolate. Jesus first gives his disciples power to cast out unclean spirits and to cure all types of sickness and disease. He does not mention here having given them the gifts either of preaching or of pastoral visitation, regardless of how important these seem to be to us. The first disciples are given by their Master the power to cure diseases and also the power to cope with sin. No matter how strong and vigorous a person is, without a transformed soul that person is little more than an animal.

Matthew is prepared only now to present the roster of the disciples. This roster contains the names of those who are later to constitute the apostolate and govern the church. At the head of the list is the name Simon called Peter. At the bottom of the list is Judas Iscariot, who betrayed Jesus.

Matthew's roster contains twelve names. Here again his Old Testament predilections are manifested. He is most careful to note this. There were twelve tribes in ancient Israel. There will be an apostle for every tribe. The new Israel of the church will be ruled by them and later by their successors.

This is the first time Matthew enters their names collectively in his Gospel, though he has already mentioned five of them. When Jesus begins his vocation, he calls Andrew and Peter first and shortly thereafter James and John (Matt. 4:18–22). The

43

fifth disciple Matthew mentions prior to this complete list is not one of the greats. He is the publican Matthew, whom Jesus called from his seat at the receipt of custom (Matt. 9:9). If the two Matthews are one and the same person, it is obvious why this fifth disciple would have been named. Matthew just could not resist this allusion to himself and the circumstances that characterized his call.

When we get the list of the names of all the disciples, it is no more than a list. It does not provide us with any information about any of them, not even the so-called greats at the top of the list. The only one about whom Matthew gives any information beyond family identity and vocation is the one whose name is last on the list, and the information given about him is such that he should not have been a disciple at all. Matthew says that Judas Iscariot is the disciple who betrayed Jesus.

More important than who the disciples were is what the disciples became. The means of their becoming, what enabled them to be what they later were, is the content of this section of Matthew.

Jesus at first delimited their mission. They were to work only as Israelites. Evidently our Lord wanted to be sure they could succeed at home before he was willing to risk sending them abroad. A person who tries to function at the general church level when that person is not influential in his or her local congregation has very little to commend him or her to anybody. Many people feel that a person who is not respected at home does not deserve a hearing abroad.

At this point the apostles are admonished to preach, and their theme is that the kingdom of God is at hand. Consequently, their message is one of urgency. The demonstration they give of its authenticity and validity as well as of their own credibility is that in preaching they at the same time "heal the sick, cleanse the lepers, raise the dead, cast out devils" (Matt. 10:8). As they have received their call and its gifts without compensation, so they will give what they have to others without price. All they are to expect is hospitality: housing, food, raiment from time to time, and, above all else, receptive minds and hearts from those to whom they minister. When they do not get this, they are to leave immediately, and God will condemn all who do not receive and heed them. Judgment and punishment are emphasized here. Those who are inhospitable to a minister of Jesus Christ and indifferent to Christ's message jeopardize their own salvation and imperil their own souls.

Nonetheless, people do not know what is conducive to their own welfare, and the prospects for the apostles in the hands of those to whom they are sent are not the best. The chances are that they will be mistreated, maligned, persecuted, misunderstood, and condemned. Feuds will break out within families. Siblings will be against siblings, parents against children, and children against parents even to the point of death. The apostles will be hated simply because they are apostles. All this evil will befall them simply because of their allegiance to Jesus. But if they can stand such abuse and remain loyal throughout it all, they will be saved. When they are rejected in one place, they must hasten to another. Their consolation lies in the fact that this cannot last too long, for the Son of man will soon return. Matthew quotes Jesus as saying: "Ye shall not have gone over the cities of Israel, till the Son of man be come" (Matt. 10:23). The nearness of Jesus and the effectiveness of his presence are more than enough to offset the most adverse of all conditions.

The disciples must realize that they cannot expect better treatment than their Master received. A servant has no right to more than his lord. Jesus warns that if society has labeled him the prince of devils, those who belong to him cannot expect any higher label for themselves.

The worst enemies of the apostles are not those who declare themselves to be enemies. The worst enemy of the apostles is fear. It is only natural for them to fear those who hurt them. But there is a limit to any damage a mere human can inflict on another human. If one goes so far as to take a human life, even then that person has not taken everything from the person who has been killed. One person cannot take another person's immortal soul. Jesus says: "And fear not them which kill the body, but are not able to kill the soul: but rather fear him which is able to destroy both soul and body in hell" (Matt. 10:28). The most important thing in life is for a person to acknowledge Jesus. If a person does, Jesus will acknowledge that person before his Father in heaven. But if a person denies him, Jesus will deny that person before his Father in heaven. Fear is relative. Our real concern should be our relationship with God rather than fearing mortals who are bent on inflicting evil.

The very nature of Christianity is divisive. The claims of the Gospel are total; there can be no compromise. There is no way to divide loyalty between Christ and another. The ones who accept Jesus within a family will by that act be set at odds with those who do not accept him. Jesus will tolerate no loyalty above loyalty to him. "He that loveth father or mother more than me is not worthy of me: and he that loveth son or daughter more than me is not worthy of me." (Matt. 10:37).

The prediction Jesus makes here that a person's enemies "shall be they of his own household" (Matt. 10:36) was literally fulfilled time and time again in the days of the early church. Take the family of Augustine, for example; his mother was a devout Christian, but his father was originally a pagan. Roman slaves became Christian. Some slaves were entrusted as nurses in pagan families. Often they won the children to Christ. The children would then try to win their fathers to Christ, but not always with success. "For I am come to set a man at variance against his father, and the daughter against her mother, and the daughter in law against her mother in law" (Matt 10:35).

The cross is the emblem of Christianity because sooner or later every Christian has to bear it. The glory of discipleship is that the person who receives the disciple and the message at the same time receives the disciple's Master and Lord.

47

## Personal Reflection

1. Many people in Jesus' day believed that the good prospered while the wicked suffered adversity. Do good things happen only to good people and bad things happen only to bad people?
2. Why is it hard to feel good about being poor in spirit or even being called poor in spirit? What character traits that are valued in our culture (for instance, the qualities that make a good executive) work at cross purposes to being poor in spirit?
3. Does being meek mean refusing to contend with others? Did Jesus refuse to confront and oppose others?
4. Matthew reports Jesus' teachings and miracles as schooling to prepare the disciples for their own ministries. Look back on your own life and name three or four things that you now see as preparation for your life today.
5. Why was the decision to follow Christ divisive in Jesus' time? Is it still divisive? Is that good or bad?

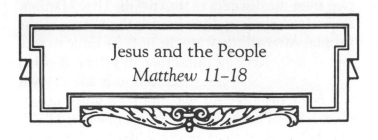

## Jesus and the People
### Matthew 11–18

The territories and towns in this portion of the Gospel are the same as in the last, but the focus is different. Although Jesus had dealt constantly with the people and performed miracles in their behalf, the disciples were always present, and Jesus explained to them all that he said and did. Indeed, the Sermon on the Mount was addressed specifically to the disciples. The closing discourse was a "brief" of their apostolate. Even the miracles done for the people were all illustrative of the Master's expectations of the disciples. The situation was similar to a teaching hospital connected to the medical school of a large university today. To be sure, the doctors in such a hospital treat sick patients, but everything they do is in the presence of their students. The enterprise is designed to teach students how to practice medicine. The primary purpose of the previous section of Matthew is to teach the disciples how to practice discipleship and to carry on the work of the Master.

In this section of the Gospel, Jesus shifts his attention from the disciples to the crowds. Here Matthew shows Jesus dealing directly with the masses of the people. After all, they are the ones he came to seek and to save. Keep in mind that this sharp division may not have been Jesus'. Indeed, it is safe to say it was not Jesus'. We do not find such a distinct arrangement of events and teachings in either Mark's or Luke's account. Rather, this is Matthew's arrangement of the materials. All three Synoptic Gospels deal with the same material. It is the way each evangelist presents his message that makes each Gospel unique. Matthew's aim is to present Jesus as the messianic king. In this portion of Matthew's Gospel we will see Jesus in relationship with his potential subjects, the people in whose behalf he came to bring the kingdom of heaven. Even the confession of Peter, which only the Twelve experience, and the Transfiguration, witnessed by Peter, James, and John, are designed as proofs of the kingdom to be proclaimed to all after the Resurrection.

1. *Recalcitrance of the Jews (Matt. 11:1-13:58)*—These three chapters portend ill for the mission of Jesus in his own country. There are signs of frustration and exasperation on the part of the Master. Those who hear his words do not seem to comprehend. The people see the miracles and even benefit from them, but they have no idea at all what the miracles indicate about Jesus.

Even John the Baptist seems to have forgotten all that happened at Jesus' baptism, including his own words of testimony that the person he baptized was far greater than he, one whose sandals he was not worthy to unloose. He seems to have come to doubt his own mission as herald of the Messiah. From prison he sends to Jesus to ask him if he really is the promised one sent by God or if he and the people should wait in expectation of another. Jesus responds by sending word back to John of all that has happened as a result of Jesus' work. Let John make his own decision about who Jesus really is. Maybe those whom Jesus has helped can supply John with the answer: the poor, the blind, the lame, the lepers, the deaf, and even those who were raised from the dead. Jesus affirms that John the Baptist, while he was active, was the greatest of all the prophets. Why was this true? Jesus does not give the answer. But it is simply this: John is the only prophet who lived to see his prophecy fulfilled. Unfortunately he is still unaware that what he proclaimed about Jesus has all come true (Matt. 11:1-15).

Jesus compares the unbelieving public to children playing games on the streets. At times they play "wedding" and so make music and dance. At other times they play "funeral" and cry and mourn. Jesus says that John the Baptist came with a sad face and preached judgment, but the people did not believe him. They said he was crazy. Jesus continues: "I preached the good news of the kingdom of heaven. I ate and drank and made merry. But then you people thought I had drunk too much wine. There just seems to be no way to reach you" (Matt. 11:16-19, AP). All the big towns around the Sea of Galilee where Jesus worked are more scandalous and reprehensible than was Sodom in Abraham's time, and they will be brought down to hell because of their recalcitrance (Matt. 11:20–24).

If the wise and prestigious members of society will not heed the Gospel, fortunately there are some who will—the simple, the openhearted, babes, as it were, whose innocence is credulous and believing. There is pathos in this prayer of Jesus, where he thanks God that he has revealed the truth at least to this precious little band of people (Matt..11:25–26). Jesus, in desperation, tells the people that they have never really come to know him; in fact, he does not think anybody really knows him except his heavenly Father. And he is certain that he is the only one who knows God. If anybody else ever comes to know God, it will be because Jesus reveals God to that person. If people only realized it, they could cast all their burdens on Jesus, and he could give them the rest they need. What he would lay on them in exchange would be a light load. "If you only knew," he says, "I am gentle, and in me you will find rest for your souls" (Matt. 11:27–30, AP). The Jews insisted on complete rest on the sabbath, anticipating perfect rest in the messianic age. Jesus says, "That rest has already come in me. The messianic age has arrived" (Matt. 12:8, AP).

The Pharisees stood aghast when Jesus and his disciples crossed through the grain fields on the sabbath, and the disciples plucked the ears of grain and ate them. This did not bother Jesus in the least, for David and his men ate the consecrated bread on the altar of the Tabernacle, and the priests changed the

twelve loaves on the altar of the Temple every sabbath and ate what they took off. Now, says Jesus,
one greater than the Temple is here, and the God of
the sabbath can determine how that day will be
spent. After all, it is set aside for God. The sabbath
was for the benefit of the people. It was made for
them. They were not made for it. Consequently,
when the Pharisees tested him in the synagogue by
pointing to a man with a withered arm and asking
whether it was lawful to heal that man on the sabbath, Jesus responded by healing him. His retort
was: You would rescue one of your own sheep from
the ditch on the sabbath, wouldn't you? Isn't a human much more valuable than an animal? When he
withdrew from town, the crowds followed him, and
he responded to all their needs (Matt. 12:1-21). He
asked them not to publicize his miracles. Jesus cautioned silence, Matthew says, to fulfill another
prophecy, and then Matthew gives the longest Old
Testament quotation in his Gospel (Isa. 42:1-4).
Many commentators think that Jesus' withdrawal
from the synagogue at this point marked his abandonment of the old Israel and his inauguration of
the new Israel through the church. However, this
thought is not expressed in Matthew, and the infer-
ence is farfetched.

Jesus returns to heal the person who had been
made blind and dumb by a devil and to show how
ridiculous was the contention of the Pharisees that
he performed this miracle through the power of the
devil. Why, said Jesus, would the devil destroy his
own work and through me tumble his own king-

dom? Jesus wants them to look at the results of his actions, which had to indicate a good, benevolent source, rather than an evil source of power. When the Pharisees ask him for a sign to prove the validity of his ministry, Jesus refuses their request. If they can not deduce from what they have already seen who he is and what he is about, no additional sign will help them. The only sign that will be given them is that of the prophet Jonah. Jesus says, ''For as Jonas was three days and three nights in the whale's belly; so shall the Son of man be three days and three nights in the heart of the earth'' (Matt. 12:40). Jonah's mission was to preach to Nineveh until Nineveh repented. That is what Jesus has been doing all the while.

Jesus says people can blaspheme against him and be forgiven, but they can never be forgiven if they blaspheme against the Holy Ghost. To blaspheme against the Holy Ghost is to refuse to believe the Gospel.

The people with whom Jesus must deal are like the Ninevites of Jonah's day. They are not different from the Queen of Sheba. However, in the end both the Ninevites and the Queen of Sheba will condemn them, because Nineveh did repent, and the Queen of Sheba left her own land and journeyed to Israel to benefit from the wisdom of Solomon (Matt. 12:41-42). These people do not realize that One greater than Solomon is standing before them. Their status will be worse than that of the man who got rid of one devil but did nothing to fill the vacuum the devil's departure had created, allowing the devil to return with seven other devils (Matt. 12:43-45).

Even Jesus' own family was not free from the unbelief that afflicted the people in general. Consequently, when he was told his mother and brothers were nearby and wanted to see him, Jesus said sadly that he had no mother or brothers other than his disciples who did believe him and were trying to do the will of God (Matt. 12:46-50).

After these various encounters, Jesus speaks to the crowds in parables, that is, in stories designed to set forth principles and truths. His parables deal entirely with the kingdom of heaven. There are here recorded seven of them. The first is about a sower who sows seed in various types of soil. The birds ate some of the seed. The rocky soil did not provide enough moisture for some plants, and they withered in the sun. The thorns choked other plants as they grew. But some seed fell on good soil and yielded a good crop (Matt. 13:3-9). Jesus explains the meaning of the parable to the disciples. Some people are too superficial to understand the word and, as its meaning eludes them, they forget what they heard just after the message has been given to them. The birds are the evil one (the devil) who snatches the gospel from them. The seed on thorny ground represents those people who rejoice when they first hear the Gospel but accept it only to lose faith when tribulation arises. The thorns represent the pleasures of this life which stifle the Gospel. The meaning of the good yield is obvious (Matt. 13:18-23).

The second is the parable of the weeds which grow

up with the plants. They cannot be removed until after harvest when they are burned. The wicked therefore will be separated from the good at the judgment (Matt. 13:24-30). The third is the parable of the mustard seed, the tiniest of all seeds, which grows up into a large tree (Matt. 13:31-32). That is the way the kingdom of heaven is. It starts off small and inconsequential, only in the end to be so large that it controls everything. Like leaven in dough, it lifts society to a higher level (Matt. 13:33). This is the fourth parable. The fifth and sixth parables, about the tares in the field and the priceless pearl, which a man sells all that he has to purchase and own, illustrate the inestimable value of the kingdom of heaven (Matt. 13:44-46). The seventh parable, of the net and the fishes (Matt. 13:47-50), is like that of the weeds and the wheat. It shows that the good and bad exist side by side, the hypocrites with the righteous, but God will separate the one from the other in the end.

Jesus tells these stories to the crowds, but they do not understand them. He explains them to his disciples. Sadly he admits that the crowds in and around Galilee will not accept him and will not heed his message. Seemingly a prophet is without honor in that person's own country (Matt. 13:53-58).

2. *Mighty Acts of Mercy (Matt. 14:1-16:12)*—In spite of the recalcitrance of the Jews, especially their leaders, Jesus continues to minister to human need wherever he finds it, and the crowds respond to his mercy and kindness. The compassion of Jesus is inexhaustible, but Matthew says explicitly that Jesus

"had compassion" only four times in his Gospel: (1) when he saw the crowds who were disorganized and helpless, "as sheep having no shepherd" (Matt. 9:36; (2) when he fed first the five thousand after healing their sick (Matt. 14:14) and (3) later the four thousand (Matt. 15:32); and (4) when he gave sight to the two blind men at Jericho (Matt. 20:34).

The news of John the Baptist's death at the hands of Herod Antipas, which Matthew treats almost incidentally (Matt. 14:1-12) in contrast to Mark's detailed account (Mark 6:14-30), causes Jesus to withdraw to a desert place. However, the news of Jesus' successes alarms Herod, for he had thought that only John the Baptist could do these mighty deeds, and so Jesus must be John the Baptist come to life again. Matthew correctly designates Herod as *tetrarch*, the ruler for Rome of only a small district. He was not a king like his father Herod the Great who ruled over the whole country, but people persisted in calling him *king* as they had his father. Herod was king to the people who were his subjects but not to the Romans whose subject he was.

The people followed Jesus to the desert place, and he ministered to their needs by curing those who were sick. At eventide the disciples wanted to dismiss the people, so that they could go back to the villages for food. But Jesus said that was unnecessary. He would feed them. He took five loaves of bread and two fish, which they had on hand, multiplied them, and fed the whole lot. Matthew says there were five thousand men in addition to the women and children, whom he does not number. This means we do not know how many were really fed, for surely the women and children ate the loaves and fish just as the men did. The significance of the story lies in what was left over. The remains of the meal filled twelve baskets. There were twelve tribes of Israel, a basket for each tribe. The food of the Gospel is for the Jews, and it is sufficient to satisfy their needs entirely. As Moses kept the children of Israel alive on manna in the wilderness, so Jesus is prepared to feed them now with bread from heaven which will provide them with strength, body and soul, for everlasting life (Matt. 14:13-21).

Jesus dismissed both the crowds and the disciples, whom he told to take a boat and cross back over the Sea of Galilee while he remained alone to pray. This is an interesting point. Here and later in the Garden of Gethsemane (Matt. 26:36-45) are the only two instances in the whole of Matthew's Gospel where Jesus is shown in the act of prayer. A storm arose. The disciples were in the boat alone. They were in danger. So Jesus walked to them across the water as if it had been dry land. Peter saw Jesus coming and called to him and asked permission and power to come and meet him on the water. In the process of doing so, Peter became frightened and began to sink. Jesus rebuked him for his lack of faith. "O thou of little faith, wherefore didst thou doubt?" (Matt. 14:31). The phrase "of little faith" is peculiar to Matthew. We use it now frequently. It is Matthew's contribution to the language of Christendom. As a result of this miracle, the disciples in the boat worshiped Jesus, saying to him: "Of a truth thou art the Son of God" (Matt. 14:33). Matthew uses this incident to emphasize his theme: the kingship of Christ.

The crowds around Gennesaret sought just to touch his garments, believing that this contact with Jesus would be sufficient to heal their diseases (Matt. 14:34-36). The scribes and Pharisees thought otherwise. They accused the disciples of transgressing oral tradition by failing to wash their hands before a meal. Jesus was outraged at their criticism. The disciples' fault was minor compared to their transgression of the sixth commandment. Moses had commanded them to honor their parents, but they used the so-called "tradition of the elders" to evade the commandment. They put their estates in trust to the Temple. They could use the revenue from this trust themselves, but nobody else could benefit from it. Therefore, they used the law to free themselves from the Mosaic obligation to care for their parents. "Thus have ye made the commandment of God of none effect by your tradition. Ye hypocrites" (Matt. 15:6-7). Once again Matthew calls attention to a prophecy of Isaiah by indicating that Jesus quoted Isaiah 29:13 in his rebuke to the scribes and Pharisees.

The real cause of defilement is not what we take into our mouths but rather what comes out of our mouths, for the words we speak reflect our thoughts and the purpose of our hearts. Murder, adultery, theft, and slander are all acts and expressions of the inner disposition of the heart. Note that these all follow the sixth, seventh, eighth, and ninth commandments of Moses. Peter asks for an explanation, which prompts Jesus to be so explicit. Before explaining, however, he shows disgust with Peter. "Haven't you got any sense?" he said. "You do not seem to have one grain of intelligence, Peter."

At this juncture Matthew records the healing of the daughter of the Canaanite woman. The disciples want to send her away, and even Jesus tells her that his mission is limited to the Jews. But when she is so humble as to say that even dogs are fed scraps from their master's table, Jesus cannot deny her. He tells her to go home, for her daughter is already well (Matt. 15:21-28). The power of Christ is for the Gentiles as well as the Jews.

On the shores of the Sea of Galilee the lame, the maimed, the blind, the dumb, and many other diseased people are healed by Jesus (Matt. 15:29-31). This time the crowds bringing all their sick people number four thousand men exclusive of women and children. People today must wonder about the male chauvinism of Matthew. Here for the second time he does not count the women and children. In this regard he was typical of the time in which he lived. Jewish society has always been patriarchal, and Matthew leans heavily on the ideas and practices of the Old Testament.

Some think that the feeding of the four thousand was the feeding of the Gentiles—that the large crowd consisted of Gentiles, not Jews, as in the case of the five thousand. Therefore they say that the seven baskets of food left over represent the seventy gentile nations, and that the four thousand people symbolize the four winds of heaven and the four corners of the earth. All this is allegorizing. There is nothing explicitly stated in Matthew's text to warrant such a fanciful interpretation (Matt. 15:32-39).

Once again Jesus refuses to give a sign to the Pharisees and Sadducees of the authenticity of his mission, telling them that they are skillful enough in reading the sky to predict the weather, but they are blind to spiritual reality and the meaning of his own authority (Matt. 16:1-4). The sign Jesus gives is that of the prophet Jonah. This means that as Jonah was in the belly of the fish for three days, so the Messiah will be in the tomb three days. The sign is Jesus' resurrection.

Jesus cautions the disciples to beware of the teaching of Pharisees and Sadducees, which he calls *leaven*. They fix on that word and mistakenly assume that he is criticizing them for not taking food with them as they once again cross over the Sea of Galilee with Jesus. He is disgusted with them. He could not possibly need food. If he could feed four thousand people as he had just done, he could readily feed twelve and himself. They have focused on material needs. He is warning them against spiritual misunderstanding (Matt. 16:5-12). The leaven of bread is quite different from the leaven of theology. Though Jesus uses *leaven* in one of his parables in a good sense (Matt. 13:33), it is used here and elsewhere in the New Testament to mean something evil.

3. *Preparation for the Establishment of the Church (16:13-18:35)*—Technically speaking, Jesus did not establish the church. He lived his life under

the ceremonies of the Temple and prayed and taught in the synagogues of Israel. The church did not come into existence until after his death, resurrection, and ascension. The birthday of the church is Pentecost.

However, Jesus conceived the church. He formulated the principles for its operation. His life was its example. His death was the means of the church's forgiveness of sin. His resurrection was its power of new life and the promise of life in the presence of God forever in the world to come. The church was to be the new Israel. It was to be the embodiment of the kingdom of heaven. Jesus was both the cause of and impetus for the church.

In this section of Matthew we receive from Jesus the blueprints for the building of the church. The divine architect himself gives the plan. Here for the first time the word *church* is used. Literally it means congregation. It is the assembly of the people of God, the followers of Jesus, the representatives of the kingdom of heaven on earth.

The confession of Peter provides the church with its theology. Peter tells Jesus who he is. "Thou art the Christ, the Son of the living God" (Matt. 16:16). This is the first confession of the Christian church. To the Christian, Jesus is God in human form. Jesus not only represents God, he is God. We need not, indeed cannot, go beyond Jesus in our understanding of the divine nature and our apprehension of the divine mind and will.

*Christ,* meaning messiah or anointed one, is technically the title of an office or position, the designation of the person who holds that office and fulfills that position. The word *Christ* becomes a name, for in Jesus person and office are inextricably one. In the Old Testament we see the change of the name of a person taking place in keeping with a change in that person's work and mission. For example, *Abram*, which means revered father, became *Abraham*, father of a multitude (Gen. 17:5); and *Jacob* became *Israel*, a name his progeny keep even to the present day. So Jesus the Christ, the messiah, the king becomes Jesus Christ, for Jesus of Nazareth is the only messiah there ever was or ever will be, and to the Christian he is king forever and ever.

Likewise, he who makes the confession has his name changed from *Simon*, the Greek equivalent of the Hebrew *Simeon*, to *Peter*, which means rock. This man, representing the apostolate, is the foundation of the church. His name always and invariably stands at the top of the list of all the apostles. Indeed, from the very beginning he was the Prince of the Apostles. The apostolate is the heart and soul of the corporate body of the church. It is to become the governing instrument of the church. It is to be the teaching authority, the ruling power, and the pastoral directive of the future church. In some Christian traditions, the episcopacy is considered to be a continuation in history of the apostolate with the bishops regarded as successors of the apostles. In other traditions, the continuation of the apostolate is more diffused among the corporate body of Christians.

The power to bind and loose was given to Peter

and to his fellow apostles. This means that the church is commissioned through its organization to forgive sin in the name of Jesus and by God's grace to make believers fit for the kingdom of heaven. The clergy have in this regard a special and peculiar privilege, for in the performance of this office they represent Christ; but at the same time they have an awesome responsibility. When the church is faithful to Christ, the church is indefectible, even infallible. Hell itself cannot prevail against the church, for the church belongs, body and soul, to Jesus Christ. That institution becomes the continuation of his incarnation throughout all history (Matt. 16:13-19).

Peter, who speaks for Christ, indeed for God, in his confession, speaks for his fellow apostles immediately thereafter. In doing so, both he and they make a serious mistake. Just after Peter's confession, Jesus tells the disciples for the first time of his passion and death. They do not understand this. They associate the Messiah with power, triumph, victory. It is inconceivable to them that the Messiah should have any relationship whatever with weakness and defeat. So Peter asks Jesus to step aside. Privately he tells him to correct what he has just said. People will misinterpret it. It will injure his work. Jesus' response to Peter is primarily the same as was his response to the devil at the end of the temptations. He calls Peter the devil, and tells Peter to get behind him. His rebuke is severe. Jesus tells Peter that he is an embarrassment to him and a hindrance to his work (Matt. 16:21-23).

Then Jesus explains the pattern of true discipleship and predicts what may happen to those who follow him all the way. Just as he will be persecuted and killed, the same fate will be theirs as well. Only people who are willing to abandon everything, even life itself, for God will discover what true life is all about. In contrast, those who work for secular reward will in the end lose everything. Those who follow Jesus will never really experience death at all, for the abundant life is unending in the kingdom of heaven (Matt. 16:24-28).

The next great event after the confession of Peter in the preparation for the establishment of the church is the Transfiguration of Jesus. We do not really know where it took place. We know that it was atop a mountain. Matthew locates the place of the confession of Peter. He tells us it was just outside Caesarea Philippi. This was a pagan city not far from Mount Hermon at the headwater of the Jordan River. Its earlier name had been Paneas, for it houses shrines of the god Pan. Titus came there to give thanks to his Roman gods for the conquest of Judea. Perhaps then Mount Hermon was the site of the Transfiguration, though Mount Tabor near Tiberias is the traditional place.

Only Jesus' intimates—Peter, James, and John—went with him to the top of the mountain. They saw him transfigured, his garments white as snow and his face aglow with the presence of God. Moses and Elijah met him there; and on that mountain with Jesus this world had juncture with the world to come.

Moses and Elijah are two of the greatest characters

THE GOSPEL OF MATTHEW

in the Old Testament. Neither died in the presence of his people. God took the life of Moses while he was alone with God on top of Mount Nebo, and angels buried his body so that to this day the site of his grave is unknown. Elijah, in the sight of his successor Elisha, was carried to heaven in a chariot of fire. These two great prophets from the Old Testament came to testify to Jesus and to relate their covenant to his.

Peter and the other two disciples, representatives of this world, see it all, and Peter wants to build three tabernacles, one for Jesus and one for Moses and one for Elijah. God spoke as he spoke at Jesus' baptism: "This is my beloved Son, in whom I am well pleased." As they descend from the mountain, Jesus cautions his disciples to keep silent about what they have seen until after the Resurrection (Matt. 17:1-13).

The Old Testament had predicted that Elijah would come back to earth to prepare the way for the Messiah. "Behold, I will send you Elijah the prophet before the coming of the great and dreadful day of the Lord: And he shall turn the heart of the fathers to the children, and the heart of the children to their fathers, lest I come and smite the earth with a curse" (Mal. 4:5-6). These are the words the angel uses to Zechariah regarding the birth of his son, John the Baptist (Luke 1:17). Jesus told the disciples that Elijah had already come, and they were correct in their assumption that he meant John the Baptist (Matt. 17:12-13).

The Transfiguration confirms the confession of

Peter. It validates and seals the theology of Christianity as being primarily Christology. Everything Christianity purports to do and all the good the church is to perform will be in the name and in the spirit of Jesus Christ.

The disciples who remained in the valley have been unable to cure a boy victimized by epilepsy. They still lack the confidence to fulfill their mission. This will be the fate of the church too, if and when that institution tries to do anything independently of Jesus and alien to the mission Jesus has given to the church (Matt. 17:14–20). Only through Jesus is the church fully the church. Trust in God is like the grain of mustard seed. Though ever so small, it is great enough to remove a mountain. The disciples had been unable to do what needed to be done because they had too little faith.

Jesus again distresses the disciples by repeating the prediction of his impending death (Matt. 17:22–23). He tells Peter to pay the temple tax for himself and Jesus, though really if the authorities understood who he was, they would not tax Jesus just as a prince is not taxed because he is the son of the king (Matt. 17:24-27).

Chapter eighteen gives us a concrete picture of Jesus' expectations regarding the attitude and behavior of Christians, requirements of his followers, and discipline for those who will constitute his church.

He uses a little child as an example of greatness in the kingdom of heaven: innocence, dependence, openness to guidance and instruction, no consciousness whatever of self-importance, willingness to be reproved, always seeking an example for imitation, devotion, and love. The basic element in Christian greatness is humility. Jesus called a little child and stood the child before his followers. "Whosoever therefore shall humble himself as this little child, the same is greatest in the kingdom of heaven" (Matt. 18:4).

The disposition of the follower of Jesus is to love little children, always seeking their welfare and happiness. Indeed, to do good to a little child is to do good to Jesus himself, while to cause injury or hurt to one is a moral and spiritual calamity, deserving the punishment of death itself. "It were better for him that a millstone were hanged about his neck, and that he were drowned in the depth of the sea" (Matt. 18:6).

Influence is powerful and pervasive. Everyone has influence. Good influences are blessings. Bad influences are curses. It is inevitable that some people will exert a bad influence. Damage to others will come because of them, because of their words and deeds, their examples, because of the evil they exert. Damnation will be their end. Therefore, carefully avoid injury to others. At the same time, carefully guard against any occasions for sinning. If a part of the human body causes a person to sin, it would be better for that person to lose that part of the body rather than commit sin. If the eye, for example, should lead one to lust or become covetous, then it would be better to lose one's sight than to yield to unwholesome desire. "And if thine eye offend thee, pluck it out, and cast it from thee: it is better for thee to enter into life with one eye, rather than having two eyes to be cast into hell fire" (Matt. 18:9).

Jesus again defines his mission in the world to seek and to save the lost and that will be the mission of the church after he has gone. Evangelism, though Jesus does not use that word nor does it as a word belong to the Gospel, is the supreme business of Christianity, namely, reclaiming the lost for God. Every person is precious in God's sight. Jesus is the good shepherd who will leave ninety-nine sheep safely in the fold and go out all night on the mountains to find one sheep that is lost. His followers cannot afford to do less. God rejoices over one reclaimed sinner more than over ninety-nine persons who need no reclamation (Matt. 18:11-13).

Jesus provides his followers with the prescription for handling mistreatment and injury at the hands of others. If a person in any way misuses a follower of Jesus, the injured person shall go quietly and privately to the offender and point out the grievance. If the offender does nothing about it and fails to provide a remedy for the offense, then the injured person is to go again with two or three witnesses. If the offender still does not provide satisfaction, the injured person is to take the issue publicly before the church. When the church renders a decision on the issue, the offender must comply with that decision or be expelled, treated as "an heathen man and a publican" (Matt. 18:17). Jesus repeats what he said earlier to Peter and this time confers the power of binding and loosing on the church itself. "Verily I say unto you, Whatsoever ye shall bind on earth shall be bound in heaven: and whatsoever ye shall loose on earth shall be loosed in heaven" (Matt. 18:18). The church, in the plan of Jesus, is definitely his agency for salvation. Here Jesus clearly teaches that outside the church there is little hope for salvation.

Though the church as an institution possesses authority entrusted to it by Christ himself and is expected to exercise that authority, the individual person does not have such authority. For a person to attempt to exercise this authority is presumptuous and dangerous. Peter, for example, asks Jesus "How many times should I forgive another person for sinning against me, say, seven times?" That, after all, is a lot of sinning. Jesus says one must forgive another seventy times seven, that is, indefinitely, just so long as that person asks forgiveness.

At this point Jesus tells the story of the king who went over the accounts of his servants. One highly placed person owed the king ten thousand talents. When the servant could not pay, the king commanded that he, his wife, and his children be sold into slavery and that all his possessions be liquidated and applied to the debt. The man fell on his knees and begged for an extension of time. The king was moved by his pleas and forgave him his debt. He did not have to pay anything. But when this servant began to settle his own accounts, he found that a fellow servant owed him a hundred denarii. This servant also asked for an extension of time, but the man would not give it to him. Indeed, he put the fellow servant in prison until he could pay the debt. The other servants who knew that the king had relieved this highly placed person of his debt reported to the king what had happened.

A talent represented the highest form of currency in Jesus' day. It was a gold piece. Ten thousand talents was an inordinate amount of money, something like a million or more dollars today. It was a fortune. A denarius was one of the lowest forms of currency. The debt of the second servant was about like a dollar today. Yet this wicked man was willing to throw the other servant into jail for this paltry sum of money.

The king was indignant. He changed swiftly from mercy to judgment, from forgiveness to condemnation and punishment. He threw his highly placed servant who owed him so much into jail. "O thou wicked servant, I forgave thee all that debt, because thou desiredst me: Shouldest not thou also have had compassion on thy fellow-servant, even as I had pity on thee?" (Matt. 18:32-33).

We cannot expect God to be merciful to us if we are unmerciful to others. Forgiveness comes from God only to those who forgive. "And his lord was wroth, and delivered him to the tormentors, till he should pay all that was due unto him. So likewise shall my heavenly Father do also unto you, if ye from your hearts forgive not every one his brother their trespasses" (Matt. 18:34-35).

The basic pattern of the church is delineated by Jesus in this portion of Matthew's Gospel. Both doctrine and discipline are explicitly set forth. Mercy and retribution, deliverance and destruction,

71

forgiveness and punishment all belong to the teachings of Jesus and therefore to the belief of his followers.

## Personal Reflection

1. Does it seem strange to you that John the Baptist doubted who Jesus was, even after baptizing him? Do you find it hard to admit your doubts when they occur? What tenets of your faith do you have questions about?
2. Using the parable of the sower, what concerns, preoccupations, or affections are most apt to choke off growth in your life?
3. Have you ever let your involvement with the church take you away from family responsibilities? How may rules be used to escape responsibility, as with the Jews who avoided caring for their parents? How does Peter's question about how many times to forgive—"Seven times seven?"—show the same attitude?
4. How many of the Ten Commandments deal with observable actions and how many with attitudes? Which are easier to change? (Exod. 20)
5. Have you ever felt "without honor in your own country" in regard to your Christian witness? Is it hard for you to discuss your faith with those closest to you?

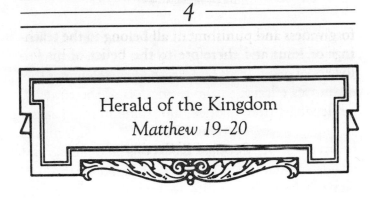

# Herald of the Kingdom
## *Matthew 19–20*

This is the shortest section in Matthew's Gospel. The material is covered in only two chapters, but it is of crucial importance. It outlines the basic principles which govern life in the kingdom of heaven. In proclaiming these principles Jesus acts as the herald of the kingdom. He does not want people to follow him for the wrong reasons. He does not choose to entice them by false expectations. Whoever would be Jesus' follower should know exactly what following him means. The ethics of the kingdom are the ethics of perfection. "Be ye therefore perfect, even as your Father which is in heaven is perfect" (Matt. 5:48).

The principles set down and emphasized in this section reflect the teachings already given earlier in the Sermon on the Mount. But here they are applied to those who desire to be subjects of the king and citizens in the heavenly kingdom.

As Matthew presents his account of the career of Jesus, these teachings and pronouncements were made after Jesus and his disciples had left Galilee and were on the road to Jerusalem. "And it came to pass, that when Jesus had finished these sayings [his discourses relative to the formation of the church], he departed from Galilee, and came into the coasts of Judaea beyond Jordan" (Matt. 19:1). This meant he went down through Decapolis and Perea and avoided Samaria. Otherwise, if he had gone through Samaria (the direct route to Jerusalem), he would not have crossed the Jordan at all.

Jesus may have left Galilee, but Galilee did not leave him. Many Galileans followed him to Jerusalem and gave him his large audiences as he taught in Perea and Judea. This was the time approaching the Passover. Some would have gone to Jerusalem anyway for the feast, but they went early to be with Jesus. And some who might not otherwise have gone, went because of him. The sick and the lame went because they knew he would heal them, and they were not disappointed (Matt. 19:2).

1. *Sexual Morality (Matt. 19:3-12)*—Jesus opens his teachings about life in the kingdom of heaven with a discussion of personal morality as it relates to sex and the use of one's sexual endowments. The kingdom of heaven here means its anticipatory stage on earth, or life in the church, the community of those who belong to the kingdom of heaven. It does not refer to the kingdom of heaven beyond death. In the next life, sex will not be a factor. There, people will not marry or be given in marriage but shall be sexless as the angels (Matt. 22:30). But here on earth sex is a factor in the determination of the quality of a

person's life and affects entrance into the kingdom of heaven while a person lives on earth.

The occasion for the teaching is a problem posed for Jesus by the Pharisees, who ask him if it is lawful under any circumstances for a man to divorce his wife. Matthew indicates that the Pharisees raised the issue in order to test Jesus. He implies that they are trying to tempt Jesus to give the wrong answer to their question, so that they might have grounds to indict him. Here their ploy would be the same as the devil's was in the temptations.

There were in Jesus' day disputes among the rabbis over divorce. Some of them questioned its moral legitimacy and doubted that it should be countenanced under any circumstances. Others laid out intricate procedures for granting divorces.

All Jesus says here is, "You know how it was in the beginning. God gave Eve to Adam, and Adam to Eve. They went through trying circumstances and terrible ordeals together, but they never sought a divorce." God made husband and wife, Jesus said, to be one—that is, one flesh. In heart and mind and will, husband and wife as they live together and love one another shall become one person. This is basic Christian teaching. It comes out of Jesus' own teaching in answer to the Pharisees. Jesus says: "What therefore God hath joined together, let not man put asunder" (Matt. 19:6).

The Pharisees object by reminding Jesus that Moses allowed men to issue certificates of divorce and thereby to separate from their wives. "When a man hath taken a wife, and married her, and it come to pass that she find no favour in his eyes, because he hath found some uncleanness in her: then let him write her a bill of divorcement, and give it in her hand, and send her out of his house. And when she is departed out of his house, she may go and be another man's wife'' (Deut. 24:1-2).

Jesus replies that it may have been Moses' teaching, but it is not God's teaching. Moses did this not because he believed it was the perfect will of God, but rather as a concession to the demands of human weakness. Even so, it is basically unfair. It gives the prerogative of decision entirely to the man.

Here Jesus delineates the difference between approval and permission. Sometimes we are forced to permit what we do not really approve. Jesus said that Moses gave permission for divorce. He did not thereby give approval. But Jesus is greater than Moses. He teaches that divorce is to be allowed only in the case of infidelity on the part of one or both of the spouses.

The disciples interrupt the discussion by saying that if there is no way to dissolve an unhappy marriage other than by infidelity, it would seem best never to get married. Jesus admits that celibacy is a legitimate and good way of life when it is a voluntary decision and is entered into for the sake of undistracted service to God and God's people. For Jesus, celibacy is not a way to avoid marriage and its obligations, as the disciples suggest. It is rather an alternative lifestyle dictated by calling and vocation. This does not mean that in the teaching of Jesus celibacy is superior to marriage, nor does it mean that the

person who never marries lives an inferior or less ful-
filling life. Both celibacy and marriage have their
own special places in the kingdom of heaven. Each
properly understood and rightly used is honored
and esteemed.

It is reasonable to assume that many of the apostles were married. Certainly Simon called Peter, or
the Rock, was married (Matt. 8:14). But Jesus never
married, and the Apostle Paul either was widowed
or single. Though Protestant ethics supports marriage for clergy, still celibacy must not be despised
any more than marriage by any Christian body.

If Jesus adorned a wedding ceremony with his
presence, he also adorned the celibate state by ad-
hering personally to celibacy all the days of his earthly life. Human sexuality is a precious but precarious
gift. Whatever use it is put to by a person must be in
order to redound to God's glory.

2. *Concern for Children (Matt. 19:13-15)*—The
intended result of human sexuality is children. The
word the Bible uses for the conceiving of children is
the word *know.* "And Adam knew Eve his wife; and
she conceived, and bare Cain, and said, I have gotten a man from the Lord" (Gen. 4:1). This does not
necessarily mean that sex between husband and wife
is reserved exclusively for childbearing. It can be precious as an expression of love between them regardless of its issue. But children are not intended by
God to be brought into the world outside the marriage bond, nor is single parenthood endorsed in
scripture as a providential way of rearing children.
The family is the proper result of the experience of

human sexuality, and the family is not a changing or intermittent relationship. It is providentially ordered to be a permanent and abiding institution into which a child is born, nurtured, and developed, until that child reaches maturity and is released in order to marry and form a new family.

> And the Lord God said, It is not good that the man should be alone; I will make him an help meet for him . . . . And the Lord God caused a deep sleep to fall upon Adam, and he slept: and he took one of his ribs, and closed up the flesh instead thereof; And the rib, which the Lord God had taken from man, made he a woman, and brought her unto the man. And Adam said, This is now bone of my bones, and flesh of my flesh: she shall be called Woman, because she was taken out of Man. Therefore shall a man leave his father and his mother, and, cleave unto his wife: and they shall be one flesh.
>
> —Genesis 2:18, 21-24

Jesus welcomed the little children when their parents brought them to him, and he was surprised and ashamed when the disciples sought to deny the children admission into his presence. It was not that the disciples disliked the children. It was simply that Jesus was in the course of his teaching. The disciples felt the children would disrupt his discourse. They thought the children could not understand what Jesus was talking about and that their Master's time could be spent more profitably.

They were surprised, and perhaps a bit hurt, when the Master rebuked them, ordered them to give the little children admittance to his presence, and said that the children belonged to the kingdom of heaven just as much as did the adults.

The church today is wise in its attitude toward children and their place in its ranks. It no longer talks of them as being the church of tomorrow, as if to say they must grow up to church membership and responsibility. Young though they are, they are already members for having accepted Christ, for having come to Christ, and they make their contributions now to the church and to the advancement of God's will. "Be as eager for me and to be in my presence," says Jesus to his disciples, "as these little children are, or else you won't be able to get into the kingdom of heaven."

The family with its children is precious in the sight of Jesus, and its preservation is essential to the kingdom of heaven.

3. *The Hazard of Wealth (Matt. 19:16-30)*— Wealth is a hindrance rather than an aid to entering the kingdom of heaven. Jesus gives this clear emphasis in the passage before us.

A man came and asked him what good thing he needed to do to obtain eternal life. The very way in which the man phrases his question captures the reader's attention. "Good Master," he says, "what good thing shall I do?" He uses *good* to characterize Jesus as a person. He uses precisely the same adjective to define the deed he needs to perform. Really the two are congruent. Good characterizes the person who performs the deed. The quality of the deed is derivative of the intention and purpose of the one who performs it.

79

Jesus does not appreciate the man's greeting. The man does not know Jesus personally and probably has never seen him before. He characterizes Jesus on the basis of his reputation. So Jesus brushes his greeting aside by saying, "Why do you call me good? Only God is good," and by implication, "You do not honestly believe I am God."

But Jesus advises him to keep five of the Ten Commandments, five that he is most likely always to have kept: the proscriptions against murder, adultery, theft, false witness, and the admonition to honor his parents. Jesus saw that this was a self-respecting man and realized that in repeating these commandments he was telling the man what he already knew, as we would say, "carrying coals to Newcastle." Jesus does add another piece of advice not contained in the Ten Commandments. It is a prescription from Leviticus 19:18, "Thou shalt love thy neighbour as thyself." The young man does not catch the significance of the addition. "Why, all of these have I kept from my youth up." But Jesus knew he had not, for the man did not really love his neighbor at all. Jesus disclosed this by saying, "Sell all you own, and give the proceeds to the poor." That would be proof that the man knew who his neighbors were and that he really loved them. The man did not stand the test. What Jesus said made the young man very sad. He was rich, and he wanted his wealth more than he wanted the kingdom of heaven.

The disciples saw and understood this. They also saw and understood that almost everyone else who had any possessions intended to keep them. That means, they thought, that the kingdom of heaven is open only to the poor. The rich cannot possibly have any place in it. Jesus admitted to them that it would be extremely difficult for a rich person to enter the kingdom, as difficult as it would be for a camel to squeeze through the eye of a needle. That, of course, is a figure of speech, an example of oriental hyperbole. No camel could ever get through a needle's eye.

Jesus says, however, that nothing is impossible with God. Therefore, some rich people will be admitted into the kingdom of heaven. Riches can be an aid rather than a hindrance if the person who possesses wealth uses it to God's will. John Wesley, for example, became by eighteenth-century standards a very wealthy man. He had an annual income larger than many wealthy estates. But he lived on the same amount of money he had lived on as a fellow of Lincoln College, Oxford, and gave all the rest to the enterprises of the kingdom of heaven.

"Where your treasure is, there will your heart be also" (Matt. 6:21). It does not make any difference how much wealth we have if that treasure is put at the disposal of God and used to enrich on earth the kingdom of heaven.

4. *God's Values (Matt. 20:1-19)*—Jesus ends his teachings on wealth with this statement: "But many that are first shall be last; and the last shall be first" (Matt. 19:30). Then he tells a story to illustrate what he means by this statement, which he repeats at the end of the story. The point of the story is that God's

81

values are not always the same as ours. Frequently, those things to which we attach the greatest importance are not at all important to God. And some things we pass by as being trivial, God looks upon as of inestimable significance.

In the busy season of harvest, the owner of a big vineyard goes to the marketplace to hire migrant workers to harvest grapes. The standard wage is one denarius for twelve hours of work a day. He offers the laborers this amount, and they consent and are employed for one day's work. Later in the morning, the owner realizes that he needs more help and comes back to the marketplace and hires another group. This time the owner fixes no pay but simply promises to be fair with them. The process is repeated off and on throughout the day, until late afternoon when the owner employs workers for just one hour.

At the end of the day, the owner tells the paymaster to compensate all the workers equally, starting with the last people hired. Each worker is to be paid a denarius, including the first ones who had worked all day, for that is the amount the owner had promised them.

The last ones hired are no doubt overjoyed at this high payment. The first are bitterly disappointed. They had not expected more than they got until they heard about the high wages of those who had worked only one hour. Then, they were disappointed and expected more. However, the owner of the vineyard said that they had no right to complain about his generosity. The money was his to do with as he pleased. All this does seem unfair to us, but we are weighing the episode on our scale of values.

Jesus says that this story illustrates what happens relative to the kingdom of heaven. God sets the standards. No one deserves God's grace—admittance into the kingdom. No matter how hard we work, we cannot earn it. In the end, it is the gift of God. Admittance into the kingdom depends on trust in God and utter dependence on God's mercy. If this comes early in life, that person qualifies and is admitted. But one can also enter just before night falls and life ends. There is no time limit for admittance during one's life. The reward for entering early is the satisfaction of work within the kingdom. One should enjoy the work and not feel that it is ''the burden and heat of the day'' (Matt. 20:12).

In the kingdom of heaven a transvaluation of all secular values takes place. From God's point of view, winning souls is far more important than the accumulation of wealth. The establishment of a church is more honorable than the organization of a new business or the transformation of a prosperous firm into a powerful corporation with multinational outreach. The heroes in the kingdom of heaven are generals who won battles over the devil rather than over human enemies. Many national heroes will do well to get into the kingdom of heaven at all, while the saints go marching in. The last in recognition here are the first there (Matt. 20:16).

The perfect example of the transvaluation by God of human values is Jesus. The Master calls the disciples aside from the crowd as they are approaching

Jerusalem to tell them again what to expect there. Jesus will be rejected by his own people. The chief priests and scribes will condemn him to death. He will be reviled and killed by human beings. But God will raise him from the dead. In the eyes of his contemporaries Jesus has no value and does not deserve to live. But in the eyes of God he is the epitome of value, the standard by which all other values are assessed. He is the last who becomes first.

5. *The Acceptance of Sacrificial Service (Matt. 20:20-34)*—The key to experiencing the kingdom of heaven is sacrificial service. There is no other way fully to participate in the kingdom. One who tries to do so in some other way is a thief and a robber.

The mother of two of the disciples gives Jesus an opportunity to teach this lesson to the Twelve, especially to her two sons. This ambitious woman, the mother of James and John, asks Jesus to promise her that when he establishes his kingdom he will seat her two sons in the chief places, one on his right and the other on his left. Evidently the two boys were standing with her when she made this request. (In Mark's account they asked for the honor themselves [Mark 10:37].) Jesus says to the mother in amazement, "Ye know not what ye ask" (Mark 10:38). And then he turns to the two boys and asks them if they are able to drink his cup—that is, to endure his suffering and shame with him, for he had just finished telling them what was going to happen in Jerusalem. The two boys self-confidently assert that they are able.

Jesus does not argue with them. No doubt he is

shocked by their arrogance. He says that, whether they realize it or not, they will all eventually drink his cup of suffering. However, the determination of greatness in the kingdom cannot be made by Jesus in advance. God will decide after all the work is completed and the quality of it assessed. The standard of determination will be service and self-sacrifice. Jesus himself will be the model, but those who consciously seek greatness and recognition are not apt to attain them. The humble and self-effacing win God's approval.

Jesus points once again to the contrast between God's values and those of society. Look, he says, at the gentile order, at the Romans who control this country of ours. They respect authority. With them the basis of authority is power. The greatest person in honor and respect with them is the one who exercises the greatest authority and demonstrates the greatest power. The lowest person is the slave who has to obey another's orders. But with God, the lowest person is the most exalted, and the highest person is the least. That means that the most important person in Roman society could be the least important person in the kingdom of heaven, and the least important person in Roman society could be the most important person in the kingdom of heaven. God will put down the mighty from their seats and exalt those of low degree (Luke 1:52). So, Jesus says to his disciples, if you want to be great in the kingdom of heaven, you must become slaves to others here on earth. If you want to be first, you must be the servant of all.

85

As Jesus and the disciples come into Jericho, passing through on their way to Jerusalem, two blind
men cry out for help from the crowds, and Jesus
touches their eyes so that they can see. Immediately
they join him, adding two more followers to his
company. In opening their eyes, he has opened their
hearts as well. They become disciples.

James and John, though apostles, are spiritually
as blind as were these two men on the Jericho road
before Jesus touched them. The two sons of Zebedee
have desired greatness without knowing what greatness is and the price they will have to pay for it.

### Personal Reflection

1. John Wesley believed in "moving on to perfection." Do you think "Be ye perfect" is an impossible command? What does the command mean
   to you?
2. How could your community of faith include
   children more fully in its public life?
3. If God were to call you to go to some faraway
   place and you agreed to go, what would you have
   to dispose of in order to travel light? How much
   more do you have than you need—how many
   pairs of shoes, how many changes of clothes, how
   many coats, blankets, dishes, towels, or books?
4. How does your sexuality affect your relationship
   with God and your response to God's call?
5. How was Jesus contrary to what his contemporaries expected in a messiah? How is Jesus contrary to what our culture applauds?

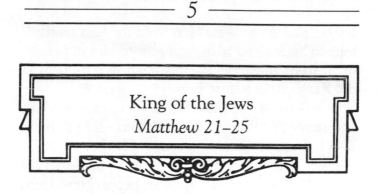

# 5

## King of the Jews
### Matthew 21–25

atthew began his Gospel with the reminder
of an Old Testament prophecy of the coming of the king and with the beginning of
the fulfillment of that prophecy in the birth
of Jesus in Bethlehem. "Where is he that is born
King of the Jews? for we have seen his star in the
east, and are come to worship him. . . . And they
said unto him, In Bethlehem of Judaea: for thus it is
written by the prophet, And thou Bethlehem, in the
land of Juda, art not the least among the princes of
Juda: for out of thee shall come a Governor, that
shall rule my people Israel" (Matt. 2:2,5-6).

In this section of the Gospel, Matthew completes
his description of the fulfillment of that prophecy
with the acceptance of Jesus as king by the people in
Jerusalem. For a brief span of time, Jesus exercises
his dominion by teaching in the Temple and proclaiming in the capital of the nation the edicts of the
kingdom of heaven.

As Jesus was born King of the Jews in the land of

Judah, where the Wise Men from the East paid tribute to his majesty with their gifts to him in Bethlehem, so he must exercise his reign in Jerusalem as did King David before him.

The Feast of the Passover is the most important and sacred of all religious observances for the Jews. This is the time when Jerusalem is filled to overflowing with pilgrims. This is the season appointed for Jesus' reign as king over his own people. Jews from all over the world are in the capital for the feast. The foreign-born sons of Abraham are assembled here with their brothers who reside in the homeland. All Jews everywhere are therefore recipients of the benefits of Jesus' presence in Jerusalem and of his rule over his people. According to Matthew, Jesus is ordained by God to be the King of the Jews.

We are indebted to Matthew for having preserved more of the teachings of Jesus, and in better order, than any of the other evangelists. He has done this in five major collections. We have examined four of these collections already (Matt. 5:1–7:29; 10:1–42; 13:1-58; and 18:1-35). In this section of his Gospel Matthew gives the fifth and last collection of the teachings of Jesus (Matt. 21:1–25:46). These are words from the throne. They are regal and majestic. They are words addressed by the ruler to his subjects. And the people to whom Jesus speaks these words are all Jews.

1. *Coronation (Matt. 21:1-16)*—Jesus' triumphal entry into Jerusalem on Palm Sunday is his coronation as King of the Jews. That is what Matthew intends to convey in his presentation of the

event. Just as in the birth of Jesus, Matthew turns back to a prophecy from the Old Testament to confirm his interpretation of that event; so now with the triumphal entry, Matthew turns again to the Old Testament to show that this is the coronation of the Davidic king.

The drama begins at Bethphage on the Mount of Olives. Jesus designates two of his disciples to go ahead of him to a nearby village to obtain an ass and a colt for his use. Zechariah had prophesied: "And his feet shall stand in that day upon the mount of Olives, which is before Jerusalem on the east" (Zech. 14:4). The two disciples find the ass and her colt in the village and bring them to Jesus as he commanded. Matthew says explicitly that this was done to fulfill prophecy, and the evangelist quotes the prophecy that is thus fulfilled: "Tell ye the daughter of Sion, Behold, thy king cometh unto thee, meek, and sitting upon an ass, and a colt the foal of an ass" (Matt. 21:5). Matthew is obviously depending upon memory for the prophecy from the Old Testament, so his statement is more a paraphrase than it is a direct quotation. He refers to Zechariah 9:9: "Rejoice greatly, O daughter of Zion; shout, O daughter of Jerusalem: behold, thy King cometh unto thee: he is just, and having salvation; lowly, and riding upon an ass, and upon a colt the foal of an ass."

This verse from Zechariah is Hebrew poetry. It is an example of parallelism, where one line repeats in different words the idea contained in the preceding line of the poem. Matthew notes that both the ass

89

and her colt were brought to Jesus, but he does not tell us which of the two Jesus actually rode upon.

The people throw their clothes in the path of Jesus as he approaches the city, and they put down palm branches before him in the road. This was a long-established act of homage. Kings in the Old Testament had been shown homage by their subjects in the same way. For example, Jehu was recognized by the people of Israel as their king in this identical manner: "Then they hasted, and took every man his garment, and put it under him on the top of the stairs, and blew with trumpets, saying, Jehu is king" (2 Kings 9:13).

The use of palm branches indicated the solemnity of the occasion. Jesus not only rode into the city of Jerusalem, he went on to the Temple. He was a priestly as well as royal king. His reign was to be messianic. Palm branches had been used at the rededication of the Temple after the return of the Jews from Exile. This was on the Feast of the Tabernacles in 141 B.C. (1 Macc. 13:51; 2 Macc. 10:7).

The response of the people was itself a litany. "Glory to the Son of David," they cried. "Glory in the highest"—that is, in heaven as well as here in Jerusalem. "Blessed is he that cometh in the name of the Lord." Jesus is our king, because God has chosen and anointed him. The music of Psalm 118:24-26 was in the hearts and on the lips of the people: "This is the day which the Lord hath made; we will rejoice and be glad in it. Save now, I beseech thee, O Lord: O Lord, I beseech thee, send now prosperity. Blessed be he that cometh in the name of

90

the Lord: we have blessed you out of the house of the Lord.''

Matthew says that the whole city of Jerusalem was moved by Jesus' great entry. Immediately after he entered the outer court of the Temple, he drove away the money changers and the merchants who sold birds for sacrifice, giving as an explanation a quotation from Isaiah 56:7: ''Even them will I bring to my holy mountain, and make them joyful in my house of prayer.'' The house of prayer, in Jesus' mind, is the Temple. Haggling, bargaining, and cheating have no place in the house of God. After driving out the money changers and the merchants, he healed the blind and the lame who came to him in the Temple. The little children kept following him about the Temple precincts, singing as they had on the road, ''Hosanna to the Son of David,'' or ''Glory to David's heir.'' *Hosanna* literally meant ''save.'' In their songs the people were asking Jesus to save them.

The chief priests became angry and upset at Jesus for what was happening. But he told them that the children had more discernment than they had. He quoted to them Psalm 8:2: ''Out of the mouth of babes and sucklings hast thou . . .'' changing ''or-dained strength'' to ''perfected praise.'' With this, Jesus walks away from their presence, leaves the Temple and Jerusalem, and returns to Bethany to spend the night.

Here there is a clear expression of regal power and majestic authority. Jesus exercises his divine rights in ejecting the moneychangers and merchants from the Temple and in pitting his authority against that of the Temple rulers.

2. *The Reign of Judgment (Matt. 21:18-22:14)*—The king is all powerful, but he is all wise, too. Solomonic in judgment, he is Davidic in the execution of judgment. Since the time of the judges, the rulers of Israel had sat at the gates of the cities, hearing the people, settling their disputes with and claims against one another, and meting out justice. The judgment seat is now the Temple. The judge is Jesus himself.

The day after the triumphal entry Jesus returns with his disciples from Bethany to Jerusalem. On the way he sees a fig tree covered with leaves and expects to find fruit on it. He has not had breakfast and is hungry. When he discovers that the tree has no fruit, he curses it so that it withers and dies. Everything in the kingdom of heaven is designed to serve the purposes of the king. Anything that fails to satisfy the purpose for which it was designed is useless and will be discarded. Consequently, the fig tree is cast aside.

"How could this have happened so quickly?" the disciples say, as they watch the little tree drying up and falling apart before their very eyes. "You can do the same thing I did," Jesus replies, "that is, if you have enough faith. By faith you can order a mountain to move out of the way and drop into the middle of the sea" (Matt. 21:21, AP).

Power belongs to the governance of the kingdom. Jesus exercises royal power now in the presence of the disciples. But they will exercise it too, in his name

92

after he is gone; and the church will continue to exercise it in allegiance to him throughout history. With the power to bind is also the power to loose. Condemnation and judgment fall heavily on the disobedient and recalcitrant, just as mercy and forgiveness are the gifts conferred on those who believe and trust. Even nature itself is under the control of God and of God's Son, Jesus Christ.

The miracle of the fig tree is unique. It is the only miracle recorded in the Gospels which demonstrates the destructive power of Jesus. There is one other, perhaps closely akin to it, where Jesus lets the devils destroy the swine and themselves as well in the sea. But here Jesus uses his supernatural power to destroy the fig tree because it has no fruit for him to eat. The disciples realize that without fruit to show for their labor, this is an example of what might well happen to them too. Jesus' own people had had their chance. He came to them. The opportunity they failed to take advantage of may now be given to others.

Jesus discredits the sincerity of the priests when they ask him by what authority he does the things he does. Countering with a question of his own, Jesus asks them whether the baptism of John the Baptist was from heaven or from people here on earth. The chief priests and elders are afraid to respond, lest their answer incriminate them with the people, who believed John was a prophet. They certainly did not believe John's baptism was from heaven, because they had ignored him (Matt. 21:23-27).

Jesus now tells two stories, the import of both of

which is the same. A father had two sons whom he asks to help him in his vineyard. One son refuses but later regrets his decision and goes into the vineyard to work. The other gladly consents to go but does not do it. Jesus asks which of the two sons obeyed his father? The first one, of course, say the Jewish religious leaders. But you, Jesus says, are like the second son. You pretend to obey God, but you did not heed the warning of John the Baptist. The tax collectors and harlots finally did hear John and heeded him, so, says Jesus to the priests and elders, they will go into the kingdom before you (Matt. 21:28-32).

The other story is about a householder who moves away but rents his vineyard to tenants—sharecroppers who are supposed to share the produce with him. Instead, when he sends his servants to collect, the tenants beat and abuse them. Finally, he sends his son, thinking they will respect him. But the tenants decide to kill the heir and seize the property. After all, possession is nine-tenths of the law. Jesus asks what will happen when the owner comes back to his property. They answer, "He will miserably destroy those wicked men, and will let out his vineyard unto other husbandmen, which shall render him the fruits in their seasons" (Matt. 21:41).

The meaning of the two stories is apparent. God will honor those who are obedient. Those who follow their own desires and ignore God's directions will be destroyed, and others will take their place in God's kingdom. The disobedient and indifferent Jews are the wicked tenants who do not give a proportionate share of the grapes to the landowner.

God is the landowner. The prophets are the servants. Jesus is the son they kill. The new tenants are
the followers of Jesus. The second story is not strictly
a parable, as we think of it, but an allegory containing several meanings. The first story is a parable; the
story conveys one meaning and has one lesson to
teach.

Jesus is the stone which the builders reject but
which nonetheless becomes the cornerstone of the
building (Matt. 21:42-44).

The chief priests and Pharisees see themselves in
Jesus' stories. Therefore, they want to arrest him,
but they realize he has won the favor of the people.
So for the time being they have to leave him alone
(Matt. 21:45-46). They fear they have another John
the Baptist on their hands.

In all these encounters Jesus maintains control of
the situation. He is the divine judge of the deeds of
those with whom he deals.

This discourse comes to a climax with the story of
the wedding feast. The son of the king is to be married, and his father sends servants to invite guests to
the wedding. Evidently the king is not too popular
with his subjects, at least those prominent enough to
be invited to court, for they laugh at the invitation
and go on about their business, one to his farm, another to his shop. Others mistreat the servants and
then kill them. The king, when he learns what has
happened, sends his army to kill the rebellious subjects and burn their city. The king sends other servants to collect guests wherever they can find them,
so that the wedding is well attended and the house is

full. Some of the guests are good, but others are
bad. At the wedding the king goes around speaking
to his guests. He finds one among them who is im-
properly clad. He does not have on a wedding garment. "Friend," the king says, "what's wrong with
you? You do not have on a wedding garment.
What's your explanation?" The poor man is speech-
less. He has no explanation. The king throws him
out. He is bound, hand and foot, and cast into outer
darkness, where he will suffer so much pain that he
will weep and gnash his teeth. Many people, Jesus
says, are called, but few of them are chosen (Matt.
22:1-14).

This is a complicated story. It, too, is an allegory.
But it has two parts. The original guests, who were
thought to be worthy of an invitation from the king,
are later pronounced unworthy because they do not
accept the invitation. Those who attend the wedding are not invited at all. They are compelled to
come. This is the first part of the story. The second
part has to do with one person present at the wedding from among those compelled to come. He is
not properly dressed, so he is thrown out and even
punished for his indiscretion. What does it all
mean?

The Pharisees, the Sadducees, the priests, and the
Levites are the elite of the people. They are the ones
who normally would be expected to receive an invitation from the king. But they make fun of Jesus
and ridicule the kingdom of heaven which he proclaims. In the end, they will all be destroyed.

Those left are the poor, the outcast, the publicans, and sinners. There are no others to constitute the kingdom. They then will fill its ranks. But the kingdom of heaven has its standards. The king expects those at the wedding of his son to show proper respect. Sinners cannot remain sinners and be citizens of this new order. When they come to the wedding, they must come prepared. They must discard their old work clothes and put on clean white garments for the feast. Those who displace the elite as guests, persons the Pharisees and their kind would never recognize as being worthy of an invitation to the king's palace, must be made worthy. In coming into the king's house these people must willingly subscribe to the king's standards and way of life, or else they too will be excluded and destroyed.

Always, when Jesus represents the kingdom of heaven, he implies its opposite, the kingdom of darkness and of evil. The wedding feast is the messianic banquet, or the kingdom of heaven as a community of saints. The ruler is God. The son is Jesus. The guests who refuse the invitation are the elite of the Jews. The others who take their place are those who believe in Jesus, heed his message, and become his followers. The man without the wedding garment represents those who, after having responded to the message of Jesus, do not live up to his standards and continue in their old way of life. The darkness outside the king's house is hell itself. If there is a heaven, there must be a hell, for the judgments of God are true and righteous altogether.

3. *The Reign of Wisdom (Matt. 22:15-46)*—The Pharisees engage surrogates to question Jesus. The

surrogates seek to slip up on the blind side of him by flattery. They falsely claim that they know all Jesus has been saying is true, that he teaches what will lead the people to God, and that he is independent of people. There is one crucial question, they say, that we want you to answer. Is it lawful to pay taxes to Caesar? Jesus sees that they are out to trick him. Paying taxes to the Romans is not popular with the Jews. In their minds, to recognize the rule of Caesar is to deny the rule of God. But not to pay taxes to the Romans means the confiscation by the Romans of all the possessions one has plus enslavement and possibly even death. "Why trick me?" Jesus says. "You know the answer already. Whose image is on the coin? It is Caesar's. So give him what belongs to him. What you owe God is different. You can still pay taxes and serve God. God does not want your money. God wants your person, your life. You and Caesar both belong to God" (Matt. 22:18-21, AP).

The Greek word for *tempt* or *ensnare*, which Jesus uses to accuse the people who ask him this question, is a hunting term. It literally means "snare" or "trap," as when one snares a bird or traps a bear. The only place the Greek word is ever used in connection with a person is in the New Testament. The disciples of the Pharisees and the Herodians sought to trap Jesus as if he had been an animal. But instead he traps them (Matt. 22:15-22).

The second effort to discredit him was a question put to him by the Sadducees. Jewish custom demanded that when a man died without children, his widow should marry his next oldest brother and seek to have a child to provide an heir to her deceased husband. The Sadducees give Jesus a test case. Suppose, they say, there are seven brothers and the oldest dies without a child and his widow marries the next, who also dies without a child, and so she goes down the line with each new husband dying without a child, until she marries the seventh and youngest brother who also dies childless. After she has buried all seven of her husbands, the widow dies too. In the Resurrection whose wife will this woman be? Here on earth she had all seven of them.

The Sadducees did not believe in life after death. In fact, this teaching is a later development in Hebrew thought. It is foreign to most of the Old Testament. The Sadducees accepted only the first five books of the Bible—the books of the Law. They assumed that the law concerning remarriage would never have been promulgated by Moses if there had been life after death, because it would cause confusion as to whose wife the widow would be in the world to come. In their minds, the Law and the Resurrection contradicted each other.

Jesus tells them that they do not understand life in heaven. There the nature of personality is different. After death, a person does not have a mortal body. There is no such thing as marriage in heaven.

Jesus also tells the Sadducees that life after death is clearly implied in books of the Law, which they accept as canonical. There God calls himself the God of Abraham, Isaac, and Jacob, long after Abraham, Isaac, and Jacob are dead. God comes to Moses in this way. Jesus says that the living God would never be introduced in terms of the dead. Therefore, Abraham, Isaac, and Jacob must be alive with God beyond the grave or else they will rise again from their graves at the Resurrection (Matt. 22:23-33).

A lawyer asks Jesus which is the greatest commandment, and Jesus tells him without elaboration: "Thou shalt love the Lord thy God with all thy heart, and with all thy soul, and with all thy mind.... Thou shalt love thy neighbour as thyself" (Matt. 22:37,39). It is interesting that a lawyer should have asked him a question about the law. This is the only place where a lawyer appears in Matthew's Gospel. In Mark there is no mention of a lawyer, but in Luke, lawyers appear six times.

Jesus then asks the Pharisees a question. "Whose son is Christ?" And they answer, "Christ is the son of David." If that be so, he says, why does David call him Lord? (see Psalm 110:1). The Pharisees could not answer him.

Jesus was the son of David if we assume that both Mary and Joseph are of the household and lineage of David. This is what Matthew believed. But Jesus was much more than the Son of David. He was the Son of God. Matthew teaches this through his account of the virgin birth of Jesus.

After this, none of the leaders of the Jews dared to engage Jesus in discussion or debate. They were not his equals. The king reigned over them in wisdom.

4. *The Reign of Counsel (Matt. 23:1-39)*—Jesus realized that a good ruler gives good advice to his subjects. The priests and religious teachers of the Jews are antagonistic and argumentative. They at-

tempt to compete with Jesus. He turns away from them and addresses the people and his disciples. His message now is to the crowds about him.

Jesus tells the people that they have been deceived by their religious leaders. The scribes and Pharisees give good advice, but they do not practice their own precepts. They put the burden of the law with all its requirements on others, but they will not lift a finger themselves. What little they do is for show—to be seen by the people and to receive their praise. These leaders court all sorts of honors and seek constant attention. They want the people to notice the scriptural verses they have tied on their foreheads and around their arms, so they make the parchment pads on which the verses are written very large. They enlarge the hems of their garments and see that their tassels are long. They want to attract attention as they perform their religious ceremonies.

The scribes and Pharisees take the chief seats in the synagogue, the seats before the ark which holds the sacred scrolls. These seats face the congregation. In that way they can see the people and be seen by them. They delight to fill Moses' seat, the chair in every synagogue where the reader for the day sits as the ruler of the synagogue. From it the law is expounded and taught and the sermon is preached. This means the scribes and Pharisees like to be the preacher on the sabbath in the synagogue.

During the week in the marketplace, these leaders want to be addressed as "rabbi." *Rabbi* means great. It is the equivalent of master or lord. The custom in Jesus' day was that a man would salute another who was his superior in the knowledge of the law. The scribes and Pharisees delighted in the daily recognition given to them in public by the people. The Jews respectfully referred to their great teachers and past leaders as fathers. Jesus instructed his followers to give up all these titles. The only person who ever refers to him as rabbi in Matthew's Gospel is Judas Iscariot. His followers must remember that they have only one spiritual Father and that is God in heaven. They have but one master, and that master is Christ, the Messiah. They themselves are just brothers and sisters. Their hallmark is sacrificial service. The greatest among them will be their servant. Those who exalt themselves will be humiliated by being debased, while the humble will be exalted (Matt. 23:1-12).

Then Jesus pronounces before the people seven woes on the scribes and Pharisees. *Woe* is the equivalent of a warning. Jesus warns the people against the sinful practices of the scribes and Pharisees. When Jesus says, "Woe to you," he vents his indignation, ashamed for what the scribes and Pharisees are doing. It is an expression of condemnation for their deeds. It is also a curse, indicating that God will punish them for their sins. Jesus is indignant that the scribes and Pharisees (1) will not enter the kingdom of heaven themselves and stand in the way of others entering it as well; (2) will do almost anything to win a proselyte only to make that proselyte twice as much a child of hell as they are; (3) confuse people by senseless oaths, telling them that if they swear by the Temple, their oath is not binding, but if they swear by the gold of the Temple, it is binding—the fools ought to realize, Jesus says, that the Temple includes all that is in it; (4) tithe some of their money but neglect justice and mercy and faith, which are weightier moral matters, when they ought both to tithe and perform these greater acts of righteousness as well; (5) are careful about outward cleanliness but careless about the inward disposition, so that they are filled with extortion and greed; (6) appear righteous but really are hypocrites, because their appearance hides all manner of iniquity inside; (7) pretend to revere the prophets of history whom their parents killed but continue to practice the evil of their parents by rejecting those whom God sends to them now (Matt. 23:13-36).

As a result of all this, Jesus breaks into a lament. His people refuse his ministry of comfort and reject his message of deliverance, and soon Jerusalem will be desolate (Matt. 23:37-39). Regretfully, he says, the inhabitants will not see him again until they are able to recognize who he really is and who it is that sent him. Only then will they be able to say, "Blessed is he that cometh in the name of the Lord" (Matt. 23:39).

5. *The Reign of Prophecy (Matt. 24:1-25:46)*—When they leave the Temple, Jesus tells the Twelve that that beautiful edifice will be destroyed. When they reach the Mount of Olives, the disciples ask him privately when this tragedy will occur. He does not answer their question but instead begins a discourse on the future and the signs that will mark the end of the world. The phrase "the end

103

of the world" is not actually used in the discourse. But we infer it from the description of events given by Jesus. We equate the second coming of the Son of man with the end of the world.

But if we use the phrase "end of the world" at all, it must have a double meaning. The fall of Jerusalem would have been the end of the world for a devout Jew. It was such for the disciples. That event, Jesus says, will take place during the lifetime of many of the disciples (Matt. 24:34). The present generation will not die before this happens.

Jesus indicates the signs preceding the catastrophe, and he warns his disciples against false teachers who claim to be Christ. He predicts wars, earthquakes, famines, and pestilence. He tells them that the abomination of desolation spoken of by Daniel the prophet will be set up in the holy place, namely, the Temple. He gives instructions to his followers to flee, to desert the city, and to hide in the mountains. Just hope, Jesus says, that this tragedy does not occur in winter, and pray that you will be in condition to flee.

All this did happen. Jesus' words were literally fulfilled. Jerusalem fell in A.D. 70. The Temple was destroyed, and the followers of Jesus did flee in advance and were scattered. Jesus did not predict the exact date.

But the end of the world has not yet taken place. Jesus says that it will not occur until the gospel is preached in all the world "for a witness unto all nations" (Matt. 24:14). The sun will turn to darkness, and the moon will not shine. The Son of man will appear in the heavens. He will come with power and great glory. When this will happen, no one knows but God, who will not share this knowledge even with the angels (Matt. 24:36).

Be ready for the Second Coming and the end of the world. Live as if your generation were the last.

Jesus' discourse seems confusing as Matthew presents it, because the description of what will take place before the fall of Jerusalem and before the end of the world is meshed and looks the same. However, the lesson conveyed by these predictions is the lesson of watchfulness and preparation.

People would not leave their houses if they knew in advance when the thief would strike. The good servant is constantly good and does not have to anticipate the master's return. It is only the evil servant who has to worry that the master might return unexpectedly. "Therefore be ye also ready: for in such an hour as ye think not the Son of man cometh" (Matt. 24:44).

It is in this vein that Jesus tells the story of the wise and foolish virgins, those five who went to the wedding with oil in their lamps and the other five who came with their lamps empty and could not purchase any oil in time for the feast (Matt. 25:1-13). He follows this with the story of the talents which the master of the house distributed to his servants in keeping with his assessment of their abilities. Two of them, in his absence, doubled the amount he had entrusted to them, while the third did nothing with his but preserve it. We are to be prepared for the second coming of Christ. Also, we are to use our time and talents profitably, so that we have something worthwhile to show for our time on earth.

We glorify our Lord and Savior Jesus Christ when we serve others. "Inasmuch as ye have done it unto one of the least of these my brethren, ye have done it unto me" (Matt. 25:40).

Rewards and punishments are both at the disposal of God who will reward the good and punish the wicked. The kingdom is not for everybody but only for those who love God and obey God's will.

## Personal Reflection

1. What emotion was Jesus feeling when he overturned the tables of the moneychangers? How do you usually handle that emotion?
2. How do you react to Jesus' cursing the fig tree? How does this miracle fit in with the way you usually think of Jesus?
3. The guests who were invited to the banquet were told to come just as they were. Do you ever feel you need to "clean up your act" in order to approach God? What do you think God requires of those who seek the Holy Spirit?
4. Jesus mourned for Jerusalem, crying for its people. Do you think God actually longs for closeness with us? How are you affected by this idea?
5. Why did Jesus not clearly draw the lines between what belongs to God and what belongs to the civil government? Who has to decide what goes in each category?

# 6

## The King of Glory
### Matthew 26–28

I n Matthew's Gospel, the passion, the crucifixion, and the resurrection of Christ are presented as a single event. Indeed, this is the only way the evangelist can justify his claim that Jesus is the King of kings and Lord of lords. To be sure, a king can be deposed by his subjects, and this is what happened to Jesus. A deposed king is generally either exiled or killed. When killed, there is no possibility of the restoration of a monarch. When exiled, there is always the chance, remote though it may seem at the time, that the ruler will come back, destroy his enemies, and take full possession of the kingdom. His reign does not end with his being deposed. Deposition is but an interlude, not a finality.

The passion and crucifixion are the deposition of Jesus as King of the Jews. At the same time, they are necessary preparation for his exaltation as the king of glory. John Wesley used to recite every Sunday from the *Book of Common Prayer:* "Thou art the king of glory, O Christ; Thou art the everlasting Son of the Father. . . . When thou hadst overcome the sharpness of death, thou didst open the kingdom of heaven to all believers.'' Christ was raised from the dead and seated at the right hand of God only after undergoing the pain of rejection, condemnation, and crucifixion.

Matthew, like the other three evangelists, had the benefit of seeing the end of the story of Jesus. He did not consider each incident in the career of Jesus as it happened, but rather saw it all in general perspective. Consequently he gives a regal cast even to the passion and death of Jesus. They stand not in the dark shadow of the cross but in the rising morning light of the Rtion. The regicide committed by Jesus' contemporaries is, then, the coronation and glorification of God's only begotten son.

1. *Conspiracy and Consecration (Matt. 26:1-16)*—Rejection and glorification are delineated together throughout the final section of the Gospel.

Jesus' work as a teacher is over. His oral message is finished. Now he is not so much the subject of action as he is the object of the action of others: his fellow countrymen and the Romans who destroy him, and God who raises him from the dead and thereby proves that he is indestructible.

Jesus again foretells his crucifixion and warns his disciples that it will be only two days hence (Matt. 26:1-2). The conspiracy against Jesus by the chief priests, the elders, and Judas Iscariot is juxtaposed with the tribute paid Jesus by the woman with the alabaster box of precious ointment.

First comes the conspiracy. The Jewish leaders confer about how they can secretly arrest Jesus and kill him. Then they agree it must not be at the Feast of the Passover, lest their action incite a riot (Matt. 26:3-5). Evidently Jesus is very popular with the people even in Jerusalem. Alongside the Jews' resolve not to do anything against Jesus during the season of the feast is Jesus' own prediction that he will die after the Feast of the Passover. This is most important in Matthew's interpretation of Jesus. The blood of the sacrificial lamb on the doorposts of the Israelitish homes in Egypt caused the death angel to pass over and spare the firstborn within those homes. Now the Lamb would be sacrificed, and his blood would spare from sin and death those who depend on it. Jesus uses the passive voice in his prediction, saying that he is betrayed in order to be crucified. But the active voice is used throughout in the conspiracy scene. The chief priests and elders take the initiative. Their plan to kill Jesus is carefully considered. The death of Jesus is premeditated.

The scene of the conspiratorial council is interrupted by another action, entirely different from it. While Jesus is eating a meal in Bethany at the home of Simon the leper, his attention is drawn to a woman with a very expensive ointment which she pours on Jesus' head. The disciples disapprove of her action. To them this seems a total waste. The ointment might have been sold and the proceeds from it given to the poor. But Jesus appreciated what she did, was grateful for her gift, and said she did this in preparation for his burial. He knew the disciples would not

109

have objected to her action had he been dead. It was customary for loved ones to anoint the bodies of their dead with precious oils and spices. When a king was anointed, oil was poured on his head. This woman by her act had anointed her king. Jesus' crucifixion and burial would at the same time be his coronation. The coronation by the Jewish crowds on Palm Sunday, which they would repudiate on Good Friday, this good woman had hailed and reaffirmed in her act of consecration in the house of Simon the leper.

What the disciples wanted to do with the ointment by selling it on behalf of the poor was laudable, but not as laudable as what the woman did with it. Jesus accepted her act as a dedicatory offering. He rebuked the criticism of the disciples with his own criticism of them. He told them that they would always have the poor with them and that there would be innumerable opportunities to help the poor. But he told them that they would not always have him. If they wanted to do something for him, now was the time.

What this woman has done will be told wherever the Gospel is preached, Jesus said, so that long after she is dead and gone, her act of tribute will stand as a perpetual memorial to her.

Except in reference to the Last Supper, this is the only time the word *memorial* is used in the Gospels, and it is used to describe this expression of love on the part of the woman for Jesus. What she did was not a philanthropic act. It was not charity in the sense of giving something to someone in need. It was not done in behalf of the destitute and needy. Instead, it was an extravagance, a waste, a display of luxury on the part of one who could least afford it lavished on one who really did not need it. Yet that act of personal tribute becomes a part of the Gospel, illustrating love for Jesus must be the highest priority in our lives.

Judas Iscariot was there, saw what the woman did, and witnessed its effect on Jesus. Nonetheless, he repaired himself to the chief priests and offered to betray Jesus to them for a price. Even in the action of Judas, Matthew sees the fulfillment of prophecy. "They weighed for my price thirty pieces of silver" (Zech. 11:12). The chief priests and the elders, the Romans, Judas—though all evil in their handling of Jesus and worthy of final judgment and condemnation—are nonetheless pawns of destiny and agents in the fulfillment of prophecy. Matthew remembers Jesus' words: "Woe unto the world because of offences! for it must needs be that offences come; but woe to that man by whom the offence cometh!" (Matt. 18:7).

The anointing of Jesus by the woman on the one hand and the conspiracy of the priests and elders and their contract with Judas on the other hand, though entirely different in motive and deed, nonetheless stand together in the Gospel. Both are essential in the fulfillment of the mission of Jesus.

2. *The Passover Meal (Matt. 26:17-30)*—The double motif is apparent at the Last Supper. On the one hand, Jesus observes the Passover with the Twelve and interprets it, not historically, but escha-

tologically (in terms of the future), where he himself becomes the paschal lamb. On the other hand, he calls their attention to the fact that there is a traitor among them.

The disciples asked Jesus where he wanted to go for the meal. He replied that they should ask a certain person in Jerusalem to invite them home for the observance. This would have been on Thursday of what we now call Holy Week, the day before the Crucifixion. On that day the lambs were slaughtered, and they had to be eaten that very evening. A day started and finished at sunset for the Jews.

Moses prescribed that the Passover would be observed by families. Each household would provide its own meal. However, if a family was too small to consume the lamb, another might be invited in to share the meal. Jesus' family was the disciples. In this instance, it is not likely that they shared the meal with the family in whose house they observed the Passover. Probably the family ate their meal together in one part of the home, and Jesus and the disciples ate theirs in another, say in a room upstairs, the upper room as it has come to be called. Matthew stated that the disciples did as Jesus had instructed them to do and that they prepared the meal (Matt. 26:19). If they had eaten with the family, the members of the family would have prepared the meal.

Matthew recalls that at the beginning of the meal Jesus predicts that one of the Twelve will betray him. This upsets the group. Each protests that it is not he to whom Jesus refers. We translate this response as a question: "Is it I, Lord? Is it I?" But what they really meant was a categorical denial, "Not I, Lord! No, no, not I!" Jesus ignores them. He goes on to say that the person who dipped his hand in the dish with him is the guilty person. In Jesus' day people ate their food by sopping a piece of bread in the dish and taking pieces of food up on the slice of bread. However at Passover, they dipped their hand in the dish and took the food out with their fingers. In all likelihood they had not noticed the person who put his hand into the dish with Jesus. The man himself knew. Jesus knew. Judas said, "You don't mean me, do you?" Jesus simply replied, "You know the person I mean." Here again the others seem not to have caught the meaning of Jesus' response to Judas. Had they understood, they probably would have risen in indignation against Judas.

Immediately Jesus took bread and blessed it and gave it to them to eat with the explanation that this broken bread was his body. He gave thanks for the wine and poured it for them to drink, explaining that this was his blood which he would shed for many for the forgiveness of their sins. He called this the new covenant. He insisted that he would never again drink wine until he had the opportunity to drink it with them in the kingdom of God. What does all this mean?

Bread and wine are the perpetual symbols of Jesus' body and blood. At the Last Supper, Jesus served the disciples the bread and wine which they themselves had prepared for the meal. The bread and wine represented the sacrifice Jesus would later make on the cross for them and for others, so that their sins might be forgiven.

This was a new covenant which would take the place of the old covenant established by Moses in Egypt when the Israelites ate the lamb and spilled its blood on the doorposts of their home so that the angel of death would pass over them. The followers of Jesus would substitute the Last Supper for the Passover meal of the Jews. They would eat bread and drink wine in remembrance that Christ their savior died on the cross for their sins and thereby effected their deliverance from sin and death.

Jesus knew that this would be his last meal on earth. He would eat no more. The next banquet he would host would be with those whom he had redeemed in God's everlasting kingdom beyond all time and all earthly existence. Thus the Last Supper anticipates the messianic banquet in the kingdom of heaven.

After eating bread and drinking wine together, Jesus and the disciples sang a hymn and walked out of the house, left the city, and came to the slopes of the Mount of Olives.

All the food and features of the old Jewish Passover are here. The ritual observances are in order and are complete. But as the meal progresses, it takes on a new character altogether. It is transformed by Jesus into a Christian sacrament. The prayers and the hymn are the same as they always were, and yet they are entirely different. This feast marks the transition from the old order to the new. The Passover in Jerusalem on the eve of the Crucifixion becomes the Eucharist, the new meal in the new Israel to establish a new world.

3. *In the Garden and before the Sanhedrin (Matt. 26:31-75)*—But the old Israel is in power now, so much so that even the heralds of the new Israel cannot resist its sway. Therefore, Jesus' first utterance when he and his disciples reach the Garden of Gethsemane is the lament that they will all desert him before this night is out. Their failure to stand by him in his passion is the fulfillment of the Old Testament prophecy, which Matthew is careful to note by including the quotation which Jesus gives when he predicts what his disciples will do. "Smite the shepherd, and the sheep shall be scattered" (Zech. 13:7).

Peter protests. He says to Jesus, "No matter what these others might do, I will never desert you." Jesus responds, "Why, Peter, you will be the very first one to leave me. Before dawn, you will deny me three times by swearing that you never knew me." "No, no, no," Peter cries, "I will die first. You mean more to me than life itself." And the other ten who are present echo Peter's sentiments.

Jesus turns away from the disciples and walks farther into the Garden of Gethsemane on the lower slopes of the Mount of Olives, but Peter, James, and John follow him. He stops them and asks them to stay together where they are and pray for him. He tells Peter and the two sons of Zebedee: "My soul is exceeding sorrowful, even unto death" (Matt. 26:38). Jesus is so steeped in scripture that he expresses himself with quotations from the Hebrew

Bible. What he says here is from Psalm 42:5. He goes farther on but stays in sight of the three disciples. When he is entirely alone, he unburdens his soul to God. He confesses to his heavenly Father that he is afraid and wants to be spared the agony that is before him, but that he is prepared to fulfill the will of God. Here we see how human Jesus really was. His reaction to anticipated pain was the same as ours would be.

He comes back to find the three disciples have fallen asleep. He shames Peter. "Remember what I told you. See, you could not stay awake praying for me just one short hour. Oh, I know your intentions are good, but you are weak. You had better pray that you do not fall into temptation."

Jesus walks away to pray again to God. He still dreads what lies before him. He comes back a second time to the three disciples. This time they are fast asleep, and he does not disturb them. It is after he has prayed alone the third time that he wakes them, for he realizes that the time of his arrest has come. "Get up," he says. "Be wide awake. I am about to be betrayed. Let us go from here."

At that point Judas Iscariot arrives with the guards of the high priest and others forming a motley crew. The noise no doubt drew the other ten disciples to Jesus. Judas had told the chief priests that he would identify Jesus by kissing him. So he rushes up to Jesus, throws his arms around him, and kisses him. Jesus says to Judas, "Friend, wherefore art thou come?"

Matthew is the only evangelist who uses the word

*friend* in his Gospel. Usually he employs the word to mean its opposite. It is used sarcastically or tongue in cheek. Jesus calls Judas friend when his act of treachery shows him to be the worst enemy Jesus could possibly have.

One of the disciples, whom Matthew does not identify, tries to defend Jesus. This disciple cuts off the ear of the servant of the high priest with his sword. John tells us in his Gospel that the disciple was Peter (John 18:10). But John wrote his Gospel after Peter was dead. If Matthew wrote his while Peter was still alive, then perhaps he did not identify him for security reasons. He did not want to expose Peter and make him liable for prosecution. Peter probably had acted so quickly that, in the dark, the crowd had not seen who had struck the servant of the high priest.

In order not to diminish Jesus' role as rightful king, Matthew is careful to record that Jesus said he could have called down from heaven more than twelve legions of angels if he had chosen to do so. He rebuked the guards for coming after him in the middle of the night with weapons when they might have taken him at any time while he taught the people in the Temple.

Jesus was brought then before the high priest and the council of the Sanhedrin, the highest governing body in Jewry. The law required that for a person to be indicted there had to be at least two witnesses to the crime. The tribunal produced many witnesses, but the evidence they gave was contradictory and insubstantial. Finally two witnesses did agree that Jesus had predicted that he would destroy the Temple and then rebuild it in three days. But this testimony became irrelevant when the high priest asked Jesus, ''Are you the Messiah?'' Jesus replied, ''You have spoken correctly, and you shall see the Messiah in power and coming on the clouds of heaven.'' This is all the Sanhedrin needed. It condemned Jesus for blasphemy.

The other disciples dispersed and fled after Jesus' arrest in the garden. But Peter followed the master and waited for him in the courtyard outside the high priest's palace. There he was accosted by two different women, each of whom said Peter had been with Jesus. He said he did not know what they were talking about. But others who stood about said, ''Your accent is Galilean. You have to be one of his followers.'' Peter swore that he had never known Jesus. The cock, herald of the dawn, began to crow. Peter remembered Jesus' prediction that he would deny him, and Peter broke down and cried.

Inside the high priest's palace, Jesus was being mocked and abused and spat upon. People would come up behind him and strike him with their hands and then say, ''Messiah, prophesy to us and tell us who hit you.''

4. *Condemnation and Crucifixion (Matt. 27:1-66)*—The trial of Jesus is unique. There has been none other quite like it before or since. Jesus was exonerated under Roman law. Nonetheless, it was the Roman penal code that put him to death.

All the Sanhedrin could do was to indict Jesus. It acted as a sort of grand jury. It could neither try a

118

case nor pronounce a sentence. It could recommend, in this case, to indict. It was up to the Romans to make final disposition of a case when the case was grave enough to carry the death penalty.

Early on the Friday morning after Passover, the Jewish leaders took Jesus to the Roman procurator Pontius Pilate, insisting that he find Jesus guilty and put Him to death. The evidence the Jews presented was so flimsy and nebulous that Pilate found Jesus innocent.

When Judas Iscariot heard that the Sanhedrin had condemned Jesus to death, he regretted that he had betrayed his master, and he returned the thirty pieces of silver to the chief priests and elders. He admitted to them that he had betrayed an innocent person. "That means nothing to us," they said. They had gotten from Judas all they needed. The traitor flung the pieces of silver on the floor before them and went outside the city and hanged himself. The Jews could not put "blood money" into the Temple treasury, so they bought a field with the thirty pieces of silver and used it as a place to bury strangers. It was known as potter's field or the field of blood.

Matthew says this is the fulfillment of prophecy. He quotes a verse from the Old Testament which he attributes to Jeremiah, but which is from Zechariah 11:12-13. He knew the verse, but his memory failed him as to its author. The name "potter's field" comes from the fact that Zechariah threw thirty pieces of silver to the potter. Matthew's confusion was due to the fact that Jeremiah went to a potter's house (Jer. 18:2) and later purchased a field (Jer. 32:6-15). The land was also called "field of blood" because the chief priests had purchased it with blood money. Matthew does not specify where Judas hanged himself. Later tradition identifies the place as this same field of blood. If so, the priests purchased the field of Judas' suicide.

Pilate asked Jesus if he was the King of the Jews, and he admitted to Pilate that he was. However, Jesus refused to respond to any of the witnesses the Jewish leaders brought to testify against him. Though his life was at stake, he offered no defense. Pilate marveled at his composure and self-control. Pilate's wife warned her husband to take no action against Jesus. She had had a dream about Him, and she was sure Jesus was innocent. Pilate realized that the Jews were trying to kill Jesus because they envied him.

Since the custom was to release a prisoner each year at the time of the Feast of the Passover, Pilate offered to release Jesus. Evidently there was only one other candidate for clemency, a notorious criminal named Barabbas. He was so notorious everyone knew his name. Nonetheless, the crowds chose Barabbas. The people would choose anyone in preference to Jesus. Only because he feared a bloody riot did Pilate yield to the demands of the crowd. He took a bowl of water and washed his hands, saying that he found no fault whatever in Jesus and could not assume responsibility for his death. The Jews in the courtyard cried out that they would take responsibility for Jesus' death.

The soldiers took the prisoner, stripped him of his garments, put a scarlet cape over him in imitation of the purple robe of an emperor, gave him a reed for a scepter, put a crown of thorns on his head, bowed before him in mockery, and taunted him as King of the Jews. Afterwards they led him out with his own cross on his shoulder. It was so heavy that a Cyrenian, Simon by name, had to be conscripted to carry it for him. Pilate had inscribed over his head on the cross: "This is Jesus the King of the Jews" (Matt. 27:37). Even in mockery, Jesus' claim was honored and the truth told.

According to Matthew, of all Jesus' followers, only three women accompanied Jesus to the cross, and Matthew does not include among them Jesus' own mother. The evangelist specifies that Jesus was led out to the place of the skull for his execution. Evidently it was a hill resembling a human skull. It was unclean because it was the place of executions. The sign Pilate put on the cross was the charge made against Jesus, the one charge Jesus admitted to. He was being executed simply because he had said that he was the King of the Jews. The Romans always attached the crime for which criminals were executed to the cross on which they were nailed.

Jesus was executed between two thieves. Here again the Old Testament prophecy is fulfilled. "He was numbered with the transgressors" (Isa. 53:12). They gave Jesus vinegar to drink mingled with gall, but when he tasted it, he would not drink. "They gave me also gall for my meat; and in my thirst they gave me vinegar to drink" (Psalm 69:21). The sol-

121

diers gambled for his clothing. This was the custom in that day, for soldiers were given the personal effects of the criminals they executed. "They part my garments among them, and cast lots upon my vesture" (Psalm 22:18). The crowds around the cross taunted Jesus, saying, "You claim to be able to destroy the Temple and rebuild it in three days. If you can do that, you ought to be able to save yourself now. If you really are the Son of God, you can come down from your cross. Do it! Prove it to us!" The chief priests, scribes, and elders joined the others in reviling Jesus. "Let's see if God will help him. He claimed to be God's son. If he is the King of Israel, let him come down from his cross, and we will believe him." The thieves, the two persons crucified with Jesus, also joined in mocking him. "All they that see me laugh me to scorn: they shoot out the lip, they shake the head, saying, He trusted on the Lord that he would deliver him: let him deliver him, seeing he delighted in him" (Psalm 22:7-8).

This went on until Jesus in desperation cried, "My God, my God, why hast thou forsaken me?" (Matt. 27:46). The people about the cross thought he called to Elijah for help, and they said, "We will see whether Elijah will come to save him." Jesus' words are the opening verse of Psalm 22. If not aloud, at least in his heart he said the rest: "For he hath not despised nor abhorred the affliction of the afflicted; neither hath he hid his face from him; but when he cried unto him, he heard" (Psalm 22:24).

For three hours before Jesus' death, there had been darkness over the land. This often happens when a storm sweeps up from the desert to the east of Jerusalem. It carries dust and sand in its wake. Before the first Passover in Egypt, when God slew the firstborn of the Egyptians, there had been darkness in the land for three days (Exod. 10:22). Amos, too, had prophesied: "And it shall come to pass in that day, saith the Lord God, that I will cause the sun to go down at noon, and I will darken the earth in the clear day" (Amos 8:9). That is what happened. It was dark on the day of crucifixion from noon until three in the afternoon, when Jesus died.

Just after Jesus' death, Matthew relates that an earthquake occurred. The quake opened graves and the saints of Israel's past awoke from their sleep, and, after the Resurrection, walked the streets of Jerusalem and were seen by many people. The veil of the Temple was rent in two and the Holy of holies was exposed. The Roman centurion and his guards saw all this and were afraid. They said: "Truly this was the Son of God" (Matt. 27:54). This "regicide," committed by the people of Jerusalem, was the beginning of the new kingdom of the Gentiles.

Joseph of Arimathea, a rich man who was a follower of Jesus, got permission from Pilate to remove Jesus' lifeless body from the cross. He deposited it in his own newly hewn tomb, and two women sat opposite the site as a stone was rolled to close its entrance. The Jews set their own guards to watch the tomb and to seal its entrance. All this was done before sunset, which was the beginning of the sabbath day. Jesus had been tried, condemned, crucified, and buried all within the span of a single day.

5. *Glorification (Matt.* 28:1-20)—Matthew adds several details in his account of the Resurrection which are not found in Mark's Gospel. The women who sat opposite the tomb know the exact site of the place where he was laid. Matthew mentions but two women, Mary Magdalene and Mary the mother of James and John, whom he calls the other Mary. He tells us that there was a great earthquake, in the midst of which an angel descended from heaven and rolled back the stone. Evidently the earthquake broke loose the seal by which the Jews had secured the stone against the entrance to the tomb. Stones used to close the entrances to the tombs of the rich in Jesus' day were big round slabs in the shape of wheels. They were set in channels, also hewn out of stone, and could, with great effort, be rolled back and forth to open and close the entrances. The stone to the entrance of Jesus' tomb had been sealed permanently by the Jews (Matt. 27:66). The earthquake and the descent of the angel had taken place before the women undertook their journey to the tomb.

Before the women arrive, the guards whom the Jews had set on watch before the tomb have all gone. They were on duty when the earthquake shook the tomb and when the angel descended from heaven. They actually witnessed what to them was a dread event. The angel's appearance was like lightning, and his raiment was as white as snow. They were so frightened by what they saw that they could not move. They either fainted or else were paralyzed by fear. This was before daybreak.

When the women arrive, the angel is sitting on

the stone he has rolled back from the entrance, and the tomb is wide open. The Matthean details which are not in Mark include the earthquake, the descent of the angel, the terror and paralysis of the guards—the preparation in advance, so to speak, for the coming of the women. Mark leaves all this out of his account, where the women are surprised to find the tomb open and venture inside before they receive news about Jesus.

In Matthew the angel dispels the fear of the two women by telling them he knows whom they are seeking and that Jesus is not here but has risen from the dead. The angel invites them to come into the tomb and see where it was that Jesus had been laid at his burial. Evidently they had not gone into the tomb with Joseph of Arimathea when Jesus' body had been carried there from the cross.

The angel commissions the women to tell the disciples what has happened and to instruct them to return to Galilee in order to meet Jesus there. The women run to bring the good news to the disciples. Jesus stops the women on the way. When they recognize him, they fall at his feet and worship him. Jesus affirms the directive of the angel that they are to tell the brethren that he will see them in Galilee.

At this point in his account Matthew returns to the guards at the tomb. They have recovered from their shock, regained the use of their limbs, and have reported to the chief priests in Jerusalem what has happened. The leaders of Israel bribe the guards to lie and to say that the disciples had stolen the body of Jesus in the night while the guards slept.

The Jews promised the guards that if the governor heard about the incident, they would be protected.

The eleven disciples journeyed to Galilee and met Jesus on a mountain. Matthew indicates that was the designated meeting place. No place is mentioned in the instructions given the women, but this mountain was the customary meeting place for Jesus and his disciples during the Galilean ministry. When they saw Jesus, they worshiped him, though Matthew admits that some doubted. This is a serious admission and is evidence of the reliability of the Gospel. The evangelist includes everything, the bad as well as the good, skepticism along with belief, doubt just as much as faith.

The Gospel concludes with the great commission. Jesus assures his disciples that he has all power both in heaven and on earth. In his strength, then, they are to go over the world winning converts, teaching these new followers even as he taught them, baptizing them in his name and in the name of God and the Holy Spirit, and promising them that he will be with them always to the end of the world.

The great commission is the climax of Matthew's Gospel. It is the culmination of its theme. Jesus of Nazareth was born to be king and was recognized as a king by the Wise Men who came to worship him in Bethlehem. Finally, after being rejected and killed by his own people, Jesus is vindicated and affirmed by God through his resurrection from the dead. He is proclaimed by the disciples as king of the whole world. The church they establish in Jesus' name will be the new Israel, and those they baptize will consti-

tute its members, citizens of a universal kingdom
that is coterminous with the whole world. This kingdom as represented by the church is a temporal institution, but it extends beyond time and beyond existence. Christ's is an everlasting kingdom. All power
is given him in heaven as well as on earth. The head
of the church is the king of glory.

## Personal Reflection

1. The disciples were concerned about the wasteful-
   ness of the woman who anointed Jesus. Do some
   of the actions called for by your faith seem waste-
   ful or irrational to you? Does your rationality ever
   hinder you in experiencing or participating in the
   mystical part of faith?
2. "Jesus' family was his disciples." Is your faith
   community your family? Why is it necessary for
   the faith community to fill the roles of family?
3. Jesus admitted his dread and fright in the face of
   doing God's will. Is it as easy for you to express
   those emotions about your faith as it is to talk
   about the comfort and strength and other more
   acceptable responses?
4. Jesus felt forsaken by God. Have you ever felt
   that way? When?
5. Matthew includes accounts of doubters and
   doubting in his Gospel. How is doubting a valuable part of faith? How can we help people ex-
   plore their doubts more openly in church?

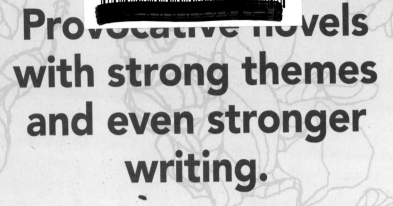

# Provocative novels with strong themes and even stronger writing.

## point of view

Check out
**www.pointofviewbooks.com**
for author interviews,
questions for discussion,
trailers, and more!

## ACKNOWLEDGMENTS

I thank the following people for jumping on the
furniture with me:

My agent, Ginger Knowlton

My editor, Catherine Frank

The Fairy GodSisters, Ink, of Santa Barbara
(Lee, Robin, Val, and Mary)

The Ventura Group for Wayward Writers
(Lynn, Laura, Dan, and Siri)

The Divine Keri Collins

Styliani Munroe, niece of extraordinary and
much-appreciated enthusiasm

Jon Chinburg, a sweet boy from down the street
and a sweet man now

and

Sonya Sones, for her belief in the importance of this
novel at a very early stage

I am always there.
But they don't care if I am
because I am furniture.

I don't get hit
I don't get fondled
I don't get love
because I am furniture.

Suits me fine.

When the garage door goes up
he's home.

We close up conversation
and scuttle off like crabs
each to our room—
Shut the door.
Shut the door.
Shut the door.

Mom alone in the kitchen
where she should be

before the garage door goes down
and we are locked in hell.

Dinner.

He knocked Darren onto the linoleum.

I don't remember his arm swing,
just Darren and his chair—
eight tangled limbs on the floor.

No reason that I could see.

But my father picked up his reasons and his
    plate and went
to eat
in the living room.

Darren picked up his chair and himself and we
are now eating
in customary ice-age silence.

When I was much younger
Yaicha and Darren
would point at my nose
and say,

"You don't look like us
your nose is different
you don't belong."

Yaicha and Darren
told me that I was
the mailman's child,

and I got so angry,
stalking away,
hot steam in my ribs.

Yaicha and Darren
told me that I was

the mailman's child

and now I am thinking
how wonderful it would be
to have
the mailman as
my father.

My mom.

At times I still want to
sigh,
curl into her,
nourish in her motherness,
especially
when she wears that
old suede jacket that
smells of fall leaves, like
      the pliable leather armchair
      left outside on the back porch.

But she doesn't welcome that.
Maybe I am not that young anymore.

And when he is there
all her motherness
has to be
spent on
him.

Oh, yay
charity day
visiting Angeline the Wimp.


I see her often enough at school.
Don't want to visit her house.


Since her dad
left her and her mousy mother
for some bouncy secretary in Texas
      mom and I
      are here
      to
      touch base, be friendly.
      Our moms met way back when we were
        in preschool.


Angeline irritates me—
she's delusional,
terrified,

weak.

the ocean has "man-eating seaweed"

the garden has "corn-barfing worms"

the fancy sound system has "thought-tracking
  speakers."

I didn't choose to be friends with her.

Angeline doesn't
have a father around

and my mom says she
really
needs one.

Maybe.

But
not
like
mine.

Scrubbing my volleyball knee pads
while I'm in the shower,
hot water,
way too much soap,
but, man,
three days of preseason training
on the sly
collected a hell of a stink.

The foam won't dry out overnight.

My knees will probably
froth in soap bubbles
if I dare set foot in tryouts tomorrow.

First day.
Ninth grade.
High school.

Honking in the parking lot,
upperclassmen back smacking,
squeals of recognition,
a grimly nodding principal.

I'm supposed to feel something more than just
rattled
by the sheer number of people in the halls, right?
Scared?

Except that I've been in and out of
   this building
a bunch of times for years—
        Yaicha's musicals,
        Darren's debate team.

I learned my classrooms from the map,

and I just spent whole days going to volleyball
   training here,
so I kind of get it already.

I like school.

Not scared.

But excited in that
         jiggering-on-too-much-hot-sauce
          kind of way
that it's time to
step out
of my old framework,
raw and amorphous,
to become something I've never thought of
   before.

*After* school is a different story.
Volleyball tryouts.

I wasn't going to do it.
Even though I crave it
I wasn't supposed to
try out
because
my father said,
"Competition is dangerous for
    a young girl's mind."

But I already like the girls from preseason
    training.
And that tenth-grader Rona saw me
growing roots
outside the locker room
dangling my new volleyball sneakers
        bought with my own money
        in secret.

Rona looked me in the eye.

"You *are* going to put on some shorts, right?"

and as she steered me
through the splintered wood door
she told me
about some player last year
who tried out with mittens on
to protect her nylon nails.

And I wasn't even nervous
because it was the same intramurals coach
from last year in eighth,
        Coach Roy,
and he had asked me to come
try out.

Passing drills
setting drills
hitting drills—
he had us try everything
with a smile
and a "one more time"
        if we didn't get it right.

I was so full in my skin,
blood pumping through,
leg muscles grinding
as I jumped and sprinted and dove.

At the end we stretched,

happy and sweaty
and on the way
to the locker room
Coach Roy said to me
"Great job!" like he did to everyone
but he meant it, too.

He looked right at me when he said it.

Swinging in the hammock,
     relaxing muscles
     heavy from tryouts,
a wild pattern
of shivering hemlock branches above me
serrating the sky.

Grasping the nearest twig
as I swing,
swing,
a few striped needles
come away
crushed
in my hand.

Inhaling their sharpness
I touch one to my tongue,
swing,
swing,
idly wondering
if this is the hemlock
people use to poison each other.

He's losing it bad tonight,
the second time this week,
chasing Yaicha out of the kitchen
holding his chair over her head—

she cowers on the living room rug.

I am close behind mom,
but it's not like I can ever do anything.

No one sees me.

Mom gets him to stop,
        with taut and twisted face, open hands,
before the chair comes down.

Yaicha runs.

He sits down, tired,
and says to mom,

"I'm sorry you had to see that."

Inevitable that he does it.

But he doesn't really want
a witness.

Lying in bed,
I am thinking that it's unfathomable,
why his anger begins
or why it ends.

There was that time
He woke us all up
at two a.m.
to go out in the street to see
the aurora borealis,

a magical flickering green spirit
dancing against the black sky
with us underneath it,
and I thought we were suddenly
a family,
woven,
peaceful.

But when we went back in
there was a raccoon in the open garage—

scuttling scared
on concrete—

and my father laughed and
shut the garage door,
roaring to send the animal
ricocheting off the rakes in the corner
in terror,
frantic for escape.

My father trapped the raccoon for the night.

Not one of us said
anything against it.

In the morning
he told Yaicha
to clean up the curling round of
raccoon shit,
cold on the
garage floor.

The foam cushions
on the old couch downstairs
disintegrate
daily
in a hush,
like each of us,

small flecks of
hardening puffs
raining mute to the floor
when I flop down to study.

And the more the couch gets used,
the less foam it keeps—

someday
just an uncomfortable
frame,
springs and other inner workings
exposed.

Silent.

Of course a full hallway.
I stub my sneaker
on the kid's heel
and we tumble like
        bowling pins,
                three of us,
        books          broadcast
                underfoot.


Dammit!


I am seventeen shades of crimson,
spitting epitaphs:

        "Here lies the girl
        whose feet grew
        their own brains
        and threw the rest of her
        over a cliff
        in front of everyone
        she'd ever known."

They call us
Nopes
      the "out" crowd,
      we don't fit their
      dog-show guidelines
      wealthy-beautiful.


We call them
Yups
      they have to
      all agree,
      yup each other
      every day on every thing.


And we say
Nope, don't
want any part
of your Yuppitude
      so tight
      society will burst
      with any change

of thought.

But being a fractured, momentary gathering
and not an actual collective,
we say
Nope
individually
with scrambled cadence

and their
Yup
is way
louder.

Those girls
over there
with Ginger Khan
know everything
about each other
        guys
        music
        toothpaste
        bra size
everything.
Look at them
huddle,
hunching their shoulders
so I can't see in.

So into themselves
they don't get it,
I don't want them
don't want
to know the day
their PMS starts,

don't want
to tell anyone
everything
about me.

"The whole *day*?" I whine.

Mom is driving with gloved fingertips.
I scraped frost off the windshield this
   morning.

"Anke, her mother may as well make the most
   of her time in Boston.
I'm sure you and Angeline will find plenty to
   do."

Right.
Me and Ange.
Whoopin' it up.

My nostrils snort
twin fog blurs on my window.

Mom glances over.
"It's Saturday, maybe Yaicha would take you

two to the mall?"

I snort again.
"Perfect, Mom.
I hate shopping,
Angeline is terrified of Yaicha,
and Yaicha is not about to agree to play
    chauffeur and babysitter."
I glare at the coming stop sign.

Mom sighs.
Honda brakes engage with rhythmic squeaks.
"Honestly, Anke. Your attitude is part of the
    problem."

I grind my teeth.
Wheels grind over gravel to a halt.
Red octagon, looming in my window.
"Sorry, Mom, but somehow I resent having a
    frickin' playdate at the age of fourteen."

Left turn onto Harper Street.

Angeline's street.
Mom taps the wheel gently with a lambskin
  thumb.
"Is she so awful, really?"

I push a breath through my lips.
Is she? Awful?

"She's fine.
But fine doesn't mean she's a friend, either."

And I don't get a choice.

"You use *that?*" Angeline squeals.

What, she's never split wood?
My shoulders are warm.
I've been at this for fifteen minutes already.

She perches on the edge of the porch to watch,
nestled in her fluffy parka
like a lost tropical bird,
knees together.

Swinging the split maul overhead,
        upper hand sliding down the shaft,
the edge lands
*CRACK* into the oak standing on end.

Blade stuck in the rippled grain,
I lift the whole shebang, maul and log,
and whack it on the stump base.
*CRACK*.

Swing,

CRACK.
Perfect thirds.

"Why don't you let Angeline try?"
How long
has my father been standing behind us?

"Oh! Oh, I don't think I could swing that
   enormous thing!"

Silently, he hands me the heavier ax,
takes mine.
Hands on Angie's hands,
he first demonstrates the swing
        as he did for me years ago,
Angie squirming, giggling.

Vessels in my heart burn,
and I turn back to my work.

Jed has wavy dark hair
eyes the ink of night
beautiful cheekbones
lean in jeans
a tilted smirk.

He lives across the street.

He says he likes me because
I just want to be friends

and I do want to be his friend
because that makes me
someone
different
from all those girls
who are dying to be more.

But no one knows
we take naps on his
damp
basement couch

after school
and sometimes he kisses me there.


It doesn't mean anything
to either one of us—
      he's a senior, after all—
but
he doesn't do it
with anyone else, either.

Final cut for volleyball,
still a mixed
carton of eggs,

cliques of chicks
all primped
bouncing
blue-and-gold hair bows
and Barbie-smooth legs,

lonely homelies
all pimpled
slouching
asparagus legs drowning in
their brothers' shorts.

But quickly quickly
    Skill
    Promise
    and
    Team Spirit

sliced through,

sniggering girly-girls
scrambled
with the rest of us
into a
glorious quiche
of mutual grins.

And as we clapped and whooped at the end,
some leftovers stood on the rim

but I am daring to be hopeful.

Trotting along the sidewalk,
salty and tacky with sweat,
I reek!

I reek with possibility.

Volleyball.

We won't find out results for a few days,
but right now,
bouncing through the neon blast of sunset,
I reek,
and
nothing can stop my grin.

Not even going home.

My Father,
Who Art Not in Heaven,
and never will be,
sometimes
doesn't come home
from work
until two a.m.

and for his own reasons
goes to my sister's room

before he goes
to his own bed.

I don't want to
hear
know
live here.

I am scared for her

but I am so glad
he doesn't

come to my room.

Yaicha is named after a song
by some group from the last century called the
  Pousette-Dart Band.

Something about a girl,
      a candle in the falling rain
      shining amidst the pain.
I kind of surprise myself
when I can picture Yaicha as that candle.

My father named Yaicha after the "haunting
  melody."

I wonder if he ever listened
to the lyrics.

I imagine living in
just the bathroom,
how I would make the bathtub my
bed at night,
a little Coleman stove to cook on,
toilet, running water,

wouldn't ever have to leave that room.

All my needs in
one
small
space.

Some kid
slams me into a locker
as he crashes through the crowd,
actually lays a hand on the side of my head
to get me
out of the way.

I lean against the locker a second,
fumble my French book,
trying to look like
I had intended to land there,

and this tall blond guy from the soccer team
Kyler
stops briefly with a light hand on my arm
to say,
"Okay?"

When I nod
he winks at me
and takes off,

but I seem glued to the cold metal door,
my flushed face turned
to follow his shoulders
weaving through the waning rush.

ImadeitImadeitImadeitImadeit
ImadetheTEAM!

I am airplaning to the school bus
laughing
      screaming
           choking
                whooping
      I don't care
ImadeitImadeitImadetheTEAM!

I burst into his basement
yelling about
making the team—
Jed smiles
in that quizzical way,
a question mark.

He could care less
about sports.

But he likes me anyway.

He pats the couch,
gestures to the TV.

*"French Flame*'s on," he says.

I snuggle in
and Jed smiles
toward the beginning credits.

"Congrats," he says.

Rona is our setter
on the volleyball team,
quick-thinking and slippery,
a fuzzy-haired elf
with fingers that are
alien long.

She and her mom rent
a rickety calamity of a white clapboard house
on the west side.
She once said
I can't go over there
because
her dad is
sometimes sober,
but
sometimes he's not.

I think we could become really good friends.

All colors of the tortured rainbow
in succession,
black
blue
purple-red
yellow-green,

my hip bone,
Rona's swollen thumb,
someone's elbow,
someone else's calf
        where she kicked herself, for Pete's sake,
all body parts covered.

Learning to roll for a volleyball
gracefully
is painful business.

The ball drops
to the floor
between me and Carmen.
We stand silent,
        guilty glances.

Coach Roy cups his ear—
the team stutters,
"My-my ball-ball-ball!"

He leans harder with his ear
eyes wider
eyebrows dancing,

we all yell,
"MY BALL!"

He points a freckled finger
and grins—

Emma "MY BALL!"
Carmen "MY BALL!"
Doneesha "MY BALL!"

When he turns to me,

the heat I'm just discovering
screams,
"MY BALL!"

Hair on my arms
stands up
and about bursts into flame.

My lungs are claiming expanding territory.

This is my voice.

It is MY BALL.

Somehow
this is worse
than the normal yelling.

Quiet and earnest,
he is squatting in front of me.
I hunch on the couch.

"I know you think you want to play volleyball.
      *—aren't I already?*
Competition creates nastiness,
      *—dissolves nastiness, you mean*
a false sense of empowerment,
  an 'I'm better than you' euphoria—
      *—my team is better than yours, maybe*
  believe me, I know.
I wouldn't want you to get caught up in that,
the hunger for control over others.
When I was young blah blah blah blah . . ."
      *—blah blah blah . . .*

My hearing sinks into a cool, soundless cellar,

my eyes watch his thin lips moving against
  each other in silence,
and I know
that Darren and Yaicha were right
when they once used our father to teach me the
  meaning of the word
*hypocrite.*

When he finishes his oration with a
"Do we understand each other?"
I say,
"Yes, Father."

*—but you didn't specifically tell me to quit.*

Darren is named after a dead person.

When my parents were first married,

my father's best friend, Darren,
died in one of those unexplained car crashes
   where there's only one car involved and no
   bad weather, with the added mystery that
   the passenger was one of my father's female
   students.
She died, too.
Her name was Sarah,
but she didn't get anyone named after her.

"Will you *stop stepping* all over me?!"
Darren is yelling,
whipping the dish towel.
After dinner cleanup is getting dangerous.

I trip all the time,
I feel like
everyone
shares my body space.

From the kitchen corner
mom says
"She's growing, Darren,
give her some room."

"There *isn't* enough room
with her around.
She's like one of those
twenty-man saloon brawls
all by herself."
He slams a pot lid .

into the cupboard.

I whisper,
"There ain't enough room
in this kitchen
for the both of us,
partner."

And mom shushes me
and says I'm not helping anything.

Sinking in my chair
staring at the carpet
as he coldly commands
that the waiter bring him
another steak,
the third one,
well
done
dammit
with
no
blood
inside,
the silence
ricocheting
from table
to table
to table,
appalled eyes
on my family.

Happy birthday,
Darren.

Rona has English before me.
"I aced it!" she exclaims,
slamming her tray next to mine at lunch.


"You usually do,"
I say,
meaning to be admiring—
        she's a great student—
but she looks hurt and slumps a little.


"You sure look tired,
it must've been hard," I try again.


Rona steals a salt-and-vinegar chip from
  my plate.
"I was up late studying."


Crunching, she amends that.
"No, I had finished studying in the afternoon,

but I was still up late.
Because my father was up late with
  his bottles."

Drinking.
My face crinkles in sympathy
        though I don't know what these bottles
        bring out in him.

"Till four thirty this morning," she adds.

Now I'm shocked.
"You didn't sleep till four thirty?"

"Almost five." She rubs her wrist across her
  nose and sniffs.

When she looks back into my eyes
her lashes seem wet,
but she's grinning.

"One hour of sleep, and I still aced it!"

I am scrunched in a corner of the cafeteria
    during study hall,
solving for $x$,
        where $x$ is the number of paleontologists
            who can fit into a bus in Malawi when
            the ambient temperature is thirty-
            three centigrade.

        Whaaa?

Actually, I am
spying
on Jed.

I see him at home,
but almost never in school,
mainly because his senior classes are in the
    west wing.

He is talking quietly
at the far end of the room

with two friends, one short guy and one petite
blonde.
His car keys jangle,
they scoot out the side door,
and I feel the rumble of his Mustang.

We can't leave campus during the school day.

None of my business.

But funny to realize
he's a total stranger to me
in school.

I look at my calculations,
and it seems that $x$ equals two paleontologists.

There must be something about
  Malawian buses
that I don't know.

In English class
Mr. Simon hands out pins,
          QUESTION AUTHORITY
in brilliant yellow
to make us think, he says.

I wear it proudly all day
so people will
ask about it

but I
wouldn't
dare
wear it home.

Chewing gum
offends my father's
sensitive nature.

My mom used to
stash a small pack
for herself
in the uppermost
kitchen cabinet,
until once when I was little
I woke up at six a.m.
and snuck some to chew
for the half hour
before my father got up.

Swallowed it
to hide the evidence.

He made a big show of smelling my
breath,
dangerously, sweetly,
wanting to know where I got it.

I quaked in my jammies
but pointed to the cabinet.
It was the only time
he ever got really mad at
mom,
ranting on,
denting the fridge when he shoved a chair.
He called her
a cud-chewing cow,
he called her
stupid
for having gum where anyone could climb
from chair
to kitchen counter
to fridge top
to get to it.

And at age five I knew
that the tears he
brought to mom's eyes
he should have
brought to mine.

I am the only one named by my mother,
   whose name is Anne.


Anke means "little Anne" in Old German
but mom just loved the sounds,
         "Ahn—" like the gentle discovery of
         "—keh" a breath of changing weather.


I like her explanation better than just being a
diminutive
of somebody else.

Snippings, pieces, smiles

I pack end-of-summer photos in
my photo album

the one time we got mom in the canoe—

> leaving out the mean shots of
>> Darren half drowning me,
>> Yaicha smacking me with her
>> paddle—

me and mom sitting with toes in the water,
me and mom cooking fish,

with captions, colored pencil, borders,

a grab at
a short history of me
in an impressive package.

I admire it

as I clean up the mess,
suffused with warmth of creation,

until Yaicha
walks in, and flips through
with derisive silence,

and at the end
says,
"There are only pictures of you and Mom!"

and I say to myself,
*Exactly.*

I grab
a package of six pairs,
and go find
Yaicha
gliding through
a sea of purses.

She fingers a popular thing
made from a shower curtain
        see-through
        with lavender and silver fish
a little smile plays on her mouth.

"They should line them,"
I say.
"You fill it with junk
and no one will
see
the fish."

Yaicha surfaces to glare
and sneer,

"Listen to the
Fashion Diva!"

pointing at the socks
in my hand.

But she purchases a purse
of flowery upholstery
instead.

Another Saturday of charity.

Angeline and I head for the kitchen
for a snack.

I open the fridge door
and poke—
yum, leftover pasta
        but that seems uncouth to offer her,
            somehow.

Angie lets out a small scream—
Yaicha is leaning
slim and silent on the back wall,
spooning up yogurt.
Yaicha's expression becomes devilish.
Uh-oh.
Scraping the bottom with her spoon,
    she warbles,
"Helloooo there, Angelllline."
She licks the back of her spoon

managing to make it a
threatening gesture.

"Um, hi, Yaicha," Angeline murmurs,
backing away one step.

My father slips in from the dining room.
"Ah, the angelic Angeline is with us."

"Oh, hello!" Angie says brightly, turning to him
in relief.

Yaicha's face slides back to sullen
as she edges sideways out of the room.

I watch her go,
wanting to follow.

In the chill evening
it builds until
he's raging at Yaicha,
and I freeze,
     the flannel cloth of my shirt
     blending me in with cabinetry.

Cyclone father
towers above her,
sucking papers off the counter,
hand raised with thunderbolts,
Yaicha crouching
on flowered linoleum,
beneath his
battering
unintelligible
roar,

and

shockingly

he's done

and walks out.

Debris swirls to the floor
around Yaicha,

and since there is nothing to say,
I put my limbs in motion,
walking woodenly
to my room.

When I was, like, five,
that redheaded girl down the street
used to ask
if she could come over.

We always played at her house.

Invite someone over?

No.

Nobody plays
at my house.

"Hey!"
Rona's yelling down the hallway,
her ponytail a copper fuzz bomb
bobbing on top of her head.

As we get closer
she says,

"The athletic slap,
not the girly whap!"

and we high-five with a cracking sound
that makes heads turn.

"Geometry." Rona holds up her book.

"Algebra." I grimace.

She shrugs, her lip to the side.
"All those word problems.
I think geometry's easier.
Doing proofs means you always know

when you're right or wrong."

Smacking my arm
she heads for class,
winking over her shoulder.
"Life should be that simple!"

Rona's humor is sometimes
          inappropriate.
She laughed out loud
when Jake's
custom chemo wig
blew off in the soccer crowd.
She got us
all giggling,
but Jake's red face
around a game grin
made me feel
kind of bad.

Rona snorted,
said
he probably needed
a good laugh—
counteract all that chemo.

Well, it *was* funny.

Our first game tonight,
at Plymouth High.

Their gym smells wrong.

I'm not nervous.
I'm not nervous.

No, really,
I'm not.

I'm a starting left-side hitter!

Jittered up, jacked up, amped up,
yes,
but
I'm not nervous.

The lights in here are pretty dim.

My god,

is that their team?
Look at that girl,
must be six-feet-something tall,
built like a jackhammer.

Okay.

I'm nervous.

We lost.

We couldn't pass the ball to save our lives,
and Plymouth just served us
to death.

Trooping onto the bus to go home,
we are all choosing
separate
seats.

Even Rona and I sit
apart,
each replaying
every bad pass, every hit into the net,
  every instance of not calling "mine."

My temple is against the rattling window,
eyes on the darkness
as we pull away from Plymouth High,

but all I see
is a white ball with blue stripes,
flying
out of reach.

"Who's depressed about Plymouth?"
Coach is standing over our leaden, silent team
while we stretch at practice.

Every hand goes up.

"What?" Coach Roy asks,
eyebrows dancing.

"I am," says Rona angrily.

I mutter the same right behind her.

"First game!" he exclaims.
"Learn from it.
But that game is over.
The rest of volleyball starts from here."

We are all looking up at him mid stretch,

our legs in Vs on the floor.

"Start fresh.
Remember we like this game!"

We smile a little,
glance at each other.

"Are you ready to play volleyball?" Coach Roy
  says.

Slowly, we stand up for our first passing drill.

"Yes."

"I can't hear you!"

*"YES!"*

I am not very big-breasted.

When I wanted
to get my first bra
        I was growing
        and they hurt
my father went berserk.

"Do they bounce when you
run across the street?"
        he roared,

        No, I said.

"Are men staring at them?"
        he roared,

        No, I said.

"Then you don't need a bra."

My mother didn't say a word

although she stood there
with me.

And the next day,
she bought me a training bra.

I was so proud.
I looked down at my breasts
snug in their new stiff bra
and thought,
*Pretty soon they'll be so big*
*I won't be able to see my feet.*

Well,
I stand by myself at the bus stop this morning,
looking down in experimentation
after more than a year of bras.

I can still see my feet.

Heavy hailstorm after lunch.
I ran outside and stood in it,
      spitting ice stinging my face,
      bitter nuggets on my tongue.

Coming back in,
gathering my language folder,
shaking out my hair,
Kyler watching me
from his locker down the hall
then turning to the back stairwell.

Squelching
sprinting
up the front stairs,
I screech to a kneel in front of class.

Retie my wet sneaker
four
slow
times,

hoping I am fast enough.

Kyler has Spanish
next door
when
I have French.

Madame DuPont
is pursing her fat lips,
tapping her watch
in the doorway.

If you don't like the weather,
wait five minutes.

Post practice
showered and clean
I step out to our backyard
lit by the sun's last rays,
my palm on the hemlock's trunk.

Ack—I'm smeared with sap,
    the bark oozing,
        shouldn't trees be going dormant
        soon?

Wipe sticky fingers on the dead lawn.
Now I'm tarred and feathered,
    furry with wilted grass
    and the bitty pinecones
    lying in a thick crunchy carpet beneath

the great tree.
My old climbing tree.

Aha!
I scoop cones into my sweatshirt pouch,
a bowlful the perfect centerpiece
for mom's fall stew.

As I step inside, cradling,
    —surprise—
    my father's home early.

He throws a glance at my loot,
says to mom,
"Tell her to take that crap back outside
where it belongs."

"I bought it with my own money."
Yaicha is backed into a corner
of the hallway,
held against the doorjamb
by our father's wrath.

"I will not have you tarting up your face
like a hooker!"
he thunders,
throwing her compact of blush
against a wall.

*But look at her,* I want to tell him.
*She knows how to make it seem natural.*

Yaicha scurries into her room.

He barrels through my shoulder as he
   stomps by,
and I am staring at

the tiny dent he made in the wall paint.

I pick up the plastic case,
slipping it into my back pocket
to give to her later.

It seems I move quietly in the darkened house
because
Yaicha doesn't hear me
come to the living room
as she sinks onto her heels by
　his favorite chair.

I watch her
open the compact
draw a fingertip across the makeup
and
luxuriantly
lovingly
smear a thick pink line low across the fabric of
　the chair back,
grinning at it wickedly.

I see Yaicha coming toward me in the school
   hallway
flanked by the two girls she's never without

and I get this funny little flutter inside,
and my hand leaps up—
"Yaicha!" I call out,
veering her way,
and she sidesteps me with a quick glare that
      glances off my temple
         and buries its blade
            in the wall
next to me.

Ah, all is good and normal with the world this
   morning.
What was I thinking,
greeting her out in the Social Open?

Kyler is ambling down the hall toward our
  algebra class
grinning at the antics of some louder
  soccer players,
in the conversation
but not being obnoxious.

At the doorway,
he lets the pack of them cram in before him,
politely gesturing,
still smiling.

I watch his tall frame disappear inside.

Suddenly
Rona is at my elbow.

"Whyoncha say something to him?"

Blushing furiously,

I wipe a hand over my hair.

Rona cocks an eyebrow.

I flip my palm up in exasperation.
"I don't know. . . ."
       What would I say?
"He's so . . .
nice."

Rona cackles and whacks my shoulder.

"Yeah, that's a real problem, all right."
And she leaves me
to walk into algebra
alone.

I pick at it
in algebra,
annoying little white thread,

and in the middle
of a square root
it lets go,

my shoulder exposed.

At the bell
Kyler pokes my skin—
"New style?"—
and grins.

I feel his touch
through lunch

raw,

charged.

Consider
picking out threads
on all my clothes,

the Fashionable
Open Seam
Look.

*Struggling with uncooperative jeans*
*this morning,*
   *thinking about yesterday when*
Angeline said she saw that I
got selected for
Student Government Day,
one of twelve students—
she did, too.

She's terrified
of course
      how do we act?
      should we study?
like it's terribly important
or something.
      *Not the blue shirt again.*
      *Is everything I own blue?*
We're just
supposed to run
the town meeting,
visit the water-treatment plant,

pass some laws.

*Should be a law against stains.*

*Is everything I own stained?*

It's kind of an honor
to be chosen by all your teachers,
but Angeline's not
who I want
to hang out with
all day.

*Hair in a ponytail? Down? Chop it off?*

I find her so irritating,
predictable,
dull,

okay, *EVERY*thing is
irritating.

Not just Angeline.

I am supposed to be getting a ride home
    with him,
but walking down Main Street
my father greets this pretty woman friend,

and I force a loud sigh,
the only irritation
I can safely show,
knowing
it will be a while.

I stare at them,
arms crossed,
and up walks Angeline
in some frilly jacket.

"Hey," she breathes to me,
adoring eyes on my father,
who acts all excited
to see her,
runs a flat gentle hand

down her back.

Angie's expression is dripping
with sugar
as he turns back to his woman,
and
my next angry
exasperated sigh
farts out
at Angie.

"Oh, *please*,"
I mutter.

Hurt cow eyes
reproach me,
and Angeline sulks away.
Over her shoulder
I hear,
"Your dad is the greatest,
and you don't even
know."

As Darren came out
of the bathroom
this morning,
pulling shirt overhead,
the bruise
half his side
glared garish mauve

and I felt
my
        upholstery
                        rip
and bits of fluff
escape
to float away

before Darren
noticed me
and yanked
his shirt down.

And yet
when I was five
before bed
he would read to me
from *The House at Pooh Corner*
in all the voices—
>my favorite was Piglet
>the only time my father had a
>soft
>high
>tender voice
with Eeyore and Tigger and
all of Rabbit's friends and relations.

And I really think
you can't read to someone like that
without
a little teeny
bit
of
love.

Mirrors suck.

From the side,
half-inch plywood
topped with
brownish brown hair
taut in a ponytail
to give my blemished Roman nose the lead,
draped in a spaghetti-spotted tee,
men's Levis
to keep up with Freakish Leg-Lengthening
  Disorder,
wooden bead earrings from Yaicha's trash
        two years ago.

Quite a package.

My grandma used to say,
        "Nobody's going to buy you."


Well, that's apparent.

Not listening, but
hearing
way too much.

Banging
beyond the wall
rhythmic
numbing
hypnotizing
amplifying
          He's in there
hurting her
          He's in there
hurting her.

Hear Yaicha's
low
unending
moan.

Why am I not good enough?

At least he loves
Darren and Yaicha
in some way

even if it's horrible,
he shows them attention

and I am furniture
I get nothing
nothing
nothing
no
thing

or
at times I get
a knife-edge glimpse of

something scary.

I think that it is supposed to be good,
that I get less
from him

but I feel



worth

less.

# PART
# TWO

Little packet by Yaicha's bed

> I've seen them before—
> Marci takes the pill before school
> laughing in the girls' room,
> proof of her
> extracurricular
> activities

But I overheard Yaicha tell her friend
she's a virgin,

never even had a boyfriend,

so I don't get it.

And she storms in
snatches the packet
raging about privacy.

Bubbling panic
I go on the offensive—

"Why should *you* take the pill?"

My insides shred
as she glares a full minute

and I stand my ground
wanting her to tell me
tell me
anything,

but when I see pain
forming
on her retinas

I decide I don't want to know.

I run.

Hunched with his calculator
pencil whispers
scowling brow

formulaic incantations
bouncing knee

jutting vertebrae
like hackles
on a gravel pit dog.


Darren carves through
nightly calculus,
sculpting another perfect grade,

the ice cream I brought him
two hours ago
now
puddling milk.

Darren is down in his room.
Yaicha is cutting through the kitchen.
I am on the edge of the rocking chair by the
  couch.

Each of us
a corner
of an equilateral triangle

equidistant

corner angle spread as far
away
from the other two as possible
without breaking apart

but in that position
we can't get any closer.

Unless maybe we step together.

Government work again.
Standing inside the mauve front door,
waiting for Angie to come down.

Fake flowers.

Silk, I think they call them.
*Hecho en Mexico*
makes me doubt any worm wove them.

A little gift card
anchored under the vase.
IN HARD TIMES FRIENDS ARE THERE.

Plastic ribs on the backs of the leaves.
Stiff wire stamens inside the
rigid papery petals.
A vibrant lily-blue never seen in nature.
Lemon Pledge–scented.

*Friends Are There?*
What friend sends false,

when false needs to be dusted?
What friend sends false,
when reality
bends toward light
nods in a breeze
feels like butter
shimmers with amethyst
smells of jelly beans, tangerines,
   and pencil shavings
finally wilts and melts so you can throw it
   away and start with something new?

I pull out the fake lily,
shove it down
behind the entry table,
as Angie tromps downstairs.

Third-floor bathroom
first stall on the left,
I am squatting
over the stained toilet seat
reading the metal walls
and catch something fresh—

> Angeline
> Peachy-keen
> The boys would taste her
> But she's too green

If a glass of milk like Angeline
gets on a bathroom wall,
the scrawlers
must be running out
of ammo.

In the between-class crush
I feel a *fwap*
    sharp and quick
    on the small of my back
and whirl
to catch
the light wink,
the tilt of his mouth
before
Jed slides to a side hallway
and away.

I embrace my biology book,
cheered by
chance encounter.

Hit-and-runs.

Rona sets the ball
     I jump and hit the ball
     (hopefully over the net)
          sprint to the back wall
               tag the wall
run back to the net
where
Rona sets the ball
     I jump and hit the ball
     (hopefully over the net)
          sprint to the back wall
               tag the wall
run back to the net
where
Rona sets the ball
     I jump and hit the ball
     (hopefully over the net)
          sprint to the back wall
               tag the wall
run back to the net—

The drill is supposed to make you stronger
but
I am so tired
after eight sprints
I stumble like a drunk
and can't get off the ground.


"Next victim!" Coach yells.

"No thinking, ladies!
You are thinking too hard!"

Coach Roy is shaking his head
at me
after I take my approach,
jump with all my might,
and hit the ball hard
into the net
again.
The ball is supposed to go
over
the net.

I never realized
till now
how hard the brain has to work
to make the body do what it asks.

Or maybe how hard the body has to work
to ignore
the brain.

In psych class
    Ms. Taft
    had us draw trees

    one tree for the traits
    we get from our
    mother's side

    one tree for the traits
    we get from our
    father's side.

    My mom's side has
    many branches,
    caring, fair, physical appearance,
      passive, calm-headed under stress.

    My father's side has
    more branches,
    athletic, questioning, impatient,
      stubborn, tightwad,

opinionated, controlling,
quick to anger,
friendly to strangers

and I stare in terror
at his massive tree,
crisscrossing branches.


If all this tree is from mom
and all this tree is from him
where do I grow
my own branches?

In the middle of a nap
a thought snaps me awake
and I stare at Jed
a moment,
his eyelashes long and still.

He is the same age as
my brother
      —I never thought of this?
and for a few more
moments
I am weirded out,
like finding out your
      turkey sandwich is actually flamingo
         meat.
But I watch Jed
asleep,
and his familiar breathing
his hand on my hip
calm me
and I lay my face again
on his warm chest.

I love the hardware store
        cool circular blade
        hefty hammer
        greasy smell.

While my father gets what he needs,
I spend a long time
running my hands
through chain-link
        like chain mail
distraction
from thinking of

last time we were here

when we ran into Marci,

        the Marci with a big chest and blue eyes
        the Marci who's had most of the greatest
            guys

and I had to introduce her to my father.

As she left with her nails or screws or
    something,
I was standing near the front door—
she leaned in to my ear
and said, all breathy,
"Your dad is soooo handsome!"
with that oozy look in her eyes.

I watched her flick her hair and go,
leaving me gulping,
leaning on the rocking display rack of
    jackknives.

His Anger stands alone
stands erect
in the
middle of the room.

We step gently around it,
a terrifying totem pole
bristling beaks, pinions, talons.

I can't remember
when it started
when firm hand
     became
     fisted liege
        became
        feral
            tyrannical
                rage
        more important than
        the rest of us,
        but

it didn't used to be this way
and that
keeps us tied to him,
guessing,
teetering,
waiting,
while stepping around
his Anger
in the
middle of the room.

"And then my mother took me to Printemps,
   you know, that makeup superstore?
And I chose, like, four different shades of eye
   shadow?"
Angeline leans over the kitchen table,
eager to please me.

I am doing my best not to snore,
tilting on my chair's back legs.

Her short delicate fingers count off.
"Let's see, um, Café au Lait,
April Skies,
Twinkle Frost,
and Satin Sheets."

She blushes on that last one,
as my father moves smoothly into the room.

"Quite becoming on you," he drips
charmingly,

hand gliding over the back of her chair.

Angie's cheeks flood a deeper shade.

I gape at the man
gently placing his mug on the edge of the sink,
smiling his way out again.

Did he just compliment makeup?

I asked Angeline
about her father
only once.

She said
all airy,
"Oh, he'll leave that
floozy
and be back someday soon."

And I thought
    *How old are you,*
    *that you believe*
*that crap?*

I'm on my third burger,
Rona's on her fourth,
sprawled in BurgerMeister,
people-watching
after practice.

A horrendously large,
      I mean,
somewhat overweight
girl from school
gets the Double Dare with Extra Sauce
and Rona hisses,
"Look at those jowls!"

I slap her on the arm
in shock.

Her lettuce-draped mouth mumbles,
"Well, so she wants a burger.
She should at least exercise."

And before I can spit out anything

Rona yells,
"Hey, I hear the wrestling team's got an
 opening!"

When the poor girl turns to look,
her lips a chubby O,
Rona salutes her with a half-eaten burger
and a serious nod.

My pickle slice slips down unchewed.

Honesty takes a stomach
with one less burger.

The snarl of a motor
and a quick
*bronnk* of the horn,
Jed's blue-sleeved arm saluting me
as he roars past me through the school lot.

Must have had someone with him.

Didn't offer a ride,
but
at least I am wavable.

Relief,
a breather from Sunday Angie-sitting,
even if it's on my father's orders.

Stepping into my clogs,
waltzing slowly slowly out the back door,
swinging the full ash bucket,
*shwwwsh*
*shwwwsh*—

Whatzit called?
Centripi—something.

*shwwwsh*
*SHWWWSH*! Too far too slow some ash flies
  out running forward to escape,
      laughing at my own stupidity.

At the compost pile
dump the bucket,

"Cinderelly, Cinderelly!"
backing away as a small poof arises.

Twirl toward the house,
spinning with both hands on the handle,
empty bucket
flying in a captive circle.

One last crisp breath—
step back inside,
bucket clanging the door frame.

Kicking off clogs
in the stifling warmth
I see Angeline and my father leaning toward
   each other over the chessboard.

He's teaching her to play.

He's teaching Angeline to play something
only
he and Darren play.

Driving home from food shopping,
me in the front seat,
Yaicha in the back,
I am shocked when
my father slows to the side
for a slippery husk of a man
thumbing a ride.

Just before the guy
gets in
next to Yaicha,
my father says,
"But young girls should never do this.
Very dangerous."

Well, first of all,
I can't drive anyway,
and Yaicha's got her license
but who lets her use the car?

Second of all,
if the guy's an ax murderer

it's very dangerous for my father to
  pick him up, too.

But he's driving smugly,
sparks of elation on his face,
enjoying the risk he's taken for us all.

Yaicha scrunches up against the car door
on her side,
legs crossed,
eyes on the pines going by.

The guy grunts
when he wants out
up the highway,

the smell of him
still hunched in the backseat
till we get home.

Mom's watering wandering Jews

and as I cut through the dining room
with my usual
          cheddar and crackers
the buffet table biffs me
in the hip—

I crumple,
cheese fumbles,

and without turning to me on the floor
mom mutters,
"Good Graces,
slow down.
That's an antique buffet."

The ancient leather
wingback chair
straddles boards on the porch.

I tuck myself
between the arms
      with Sleator, Asimov, Sones.

Then I see
tufts of stuffing
billowing from the hole in the seat

and something gray
running in panic
  —a mouse.

No,
not with that snakey naked tail.

I jump up,
my books drop.

They're rats.

Rona and I push off from my locker and head
  to practice.

Struggling with the strap on my gym bag,
I hear Rona say softly,

"Zat a bruise on Yaicha's chin today?"

My heart cramps up and can't do its job for
  one long beat.

"Yes" comes out in a hoarse whisper.
I give up on the strap,
letting it dig into my shoulder.

"Your dad?"


"Yes." How does she know that?

Rona starts swinging her duffel,
looking around nonchalantly

as we enter the gym.

"*You* never seem to have bruises."
And Rona would know,
we see each other changing clothing every day.

"He likes my sister and brother
better than he likes me."

Did I just say that out loud?

Rona asks questions all the time.

Things I don't really want to answer,
but I have to, somehow.

She's the only one I feel compelled to tell my
   reality to.

If I could just open my mouth wide enough
to allow those gagging blobs of truth
their slow, tar-seep passage
up through my gullet,
        with barely enough oxygen to keep from
           passing out
        while they glorp over my tongue,
those truths would reach my teeth,
        where if my jaw weren't unhinged,
I might bite them off
so I could
breathe again.

Sprained my right thumb
in last night's game
          —we pounded the Red Hawks—
so I proudly tape it up for school,
until some guys
jeer that I'm a pansy.

Which I'm not.
I mean, I can still play with a sprained thumb.

I rip off the tape
before French.

As I slip into my seat
Angeline points gently at
the darkening thumb
and whispers,
"Ouch. I mean, *ouille*!"

I shrug like I'm fine,

grant her
a quick grin

but at the boundary of
her sympathy
and
my irritation,
I take the grin
back again.

Dreaming of
rolling
rolling
rolling down
a warm grassy slope
laughing
rolling faster
rolling
rolling
into shadow
rolling
rolling
fear
rolling
cold
rolling
*SMACK*
into a tree.

I awake
on the living room floor,
moonless dark,

heart pounding,
my head leaning
against the leg of my father's chair.

Darren came into the kitchen
this morning,
black circles
around wavering eyes,
and he wouldn't look at any of us.

Mom said he was sick

but he's not sick.

I've seen this
a few times before

always after he and my father fight

and then

my father "talks" to him
in private

in his room
for hours

but most of the time
I don't hear their voices.

We are drinking Diet Coke
on the couch after dinner,
Mom and I.

She smoothes the black wool surface
with her wedding hand,
and says
before they splurged and bought this
furniture
when they got married,
my father
had an enormous broken armchair
they both squashed into,
and someone else's television box for
   a side table.
She says
they would read to each other
from a book of Ogden Nash,
my father stroking her hair.

I am floored.

Floored by her butter-soft eyes,

her caressing hand,
her fondness for the furniture
they bought together
in a time
of kindness.

I belong,
sweating team effort,
when the pass is right to Rona
when I run to her and spring
when my arm swing is on
when our timing is perfection
when I smack
        that ol' white leather butt
and the
opposing team scrambles,
stands erupt,
high fives all around,
singing together in the locker room.

    I ran track last spring,
    nervous
    every meet
            out there all alone
            against seven other girls
            on a narrow track.

    The strength felt good

but nothing
nothing
like this.

Only working together.
Only these girls.
Only volleyball.

*YES!* What a hit!
Oh no,
Oh no,
Oh shit, she's down.

What a glorious hit
great form
great grunt
hand on
ball down
straight down
      in her face,
      six-packed,
      floor-flat,
      disoriented,
      fighting tears,
      bloody nose,
I'm rushing in
offering aid—
      Can she feel it?
      Elation running slicing through me

through my hand
to her hand?

She only sits
on her haunches,
hand staunching
the river red
flowing south
to her mouth.

I grimace guilty apologies.

But *YES!*
A frickin' glorious hit!

After an hour of silence
in the library
studying
fake oak grain on cubicle walls,

I love the way my voice sounds
      startling
      strong
      confident
as I give a woman in teetering heels
directions
to the school office.

We just happen to be walking to
  the east wing
at the same time.

Finally Angeline says,
"You're tall, you've really gotten tall."

I hmph.
I mean, duh.

Now she's walking sideways to face me,
earnestly explaining herself.

"No, really! You've grown so much lately!
It's so incredible!"

I stop in the middle of the hall
fist on my hip—

"Believe me, Ange,

I am aware that I have grown!"

I set my size-ten feet in motion as she reels in
  her shock
and scampers after me.

"But, really, tall looks good on you.
You're going to be beautiful!"

I peel off at psych class as she continues to
  world history.

Angie was digging a hole for herself,
but I find myself
wanting to
believe
the last thing she said.

I can see from my bedroom window
that his Mustang is not parked under the
  oak tree.

Where is Jed?

We haven't had our nap in days.

Possessed for three seconds.

Some demon jumped
into my mouth
flapping my tongue with its claws
to say
words I'd never thought of—

"Yaicha, I was talking
to *mom*.
You don't give a shit
about my life, so
why don't you just *shut up*?"

—and my jaw drops down
and Yaicha's
and Mom's.

And then the demon is gone,
so I can mumble
"sorry"

to my sister.

And I stand here
in dumb
confusion
while they continue conversation.

Where the hell
did that come from?

My father pokes me
nastily
in the side.

"You'll probably
never
get the nice rounded
curves of
a full woman.

You've always
been skinny,
always will."

I can feel
each
reclusive
bone
poke through,

the bones of
Embarrassment,

Anger,
Relief.

I push some back in,
but leave
Anger
sticking out.

Walls are thin.

Doesn't matter
what they are made of—
wood and plaster
wood and plaster and concrete block
wood and plaster and concrete block and
        corky soundproof panels
        like in the music room at school.

Doesn't even matter
which wall the bed is against,

I can hear
everything.

I mean,
*WHY* can't she just tell on him?
It's just words.

Just
open her mouth
and out come those words.

And then he'd be stopped.

Right?

I stare hard at Yaicha
during breakfast.

She's good with makeup
really good
from being in plays and musicals.

I stare at the smudge,
purpling black
on her jaw,
barely buried under makeup.

Okay.
She isn't
good at it
just because of plays.

It's cold enough this morning
to want to stand
in front of the woodstove
after stoking it for the day.

"Hey, quit
soaking up
all the heat!"

Darren and I
say that every time
and shove each other
in jest,
and every time
Mom says we deserve each other.

It's one of about
only three
things I know how
to do
with my
brother.

Jed's peeling out
in the school parking lot.
Why doesn't it
make me laugh,
      twirl,
    shout!
like
Ginger and Marci?

I stand alone
crossing my arms
eyes rolling
making that
      "you are such an idiot"
      sound with my tongue.

When Jed has left just a cloud,
Ginger and Marci
glance at me,
then pointedly roll eyes at each other.

Something as dumb as

burning rubber
rattles
my cardboard box of structure.

This is why
I am not popular,
I think.

Untwisting my bra strap
in the middle of the hallway

and there is Jed coming out of room 32
in serious discussion with another guy.

I blush his way,
feel a little thrilled at showing off my bra strap
  in front of him

but his eyes glide over my head
as he answers a question,
missing me entirely.

I got an A on the third quiz in
  American history,
an A,
dammit.

Last time I got a B

up from a C

and my father said,

"If you can get a C
you can get a B,

If you can get a B
you can get an A."

So I got an A in American history,

which I only studied hard in
because Mr. Parks is more like
  a friend to everyone

than a teacher
and we got to interview this
  hundred-year-old man
who's lived here
forever
and remembers when Cartwright Street
was only a horse trail
and the mill at Mill Pond
actually worked.

I got an A
and my father said,

"Grades don't mean anything."

He was reading in his chair
I was reading on the couch
both of us reading
and drinking hot tea
in the evening
just like a peaceful father and daughter.

I bumped my cup
and scalding tea sailed
all into my jeans
burning hot
burning me
and he slammed his book down
yelling,

"You are so stupid!

What a stupid thing to do!"

Like I did it on purpose
to spoil his night

Like I wasn't in enough pain

And I started to cry
running away to rip off my jeans
ice my leg
ice it
ice it.

When I washed my angry face
and came back
he was reading in his chair
ignoring

the puddle of tea
the fallen cup
still wallowing on the couch.

I am
dumb
as wood,
old
dry
brown
hardened
splintering
flammable
unfeeling
resistant
jammed
un
speak
ing

table
bench
chair


footstool.

Long ago
we stood in the kitchen,
my mother
my father
and I,
hugging in a cluster
when my father
came home from work.

From their knees
I leaned way back to see
warm soft gazes for each other's faces,
and the velvety kiss,
until I pulled their attention
to me
down low.

They laughed,
tousled my hair,
and
we all said
I love you.

Knee pads at my ankles,
covered in the brine of practice,
I tromp into the kitchen
and he's there.

Shit.

Why is he home so early?

My father downs what seems like an entire
    quart of water
in one long swallow,
staring around his tall glass at my damp
    person.

He carefully places the empty tumbler on the
    counter,
turns precisely on one foot,
leaves the kitchen

without a word.

So.

Before,
he didn't want me to play
and there was almost a conversation going.

Now he for sure knows I am still playing.

Why doesn't he say anything?

Yanking jeans over sweaty postpractice skin,
knowing taking a shower would amplify
where I've been.

I come out of my room,
Darren comes up the stairs,
and our father comes from the bathroom,
        a damp bath towel dangling
            from forefinger and thumb.

"Whose," he intones at me in the hallway,
    "is this?"

Darren holds out his hand.
"Mine," he whispers.

Our father looks surprised.
Did he think it was mine?

He breathes in,

launches the offensive at Darren.
"HOW MANY TIMES HAVE I TOLD YOU TO
   HANG THIS . . ."
louder and louder
words crushing together
in a piling roar
except in excerpts
"YOU THINK YOU CAN JUST DO WHAT YOU
   WANT . . ."
"I AM THE ONE WHO KNOWS WHAT'S GOOD
   FOR YOU . . ."
and suddenly I realize
he's actually yelling at me
         about volleyball.


I want to make him turn to me
yell at *me*


I want to yell at *him*
         I am here
         right here

I am not furniture—

But when his hand
smothers Darren's face with the wet towel,
shoving him hard into the wall,

I am backing away.

Darren is tromping upstairs
in work boots
and a black scowl,

heading out back to split wood

and as he cuts through the living room
swerves toward our father's chair

gives the leg a vicious kick
so the chair rocks up on two legs
and
bangs down again,

Darren already jerking open the back door
to a blast of fresher air.

Indian summer
crowding
at the farmer's market,
Mom's requested squash in a string bag
scraping the goosebumpled skin
  below my shorts.

I crush
lemongrass
with my thumbnail,

breathing
sharp cleansing.

Mr. Ogawa
nods,
gestures with a bok choy
toward my calves.

"Leg like deer!"
bobbing

grinning
his compliment.

I flush pride at my volleyball strength,
bob my head, too.
What a sweet gentle man.

The best smell in the whole world
is
hot
popcorn
      slathered in decadent
      criminal amounts
      of butter
cooked in the old copper-bottomed pot.

Lights off.

I bury my face in my bowl,
the three of us kids
      watching
      *Some Like It Hot* with that
        hysterical Jack Lemmon,

munching together

parallel gazes.

Man, I'm Starvin' Marvin
running to meet Rona,
there she is,
close to the front near the salad bar
but
oh,
Angeline just behind her.

I stop mid hurry
        a girl slams me from behind,
        we murmur sorry
but all sound dims as I watch unnoticed,
        my best friend
        and
        my constant twitch

        the daring
        and
        the whimpering

        the architect
        and

the timber rot

the solid earth
and
the space walk, holding your breath
   because you forgot your helmet.

Maybe they said hello
when they first got in line.
Now they simply ignore each other,
inches apart with their trays.

We don't need to be a threesome.

I sidle into the ragged tail of the lunch line.

"So who the hell cares?"
Rona throws three carrots down with minimal
  crunching.
"Not like she's a friend
*or* an enemy, right?
She's nobody.
So why does Angeline bug you?"
She whips those blue eyes my way,
and all I can do
is swallow my hummus
and shrug.

A thought forms—
I shove it down.

Something about
my father.

Errands on the way home.
My father jogs across pavement to his office,
I stay in the parking lot
watching sparrows' rusty
heads
pop-in-pop-out
of car grills

nibbling bugs
spitting out papery wings
wiping grubby beaks.

On each car
a tiny
bird-sized neon sign:
DINNER BUFFET!
SMORGASBORD!
EAT AT JOE'S GRILL!

My father reappears,
hugging some blonde
half his age good-bye

kissing her fully longer,
sexier
than a married man
should even imagine.

He walks to our car,
smug.
I turn back to the birds,
glance at their
happy meal
and feel
a familiar familial nausea.

Homework.
Efficiency models
for the environmental psych unit.

## What I Can Live Without

cars
cell phones
wall-to-wall carpet
furniture
whitening toothpaste
grape soda
Polo cologne
growing at the speed of giant kelp
that glue smell from the woodworking shop
Ginger's snorky giggling
Madame DuPont's fish-pale eyes
Angeline's whiny voice
choosing sides
a father

There's Jed
strolling up his driveway
with a senior buddy
in the indigo evening.

He wasn't home
all afternoon
and I am
suddenly
furious and garter-snake-striped with jealousy.

I want to run out there,
plant a real estate
SOLD
sign
between this guy
and Jed.


That's it.
I'm officially nuts.

Both hands in
Yaicha's wastebasket,
digging
while she's down
in the laundry room.

Crinkly Snickers wrapper
plastic promo case
sleek Clinique compact
        corners still packed with Sugar Toast
stained satin ribbon
Fashionista receipt
fermenting apple core

I stop at the racy lacy bra
        —no way did mom buy that—
worn to weariness,
elasticless.

I usually don't find much
but

search under pressure,
my heart-pounding glimpse
of
Yaicha's world.

"Let's go camping tonight,"
I say softly
to Yaicha,
starting the game
       where I reach out
       and she does what she wants
       with it.

Her eyes pointy and dark
she throws words out of her mouth.
"I hate camping."

Staring back
I whisper
"I hate this *house*."

"You don't know anything.
He'll never let us go."
She thunks the back of her head

against the kitchen wall.

"He'd never let *you* go.
He'd never notice
if I was gone."
I try a small smile,
nudge her,
"He's got a meeting.
Mom'll let us go.
I'll get the tent."
I hold my breath.

Thunk
with her head,
she turns away.
"I hate camping."

Game over.

In the attic
watching my exhales fog and dissipate
over a stage of life,
a cast of
cast-off
furniture and relics,
a dull palette of gray
in the worn-out gloom.

The ancient pine banana box
filled with Grandma's tea pieces,

the huge empty rococo frame
        garish even in dust,

the oak stool, folding table, sagging armchair
        from Aunt Sepha's house,

all unnecessary,
superfluous,
not worthy of life downstairs,

hidden away
like unused emotions

chilled to a crisp.

Unhappily comfortable here,
cold tears course
trails over my cheeks
like Olympic skiers,
crashing over the precipice of my jaw
in a spectacular
agony of defeat.

Yesterday afternoon
my father and I
tiled the bathroom floor
while everyone was out.

No praise.
No critique.
No words.
No one there worth talking to.

His section of tile was perfect.
My section of tile was perfect.

He didn't show off our work
when everyone got home.

I showed mom which section
was mine,
but I don't think she believed me.

After dinner
I chiseled a chip

out of one of his tiles
next to
the toilet.

Transparency girl.

Darren even sat in my chair for his breakfast,
my glass of OJ right there in front of him
waiting for me.

Walking to school
instead of waiting for the bus
because I am
so
damn
grumpy
this morning,

hoping
the smell of autumn
will revive me.

"Red-and-yellow,
gold-and-brown,
autumn-leaves-are-falling-down,"
in time with my feet,

knowing it sounds juvenile,
even saying it
out loud
convincing, convincing,

but pretty soon
it's just a jumble of
consonants,

a rhythm
for my
brain to pound by.

I have stopped for a mocha at Johansen Java,
lower lip on smooth plastic lid,
listening to Tight Yoga Suit explain to
   Over-Dyed Poodle Perm how starting up
     a gallery for her son's artwork is not a
     selfish act,
smelling warm raisins as the elderly man next
   to me breaks open a steaming scone,
       mumbling that he's fine, he's fine,
      he'll stay in his house no matter what
       that goodfernothin' son says,
patting some little boy with bedhead as he
   chokes on crumbs,
      his tattooed mother yapping into her
     phone about the water bill,

and I feel a fuzzy warmness toward humans.

Disparate,
fascinating,

bonding with a cup of joe in the same place.

Eavesdropping on strangers
gives more insight into a life
than having a conversation with someone you
   know.

People are more honest
when they don't know you are listening.

"I don't know, she just—
she just doesn't interest me."

Kyler is sitting behind me in algebra,
answering a grilling by his friend.

"Fake nails,
all that white skin,
doesn't she go outside?
A person should go outside sometimes,
feel the weather."

His pencil eraser is bouncing
*tok*
*tok*
*tok*
on the desktop.

"I mean, yeah, she's hot,
but . . ."

The teacher clears her throat and Kyler goes
  quiet.

I like the "but."

Rona and I
each in our own bus seat
lie on our backs
feet out the open windows
as we head back home.

We just barely won
against Raeburn
and we didn't "play up to our potential"
but hey
another win.
Our 8-2 record has us heading for the state
   tournament.

Rona and I
hang our heads off our seats
into the aisle,
watching a Barbie player
put makeup on her sweaty face,
and roll our eyes at each other.

Probably forgot to bring deodorant

but her face
will be all dolled up.

Smoothing on lipstick,
Barbie catches my eye and shrugs,
and we grin at each other.

To see her primp
you'd never know how tough she is on the
  court.

One of the toughest.

Sweaty in my sweats,
I step into the kitchen.

"Where'd you come from?"
Darren asks,
dish towel dangling.

Yaicha butts in,
all business at the sink,
"She's playing volleyball."

Darren's eyebrows fly up.
"Yeah? Cool,"
and
with a fierce scowl
he snaps the towel
at me.
I dance away
suddenly agile
and he flicks the table leg
instead of mine.

Snuck out to a party
at the Forsters' half-framed house—
snuck,
          yeah,
                    like anyone at home noticed I left.

Tired of meandering
between
knots of dull conversation,
I hunker down onto the unfinished porch steps
mittens around my two-hour beer,
listening to Kyler explain to someone
where the back trailhead is for Mount Logan.

"No, that's the main trailhead you're
   thinking of."
Kyler is itching his head
          through his hand-knit hat.

Before I can think, I say,
"The back trailhead starts off the highway,

near the twelve-mile marker."

Kyler turns,
earflaps swinging.
"You've done that hike?"
He lets out a whistle,
reaches over to push my thigh with a gloved
  hand.
"All the way to the top?
You're strong, volleyball girl!"

"Good oxygen up there in July," I say,
grinning madly at his compliment.
"And we had a black-mama-bear encounter
  halfway up."

The other guy snorts,
"Bet you ran with your tail between your legs."

Kyler's warm brown eyes examine mine.
"No, she didn't," he says.

"You don't run from black bears,"
   I say to the guy,
but I'm gazing at Kyler,
heart thumping.

No one is home.

I stand poised
midroom,
woofers buzzing the windows.

And when
shrieking guitar strings
rip me free
I begin with the desk chair,
throw it to the side,
spin the desk
        to the center
                of the room,
shove the bed
        momentarily in front of the bedroom
          door
        then against the far wall,
plow the desk smack against baseboards,
ram the chair home,
crash the dresser in the corner,
flop the carpet open to the left,

whirl
with fingers wide,
the beat fades,

and
I stand poised,
arm hair on end,
in a new country.

Startled out of a light nap,
my face against the couch back.

Jed wraps an arm around my shoulders
to roll both of us
so he can reach the ringing phone.

I consider grumbling.

"Yuh. Yuh. No, nothing important,
just napping."
He yawns.
"Sure, let's go now. Yuh. See ya."

He tosses the phone to the other end
   of the couch,
tapping my back three times,
Jed language for "I need you to move."

I shift,

squinching my eyes like I had been sleeping.

He eases out from under me and stands,
"I gotta go,"
stretching long arms,
another long yawn with canines showing,
and he tosses his coat over his shoulder.

"See you tomorrow, I guess," and he's loping
   out the door,
leaving me sprawled,
unnapping,
alone in his basement.

I glare at the texture of the ceiling,
trying not to cry.

Last night
a group of us from volleyball and some guys
saw that movie
about all the world's nuclear power plants
  gone wacko
and the guy next to me
actually took my hand
early on
and didn't give it back.
We held hands through most of the movie
for some reason.
When the reactors melted down in
  enormous explosions
he gripped my fingers so hard
my rings bit me
and I pulled back.
He let go and kind of stretched.
I was able to enjoy
the rest of the nuclear meltdown with
  feeling in my fingers,
but I felt

like I was the only one in the theater.

And at the end of the movie
the boy-romantic-interest lived,
of course.
The girl-romantic-interest passed out from
   radiation exposure
and it was clear
she'd never make it.

Lying on my side
in my old running tights
on the black couch,
        elbow cocked
        head propped
reading, my usual
escape.

My father walks in,
stops in the middle
of the carpet,
contemplating me.

"You are getting to be
very sexy," he says
quietly
in a reverent tone
I don't like at all.

I sit up fast
snap shut my book
fist clenched

mouth dry
controlled walk past him
down the hall
to my room
close the door
back away
back away
breathe.




Don't look at me.
Don't look at me


ever


again.

The boys' soccer team swaggers by our
   pregame warm-up.

"Whoa!
Did you see—
that girl can *hit*!"

The team clown is performing loudly for us.

"What's her name?
What?
Anke?"

Kyler jostles him
to keep him moving,
and throws a wave and a smile to me.

The guy is still at it as they amble out
   to the fields,
"I want her on my team!
Hey, Anke!
Wanna be on my team?"

I am blushing
as I run back to the end of the hitting line,
blushing
but grinning.

Guys sure are obnoxious.

Swapping
ProBars after our big win,
        half my peanut butter
        for
        half Rona's chocolate malt.
We chuck the crumpled wrappers to each other
grunting,
super slo-mo,
grunting
like we're hitting the volleyball.

I holler
*"MINE!"*
as her wrapper flies to me,
and toss it back
over her head
"Go, Rona, *GO!*"
screaming at her
as she
dives to the grass

and rolls to a stop at the foot of the tree.
*"YEAH, RONA!"*

Her on the ground holding up the wrapper,
me with my hands up in victory,
*"The CROWD GOES WIIIILLLD!"*
Two senior guys stroll by,
        eyebrows raised.
We grin.

Volleyball has taught me to yell.

Yawning at my locker,
gathering English books,
when a long body grazes my back and
   there is Kyler,
looking a little breathless.

"Hey, caught you," he says, flashing a grin.

"Hey, Kyler!"
Was that too enthusiastic?
*And I love that green shirt on you.*

He rubs a hand down his sleeve.
"I was wondering if you were going to the
   Harvest Dance."

Okay, panic.

"I, um, yeah, I'm going.
Probably with Rona, you know,
not as a date, ha! but, well,

I don't think I should go and just dance with
   one person all night,
you know?
So I was going to go with friends
and just dance with whoever I want."

Way too much talking.

But Kyler is nodding,
"Yeah, that's what a bunch of us are doing,
   as well.
But I was hoping you'd save me a dance?
Or two."
Squeezes my forearm and laughs a little.

"Sure! Thanks!" I squeak.
Dammit—I hate squeaking.

"Great!" he says,
sliding his hand off my arm
in a trail of warmth,

"Gotta get to chemistry."

He walks down the hall backward
hands gesturing rising bubbles
with a pop-pop-pop of his lips,
then he waves
and turns the corner.

Changing into
my uniform,
ignoring all the locker-room babble,
thinking of Kyler,
wondering
why he seems to like me.

Thrilled he might like me!

But I don't get it
and
I don't really believe it
because
there are so many cute girls
and I am basically
a nothing freshman with big feet and a newly
  discovered pimple on the side of her nose.

On the bus
to an away game with Robins-Hancock,
zoning to tunes,
teammates around me
bouncing in their seats.

My mind travels to
this family of crows
in the woods next door,
cackling, chuckling, creating ruckuses and
　general wild rumpuses,
each one
involved with the next one,
knowing who likes to sit next to who among
　the pine needles,
shuffling in a file on the limb
so everyone is finally comfy.

I smile, watching,
as they ruffle and rattle their feathers,

all their emotions
laid out on the branch,
      so to speak,
no secrets,
no wondering what the crow beside you
  is feeling.

Kind of like my volleyball family.
Just as noisy.
Fewer feathers.

Rona drops me off
into windy darkness at the bottom
   of the driveway,
a shuffle of leaves
blown against my feet,
and I stand still,
listening.

Acorns plopping onto damp asphalt,
moaning of hemlocks,
a high whine of air
        whisking around the corner
           of the house.

It's stirring energy out here.

A yellow angle of light from the kitchen
scrapes the back lawn.

My ponytail whips my face
with the first smattering of drops,

so I head in
before the deluge,

though I'd rather stand out here
to hear rain pelting the oak trees,
than go inside
and hear what's there.

Yaicha is crying gently
in the bathroom.
Darren,
hesitant,
goes in.

What I hear,
        flat against the hall wallpaper,
is the lift at the end
of Darren's soft sentence,
        a question.

And Yaicha's voice
flat as mud at low tide,

        "I'll live for now.

        You know
        he said he'd kill me
        if I told.

        He'd kill me."

And I hear it,

a wooden mast snapping
from years of termites below—

I hear it
and know

it is true.

He would kill her.

Can't sleep through it
so I pad to the kitchen.

Earphones on
huddling on the stool
cuddling hot chocolate.

In she comes,
glazed
and frayed,

leans on the
butcher block
then lays her cheek
on the smooth
scored
wood.

I am still
as brick
and then crack,

click off my music,

push my steaming cocoa
across the maple
to Yaicha.

Her fingers wrap
the scalding mug,

eyes closed.

. . . and i'm jealous!
with a sick
acidic
burbling
bile
i want what they have

as horrible
curdling
vile
as it is
darren and yaicha
get more
than
me.

Sometimes
first thing in the morning
when I walk down the hallway before class
shouts and hurrying footsteps and laughter
  spin off,
sucked away by a whirlpool,

and I could be alone,
deaf,
a different sort of fish
in this vast school of shining matching silver.

And it takes something physical—
      the vice principal's hand on my arm,
      "You all right, Anke?"
to bring me back.

Walking home alone,
cooling sweat.
An odd afternoon of fog
slaps softly like a damp paper towel.

My breath feels thick,
striding past the soggy soccer field,
around the goal post
off the edge of the grass.

Entering birch trees,
a dove careens by,
mockingbirds holler,
wind washes the carpet of yellow leaves.
Rounding the path's curve
a slice of fall glances my jaw
and my nose opens
to take in something sharp,
something easier to breathe,
an acrid, lively, nervous smell
that says something cutting and different
is on its way.

He went into Yaicha's room
last night
after he hit her
across the mouth
for reading
*Cosmo* magazine.

I burned in my blood,
I turned to Mom
as we stood in the hall
and inside my head screamed,
          *DO something!*

Her eyes glazed and wide
like an injured cat,
her mouth pulled tight,
Mom sighed in a voice that didn't match,

"It'll be okay.
He's just making peace with her."

And she walked away.

It just occurred to me.

It's her choice.
Yaicha chooses not to tell anyone
and Darren does too

and Mom.

Am I the only one bothered by this?
I mean
bothered enough to think about it?

So all the pressure is on me,
the Youngest and Most Bothered.
Or maybe I am just
outside enough,
being the footstool observing from the corner,
that I have a view of reality.

And I can't stand it anymore.

Why me?
I don't need this crap.

Then
why don't I tell on him?

If they don't,
why don't I?

Because.

Because I am safe this way,
silent
unnoticed.

Because my family would crack
snap
shatter
        like pine boughs in an ice storm
jagged pieces scattered,
irreparable,


and there would be no family

and I don't want that on my head.

What we have is better than that.

Right?

Squid ink black dreaming,
Running hard,
running from,
from my father
in that mask,
running to,
to the school
bell's ringing
incessant ringing,
late late late,
volleyballs
rolling in the hall,
Angeline
Angeline
pestering
pestering,
pushing by people
to get to me,
I am panting
with exertion
backed up against it,
Jed slouching

against my locker,
pointing at me,
no expression,
pointing,
I wear no clothes,
the entire
student
body
halts
to stare in silence—

bursting to breathe,
I look down to find
I have
a penis.

# PART
# THREE

I should have worn polypro liners
inside my work gloves this morning.

Brittle frost,
and I am lugging dead branches from
  the front yard
into the side woods.

Usually I just haul ass and get it done,
keeps me warm.

Today I am shivering in my plaid flannel shirt,
staring into the windows of our house,
my perspective skewed
to an outsider's.

Why am I suddenly uncomfortable?

Up till now
life was just normal.
Maybe not normal for everyone,

but *my* normal.

I used to feel solid,
knowing my job in this house—
       silence, blinders, stillness.

Now
I feel like a lumberjack
with a nail file instead of an ax,
out of context,
frustrated,
looking around me to kill time.
Except that I am noticing things.
And being bothered by them.

I don't like it.

I don't want to think about it.

"Hey," I say, shifting my backpack,
standing in his basement doorway.
"No practice today, lighting repairs."

Jed pats the couch,
eyes on the television.
"Have a seat," he says absently.

Wow.

What an invitation.

"Um, no thanks.
I have algebra problems to finish."

I have never made an excuse before.

"Oh. 'Kay, do a good job."
He smiles,
but his eyes swing back to the TV,

and I am so out of here.

I've been telling Rona all about Kyler,
having talked to him, like, what, twice?

Peeling a pale slice of tomato off her sandwich,
she slaps it onto her tray.
"So why is he in chem class as a freshman?"

Trust Rona to point out I don't know him at all.
"Must've tested out of bio?"

Rona whacks her sandwich back together,
chomping through the middle with gusto.
"Musht be shmart," she mumbles.

I nod,
blowing steam off my chili.
"He was nervous, even asking me for a dance."
I dump the spoonful back in,
feeling disappointed.
Aren't guys superhuman about their feelings?

"Well, no shit, Anke,

you're this tall, gorgeous, amazing
  volleyball player,
even if you are a freshman."

I roll my eyes.

She waves her milk,
spraying liquid from the straw.
"You are, even if you're too blind to see it.
And he's smart, not asking you for a
  big commitment,
just a dance or two.
But if you'd said no, how devastating would
  that be to a good-looking guy?
I mean, not that he's really popular or
  anything,
and neither are you—"

"Gee, thanks for reminding me."

"—but he's supposed to be a great
  soccer player,

and his buddies would sure give him shit if you
    refused to dance with him."

Like I *would* refuse to dance with him.
Flexing the styro bowl,
it finally cracks.
"Wanna go to this Thursday's soccer game
    with me, Rona?"

Under lights on Thursday night,
end of the second half,
tied with Westland 3 to 3,
shouts of fans crystallizing midair
at the coldest soccer game on record.

Rona shrieks through her scarf,
razzing the ref.
I am hopping for circulation,
clapping mittens,
      thinking how smart I am,
      wearing tights under my jeans.

Kyler is back in the game with less than a
   minute to go,
right wing,
he has the ball,
a fluid body speeding downfield.
Westland is on us,
but Kyler does this special spin,
taking control again,

his defender lurching—
　　　without thinking I belt out,
　　　"GO, KYLER, GO!"
　　　up on my toes—
and suddenly he feints left,
passes to our center,
who passes back,
Kyler taps it once,
then kicks the ball past the goalie's glove into
　　the high left corner of the net in the last five
　　seconds and we've won the game!

"Yeaaaah!"
I grab Rona's shoulders,
bouncing together
in a screaming mass of elated faces.

As players flow to the side
Kyler catches sight of me,
　　　his eyes light up in recognition,
　　　the widest smile ever.
Pulling off a mitten to give a thumbs-up

I grin back
and he's carried on with the
crowd's enthusiasm,

but he smiled right at me,
me,
personally.

Oh my god
that's Darren
leaning against the stage
at the far end of the court.

I've never seen him in the gym.
Ever.

His arms are folded over a textbook,
and he's doing his
breathing through his nose thing
like he's checking the atmosphere for foreign
   substances in parts per million,
no expression I can see from here.

We finish our drill
and I manage not to shank the ball
   into the bleachers
in front of my brother.

Now we go over hitting coverage
and I feel a bubble of elation

for some reason
as Darren watches us.

He stands there the whole drill.

I pretend to suddenly see him,
raise a casual from-the-hip wave.
His small smile flashes
and he pushes off the stage
to head to debate club.

I lean to the girl next to me.

"That's my brother, Darren."

After volleyball practice
I spot Jed walking parallel to me across the lot,
and he angles over.

"Want to walk home today? It's pretty warm,"
  he says,
throwing an arm over my shoulders.

It's been days since he's even said hello.
"Careful," I say, grimacing,
"you're touching a freshman in public."

That crooked lip sets my heart dancing,
dammit.

"So? Senior guys can get away with it.
It's the young girls who get the reputation."

I pull out from under,
pissed.
"That's exactly it,"

and I walk three steps out to the side of him,
arms folded.


Jed pulls at my arm,
laughing,
trying to uncross me.
"C'mon, Ank, you of all people don't have a rep."


Wondering
if that's good or bad,
I let him release one tucked arm.


"Aaaah, I need a nap," he says in a yawn,
squeezing my forearm and letting it go.


Does he ever do anything else?
"Hey," I say, bopping his bicep,
"let's walk home through College Woods!
        Take off our sneaks, put our toes in the
            icy brook."

His right eyebrow goes up.

"In October?"

Not his thing.

But napping is.

I wish I'd taken the late bus home.
Jed can't possibly be this worn-out after
two or three of my kisses,
I'm not that good.

But he's snoring.

Do I need a nap?
No.

Do I need kissing?
Definitely.

There has been an imbalance
   between the two lately.

And maybe there's another guy out there
who might enjoy
kissing me more.

When I come into the dining room,
French book in hand,
Yaicha doesn't even register me.

All these cool charcoal rubbings
cover the table
and she hovers on tiptoe
darting in
moving one pattern close to another
tipping back for a different perspective
moving a piece minutely
knocking her rings on the table
    as she contemplates.

I glide into view.
She shuffles through wall textures
heating grates
fig leaf veins
sneaker soles

and shifts focus toward my face.
I gape when I see the bright bruise

under her left eye.

Un-make-upped.

She glares defiance,
says nothing.

It's not really that Yaicha sat before everyone
  else at the table.

This time it made him angry.
Next time it might not.

I know it's not Yaicha.
Or Darren.
Or me.
Or mom.

It's him.

Inflict.
Dominate.
Impair.

It's all him.

Psycho-man.

And live-in victims

assuage him,
keep him hidden
from
the rest of the world.

I suppose in that way we are useful.

"Your father must have
info like that."
Angeline is at me
again.

Mom is making me work with her
on topics for government
and Angie is
forever formulating festering questions
to present
to Authorities,
Officials,
and suspicious
Politicals.

"He must have
books and books,"
Angie is pleading.
"He's a professor."

I'm not asking
him

for anything.

I want to say,
    *Get over your goddamn crush,*
    *Angie,*
    *you have no idea*
    *who he is.*
But my jaws
clamp.

"You're grumpy.
I'll call him,"
she offers
and digs out
a sparkly blue cell phone.

Well why not?
She's already more a part of my family
than I am.

She gets his answering service.

"No, no, his mom invested in that waterfront
   thing and now it's belly-up.
They already took out, like, a second mortgage
   on the house.
My mom knows the real estate broker.
I mean it.
Jed's family is flat broke."
Cherry-blossom lip gloss glues Marci's mouth
   into a smirk.

I am at the next table
shielded by a forkful of spaghetti special
and an escaped swath of hair.

Jed is broke?
He's always buying one of the guys a Coke,
gas for someone's car,
the latest music.

I glance around
and there's Jed at the back

listening to a buddy tell a story.
A slight smile on his lips
but a faraway look.

I'm staring.

Because isn't it incredible,
how you don't know much
about the people you spend every day with.

Watching mom's hair curl
in the steam from the broth,
biting my upper lip.

I offer my pyramid of meatballs
and finally stutter,
"Would you,
maybe,
come to
my game
Friday?"

Distracted in her timing
she sighs,
"Oh, I don't know.
Fridays are so busy."

I back away,
sandpaper mouth,
stumbling in my newly enlarged feet,
grasping the table

smeared with raw meat.

Right.

Mom is usually
home alone
on Friday nights.

I think
of mom as an oasis,
center of calm
in raging rapids.

But what a deception

because if I tread water in that spot
with her too long
I am lulled in froth,
mesmerized,
brain waves whirlpooled
to stay there
too,

watching petals
feathers
branches
whirl by.

Why does she stay there?

Saturday night,
dejected in the dark,
dancing halfheartedly with an embarrassingly
  eager guy
       a full head shorter than me,
        his body gyrating with abandon,
when I finally catch sight of Kyler
leaning on the wall near the front speakers.

This is terrible.
How do I nonchalantly happen to go by him
  when he's standing so far from any
  path of travel?
Has he been there all night?
Harvest Dance is already more than half over.
Maybe he changed his mind,
he's staying out of the way.
    Maybe I should just slink out the back at
      the end of this stupid, endless song,
         right about now.
Maybe—

Wait.

He's pushing off the wall,
heading right for me!

The heavy beat of the song fades,
my own internal beat heating up.

Eager Short Kid slugs me in the arm,
"Hey, how 'bout another one?"
I think I murmur no thanks,
pushing through people toward the smile on
   Kyler's lips.

Taking both my arms in his hands,
he laughs,
"An opening at last!
You are a popular girl!"

I open my mouth to protest
that I was just biding time waiting for him,

but in my wisest decision to date,
I close my mouth again
as he pulls me in for what happens to be a
slow
song.

Swaying,
        turning in that
                slow
        dance
circle.

My heart thumping,
or his?

It seems the same rhythm,
chest to chest,
my cheek at the bottom of his jaw.

If it's my heartbeat
I need to slow it down,
seem relaxed.

If it's his heartbeat,
he's as excited as I am to be dancing together,
and I am thrilled by this,
and nervous

that he's nervous.
He smoothes his hands over my lower back.


And then I feel it.

Our legs are the same length
so our hips are the same height.

I feel it,
panic,
try to pull away just enough so I'm not
  pressed up against it
without being too obvious.

Kyler pulls back a little too—
now we're both
embarrassed.

At the end of the song I chirp "Thanks!"
running for the safety of the girls' room.

What did that mean?

Doesn't an erection
mean
he wants to have sex?

I don't know him enough for that.

Dammit.

I liked him so much before this happened.
He's warm,
      like buttered pancakes and bacon
        snuggled on the plate,
      like a Synchilla jacket in the frost of
        morning,
      like the scent of cedar smoke from a
        chimney.

But this other thing.

I don't know how to put them together in the
  same person
and still like him.

Last to shower
Sunday morning,
who knows where my family disappeared to.

There's a note for me to do laundry.

Yay.

It's going to take more than stinky clothes
to wipe my mind of Ky—
        don't even think his name.

Banging around the kitchen,
I finally throw down a handful
  of Oat Crunchers,
        wonder what he eats for breakfast—
        don't—
and munching loudly,
pound downstairs to start the
  washing machine.

My knee pads are still wet

on top of the dryer
so I toss them in even though heat'll
   kill elastic—
          Kyler elastic—
          DON'T—
and I press the button,
lean against the rumbling metal,
listening to the *kathunka-thunka* of two knee
   pads making the rounds.


Going to be a long day


and I'm already sick of myself.

Amazing
how you can spend so much of the school day
hoping
to see someone,

and when things go wrong
how you can spend so much of the school day
desperate
to avoid them.

Kyler is watching me
as I am trapped in the lunch line—
        please don't talk to me
        please don't talk to me
—his eyes full of hurt,
and I feel bad,
but it's so much easier
when Rona arrives and cuts in front of me
so I have someone to yell at,
joke too loudly with,
shove around,
and I don't have to look at his eyes.

He actually comes to my locker.
"Can I please talk to you for a minute?"
Kyler's face is squinched up.

I feel my face go white and paper thin
as I nod,
and he takes my elbow
          in a gentle, nice way,
moving us around a corner to the back
   stairwell.

All I can think of is
this is where couples kiss,
but that is so obviously not
   what he wants right now.

He lets go of my elbow,
grasps my hand just for a second and
releases it,
a trace of a grimace.

He leans against the wall

with a whoosh of breath,
rubbing the sleek part of his neck with a
   long hand,
and looks up at me from a ducked head—
"I'm sorry."

I feel my jaw drop.
"I'm the one who ran," I retort.

He smirks a little.
"I don't blame you.
I just like you so much and—and—and—
I don't seem to have a lot of control over what
   that, um, does to me."

His widened pupils flicker from the floor to me
   and back again.
I blush.

"I just like you, Anke.
I just want to do stuff together sometimes,

        maybe.
We like the same things, like hiking."


"So we could be . . . good friends, then,"
    I manage to say.


"Yeah!" he says with a relieved grin,
and I am angry at myself          for saying it,
and disappointed in him          for agreeing.

At the beginning of the night
my father put on his horrible mask
and made me hide behind him in the doorway
so I could see
their little terrified faces
and trembling bags of goodies.
"Trick or treat?"

He was unrelenting,
not saying a word,
just breathing,
        a beast smelling carrion.

Several ran away without candy
causing him
great glee.

Then he got bored
closed the door,
one naked outside bulb on,

and played the recording
of wolves howling

and no one came
after that.

"What if he died?"
Words bounce off the wall, the dryer,
  the concrete floor,
land with a *poof* in the pile of laundry
  we're folding.

Yaicha swings to stare at me in shock.
"I can't believe you'd even say
that
out loud."
She whispers like he's in the next room.

I shrug,
for once looking her in the eye.
"So. What if he did?"

Her lashes sweep down.
"It's not going to happen."

I'm feeling ruthless.
"Just go with it."

I blow my hair forcefully out of my vision.
"What if he died?"

The whites of her eyes show
so that her irises seem very small,
      like a cartoon character who realizes
      they've just stepped off the cliff of the
            Grand Canyon.
"Tell me you aren't going to try and—
and—
kill him," she hisses.

She is so out there.
"I said 'died,' Yaicha, not 'I'm going to kill him.'
  Think about it. What would we do?"

She breathes hard through her nose,
then turns away,
picks up her stack of laundry
in a sweep of sudden washerwoman authority.
"Only the good die young.
He'll live to be a hundred and twenty."

Stretching on the living room floor
contorting myself
to relax my left gluteus minimus.

Switching legs,
my head is almost under
his chair.

I start to scootch away,
then stop,
noticing upholstery staples in a line
under the seat.

One is loose.

Reaching under,
I pick at it.

It's out.

Look, that one's loose, too.

It's out.

And another
and another
and one more

and the under-fabric is sagging.

Think I'm finished stretching.

Burst of energy—
scramble full tilt downstairs to the garage
to sprinkle
        staples
                over cold fish bones
at the bottom of the trash can.

State Quarter Finals!
A home game!

Rona is always in uniform first,
running in and out
to warm up
and report who's arrived in the stands.

She trots in
with the update
of our fans.
"Jackie's mom,
Ellen's mom,
Irene's two hot brothers!"
and her eyes slide
over me.

"No one yet."


They won't come.

They never do.

My father
says
competition is bad

but in biology class
we talked about
how
without competition
there is no
natural selection
and
we all could have
died
out
because we didn't fight back
when some angry ape
slapped us around
or
pillaged our bananas.

Survival
depends on

contesting the despot,
competing for the best bananas,
fitness in the fight.

Works for me.
I am ready for the opposition.

We won the match in two games,
and I soared,
I soared!

I jumped so high,
tendons of steel,
I pounded that Molten right
  into the floorboards,

our home crowd was enormous,
stamping, yelling,

I was fierce,
a warrior,
dominant!
Dominant!

On to the semi-finals!


Afterward,
Coach raised an eyebrow.

"What got into you today?
Quite the performance."

Weird—
I am not sure,
but he seemed
a little
concerned.

Feeling out of sorts,
uneasy,
Sunday bluesy,
low-down,

and I shouldn't be, right?

Great volleyball on Friday night,
moving on to the semis—

but I am in a funk,
raking the last of the rain-mashed leaves,
watery snot dripping off my nose.

The bubble of game greatness has popped

and I am back to plain old me,
alone and soggy on the lawn,

a drizzle beginning to fall.

Thanksgiving is coming this month
and in some doomy-gloomy premonition
I feel like
I have nothing to be thankful for.

I am annoyed
in my underwear
when Angeline comes into the locker room
  before Monday's practice,
clutching her pale pink sweater,
breathlessly spilling
that we could pick up government law info
at my father's office.


"He said 'Sure!'" she squeals.


His specialty,
and grudgingly I am thinking it *would* help us
on Thursday, Government Day.
I grunt on my knee pads.


He'll leave a folder on his desk because,
sigh,
"he might have a meeting."
She is briefly bereft.


I say I'll meet her in the lobby after practice.

"Oh, I told him I'd go, I don't mind."

Grrrr.
He *is my* father.
"No, I'll meet you," I throw at her
retreating back
but she's gone.

Cock my foot to lace my left sneaker.

"Why don't you just frickin' move in with us,"
  I say out loud.

I'll be glad when this government thing is over,
this annoying extracurricular supposed honor
that forces me to spend
even more time
with Angeline.

I'm a little late
getting to my father's building
after hanging out in the locker room
  with Rona, reliving every play
  from the Quarters
        and making up a few.
I scan for Angeline in the lobby
then sprint up the three flights
        on postpractice elation's momentum.
Coming to the DR. LARUS FELD etched on his
  frosted door,
I hitch up my sweatpants,
hoping he's not in.


Tapping lightly,
turning the knob,
the door swings in silence, fangs of light
  glinting in the glass.


Then I hear—

I hear—something—soft crying somewhere.

Angeline?

    Clamping gym bag to my body,
    sneakers on carpet,
       carpet,
       carpet,
    lean around the bookcase—

My
father with a small smile
leaning toward the armchair,
zipper on its way down,
Angeline, her skirt tweaked,
swelling closing one eye,
pleading softly, no, no,

"NO!"
Dr. Feld is shock still.
I take another lungful,

"NO!"

       Angie slides to standing,
       gathering her book bag,
       running for the exit.
Raising brows, he mocks me,
but, dammit, he will hear me,

"NO!"

Slamming by the bookcase
tearing through the doorway
pounding down the stairwell,
no-no-no-no,
NO-NO-NO.

She is gone when I get outside,
so I'm running toward home
along the railroad tracks,
gym bag whacking my back,
not smelling the oily rails,
crows muted,
sun dim,
tunnel vision only two feet
in front of my feet,

my only companion
that shrill pitch above me,
the one they use
in movies
when something terrible is revealed.

Throwing my gym bag down
by the brook
with a crunch of fine ice,
I double over,
dry heaves
on my knees.

What did I see?
What did I see in his office?

How could he, to
poor Angeline?

I sink onto a rock near the water,
taking a blood-red
maple leaf
and dunking it under,
holding it beneath the frigid liquid.

Poor Angie.

She was supposed to be outside our

house of horrors
and I let her in.
I should have kept her away from him.
He went outside.

And the tears burst through
heavy as mercury,
heated by guilt,
and I take the leaf out of the water,
sobbing.

Angeline,
Angie,
I'm sorry.

Trudging
trudging up the driveway,
patches of ice,
Darren sweeping
patches of wood chips.

"Go look out back,"
he says with a jerk of his head,
stamping the broom,
and I am
standing,
staring . . .

"Go look," he says.

. . . then trudging
past,
saying nothing,
peeling my coat
to cool myself down.

From the dining room
I gape at the backyard,
suddenly so vast and bright
even in twilight,

the old hemlock tree gone.

Stump and sawdust.
Cut off at the knees.

"It had that disease,"
Mom says,
"it might have spread.
The tree had to go."

I flash with incendiary anger at her.
Then, pressing my forehead
to the chilled glass of the sliding door,
an ice block

forms in my chest.

My climbing tree.
My pinecone supply.
My hiding spot in the middle of the yard.
Gone.

Pushing open the bathroom door
I take two steps toward Yaicha
who is wrestling with her hair.

"I saw him hurt Angeline."

The brush stops moving.

"At his office today."

Small sounds
        like a dying cricket
come from Yaicha's lips.
"I'm sure you were mistaken," she says
    to her brush.

My ears pin back—
*"MISTAKEN?*
I know who Angie is, Yaicha.
I know who our father is, Yaicha.
He hurts people, he hurts you,

you never do anything!"
My claws scrape the wall paint.

She turns with soft rabbit eyes.
"He'll kill me."

"He's already doing that!"
I am growling, grabbing her sleeve,
"Every day,
every day he rips you open,
chips off pieces week by week,
till a few years from now you are not even a
  mouthful of sawdust.
A drawn-out killing.
Well, I'm tired of all of us doing nothing.
He has to be stopped."

Yaicha's eyes have flinched a few times
but soften again.
"Nobody can stop him."

My teeth show.

"Nobody can stop him?
Good.
To him I have always been
Nobody."

"No-no-no-no, Anke,
What're you going to do . . . ?"
Yaicha is whispering, pleading.

I storm outside
to visit the stump
and hear her hammer downstairs and streak
  out the garage to tell Darren.
In a weird echo along the hedge
I hear him say,
"No, she can't. . . .
Let's talk to mom."

And in the gathering night
I stand on dying chips,
stare at the new cut
oozing plasma,
sticky,
drying in the chill.

The family secret,

      carefully contained for years,
out in the open air.

Now Yaicha and Darren are talking to mom
in the living room.

I hear his car
slow for the gravel turn
at the bottom of the driveway
and I head
inside.

Where is the safe, cuddling daddy
who
sang "I'm Being Swallowed by a Boa
    Constrictor" to me

                    when I had a fever?


Was that man molted off
like scales that no longer
lie smoothly
around the shape of what he has become?



I want my daddy back.




Too bad for me.

# PART
# FOUR

They all swivel to me—
Mom, Darren, and Yaicha—
as I come through the sliding door.
Mom's mouth opens
then closes
when the garage door
goes up.

Then comes down.

Footfall,
Darren frozen, eyes on the baseboard,
Yaicha melted against the stereo cabinet,
as he steps lightly up the stairs.

"Sorry I couldn't give you
a ride home,"
he says to me,
sliding into the living room
with his briefcase,

"I had a meeting."

His eyes dare me.

Dare me.

Slow        motion
twitching
        twitching
                hissing burning
                blood pushing
                itching skin
                        pushing out
                        something scary
                        pushing out
                        something stronger.

I stand behind his chair.
"Liar,"
    under my breath.


    His eyebrows rise,
    pupils sharpen.


"You weren't at a meeting,"
    take a breath, gain speed, bursting,
"You were with Angie in the office.
I saw you. I saw you.
You clamp us down,
you think no one knows.
You hurt my brother! My sister!
You hurt my friend! Small trusting prey, huh?
You had to squash some weak person
  already in pain,
    thinking she loved you.
You could have chosen to hurt *me*!

But I'm not worth enough I never am and
   you picked poor Angie,
   you were going to RAPE her,
   I SAW YOU TRY TO RAPE ANGIE,
   you fucking MONSTER!"

      I shove his chair forward
      with the force of my words,
      the wooden leg touches
      his foot.

      Stillness. Shaking.

      White-faced, cold,
      slowly
      he picks it up by the seat.

      Suddenly spinning the chair in air
      he smashes it on me

hard—

with a great crack
I go down,
splinters of wood
splinters of bone
my leg showing bone,

and finally
I
roar.

Coming out of anesthesia,
throwing up
as the doctor
explains
one rod, two plates, eight screws
he planted
in my leg bone.
A recipe for repair.

"No duct tape?" I croak.

Leaning off the hospital bed,
convulsing again.
Throwing up
feels
strangely
good.

In the sweeping blur
the doctor's

purple high-tops
swim into focus.

I can barely hear his grin.

"Nope, no duct tape."

The teeny card attached
        with a green Band-Aid on a heart
says *from*
*Coach Roy and Rona and the Team*
in florist script.


An arrangement bursting
with
stripy-throated trumpety flowers
the exact color of
salmon sashimi.
        Alstroemeria, Mom called them.


I am grinning.


My team.


My first real bouquet.

Mom perches
on the gurney edge,
flicking, straightening the beautiful
one perfect
flame-colored rose
she brought.

"I threw him out, Anke.
Out."

Softly, fiercely,
she rips a petal.

He's been arrested.

In jail.


Such an odd disconnect

to feel so relieved
and so guilty,

yet so cold about the whole thing,
like concrete,
like a nuclear reactor decommissioned
        and left by itself to withstand the
            winter.



I wonder if he has to wear one of those
    bar-striped suits.

I scootch up straighter.
Mom props pillows
and then they stand there,

Mom, stroking my hair,
Darren, staring at me
      like he suddenly sees my eyes are brown,
Yaicha, wearing pink, squeezing my toes,
      looking at me,
      then out the hospital window.

I am
grateful they came,
embarrassed they wanted to.

I want hugs,
I want
to ask them to leave,
but when they finally go
I am lonely
again.

I can't be
still
in this antiseptic bed.

I knock my new
shocking green cast
against the metal rails
even though it hurts
to do it,
rocking my leg
        back and forth, *whack*
        back and forth, *whack*
        back and forth, *whack*.

I did it.

        back and forth, *whack*

I filed
a restraining order
against

my own father.

     back and forth, *whack*

He's out on bail
and needs more than restraining.

     back and forth, *whack*, *WHACK*.

But it's
a damn good
start,
and

I did it.

Angeline has a lawyer

and
I have a doctor
and
    strong pain medication
    for where my bone
    punched through to the open air,
    a desperate method
    of escape,
    and I'm a little proud of it.

Angie has a therapist
too

and
they want one for me.

But I told them I need
to think on my own
first.

I am staring at the nothingness of the
    hospital room
when a fluttering of yellow
catches my eye.

Long fingers curve around the door frame
waving a birch leaf.

I prop myself,
grinning,
wondering.
"Hello?" I call.

Blond hair and one crinkled light brown eye
    show next to the doorjamb,
then the rest of Kyler's smiling face.

"Hey," he says gently.

"Hey!" I say,

my heart skipping up in tempo.

Stepping into the room,
Kyler reaches gingerly into the chest pocket of
   his flannel shirt,
drawing out a handful of autumn leaves.

"For me?" I say gleefully,
palms up for him to lay them on.

He sits easily on the side of the bed,
watching me go through beech, oak, maple.

"I didn't know your favorite flower," he says,
like it's an apology.

I raise the pile of leaves and breathe
   their scent,
looking up into Kyler's eyes.

"These *are* my favorite," I say.

Lying spread eagle,
anchored
by my leg cast
to the driveway
      still barely warm
      from an unseasonal day.

Staring into the starred darkness
makes me feel
stronger,
a simple truth.

With all the
dizzy galaxies
      hot gases
           dust at the speed of light
               neutrinos running through
               everything,

no matter how powerful somcone is
    here on Earth

they are just as small as me
to the vast greatness of
outer
space.

Strangely calm
about missing the State Semi-Finals.

We lost.

It's too bad,
but I secretly feel kind of proud
that maybe we lost
because
I wasn't there.

And I'll be back next year.

An envelope
under my door
in the morning.

*Anke,*
in my mother's
small script.

Inside, a love letter:

> *I am sorry I let you down.*
> *Your strength has always been immense,*
> *I think I believed your father*
> *needed me more.*
> *He is in such pain, and I chose not to*
>   *see some things he did to feel better.*
> *Shielded by my love for him,*
>   *I always did what I thought was best*
> *for my marriage—*
> *I see I failed you, my daughter.*
> *I sacrificed my children.*
> *Please help me*

*be a better mother to you now.*
*I love you, I need you.*

And I am crying
stumping out to the hall
enveloping Mom in a smothering of
  pajama arms,
pounding her shoulder with my fist,
pounding,
damn you,
mingling tears,
I love you, too.

I wish I could ask Yaicha
what it was like
what she was thinking
what she was feeling
what made her lie still
while he hurt her so badly.

I wish I could
but I don't know how to bring up
such horrible questions.

Maybe they are none of my business.

Maybe she is wanting someone to ask.

Do I just open my mouth over homework,
brushing teeth,
folding laundry?
Do I just plunk myself on the edge of her bed
  one morning
and ask?

I find myself crying all the time—
right now,
for instance.

It comes over me at the weirdest moments,
like boiling water for tea
or chopping wood for the fire.

At first I thought it was just leftover reaction.

But I feel like I'm breaking into a thousand
    random pieces, unsolvable.

And Darren is at the door of my bedroom
with a sad face,
and he comes and puts his arm around me—I
    can't remember when he's ever done that—

and I realize he loves me maybe and I haven't
   ruined the whole family and ripped us all
   to shreds and maybe they don't hate me and
   it'll be okay and now I'm crying even harder,
   sobbing on Darren,
   holding him around his neck
   like I'm ten years old,
   and he says
"Add some soap, you'd be a great washing
   machine."
and I am laughing and crying and I am so glad
   I have my brother.

The turkey seems way too big this year.

Did just one person
take up
that much table?

The steam leaks from a vent in the crackly skin
just like a touched-up photo
in *Chef's Fare*.
But we are not in a magazine.

I thought maybe
we'd all know what we're thankful for.
He's *gone*, isn't he?

It was Yaicha's idea.
Mom said,
"Just the chair!"
and something about pumpkin pie having gone
  to our heads.

But Darren finds a broken crate,
leftover shingles,
a branch of cedar,
to jumpstart the bonfire,

so our father's teak armchair
will really burn,
burn completely away.

The fire howls to life,
cedar sap snapping,
and when it is so hot
we have to shield our faces,
Darren helps me throw on the chair,
upholstery down,
shattered frame to the blackening sky,

flames lapping
three unbroken legs
      awkward in the air.

The three of us let out a cheer
dancing, me stumping, in a crazy circle
fed by the blaze,

and Yaicha sings,
"Ding-dong, the wicked witch is dead!"

And then the silliness stops.
Yaicha
Darren
and I
are standing
with our scarves to our noses,
saying nothing
thinking everything
eyes glued to the pulsing core of the fire.

I nudge
a burning twig with my toe,
reflecting
on my father himself.
I have loved him,
feared him,
loathed him,
for so long.

But what does he have
to give me

now
that I would actually want?

The final chair leg tumbles
to the coals,

and I can't come up with
one
thing.

Yaicha and I
sit against the big hemlock stump
heads nearly touching
through the feathery needled sprout
between us.

Darren is silhouetted,
standing,
arms folded,
facing the fire.

"Come sit with us,"
I tell him,
patting the ground
like he's a small child.

And he comes!
He sits on my other side,
arm around the scratchy bark,

throwing tiny chips into the coals.

Three of us,
facing the embers,
leaning on the scent
of fresh-sawn wood.

They head into the house,
Darren patting my shoulder,
Yaicha touching my hair.

Resting my cast on a smoldering shingle
I stare into coals,
eyelids drying,
small pulsing flames emblazoned on my vision
  when I finally blink.

I shiver
with contrasts
like the planet Mercury,
        one side boiling
        one side frozen

and here I am crying again
because that sounds so lonely,
I am tired of
being lonely,
so done with

being lonely.

And yes!

I *am* done with being lonely
because there,
sticking their heads out the sliding-glass door
are my mother,
my brother,
my sister,
calling me
      "Come in!"
           "It's cold out there alone!"
                 "We're making hot chocolate!"

Wrapped in a grin,
I douse the last embers
and turn on my cast
away from ashes.

Toward offered afghan.
Toward mug of frothy warmth.
Toward my family.

# DISCUSSION QUESTIONS

- *Because I Am Furniture* is a verse novel—a collection of poems that work together as a complete story. Identify several passages in which the visual layout of the lines contributes to the mood and/or emotion of the story. What effect does the layout of these lines create? What role does punctuation play?

- Conflict is central to a story. *Because I Am Furniture* addresses three forms of conflict: person against person; person against self; and person against society. Discuss how each type of conflict applies to the story.

- Describe Anke's relationships with her brother, Darren, and her sister, Yaicha, in Part I of the story. In what way is she "furniture" to them? Why?

- Anke makes the volleyball team and becomes an exceptional player. How does being a member of the team shape her identity?

- Compare and contrast Anke's perceptions of her mother with those of her father. How are they alike? How are they different? Does Anke seem to love one parent more than the other? Explain.

- Anke is aware of her father's abuse of her sister and brother and has conflicting feelings about her own relationship with him. At one point she says, "I think that it is supposed to be good that I get less from him but I feel worth less." Why do you believe she feels this way? Is her response normal?

- One might argue that Angeline is a character foil for Anke. How does Angeline's perception of Anke's father contrast with Anke's feelings?

- Anke's mother remains silent about the abuse, and yet Anke calls her mother an "oasis." What do you think contributes to Anke's contradictory feelings about her mother? Is Anke's mother a good mother? Support your response with passages from the novel.

- In what way is school a haven for Anke? In what way does she feel threatened while there?

- At one point in the story Anke says Rona is the only person to whom she could tell the truth. Compare and contrast Rona and Angeline. Why does Anke feel safe with Rona? Why does Anke distrust Angeline?

- Compare and contrast Anke's feelings for Jed and Kyler. Make a case for one boy being "furniture" in Anke's life. In what way might Anke be like her father?

- Anke's parents do not support her efforts to play volleyball, but she excels at the sport anyway. Discuss the scene in which Darren comes to watch Anke practice volleyball. What is Anke's response? Why do you think Darren comes? Does this scene create a turning point in their relationship?

- One morning after her father has beaten Darren, Anke notices the bruise on his torso. She describes her feelings: " . . . and I felt my

upholstery rip and bits of fluff escape to float away." What does Anke mean? Find other references to furniture and discuss how they contribute to the overall meaning of the story. How are chairs in particular symbols or metaphors for Anke's life? For that of her father? For their relationship? Find passages to support your response.

- Victims of domestic violence become caught in the abuse cycle because they buy into the belief that the abuser abuses because he/she loves the victim. Does Anke fall into this cycle during any point in the novel? Why or why not? In the end, Anke breaks the cycle for her family. How might her role as an outsider give her courage? In your response, consider the passage, "Or maybe I am just outside enough, being the footstool observing from the corner that I have a view of reality."

- At the end of the novel, Darren, Yaicha, and Anke build a bonfire in the backyard and burn

their father's chair. Explain the significance of this scene.

- The story takes place in the fall, and numerous references are made to autumn colors (e.g., reds, yellows, and browns). How does this color imagery contribute to the story? Many references are made to ice and fire and similar oppositions (e.g., cold and heat). What purpose do these images serve? How does the author's use of sensory imagery contribute to the overall tone and mood of the book?

- Symbolism abounds in references to wood, leaves, and trees. Identify several passages containing these motifs and discuss their meanings. Pay particular attention to the old hemlock tree and what happens to it toward the end of the story.

- Near the end of the book, Anke, Darren, and Yaicha sit together against the hemlock tree stump. How does this scene bring closure to the story? To this time in the family's life?

- How do you envision Anke's relationship with her mother in five years? Her father? What about her relationships with Darren and Yaicha?

# PART
# ONE

# Because I Am Furniture

Only fiction and truth were used in the crafting
of this book.

To
my mother
my brother
and
my sister.

I write
now
what I could not do
then.

SPEAK
Published by the Penguin Group
Penguin Group (USA) Inc., 345 Hudson Street, New York, New York 10014, U.S.A.
Penguin Group (Canada), 90 Eglinton Avenue East, Suite 700, Toronto, Ontario, Canada M4P 2Y3
(a division of Pearson Penguin Canada Inc.)
Penguin Books Ltd, 80 Strand, London WC2R 0RL, England
Penguin Ireland, 25 St Stephen's Green, Dublin 2, Ireland (a division of Penguin Books Ltd)
Penguin Group (Australia), 250 Camberwell Road, Camberwell, Victoria 3124, Australia
(a division of Pearson Australia Group Pty Ltd)
Penguin Books India Pvt Ltd, 11 Community Centre, Panchsheel Park, New Delhi - 110 017, India
Penguin Group (NZ), 67 Apollo Drive, Rosedale, North Shore 0632, New Zealand
(a division of Pearson New Zealand Ltd)
Penguin Books (South Africa) (Pty) Ltd, 24 Sturdee Avenue,
Rosebank, Johannesburg 2196, South Africa

Registered Offices: Penguin Books Ltd, 80 Strand, London WC2R 0RL, England

First published in the United States of America by Viking,
a member of Penguin Group (USA) Inc., 2009
Published by Speak, an imprint of Penguin Group (USA) Inc., 2010

3 5 7 9 10 8 6 4

Copyright © Thalia Chaltas, 2009

THE LIBRARY OF CONGRESS HAS CATALOGED THE VIKING EDITION AS FOLLOWS:
Chaltas, Thalia.
Because I am furniture / by Thalia Chaltas.
p.  cm.
Summary: The youngest of three siblings, fourteen-year-old Anke feels both relieved and
neglected because her father abuses her brother and sister but ignores her,
but when she catches him with one of her friends, she finally becomes angry enough to take action.
ISBN 978-0-670-06298-0 (hardcover)
[1. Novels in verse. 2. Child abuse—Fiction. 3. Child sexual abuse—Fiction.
4. Family problems—Fiction. 5. High schools—Fiction. 6. Schools—Fiction.] I. Title.
PZ7.5.C38Be 2009
[Fic]—dc22
2008023235

Speak ISBN 978-0-14-241510-8

Printed in the United States of America

Book design by Nancy Brennan
Set in Egyptienne

# Because
# I
# Am
# Furniture

BY

## Thalia Chaltas

**speak**

An Imprint of Penguin Group (USA) Inc.

## OTHER BOOKS YOU MAY ENJOY

| | |
|---|---|
| *Dreamland* | Sarah Dessen |
| *I Hadn't Meant to Tell You This* | Jacqueline Woodson |
| *Impossible* | Nancy Werlin |
| *Just Listen* | Sarah Dessen |
| *Lock and Key* | Sarah Dessen |
| *Looking for Alaska* | John Green |
| *Looks* | Madeleine George |
| *The Rules of Survival* | Nancy Werlin |
| *Speak* | Laurie Halse Anderson |

# POSSIBILITY

Trotting along the sidewalk,
salty and tacky with sweat,
I reek!

I reek with possibility.

Volleyball.

We won't find out results for a few days,
but right now,
bouncing through the neon blast of sunset,
I reek,
and
nothing can stop my grin.

Not even going home.

political party formed in 1833 to oppose the policies of President Andrew Jackson. It was her first political convention, and she "enjoyed every moment of it."

## *"Yes, Here Is the Conflict"*

In her diary, Susan recorded her social life of suppers and dances and horse-and-buggy rides. An excursion to Saratoga Springs, an idyllic town with many natural mineral springs, was not as much fun as she anticipated because the young man she liked invited another young woman to ride in his buggy. Susan ended up riding in the buggy of a man she considered far less appealing. Nevertheless, she tried to be "agreeable," until he pressed her to give up teaching and marry him.

She spent several months in Vermont with relatives and recruited her cousin Moses Vail to teach her algebra. Hearing about her accomplishment, her brother-in-law Aaron McLean said that he preferred that she continue to bake her delicious biscuits.

"I'd rather see a woman make such biscuits as these than solve the knottiest problem in algebra," Aaron told her.

"There is no reason why she should not be able to do both," Susan replied.

In the summer of 1845, she rejected another marriage proposal, this one from a wealthy widower who tried to entice her with visions of his fine farm, large house, and sixty dairy cows. He was taken with her, he said, because she reminded him of his dead wife. That same summer her sister Hannah announced her engagement to Eugene Mosher. As with Guelma's marriage, Susan struggled with her feelings of loss of her intense sisterly bond with Hannah. In a letter to her parents, she first expressed her concern that Hannah "seems so swallowed up" in herself.

But in her typical self-reflective way, she ended her letter with the insight that she needed to accept Hannah's love for someone outside their tight family circle: "Yes, here is the conflict, I hope after having seen her and Eugene I shall feel different and give it up." In time she accepted Eugene, although she continued to think that "no one is good enough for my Hannah."

### "Cold and Cheerless Day"

For five years, the Anthonys struggled to recover from bankruptcy. Daniel tried to earn a profit from two small mills and a logging camp. Lucy took in boarders. She spent weeks at the camp and cooked for the workers. Susan sent him money from her meager salary. But to no avail. In search of new opportunities, Daniel traveled to Michigan and Virginia, but found nothing.

Finally Lucy's brother Joshua Read (who had saved their essential items from the bankruptcy auction) suggested they look at a farm for sale near Rochester, New York. They liked it, and Joshua used money for the down payment that Lucy would have inherited from their parents if she had not been a married woman.

Susan, her sister Mary, her brother Merritt, and their parents moved in early November. They went by stage and railroad to visit Joshua and his family in Palatine Bridge, New York, a village on the Mohawk River. From there they boarded a "line-boat" that was loaded with all their possessions, including their "old gray horse" and their wagon, to travel on the Erie Canal to Rochester. Arriving late on a "cold and cheerless day" and unable to afford a hotel, they hitched the horse to the wagon and headed to their farm, three miles to the west. The "roads were very muddy," Susan later recalled, and it was "quite dark" when they arrived. For dinner, Lucy made "a kettle of mush" from cornmeal and milk. That night, she and Daniel shared the only bed. Susan and her siblings slept on the floor. Beds and other household goods were delivered the next day. Soon a "long and lonesome," cold and snowy winter arrived. For months, Susan and her family felt "very sad and home-sick."

Springtime boosted their spirits. The fruit trees and bushes—peach, cherry, quince, currant, and gooseberry—bloomed. They were befriended by Quakers from Rochester who shared their antislavery sentiments. Their house soon became a popular gathering place for reformers and abolitionists.

In 1846, Susan moved to Canajoharie, New York, a town across the Mohawk River from Palatine Bridge. The Mohawk chief, Joseph Brant, had translated "Ca-na-jo-ha-rie" to mean in English "the pot that washes itself," an apt description of a large circular pothole carved by rushing water in the Canajoharie Creek Gorge. Susan accepted an offer to head the Female Department of the Canajoharie Academy, a private high school with forty boys and twenty-five girls. Her uncle Joshua was a trustee of the school. She worried about doing a good job. Did she know enough to teach older students? Would she disappoint Uncle Joshua? What about the parents? Uncle Joshua reassured her. The secret to success, he said, was "thinking you know it all."

## *"There Were Plenty of Them"*

Susan spent three transformative years in Canajoharie. She gained confidence in her ability to teach a variety of subjects: reading, spelling, writing, grammar, arithmetic, botany, philosophy, and history. Her students excelled at the regular public examinations that were attended by the principal, trustees, and parents. She took them on field trips to "the pot that washes itself" and other local sites. One year she directed her students in a play about the difference between country and city girls. She assembled the costumes—plain ones for the country girls and fancy ones with "splendid hats, trimmed with wreaths and plumes," for the city girls. The play was a hit.

"Can you begin to imagine my excitement?" she wrote to her parents. "Who ever thought that Susan Anthony could get up such an affair? I am sure I never did, but here I was; it was sink or swim, I made a bold effort and won the victory."

She no longer had to send money home because her father had gotten a job with an insurance company in Rochester. With the highest salary she had ever earned, $110 dollars a year (about $2,967 in today's dollars), Susan discovered she had a flare for fashion. She bought a "new pearl straw gypsy hat trimmed in white ribbon with fringe on one edge and a pink satin stripe on the other, with a few white roses and green leaves for inside trimming." For winter wear, she purchased a broché shawl, a gray fox muff, and a white ribbed-silk hat, and had a new dress made out of plum-colored merino wool. The hat, she told her parents, made "the villagers stare."

Her embrace of fashion was very un-Quaker-like. She also took up dancing. Susan, however, did not start drinking liquor. After one escort drank too much and made "a fool of himself," she vowed that she would only attend events with "a total abstinence man."

She was not lacking for suitors. Soon after her arrival in Canajoharie, she spent an evening with a Mr. Loaux. "Well, I passed the fiery ordeal," she reported to her parents, "no doubt he thought I was <u>handsome</u>." Later she mentioned a Mr. Wells, Mr. Stafford, and Dan S., but provided scant information about them. Many years later, her biographer, Ida Husted Harper, asked her why her diaries were not "full of 'beaux' as most girls' were."

Susan replied, "There were plenty of them, but I never could bring myself to put anything about them on paper."

## 7

# "To Do and Dare Anything"

### ELIZABETH CADY STANTON
#### 1848–1850

DURING THE SUMMER OF 1848, Lucretia and James Mott were in the Seneca Falls area. They attended a Quaker meeting, traveled to communities of escaped slaves in Buffalo, New York, and Canada, spent time with the Seneca Indians in Cattaraugus, New York, visited prisoners in the penitentiary in Auburn, New York, and stayed with Lucretia's sister Martha Coffin Wright, who lived with her husband and seven children in Auburn, where she was active in the Underground Railroad.

Early in July, Elizabeth had tea with Lucretia, Martha, Jane Hunt, and Mary Ann M'Clintock at the Hunts' house in nearby Waterloo, New York. In the presences of such "earnest, thoughtful women," Elizabeth expressed her anguish with such "vehemence and indignation" that she stirred herself "as well as the rest of the party, to do and dare anything." And they did; together they wrote a call, or an announcement, of "a convention to discuss the social, civil, and religious condition and rights of woman" to be held in Seneca Falls on July 19 and 20.

Three days before the convention, Elizabeth took her draft of an opening statement and resolutions to the M'Clintocks' house in Waterloo. She sat at a small, round mahogany table and, with input from the M'Clintocks, worked to produce the Declaration of Sentiments. Using the Declaration of Independence as a model, she revised the famous five words, "all men are created equal," to read "all men and women are created equal," then described eighteen grievances and ended with eleven resolutions, including woman's "sacred right to the elective franchise," or the right to vote.

## *"With the Merry Eye"*

Elizabeth was well prepared for her role. For years she had studied law, economics, history, and politics. She had read books by the great writers and philosophers on woman's rights—Mary Wollstonecraft's *A Vindication of the Rights of Women*, Sarah Grimké's *Letters on the Equality of the Sexes, and the Condition of Woman*, and Margaret Fuller's *Woman in the Nineteenth Century*. She read Judge Elisha Powell's essays strongly supporting woman's rights, and Reverend Samuel J. May's sermon "The Rights and Conditions of Women." In the mid-1840s, she, along with Ernestine Rose and Paulina Wright Davis, had lobbied New York legislators to pass an act allowing married women to retain property they brought into the marriage or inherited during it. The act—the Married Women's Property Act—had just been approved by the state legislature, the first in the country to take this step.

Lucretia warned Elizabeth that people might not attend "owing to the busy time with the farmers' harvest." But hundreds came. Some walked; others rode horses or traveled in horse-drawn vehicles—surreys, heavy farm wagons, and democrat wagons (lightweight flat-bottom wagons with two or more seats).

Thirteen-year-old Mary Bascom was there with her parents. Years later she remembered the scene "as vividly as if yesterday,—the old chapel with its dusty windows . . . the wooden benches or pews, and the platform with the desk and communion-table, and the group gathered there; Mrs. Stanton, stout, short, with her merry eye and expression of great good humor; Lucretia Mott, whose presence then as now commanded respect wherever she might be; Mary Anne McClintoc [sic], a dignified Quaker matron with four daughters around her, two of whom took active part in the proceedings."

## "So Timely, So Rational, and So Sacred"

For two days, they listened, discussed, debated. The Declaration of Sentiments was adopted and signed by sixty-eight women and thirty-two men. Only one resolution caused a bit of a stir, and that was the one Elizabeth insisted on—the right of suffrage. Henry said he would leave town if she proposed it. She did, and he absented himself. Lucretia worried that it was too radical. Frederick Douglass, however, supported Elizabeth's demand for the vote and spoke up during the debate. "In due time," she said, "Douglass and I carried the whole convention."

It was inconceivable to Elizabeth that a convention that she considered "so timely, so rational, and so sacred" would be the brunt of "sarcasm and ridicule." But it was. Hyperbolic accounts appeared in newspapers across the country: The convention was "a most insane and ludicrous farce" and the participants were "erratic, addle-pated comeouters." The women's demands would "prove a monstrous injury to all mankind."

Some newspapers heralded the convention. The editor of the *Herkimer Freeman* wrote, "Success to the cause in which they have enlisted! . . . I hail it as a great jubilee of the nation." The *St. Louis Reveille* proclaimed, "The flag of independence has been hoisted for the second time on this side of the Atlantic . . . by a convention of women at Seneca Falls, New York." Horace Greeley, editor of the widely read *New York Tribune*, wrote, "It is easy to be smart, to be droll, to be facetious in opposition to the demands of these Female Reformers." But, he conceded, although their demands are "unwise and mistaken," they are based on the "assertion of a natural right," as are the words "all men are created equal" in the Declaration of Independence.

## *"The Right Is Ours"*

Energized by the Seneca Falls convention, Amy Post, a prominent reformer, organized another one that was held two weeks later in Rochester. Although Elizabeth later said she attended "with fear and trembling" because of the hostile press, she was there, along with Lucretia and Frederick. Whereas men had presided at the Seneca Falls convention, Amy nominated her friend, the activist Abigail Bush, as president. Worried by such unwomanly behavior, Elizabeth and Lucretia left the platform and sat in the audience. Undeterred by their action, Abigail competently performed her duties. Afterward, Lucretia tenderly held Abigail in her arms and thanked her for presiding. Elizabeth wrote an apology to Amy: "I have so often regretted my foolish conduct." Her behavior, she said, was due to a lack of experience in seeing women "act in a public capacity."

The success of both conventions gave Elizabeth "great encouragement to go on." The question she asked was "What are we next to do?"

The answer was a whirlwind of activity. She printed the directions "Read and Circulate" on copies of the minutes of the Seneca Falls convention and sent them to her friends. She wrote letters to newspapers, organized a petition campaign, and gave her first major speech on woman's rights at a Quaker meetinghouse in Waterloo. Again she called for the right to vote—"The right is ours. Have it we must. Use it we will." After giving that speech a few times, she tied a ribbon in her favorite color—pale blue—around the manuscript and put it away. Years later she gave it to her two daughters with the hope that "they will finish the work which I have begun."

No longer intimidated by hostile press, Elizabeth cut out articles and pasted them in a small red-backed scrapbook (which is now in the Library of Congress). She welcomed any publicity because it spread their ideas and that would "start women thinking, and men too; and when men and women think about a new question, the first step in progress is taken. The great fault of mankind is that it will not think."

Her house was a place where young people gathered to talk and dance. On Saturday nights, people met for "conversation-als," or discussion groups, on a different topic each week. She put a billiard table in the barn, started a dancing school, and put up swings and bars for exercise (a novel idea at the time). Years later, her children described her as "a most devoted mother; she sang and played for us on both piano and guitar, and told us wonderful stories."

### *"Great Effort and Patience"*

Elizabeth had a miscarriage in March 1849. We know that from a letter Martha Wright wrote to her sister Lucretia with the news that Elizabeth "has miscarried at 5 mo. with a little

girl—a great disappointment." Despite her sadness, Elizabeth
kept up her whirlwind of activities.

Since January, she had been writing articles for the *Lily*,
a temperance newspaper published by Amelia Bloomer, the
deputy postmaster of Seneca Falls (her husband was the postmaster). Amelia had attended the Seneca Falls convention,
but she had not signed the Declaration; instead she had "stood
aloof and laughed." Undeterred and characteristically strategic,
Elizabeth set about with "great effort and patience" to infuse
the *Lily* with woman's rights ideas. Within a year, she published
"Woman," the first of many provocative articles about every
aspect of women's lives—voting, housekeeping, dating, and
sewing.

Her writing style was as bold, good-natured, and as colorful
as her personality. Typically in both her writing and speaking,
she posed questions, undoubtedly to provoke readers to think.
In "Sewing," she wrote, "What use in all the flummering, puff-
ing, and mysterious folding we see in ladies' dresses? What use
in ruffles on round pillow cases, night caps, and children's
clothes? . . . It will be a glorious day . . . when men and boys
make their own clothes, and women make theirs in the plainest
possible manner."

## *"The Point to Attack"*

In Ohio in 1850, a group of delegates—all men—was slated to
meet to revise the state constitution. Determined to convince
them to add woman suffrage to the constitution, a group of
women held the first Ohio Women's Convention on April 19
and 20 in Salem, Ohio. Elizabeth was invited to speak. Thrilled
by the invitation, but not free to leave her children, she wrote
a letter that was read to the convention. In it she underscored

both the importance of and resistance to woman suffrage: "Depend upon it, this is the point to attack the stronghold of the fortress—*the one* women will find the most difficult to take, *the one* man will most reluctantly give up."

Although men had been allowed to participate in the conventions in Seneca Falls and Rochester, they were silenced in Salem by President Betsey Mix Cowles, a pioneering kindergarten teacher, operator in the Underground Railroad, and one of the Cowles Family Singers, along with her sister Cornelia and brother Lewis. "No men were allowed to sit on the platform, to speak or vote," recalled one participant. "They implored just to say a word; but no, the President was inflexible. . . . For the first time in the world's history, men learned how it felt to sit in silence. . . . They gamely founded their own suffrage association, where they promptly endorsed all that the women had said and done." (These efforts, plus petitions with eight thousand signatures, failed to get woman suffrage into the state constitution.)

Six months later, the First National Woman's Rights Convention was held in Worcester, Massachusetts. More than a thousand people attended. But not Elizabeth; again she wrote a letter that was read to the convention and published in the *Lily*. Why was she unable to attend? She was five months pregnant with her fourth child.

## 8

# "OUT OF SORTS WITH THE WORLD"

## SUSAN B. ANTHONY
### 1848–1850

ALTHOUGH SUCCESSFUL IN CANAJOHARIE, Susan was increasingly discontented. In the spring of 1848, she wrote to her parents, "a weariness has come over me." She was feeling "out of sorts with the world." What could she do? A new hat did not lift her spirits; neither did a visit home. She had little energy left for teaching, having taught since she was fifteen years old, always for less than what men were paid. Marriage did not appeal to her. Susan was restless and unfocused. News of the gold rush in California prompted her to wish "Oh, if I were but a man so that I could go!"

The year itself—1848—was unsettled. Revolutions swept Europe: Sicily, France, Germany, Hungary, and the Hapsburg Austrian Empire. Ireland was still in the throes of the Great Famine that killed a million people and forced hundreds of thousands to immigrate to America. Mexico lost the Mexican-American War and ceded vast territory, including California, in the Treaty of Guadalupe Hidalgo.

By 1848, the country was connected by thousands of

miles of canals and railroads. Trips that used to take days, now took hours. In 1844, communications had been transformed by the introduction of the telegraph that instantaneously transmitted messages, information, and news. By 1848, a telegraph line connected New York City and Chicago.

The rapid industrialization, growth of cities, westward migration, and huge influx of immigrants brought new opportunities for Americans. These changes intensified a range of existing problems: wretched living conditions, abject poverty, drunkenness, and vices such as prostitution, lewdness, and gambling. A reform movement rooted in religious revivals arose to ameliorate these problems. Women were the backbone of the movement; they formed hundreds of moral reform societies that focused on everything from helping prostitutes to establishing orphanages.

## "There Is No Neutral Position"

By the 1840s, involvement in a reform movement seemed to offer educated women like Susan an alternative to marriage or teaching. Perhaps that was why she decided during her unsettled time to join the Canajoharie Daughters of Temperance. It was a logical choice. She had grown up in a temperance household. Her father had been involved in the movement for years. On March 1, 1849, she gave her first public speech to two hundred people at a supper sponsored by the Daughters of Temperance. On one wall of the Hall of Temperance, her name was "printed in large capitals of evergreen [branches]." She told her audience that "all that is needed to produce a complete Temperance and Social reform in this age of Moral Suasion, is for our Sex to cast their United influences into the balance. Ladies! there is no Neutral position for us to assume."

The next day the streets were abuzz with the opinion that "Miss Anthony is the smartest woman who ever had been in Canajoharie."

Susan lived in Canajoharie with her cousin Margaret and her husband and three children. Margaret was like a sister to her, supporting and encouraging her. She helped Susan get ready for a public examination of her students. She braided Susan's hair in four long braids and wound them around a big shell comb. She pinned her watch with a gold chain and pencil to Susan's dress.

### *"I Have Lost the Only Friend"*

On March 7, six days after Susan's successful speech, Margaret gave birth to a baby girl. It was a difficult birth. Afterward Susan wrote to her mother, "It is rather tough business, is it not Mother. Oh, I am so glad she is through with it." Susan devotedly tended to Margaret for seven days, but then she died. Susan wrote to Hannah, "Sister, I feel that I have lost the only friend that I had (out of our own family circle) who loved me because of union of soul, of sympathy, of spirit, but that friend is gone."

Susan resigned her position. That summer she visited friends. In the fall, she returned to Rochester to run the farm for a while. She wanted to make temperance reform her life's work. How could she do that and be self-sufficient? That question was on her mind as she tended the fruit trees and gardens, cooked and cleaned, and cared for her ailing mother.

On Sundays, abolitionists and reformers gathered at the Anthonys' house to eat and talk. Susan developed important friendships with people like Frederick Douglass, who was a close friend of her father and Amy Post. She heard talk about the woman's rights conventions in Seneca Falls and Rochester and Worcester. In fact her parents and sister Mary had attended the Rochester convention. Her cousin Sarah Anthony Burtis had been the secretary. They had all signed the Declaration of Sentiments. Although Susan thought temperance and abolition were more important than woman's rights, she was intrigued by all the praise she heard about a woman named Elizabeth Cady Stanton.

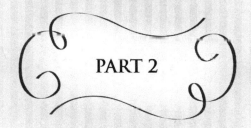

PART 2

# 9

# "AN 'INTENSE ATTRACTION'"

## ELIZABETH AND SUSAN
### 1851–1853

Susan B. Anthony and Elizabeth Cady Stanton had many mutual friends, including Amy Post, Frederick Douglass, and Amelia Bloomer. Eventually one of them was bound to introduce them. It was Amelia who invited Susan to visit and attend an antislavery meeting in Seneca Falls, in May 1851. The speakers were William Lloyd Garrison and George Thompson. Elizabeth, who had given birth in February to her fourth son, Theodore Weld Stanton, known as Theo, also attended.

After the meeting, Elizabeth encountered Amelia and Susan, who were standing on the corner of the street waiting to greet her. Amelia and Elizabeth were wearing bloomers, the new, comfortable but controversial fashion of a below-the-knee-length skirt worn over pants that dress reformers were promoting.

Years later, Elizabeth vividly recalled her first impression of her "future friend and coadjutor" and wrote, "There she stood, with her good, earnest face and genial smile. . . . I liked her thoroughly."

Susan later recalled that there was an "intense attraction" between them. She did not, however, yet share Elizabeth's passionate commitment to woman's rights.

Susan's lesser commitment to woman's rights was the result of several factors. Her Quaker upbringing had inoculated her with the idea of equality between women and men. Unlike Elizabeth's father, Susan's father did not value his sons more than his daughters; both were expected to be self-sufficient. Her parents supported her decision to leave teaching and take up reform work, including providing financial backing. As for voting, Quakers traditionally disavowed involvement in partisan politics. As pacifists, many Quaker men refused to vote as a protest against governments that engaged in wars.

Another factor was that Susan was just beginning to be immersed in the whirlwind of political debates, stimulating conversations, and new ideas that Elizabeth had been exposed to much earlier. Recently she had written to her father that she wanted to be "associated with those whose ideas are in advance of my own" because then she would "develop so much faster."

Of course, Susan had experienced some of the inequalities; she herself had been paid much less than male teachers. She knew that although her mother's money provided the down payment for the farm, her name could not be on the deed. Her organization, the Daughters of Temperance, was considered merely an auxiliary to the Sons of Temperance. But, unlike Elizabeth, Susan had not yet thoroughly delved into understanding the legal, social, civil, and religious status of women, and had not personally dealt with the "practical difficulties" of managing a household and raising children.

Susan was also well aware of the other great social movement: antislavery. But of the three—antislavery, temperance, and woman's rights—she remained most committed to her temperance work. That is where she thought she could make a difference. She soon learned otherwise.

### *"Come and Stay with Me"*

Susan's first jolt of awareness came at a Sons of Temperance meeting. She was there because the Sons had invited the Daughters to send delegates. The women were welcomed, until Susan stood up to speak. "The sisters were not invited there to speak," the presiding officer told her, "but to listen and learn." Uncowed and indignant, Susan walked out. A few women followed her, but most remained seated, some remarking that Susan and the women who left with her were "bold, meddlesome disturbers."

The upshot of the incident was Susan's decision to organize an independent organization, the Women's New York State Temperance Society. She recruited Elizabeth to write her a lecture and to serve as president. "I will gladly do all in my power to aid you. Work down this way, then you come & stay with me, . . ." Elizabeth responded. "I have no doubt a little practice will make you an admirable lecturer. I will go to work at once & write you the best lecture I can. Dress loose, take a great deal of exercise & be particular about your diet, & sleep enough, the body has great influence upon the mind. In your meetings if attacked be good-natured & cool, for if you are simple & truth loving no sophistry can confound you."

As for her own speech as president, Elizabeth warned Susan that "anything from my pen is necessarily radical." If Susan needed to dissociate herself from what she said, that was all right; Elizabeth was "ready to stand alone." She did not "write to please any one . . . but to proclaim my highest convictions of truth."

### "Half Man and Half Woman"

The convention met in Corinthian Hall in Rochester, New York, on April 20, 1852. More than five hundred women showed up, a testament to Susan's remarkable skills in organizing events: She had written countless letters, gotten press coverage, traveled to spread the news by word of mouth, invited prominent speakers who would attract a crowd, secured a hall, and supervised every detail from the program to the flowers. Men were there too, although they were not permitted to hold office or vote.

Elizabeth was elected the president. Wearing bloomers and with her hair newly cut short in a bob, she gave a "powerful speech," parts of which "acted as a bombshell not only at this meeting, but in press, pulpit and society." She proposed that women be permitted to divorce a "drunkard," at a time when divorce was a taboo subject. She also urged women to shift their support of religious charitable work from missionary work in other countries to "the poor and suffering around us," a heretical proposal at that time. Despite the uproar about Elizabeth's words and her bloomers and her bob, Susan stood with Elizabeth.

Two months later, Susan and Amelia were invited to another Sons' meeting. Their friend and supporter Samuel J. May had assured them that they would be welcomed; instead when they arrived in the hall their presence was denounced by others in the group. One particularly agitated clergyman proclaimed that they, indeed all women involved in temperance work, were "a hybrid species, half man and half woman, belonging to neither sex."

## *"A Brilliant Galaxy"*

After the Seneca Falls convention, woman's rights conventions had been held in Ohio, Indiana, and Pennsylvania. Delegates from many states and Canada attended two national conventions in Worcester, Massachusetts. Although too busy with her children to go to any of them, Elizabeth was never too busy to write a letter that was read aloud to the audience. In the fall of 1852, Susan attended her first woman's rights convention, the third national one, which was held in Syracuse, New York. Elizabeth, who was eight months pregnant with her fifth child, asked her to read the letter.

By this time, Elizabeth was widely known and greatly admired; so the fact that Susan stood on the speakers' platform and read her letter to the audience added to the cachet she had already acquired through her temperance work. It also associated her with Elizabeth's radical ideas, such as proposing that colleges accept women, which "raised the usual breeze in the convention." Unconcerned by controversy, Susan chose to stand by Elizabeth, and she read the letter with "hearty approval."

It was perhaps easy for Susan to support Elizabeth because she too was bold and willing to stand alone when necessary. That was how she blocked the election of Elizabeth Oakes Smith as president of the convention.

An elegantly stylish woman, Elizabeth Oakes Smith was a

poet, novelist, and lecturer. She and her close friend Paulina Wright Davis, who had organized the convention, arrived wearing matching short-sleeved, low-necked white dresses with loose jackets, one embroidered in pink, the other in blue. Susan, like most women, shrouded herself in layers of clothes because it was unthinkable at that time for a woman to bare her arms and neck in public. When Paulina nominated Elizabeth Oakes Smith for the presidency, Susan objected because "nobody who dressed as she did could represent the earnest, solid, hardworking women of the country." Although no one else spoke up, Susan clearly prevailed—the plain-dressing Quaker Lucretia Mott was elected president.

Lucretia was just one of the many extraordinary people Susan met and listened to at the convention. Lucy Stone, a graduate of Oberlin College and a spellbinding orator; Matilda Joslyn Gage, a freethinker with a dry wit; and the charismatic Ernestine Rose, known at the time as "the queen of the platform," were among the many dynamic speakers. All in all, it was a "brilliant galaxy of men and women" who discussed woman's rights from "every conceivable standpoint."

By the time the convention ended, Susan had embraced the centrality of suffrage. She had realized that, without the vote, women were powerless to influence politicians and to effect changes in laws and policies. Although she continued her temperance work, her focus had shifted.

### *"Oh! How I Wish"*

Whenever Elizabeth had a baby, so the story was told, she flew a flag—red for a boy, white for a girl. Her first white-flag baby was born in 1852. She named her Margaret Livingston, after her mother. "Rejoice with me all womankind," she wrote to Lucretia, "for lo! a champion of thy cause is born." She recounted how, with the help of Amelia Willard, her full-time housekeeper, she gave birth in about fifteen minutes.

With four boys ranging in age from ten years to twenty months, a newborn, and a frequently absent husband, Elizabeth had her hands full. Rejecting the strict parenting style that was in vogue, she had developed her own commonsense approach. Shunning physical punishment, she stressed self-control and self-discipline. By the time Margaret, known as Maggie, was born, Neil and Kit were spending the school year at a coeducational boarding school run by Angelina and her husband Theodore Weld and her sister Sarah who lived with them and taught at the school.

The boys received long letters from their mother full of love and advice. In one, Elizabeth responded to Neil's request that she not wear her bloomers when she visited them at school. First in her letter, she asked him to imagine that they were walking in a field and a bull began chasing them. While Neil could run away fast unencumbered by petticoats, she could not. "Then you in your agony, when you saw the bull gaining on me, would say: 'Oh! how I wish mother could use her legs as I can.' Now why do you wish me to wear what is uncomfortable, inconvenient, and many times dangerous? I'll tell you why. You want me to be like other people. You do not like to have me laughed at. You must learn not to care for what foolish people say."

## *"Bigger Fish to Fry"*

Throughout the 1850s, Elizabeth's domestic responsibilities constrained her ability to think and write and speak on woman's rights. Although she had the invaluable help of Amelia, she needed a physical link to the outside world to avoid being "wholly absorbed in a narrow family selfishness." That link was Susan, who not only brought her firsthand reports, but also willingly relieved her of her domestic demands and duties so that she could think and write. "But for her pertinacity I should never have accomplished the little I have," Elizabeth reflected years later. In turn, Susan loosened up under Elizabeth's influence. In December 1852, she started wearing bloomers; then she got her hair cut in a bob.

Susan and Elizabeth wore their bloomers to the first anniversary meeting of the Women's New York State Temperance Society in June 1853. It now had over two thousand members, thanks to Susan's hard work. As the president, Elizabeth addressed the hotly debated issue of talking about woman's rights at a temperance meeting. It was necessary, she said, because many people questioned whether women should be allowed to talk on any subject. She also raised the inflammatory divorce issue again.

Then a motion was made to change the constitution and allow men to be elected as officers. Elizabeth and Susan supported the change with the hope that the men "would modestly permit women to continue the work she had so successfully begun." That was not to be. The men, with the support of many women, took over. They changed the name to the People's League and rejected any connection to woman's rights. Elizabeth was defeated for reelection as president, and she refused the vice-presidential position that she was offered instead. Susan refused her reelection as secretary. Together they walked away from the organization that Susan had founded.

Susan returned to her home in Rochester disheartened and worried that Elizabeth was "plunged in grief" by her defeat. Not to worry, Elizabeth reassured her. She was happy to shed the responsibility and satisfied that she had brought up the divorce issue. "Now, Susan," she wrote in a letter, "I do beg of you to let the past be past, and to waste no more powder on the Women's State Temperance Society. We have other and bigger fish to fry."

## 10

# "Do You Not See?"

## A WOMAN'S RIGHTS POINT OF VIEW
## 1853–1854

Elizabeth had ambitious goals, but first she needed a break. "I forbid you to ask me to send one thought or one line to any convention, any paper, or any individual," she wrote to Susan, "for I swear by all the saints that whilst I am nursing this baby I will not be tormented with suffering humanity."

For now Susan heeded her friend's admonition and joined forces with Lucy Stone to organize a temperance convention where both women and men could speak. Her idea was to schedule it to coincide with the World's Temperance Convention in September 1853 or, as Susan put it, when "the Old Fogies hold their convention." The "Old Fogies," of course, were the people who refused to allow women to speak. But, first, Susan wanted to stir up the women at the New York State Teachers' Convention.

### *"I Wish to Speak"*

The teachers' meeting was held in August in Corinthian Hall in Rochester. Anyone who paid a dollar could participate. Susan paid and sat without saying anything for a day. She later described her "grief and indignation" that although two-thirds of the five hundred attendees were women, they did not even try to participate in the proceedings; the handful of men teachers did everything: presiding, pontificating, debating, and voting. That was bad enough, but what was worse for Susan "was to look into the faces of those women and see that by far the larger proportion were perfectly satisfied with the position assigned to them."

On the second day, she stood up and said, "Mr. President," causing shockwaves to ripple through the audience.

"What will the lady have?" replied the president, Charles Davies, a professor at West Point who was wearing his full-dress uniform.

"I wish to speak to the question under discussion," she said.

"What is the pleasure of the convention?" he asked the group.

"I move she shall be heard," one man said; another man seconded the motion, which was then debated for half an hour. Susan remained standing, afraid to appear to be giving up by sitting down. Finally the men voted and by a small margin the motion passed. Susan had permission to speak on the question under discussion, which was "Why the profession of teacher is not as much respected as that of lawyer, doctor or minister."

In a voice that carried to every part of the hall, she said, "It seems to me you fail to comprehend the cause of the disrespect of which you complain. Do you not see that so long as society says woman has not brains enough to be a doctor, lawyer or minister, but has plenty to be a teacher, every man of you who condescends to teach, tacitly admits . . . that he has no more brains than a woman?"

69 ~

Susan was not greeted with applause; instead she heard comments such as "Did you ever see such a disgraceful performance?" and "I was never so ashamed of my sex." Two teachers, however—Mrs. Northrop and her sister Mrs. J. R. Vosburg—told Susan that she had "taught us our lesson and we propose to make ourselves heard." They did just that the next day by offering two resolutions. One recognized the rights of women teachers to fully participate in the organization, and the other dealt with providing equitable pay for women teachers. To Susan's satisfaction and Charles Davies's shock, both resolutions passed.

### "The Uproar Was Indescribable"

New York City was abuzz with excitement in September; huge crowds were attending the Exhibition of Industry of All Nations in the Crystal Palace, a spectacular new building made of glass and iron with a dome one hundred feet in diameter. Over five thousand exhibitors from every part of America and twenty-three foreign countries were showing off steam-powered machines, marble statues, fancy home furnishings, paintings, and specimens of ores and minerals, including California gold.

Hoping to attract the crowds to their cause, various reform groups held their conventions at the same time—two temperance, one antislavery, and one woman's rights. The temperance convention organized by Susan and Lucy was a great success. The other one, the World's Temperance Convention (or the Half-World's Temperance Convention, according to Susan and Lucy), spent most of its time arguing over whether or not to allow Antoinette Brown, the first woman to be ordained a minister, to speak. As one newspaper described it, "This convention has completed three of its four business sessions and the results may be summed up as follows: First day—Crowding a woman off the platform; second day—Gagging her; third day—Voting that she shall stay gagged."

As usual there were aggressive rowdies at all the conventions, especially at the two-day woman's rights convention. Hostile spectators hissed, whistled, and cried "shut-up" and "get out." Susan later told her biographer that the "uproar was indescribable, with shouting, yelling, screaming, bellowing, stamping and every species of noise that could be made." Henceforth it would be known as the "mob convention."

### *"A Purse of Her Own"*

That fall Susan attended one more convention, the Fourth National Woman's Rights Convention in Cleveland, Ohio. In dramatic contrast to the "mob convention," it was peaceful and orderly. She was appointed to a committee on finance and business. Now fully committed to work for woman's rights, she revisited the counties in New York where she had already organized women to work for temperance. But all the groups had fallen apart. The reason, she was told, was that the women, all wives, had no money of their own to continue the work. She wrote in her journal that as she traveled "from town to town," she "was made to feel the great evil of woman's utter dependence on man for the necessary means to aid reform movements."

Reflecting on that insight, Susan had an epiphany—"the grand idea of pecuniary independence. Woman must have a purse of her own." To do that, she realized, women had to have equal property rights. Fired up, she organized an extensive petition campaign to secure married women the right to their own wages and equal guardianship of their children. For months, she and sixty women canvassed the state getting signatures. Her plan was to present the petitions to the New York State Legislature when it was in session in Albany in February 1854. In addition, she scheduled a woman's rights convention in Albany, on February 14 and 15. Determined to spur Elizabeth into action, Susan presented her plan to her and insisted that she give an address on the legal disabilities of women to both the convention and a joint session of the judiciary committees of the Legislature.

"I find there is no use saying 'no' to you," Elizabeth responded and asked Susan to find a sympathetic lawyer who would identify eight of the "most atrocious" laws affecting women. Elizabeth could, she told Susan, "generalize and philosophize by myself but I have not time to look up statistics . . . surrounded by my children, washing dishes, baking, sewing, baking."

### "Because I Am a Woman"

Susan's friend Judge William Hay sent Elizabeth thirteen laws and added his agreement that she was admirably suited to write the address. Echoing Hay, Reverend William Ellery Channing, a reform-minded minister in Rochester, wrote to Elizabeth that no one could tell the "story of woman's wrongs as strongly, clearly, tersely, eloquently" as she could.

This speech, Elizabeth later wrote, was "a great event" in her life and she felt very "nervous." Susan suggested she go to Rochester and confer with Reverend Channing. That she did, while Susan stayed with her children. Channing enthusiastically endorsed her speech. Her father was another matter.

Judge Cady had read an announcement about Elizabeth's

upcoming speech in the newspaper. There are two versions of what happened next. More than forty years later in her auto-biography, Elizabeth portrayed a positive, even tender, encounter that included "tears filling" Judge Cady's eyes as he listened to her speech. He offered some suggestions and said he could find her even "more cruel laws" to quote. Then they "kissed each other good-night." In the other version, Judge Cady strenu-ously objected, offered her bribes, and threatened to disinherit her.

The later version is perhaps more plausible because of a let-ter she wrote to Susan several months after her speech: "I passed through a terrible scourging when last at my father's. I cannot tell you how deeply the iron entered my soul. I never felt more keenly the degradation of my sex. To think that all in me of which my father would have felt proper pride had I been a man is deeply mortifying to him because I am a woman."

What was her mother's reaction? For that time period, there is no record. But she most likely supported Elizabeth based on her actions after her husband's death when she tended to her grandchildren, thus freeing Elizabeth to travel; donated money; welcomed reformers in her home; and signed a suffrage petition.

### *"Heads About the Size of an Apple"*

Elizabeth gave a stirring speech. Proclaiming women as "daughters of the revolutionary heroes of '76," she demanded "a new code of laws." She described the "position of woman" from four perspectives: "woman as woman," "woman as wife," "woman as widow," and "woman as mother." She debunked the frequently cited argument that only "a few sour, disappointed old maids and childless women" demanded equal rights with a series of rhetorical questions, including "Think you that the woman who has worked hard all her days in helping her husband to accumulate a large property consents to the law that places this wholly at his disposal?"

Elizabeth's speech was generally well received. Susan had had fifty thousand copies of the speech printed in pamphlet form. Each legislator got a copy; the rest Susan sold to earn money to cover the printing cost. The press coverage ranged from favorable to hostile. Negative articles did not bother Elizabeth; she dismissed them as accounts from the pens of reporters whose heads "were about the size of an apple." As for a group of women who accused her of abandoning her children to give the speech, she calmly replied that hers were nearby in a hotel with their nurse. Where, she asked the women, were their children?

Despite Elizabeth's persuasive speech and petitions signed by thousands of people, the legislators refused to change laws that discriminated against married women. Doing that, most of them believed, would "unsex every female in the land" and overthrow the divinely ordained institution of marriage in which man was the head.

### "It Is Not Wise"

For this great event, Susan had worn her bloomers. Elizabeth, however, had recently stopped wearing hers; instead she wore a black silk dress with a white lace collar and a diamond pin. She had loved wearing bloomers, a style she had copied from her cousin Libby, who is credited with being the first to wear them. "Like a captive set free from his ball and chain," she recalled, "I was always ready for a brisk walk through sleet and snow and rain, to climb a mountain, jump over a fence, work in the garden, and, in fact, for any necessary locomotion." But "the physical freedom," she later explained "did not compensate for the persistent persecution and petty annoyances suffered at every turn."

Gangs of boys jeered and threw stones at women wearing bloomers. Crowds of men accosted them. Friends and family members expressed disapproval and embarrassment. The press derided their appearance. After one of Elizabeth's speeches, she was described as "resembling a man in her dress, having on boots like a man, dickey like a man, vest like a man." Two years of that had exhausted her patience.

Susan had had it too, but she stubbornly refused to give in to public pressure. Finally, however, in early 1854, she heeded Elizabeth's admonition to "let down a dress and petticoat. The cup of ridicule is greater than you can bear. It is not wise, Susan, to use up so much energy that way."

### *"Brilliant Conversation at the Table"*

After the New York State Legislature refused to heed their petitions, Elizabeth once again curtailed her involvement in the woman's rights movement. "My whole soul is in the work," she told Susan, "but my hands belong to my family." Henry continued to be away for months at a time conducting legal business, attending meetings for various causes, and immersing himself in the politics of the new Republican Party. He wrote many more letters to Elizabeth than she did to him, perhaps because he was not encumbered with managing a household of lively children.

In a letter addressed to "Margaret Livingston Stanton" (Maggie, who was four years old at the time), Henry wrote

*My dear daughter*

*I want your mother to write me a letter. I have told her so several times; yet she does not write. Now, my daughter, if she does not write to me immediately, I want you to take a pen & sit down & tell me all the news.... Tell your Mother that I have seen a throng of handsome ladies, but I had rather see her than the whole of them; but, I intend to cut her acquaintance unless she writes me a letter. Kiss the baby & the boys for me.*

*Your affectionate father Henry B. Stanton*

When Henry was home, he played with the children and worked in the garden and orchard. In the evening, he insisted on uninterrupted time to read the evening paper. Afterward, they might all play games, one of Elizabeth's favorite activities. "She always played to win," her children later recalled, "and was sorely disappointed when she did not succeed."

The annual National Woman's Rights Convention was meeting in Philadelphia, Pennsylvania. Lucretia requested Elizabeth's presence: "Cant thou take thy baby, & come to our Woman's Convention? We shall need thee and all other <u>true</u> women." No, she couldn't, Elizabeth replied. Susan, however, planned to attend, and accepted Lucretia's invitation to stay with them:

*It will give us pleasure to have thy company at 338 Arch street, where we hope thou wilt make thy home. We shall of course be crowded, but we expect thee and shall prepare accordingly. We think such as thyself, devoted to good causes, should not have to seek a home.*

Twenty-four people stayed with the Motts. During meals, Lucretia sat Susan at her left hand; William Lloyd Garrison was at her right. Afterward, a little cedar tub filled with hot sudsy water was placed in front of Lucretia. She washed the silver, glass, and fine china. Susan dried them on "the whitest of towels, while the brilliant conversation at the table went on uninterrupted."

## 11

# "WHERE ARE YOU?"

### CHALLENGING TIMES
### 1854–1859

O N CHRISTMAS DAY, SUSAN EMBARKED on a mission to get support for the woman's rights petition. She planned to canvass fifty-four counties in New York. Wendell Phillips loaned her fifty dollars. Elizabeth continued to write letters and articles for newspapers, but as for doing more than that, she warned Susan, "As soon as you all begin to ask too much of me, I shall have a baby. Now be careful; do not provoke me to that step."

Susan's family helped her get ready to undertake her mission. During the coldest and snowiest winter in ten years, she planned to travel for five months, to small towns and villages where most people had never seen a woman speaker. There was so much to do: handbills advertising her meeting, along with a letter from her requesting it be displayed two weeks before her arrival, needed to be folded, addressed, and mailed to local sheriffs and postmasters. Sheaves of woman's rights literature and copies of the petitions had to be packed in her carpetbag. Then there were her clothes—a shawl, a bonnet, a simple black silk dress with a basque waist (a waistline that dipped to a V in the front), and shoes.

The diary and records she always meticulously kept included details of her adventures: "the day very cold, snowy, sleighing very poor . . . could not [get] a church, school house or academy [to] speak in—held meeting in a dining room of landlord." A newspaper reporter described her as having "pleasing rather than pretty features, decidedly expressive countenance, rich brown hair very effectively and not all elaborately arranged, neither too tall nor too short, too plump nor too thin."

After she spoke in Albany, a gentleman in her audience joined her for the stage ride to Lake George. A solicitous companion, he provided a heated plank on which she could warm her feet. After her meeting, he took her in his sleigh filled with robes and drawn by two spirited gray horses to his house to meet his sister and spend the day. For the next several days, he drove her to meetings and tended to her needs; then he proposed. She was not tempted by the well-cared-for life he offered her; instead it prompted her to "strongly continue in her chosen work."

## *"Struggle in Deep Water"*

Although Elizabeth stayed close to home, she continued spreading the woman's rights message through her letters and articles. A prolific writer, she wrote for the women's papers, the *Lily* and the *Una*. Her articles regularly appeared in the national newspaper the *New York Tribune*. At first, she asked for Henry's opinion before submitting her pieces, but not for long. "Husbands are too critical," she wrote to Susan.

In March she wrote to Lucretia about her plan to write a book about the history of the woman's movement. "This is the right work for thee, dear Elizh.," Lucretia replied. "Do thyself justice. Remember the first Convention originated with thee." The book did not get written, at least, not then; it was too big a project, and Henry was pressuring her to give up her woman's rights work.

In a letter that she asked Susan to keep "strictly confidential," Elizabeth wished she "were as free" as Susan. Then she "would stump the State in a twinkling." But, she confessed, she could not because Henry objected to "all that is dearest" to her. He was "not willing that I should write even on the woman question. . . . Sometimes, Susan, I struggle in deep water." Ever optimistic, Elizabeth ended her letter, "However, a good time is coming and my future is always bright and beautiful. Good night."

In her letter to Elizabeth, Lucretia had noted the recent "rapid progress" of the woman's rights movement and the number of talented women leaders "already in the field." That number significantly decreased in 1855 when both Lucy Stone and Antoinette Brown got married. (Best friends in college, they married the Blackwell brothers. Lucy married Henry, but kept her own name, a scandalous act in those days. Antoinette married Samuel.) Susan felt "great regret." Of course, both Lucy and Antoinette reassured her that they would continue to work for woman's rights, but she had seen one effective leader after another get overwhelmed by the demands of marriage and then children. The prime example was her dear friend Elizabeth, who, once again, was pregnant.

## "The Life Is a Very Good One"

Susan herself was struggling to keep up her pace. Her arduous speaking tour throughout New York had left her with back pain. She managed to attend two conventions: the annual teachers' convention and the annual state woman's rights convention. But no more; worried that the pain would eventually prevent her from continuing with her "life work," she entered the Worcester Hydropathic Institute, run by her cousin Dr. Seth Rogers, a supporter of woman's rights and a practitioner of the "water cure," a four-to-six-week regime of rest and outdoor exercise that included a limited diet, no alcohol or tobacco, and copious amounts of water used for washing, bathing, soaking, and drinking.

Gradually Susan improved, although she complained that her day was "so cut up with four baths, four dressings and undressings, four exercisings, one drive and three eatings," that she did not have time "to put two thoughts together." She did, however, manage a trip to Boston, the city where Elizabeth had been so stimulated. Susan was too. In a letter to her family, she described the sights: Mount Auburn Cemetery, the Bunker Hill Monument, and the library of sixteen thousand books belonging to Theodore Parker, the reform-minded minister Elizabeth had heard preach when she lived in Boston.

When Susan returned to Rochester, she took out a life insurance policy that required a medical certificate. On December 18, the doctor recorded this information about her at the age of thirty-five: "Height, 5 ft. 5 in.; figure, full; chest measure 38 in.; weight, 156 lbs.; complexion, fair; habits, healthy. . . . The life is a very good one."

## *"Do Get All on Fire"*

Elizabeth gave birth to another white-flag baby, Harriot Eaton Stanton, known as Hattie, in 1856. She was, she wrote to Susan, "very happy, that the terrible ordeal is passed & that the result is another daughter." Hattie was a month old when Elizabeth vented her frustration in another letter to Susan: "Imagine me, day in and day out, watching, bathing, dressing, nursing and promenading the precious contents of the little crib. . . . I pace up and down these two chambers of mine like a caged lioness longing to bring nursing and housekeeping cares to a close." Susan could not wait for that day to come; she had urgent work for Elizabeth to do.

The next state teachers' convention was fast approaching, and Susan was unable to write the speech she had been asked to give. Writing to Elizabeth, she pleaded for help, "So for the love of me, & for the saving of the <u>reputation of womenhood</u>, I beg you with one baby on your knee & another at your feet & four boys whistling buzzing hullooing <u>Ma Ma</u> set your self about the work. . . . <u>don't</u> say <u>no</u>, nor <u>don't delay</u> it a moment, for I must have it done. . . . Now will <u>you load my gun</u>, leaving me to pull the trigger & let fly the powder & ball . . . do get all on fire."

"Come here," Elizabeth replied, "and I will do what I can." Together they juggled household and writing tasks and produced another bold speech that called for coeducation because girls and boys were equal in intelligence. It also castigated women teachers for passively accepting salaries below what men received.

At the convention, many of the women rejected the call for equal pay because that would be unfeminine. "What an infernal set of fools these school-marms must be!! Well, if in order to please men they wish to live on air, let them. The sooner the present generation of women die out the better. We have jack-asses enough in the world now without such women propagating any more," Elizabeth wrote to Susan.

## "To Do Battle Alone"

While Elizabeth was tending to her children, Susan accepted an offer from the American Anti-Slavery Society to be an agent for ten dollars a week, as long as she could continue her work for the woman's rights movement. She fretted that Lucy (who was pregnant) and Antoinette (who had had a baby and was pregnant again) had abandoned the movement and left "poor brainless me to do battle alone." Elizabeth counseled her, "You, too, must rest, Susan, let the world alone awhile."

That was impossible. The country was tearing itself apart over the issue of slavery. Congress had passed two bills that inflamed and divided public sentiments—the Fugitive Slave Act in 1850, which included steep penalties for anyone who helped a slave escape, and the Kansas-Nebraska Act in 1854, which opened up land to slavery where it had been prohibited by the Missouri Compromise of 1820. In 1857, the U.S. Supreme Court ruled in the Dred Scott case that slaves were property, not people, and that Congress did not have the right to prohibit slavery.

Susan hired white and black antislavery speakers; together they went on lecture tours. But she outlasted all of them as each one succumbed to the hardships: miserable weather, taxing transportation, hostile crowds, illness, and unpalatable food. "O, the crimes that are committed in the kitchens of this land!" she complained.

In March she went to Maine to speak on woman's rights for

the unprecedented fee of fifty dollars. Arriving at the snowy, slushy, muddy time of year, she spoke in Bangor and surrounding villages. "Many a woman, and man too," one newspaper reporter wrote, "went home that night with the germ of more active ideas in their heads."

## "I Will Do Anything to Help You"

Before Susan's next annual appearance at the state teachers' convention, she and Elizabeth wrote resolutions that denounced the exclusion of "colored youth from our public schools," protested the firing of a woman teacher when it "was discovered that colored blood coursed in her veins," and denounced the fact that "teachers and pupils of the colored schools of New York City were denied access to free concerts."

Susan first introduced these resolutions, then she threw "another bomb" and put forth this demand: "That it is the duty of all our schools, colleges and universities to open their doors to woman and to give her equal and identical educational advantages side by side with her brother man."

That would be "a vast social evil," declared Charles Davies, president of the state teachers' association. The resolutions were soundly defeated.

Elizabeth was delighted by Susan's performance. "I did indeed see by the papers that you had once more stirred that pool of intellectual stagnation, the educational convention. . . . I glory in your perseverance," she wrote to her. "Oh! Susan, I will do anything to help you on. . . . You and I have a prospect of a good long life. We shall not be in our prime before fifty, & after that we shall be good for twenty years at least."

Earlier that year she had promised Susan that "in two or

three years I shall be able to have some hours of each day to myself. My two older boys will then be in college or business and my three younger children will be in school." (Susan undoubtedly noticed when she read this that Elizabeth forgot to count her baby Hattie.)

### *"I Do Long to Be with You"*

Susan needed Elizabeth's reassurance. She was discouraged and disheartened by the struggle to recruit people to speak at the next annual national woman's rights convention. "How I do long to be with you this very minute," she wrote to Elizabeth, "to have one look into your very soul, & one sound of your soul stirring voice. . . . I have <u>very weak moments</u>. . . . [H]ow my soul longs to see [you] in the great Battlefield. . . . If you come not to the rescue, who shall?"

Elizabeth had announced that Hattie was her last baby, but, at the age of forty-two, she was once again pregnant. Susan expressed her feelings in a letter to Antoinette, "[A]h me!!! alas!! alas!!!! <u>Mrs. Stanton</u>!! . . . For a <u>moment's pleasure</u> to herself or her husband, she should thus increase the <u>load of cares</u> under which she already groans."

Her last red-flag baby, Robert Livingston Stanton, known as Bob, was born in 1859. "You need expect nothing from me for some time," she wrote to Susan. "I have no vitality of body or soul. . . . You have no idea how weak I am & I have to keep my mind in the most quiet state in order to sleep." Undoubtedly unwilling to lose her connection with Susan, she wrote, "I am always glad to hear from you & hope to see you."

Elizabeth soon bounced back. "I am full of fresh thoughts and courage and feel all enthusiasm about our work," she wrote to Susan. "I hope to grind out half a dozen good tracts during the summer. . . . The children are all well. The house is cleaned. The summer's sewing all done and I see nothing now to trouble me much if all keep well." Six weeks later, however, her servants quit, her older boys came home from school, and Susan needed the tracts. Although Elizabeth said she was no longer in a "situation to think or write," she agreed to exert herself. "When you come I shall try," she wrote to Susan, to "grind out what you say <u>must</u> be done. I expect to get my inspiration facts & thoughts from you."

### "I Have Looked for You"

In the fall of 1859, shock waves reverberated throughout the country with the news of John Brown's bloody guerrilla raid on the federal armory in Harpers Ferry, Virginia. Brown's plan to incite a general slave uprising failed, but his attempt convinced Southerners that abolitionists would stop at nothing to end slavery, an institution that they believed was protected under the Constitution and that benefited Northern businesses and consumers. Many Northerners, including Elizabeth and Susan, heralded John Brown, who was captured, tried, and executed, as a martyr. Public opinion was aflame with fiery rhetoric; the country was on the cusp of dissolution and civil war.

Gerrit Smith was one of the Secret Six who had funded Brown's raid. Distraught over John Brown's fate and the fact that he might face legal charges, Gerrit committed himself to an insane asylum. Within weeks of these calamitous events, Elizabeth's father died, compounding the emotional turmoil she already felt. Christmas was approaching, and, as usual, Henry would be away. But Susan had promised to come. On December 23, Elizabeth wrote to her: "Where are you? Since a week ago last Monday, I have looked for you every day . . . but lo!

you did not come. . . . The death of my father, the worse than death of my dear Cousin Gerrit, the martyrdom of . . . John Brown—all this conspires to make me regret more than ever my dwarfed womanhood. In times like these, everyone should do the work of a full-grown man."

Susan arrived in time for Christmas, and, as always, she fired up Elizabeth to continue to fight for the freedom she coveted.

## *12*

# "NEVERTHELESS YOU ARE RIGHT"

### CONTROVERSY
### 1860

SUSAN WAS IN ALBANY LOBBYING the legislators when the chairman of the judiciary committee, Anson Bingham, told her that "Mrs. Stanton must come" because it appeared that legislators might approve the bill extending woman's rights that had been defeated in 1854. Afraid to leave and relax her constant lobbying efforts, Susan asked Martha Wright to go to Seneca Falls and persuade Elizabeth to write a speech. The women of New York, Susan wrote, depend "upon her bending all her powers to move the hearts of our law-givers at this time."

Evoking the name of the famous French general, Elizabeth replied, "If Napoleon says cross the Alps, they are crossed." However, she insisted that Susan come to Seneca Falls to help her. "In thought and sympathy we were one," Elizabeth later recalled, "and in the division of labor we exactly complemented each other. . . . She supplied the facts and statistics, I the philosophy and rhetoric." Their method, Susan later told her biographer, was to "sit up far into the night arranging material and planning their work."

The next day, Elizabeth would "seek the quietest spot in the house and begin writing." Susan "would give the children their breakfast, start the older ones to school, make the dessert for dinner and trundle the babies up and down the walk, rushing in occasionally to help the writer out of a vortex."

By the time Elizabeth arrived in Albany, the Married Women's Property Act of 1860 had passed. A momentous achievement, due to the relentless efforts of Susan and other activists, the bill gave a married woman in New York the right to own property, collect her own wages, engage in her own business, enter into contracts, and sue and be sued. She would have the same "powers, rights and duties in regard" to her children as her husband had; upon the death of her husband she would inherit the same property rights that he would have inherited upon her death. Elizabeth devoted her speech before a joint session of the judiciary committees to demanding the "sacred right" of woman suffrage.

### *"He Had No More Right to Whine"*

The Tenth National Woman's Rights Convention convened in May at Cooper Institute in New York City. On the first day, Susan was lauded for her arduous petition campaigns and lobbying efforts that culminated in the recent passage of legislation for married woman's rights—except for the man who yelled out, "She'd a great deal better have been home taking care of her husband and children." The next day Elizabeth "set the convention on fire" with a speech in support of resolutions in favor of liberalizing divorce laws to allow women to divorce husbands who were violent or habitually drunk, or who abandoned them.

Wendell Phillips, a longtime friend and ally, was outraged.

The issue of divorce, he said, had nothing to do with woman's rights because the laws of divorce did not rest unequally upon women. He made a motion not only to defeat Elizabeth's resolutions but also to expunge any mention of them from the written record of the convention proceedings. Stunned by Wendell's disapproval, Elizabeth later wrote that her "face was scarlet" and she "trembled with mingled feelings of doubt and fear." Noting her distress, the Reverend Samuel Longfellow (brother of the famous poet Henry Wadsworth Longfellow), who was sitting beside her, leaned over and whispered in her ear, "Nevertheless you are right, and the convention will sustain you."

Wendell's motion was defeated, but the controversy over liberalizing divorce laws raged on in the press and from the pulpit. Elizabeth and Susan stood their ground. Elizabeth wrote letters to hostile newspaper editors. Susan dealt with Reverend A. D. Mayo, an abolitionist, who told her, "You are not married, you have no business to be discussing marriage."

"Well, Mr. Mayo," she replied, "you are not a slave, suppose you quit lecturing on slavery."

During the controversy, a few longtime allies supported Elizabeth and Susan. Lucretia wrote that she had the "fullest confidence" in their "united judgment." In response to Amy Post's encouragement, Elizabeth replied that she was glad she had not anticipated Wendell's disapproval because, she wrote, "The desire to please those we admire and respect often cripples conscience."

When Elizabeth heard that Wendell was continuing to criticize her for bringing up the issue of divorce, she wrote to Susan, "He has no more right to whine than I would have if I had been defeated. The fact is he over-rated his personal power, and was mortified to find it so little." Susan attributed his position to the fact that "he is a man and can not put himself in the position of a wife; can not feel what she does under the present marriage code."

Elizabeth agreed. "The men know we have struck a blow at their greatest stronghold."

The divorce controversy prompted a group of women to hold another convention with a ban on controversial topics, such as divorce. "How," Elizabeth wondered in an article she wrote about that convention, "can an earnest soul, in search of truth, set bounds to its investigation?"

The convention was a dud, and the energy for follow-up gatherings fizzled out. That did not surprise Susan, who wrote, "Cautious, careful people, always casting about to preserve their reputation and social standing, never can bring about a reform. Those who are really in earnest must be willing to be anything or nothing in the world's estimation, and publicly and privately, in season and out, avow their sympathy with despised and persecuted ideas and their advocates, and bear the consequences."

For now, the disagreement did not rupture the relationship between the factions. Wendell sent money from the Hovey Fund (money left by Charles Hovey, a Boston businessman, to promote antislavery and other causes) that Susan requested to publish the proceedings of the convention, including Elizabeth's speech and resolutions. Elizabeth invited him to visit during the winter. William Lloyd Garrison, who had sided with Wendell, agreed to publish Elizabeth's speech in his abolitionist newspaper the *Liberator*.

The tensions resurfaced in December when Susan came to the aid of a desperate woman whose face was shrouded by layers of veils.

## "Legally You Are Wrong, but Morally You Are Right"

The woman was Phoebe Harris Phelps, the author of several children's books and the former principal of a girls' academy in Albany. Now, with her thirteen-year-old daughter, she was in hiding from her brother, Ira Harris, and her husband, Charles Abner Phelps, both very prominent men. Her troubles had started when she confronted her husband, a member of the Massachusetts legislature, about an affair he was having with another woman. Infuriated, he threw her down a flight of stairs. He continued to abuse her and finally had her committed to an insane asylum, an easy and all too common thing for husbands to do in those days. Finally after a year and a half, her brother, a member of the U.S. Senate and a lawyer, got her released and brought her to his house.

After Phoebe pleaded to see her children, her husband allowed her son to visit her for a few weeks, then her daughter. She asked to extend her time with her daughter, but her husband refused. Her brother would not intervene; instead he said, "The child belongs by law to the father and it is your place to submit. If you make any more trouble about it we'll send you back to the asylum." With that threat, she fled with her daughter.

Finding refuge with a Quaker family in Albany, Phoebe and her daughter stayed there until her husband found out where they were. That is when she sought out Susan, who was staying with her friend and coworker Lydia Mott. They discreetly checked with people who confirmed the woman's story, but added that they were too afraid of the brother and husband to get involved. Unafraid of anyone, Susan and Lydia decided that Susan should find a hiding place for the woman and her daughter in New York City. Disguised as an old woman wearing a tattered shawl and green goggles with her shabbily dressed daughter, Phoebe boarded the train on Christmas afternoon. Susan boarded shortly after they did, only to find Phoebe traumatized from having seen her brother, who was sending his son back to boarding school. Fortunately her disguise fooled her brother.

They were turned away from one hotel after another in New York City because they were unaccompanied by a man. After hours of trudging through slush and snow, Susan told a hotel clerk that they would spend the night in the lobby. He threatened to call the police. She called his bluff and said, "Very well, we will sit here till they come and take us to the station." With that, the clerk rented them an unheated room. The next day, after an exhausting search, Susan found someone who would shelter the mother and her child.

Satisfied that she had done all she could, Susan returned to Albany. The woman's family soon figured out Susan's role in the affair and began to badger her about revealing the hiding place. They publicly said that she had "abducted a man's child and must surrender it." They threatened to have her arrested. Worried that her involvement would taint the antislavery cause, Wendell sent her a telegraph with the message "Let us urge you at once to advise and insist upon this woman's returning to her relatives."

At an antislavery convention, William Lloyd Garrison confronted Susan. "Don't you know the law of Massachusetts gives the father the entire guardianship and control of the children?"

"Yes, I know it," she replied, "and does not the law of the United States give the slaveholder the ownership of the slave? And don't you break it every time you help a slave to Canada?"

"Yes, I do."

"Well, the law which gives the father the sole ownership of the children is just as wicked and I'll break it just as quickly. You would die before you would deliver a slave to his master, and I will die before I give up that child to its father."

Susan felt betrayed by "the two men whom I adore and reverence." Her father was the only important man in her life who stood by her. "My child," he wrote, "I think you have done absolutely right, but don't put a word on paper or make a statement to any one that you are not prepared to face in court. Legally you are wrong, but morally you are right, and I will stand by you."

Phoebe and her daughter were safe for a year. Then, on a Sunday morning, as the girl walked to church, her husband's men abducted her. The girl and her mother never saw each other again.

### "I Think You Risk Your Lives"

Abolitionists were worried about the newly elected president of the United States, Abraham Lincoln. Instead of embracing their single-minded commitment to immediate emancipation as the way to end slavery, Lincoln articulated a mix of positions: He opposed the extension of slavery, but he promised to enforce the odious Fugitive Slave Act that allowed for the return of escaped slaves; he said he believed that slavery was wrong, but he also said that the government should not interfere with people who thought slavery was right.

Slaveholders were not reassured by what Lincoln said. To them, his election and the ascendance of the Republican Party, a party formed in 1854 to oppose the expansion of slavery, left them no choice but to break away from the United States. In January 1861, four slaveholding states seceded: South Carolina,

Mississippi, Florida, and Alabama. Georgia, Louisiana, and Texas joined them on February 1.

Worried that Lincoln might make compromises to lure the slaveholding states back, abolitionists launched a campaign in January under the slogan "No Compromise with Slaveholders! Immediate and Unconditional Emancipation!" Susan put together a team of lecturers to tour New York that included Samuel J. May, a staunch abolitionist and woman's rights advocate, and Elizabeth, who finally felt free to go. Her older children were away at school. Amelia Willard, her live-in housekeeper, was more than capable of running the house and caring for the younger children. Henry was in Washington, DC, covering the tumultuous events as a newspaper correspondent.

Hissing, hooting, yelling, bellowing mobs of boys and men met them at every stop from Buffalo across the state to Albany. In Syracuse, ruffians threw rotten eggs, broke benches, and brandished knives and pistols. Obscene effigies of Susan and Samuel were dragged through the street and burned in the public square. Mayors and police refused to protect them. Alarmed by the newspaper reports, Henry wrote to Elizabeth, "I think you risk your lives. . . . The mobocrats would as soon kill you as not."

Undeterred, Elizabeth shifted her emphasis in her speeches from abolition to the right of free speech. In Albany, they finally met a mayor who was, in Elizabeth's words, "a man of courage and conscience, who said the right of free speech should never be trodden under foot." To protect that right, he sat on the platform with a revolver across his knee and dispatched police officers throughout the audience with orders to arrest any troublemakers.

In the spring of 1861, Wendell, perhaps in a gesture of reconciliation, offered to use the Hovey Fund to send Elizabeth on a three-month speaking tour to Europe. She longed to go; the trip would give her "new life and inspiration." Susan offered to stay with the children, and Elizabeth replied that she would leave them with her "without the least hesitation." But in the end she refused; war was imminent. Her older boys—Neil, age nineteen; Kit, age seventeen; and Gat, age sixteen—were drilling with a military regiment in Seneca Falls. From his vantage point as a reporter in Washington, Henry was writing letters describing the rising war fever.

Elizabeth embraced the idea of a war to end slavery. She also agreed to a request from Wendell and other abolitionists to suspend the campaign for woman's rights and focus on the war effort. Not Susan. She held fast to her principles as a pacifist. She also insisted that they must not suspend the fight for woman's rights. But when Elizabeth and the other speakers pulled out of the Eleventh National Woman's Rights Convention, Susan was forced to cancel the event. "I have not yet seen one good reason for the abandonment of all our meetings," she exclaimed in a letter to Martha Wright, "and am . . . more and more ashamed and sad."

## 13

# "PUT ON YOUR ARMOR AND GO FORTH!"

## WOMEN RALLY
## 1861–1866

ELIZABETH AND SUSAN WERE AT LOGGERHEADS. Each one argued for her point of view, neither one bending. Elizabeth believed that if women worked for the war effort, they would be rewarded with suffrage. Susan knew better, perhaps because she had spent ten years in the trenches trudging door to door with petitions, lecturing in remote places to people who came to gawk at a woman who dared to speak in public, struggling to raise money to rent halls, print tracts, and provide for her travel, meager food, and primitive lodging.

Whatever differences Elizabeth and Susan had about motives, goals, strategies, or tactics, they resolved them in private. "We have indulged freely in criticism of each other when alone, and hotly contended whenever we have differed," Elizabeth later recalled. "To the world we always seem to agree and uniformly reflect each other. Like husband and wife, each has the feeling that we must have no differences in public."

## *"I Long for Action"*

The Civil War began in April 1861. Elizabeth was in Seneca Falls tending to her children with the help of Amelia. Neil, Kit, and Gat continued to drill. Susan had returned to the farm in Rochester. While she was there to tend the farm and her invalid mother, her father left to visit his sons who lived in Kansas. Susan's diary reveals both the hard work she had undertaken and her restlessness with her life: "Tried to interest myself in a sewing society; but little intelligence among them. . . . The teachers' convention was small and dull. . . . Washed every window in the house today. Quilted all day . . . stained and varnished the library bookcase today. . . . The last load of hay is in the barn. . . . Fitted out a fugitive slave for Canada with the help of Harriet Tubman. . . . To forever blot out slavery is the only possible compensation for this merciless war."

Susan and Elizabeth were avid readers of newspapers, magazines, tracts, nonfiction books, poetry, and novels. During this time, Susan noted in her diary that she was reading the forty-four love sonnets, *Sonnets from the Portuguese*, by Elizabeth Barrett Browning, a renowned poet then and now. She also read *Adam Bede*, the first novel by the acclaimed writer George Eliot (the pen name of Mary Ann Evans). Hetty Sorrel, a beautiful young woman; Captain Arthur Donnithorne, a dashing squire; and Adam Bede, a handsome carpenter, are the love triangle at the heart of the story. The plot involves an out-of-wedlock pregnancy, infanticide, a murder trial, a last-minute reprieve, and ends with the marriage of Adam and Dinah Morris, Hetty's cousin and a Methodist lay preacher.

"I finished *Adam Bede* yesterday noon," Susan wrote to Elizabeth. "I can not throw off the palsied oppression of its finale to poor, poor Hetty—and Arthur almost equally commands my sympathy. . . . It will not do for me to read romances; they are too real to shake off."

"You speak of the effect of *Adam Bede* on you," Elizabeth replied. "It moved me deeply. . . . O, Susan, are you ever coming to visit me again? It would be like a new life to spend a day with you. How I shudder when I think of our awful experience with those mobs last winter, and yet even now I long for action."

### *"I Am Sick at Heart"*

In January 1862, Susan attended a state antislavery convention in Albany, but she was not able to generate any support for a woman's rights convention. Worried that she was settling into the routine of her life on the farm and losing her passion for "public work," Susan left Rochester to give antislavery lectures.

While Susan was traveling, Elizabeth was getting ready to move to New York City. Henry had a new job as a deputy collector for the Custom House Office. In April, Susan arrived at Seneca Falls to help with the packing. Then she went on ahead with four of the boys and took care of them until the rest of the family arrived. When Elizabeth hired a private teacher to educate her children at home, Susan castigated her: "Any and every private education is a blunder, it seems to me." Yes, she agreed that public schools had "short-comings," but they were outweighed by the benefit of learning "side by side with the very multitude with whom they must mingle as soon as school days are over."

On April 10, 1862, the New York legislature repealed parts of the bill that had passed in 1860, including giving mothers the same rights as fathers to make decisions regarding their children. Susan felt that the legislators had been emboldened by the cessation of the campaign for woman's rights. "While the old guard sleep, the young 'devils' are wide-awake, and we deserve to suffer for our confidence in 'man's sense of Justice,'" she wrote to Lydia Mott. "I am sick at heart."

That summer Susan attended her last state teachers' convention, satisfied at what she had accomplished for women teachers. In the fall, she continued to give antislavery speeches on the topic "Emancipation: The Duty of the Government." Then, on November 25, 1862, she suffered the worst blow of her life—the unexpected death of her beloved and supportive father. For a time, Susan felt "stunned and helpless," but fueled by the belief that her father would want her to carry on, "her old strength came slowly back."

### *"A War of Ideas"*

The war wore on. For two years, President Lincoln had refused to oppose slavery because he did not want to antagonize the border states that remained in the Union—Kentucky, Missouri, Maryland, and Delaware—where slavery was legal. The war was being fought, he said, to restore the seceding states to the Union. In a Fourth of July speech, Susan had denounced Lincoln. The war, she said, was "not simply a question of national existence, but of the value of man."

Finally, on January 1, 1863, President Lincoln issued the Emancipation Proclamation, which freed the slaves in all the Southern states fighting against the Union. He did not free slaves in border states or in Southern states under Union control on the grounds that these areas were not waging war. Slaves themselves had pressured Lincoln to issue the Emancipation Proclamation by "self-emancipating" themselves in large numbers and fleeing to Union forces. Under the proclamation, the freed slaves could join the

Union army, and hundreds of thousands did. Although abolitionists welcomed the Emancipation Proclamation, they knew that it did not apply after the war ended and that slavery would still be protected by the Constitution. They were not even confident that the Union would win the war. The army had suffered a series of setbacks. Casualty rates were appallingly high. An increasingly vocal group of Northern politicians were promoting a peace movement that would allow slavery. They called themselves Peace Democrats; abolitionists labeled them Copperheads, likening them to the venomous copperhead snake. Confusion over the purpose of the war was undermining support for it among civilians and soldiers, who were deserting at the rate of two hundred men a day.

In mid-January, Susan received a letter from Henry Stanton, who was still in Washington, DC, working as a journalist. "The country is rapidly going to destruction," he wrote. If the Union lost, slavery would endure. "Here then is work for you," he wrote. "Susan, put on your armor and go forth!"

By February, Susan had moved into Elizabeth's home in New York City. Together they formed a new organization—the Women's Loyal National League. Women were already raising money, knitting socks, sending foodstuff, tending to wounded, sick and dying soldiers, working on farms and in factories, spying on the enemy, and disguising themselves as men and fighting on the battlefield. Now Elizabeth and Susan planned to enlist women in a "<u>war</u> of <u>ideas</u>"—emancipation for all slaves.

They sent out a "Call for a Meeting of the Loyal Women of the Nation" to be held in New York City. Women from all over the North attended. Elizabeth spoke. The Hutchinson family sang rousing freedom songs. Susan boldly stated, "Shame on us if we do not make it a war to establish the Negro in freedom."

A series of resolutions were introduced, including one in favor of extending "civil and political rights to all citizens of African descent and all women." Including "all women" was going too far, some participants angrily objected. Not so, Susan pointed out. "It is the simple assertion of the great fundamental truth of democracy that was proclaimed by our Revolutionary fathers." The resolutions passed, and the women pledged to "give support to the government in so far as it makes a war for freedom."

From an office at the Cooper Institute, Susan spearheaded a massive campaign to collect millions of signatures on petitions for a law abolishing slavery. Scores of volunteers were exhorted to "go to the rich, the poor, the high, the low, the soldier, the civilian, the white, the black—gather up the names of all who hate slavery, all who love liberty, and would have it the law of the land, and lay them at the feet of Congress."

They worked throughout a miserably hot and humid summer. As the petitions were returned, Elizabeth enlisted her three younger sons to roll up each one and mark the number of signatures on the outside. Susan ran the day-to-day operation, which included raising money to pay rent, printing costs, postage, and other expenses. Her salary was a meager twelve dollars a week. She saved money by staying at Elizabeth's at a reduced rate. Every day for lunch she spent thirteen cents at a restaurant for a dish of strawberries with two tea-rusks (a hard, dry biscuit) and a glass of milk.

## *"Terrible Times"*

On July 13, 1863, mayhem broke out in New York City as violent mobs protested a new draft law that created a lottery to select male citizens for military duty. Black men were exempt because they were not citizens. Wealthy white men could avoid serving by paying the government three hundred dollars or by hiring a substitute. The law infuriated white workers in New York City, many of whom were proslavery because they feared competition for jobs from an influx of freed slaves. The rampage lasted for a week. Murderous rioters attacked black people, threatened abolitionists, and burned down buildings, including the Colored Orphan Asylum, one block from Elizabeth's house.

Elizabeth's son Neil was standing outside her house when the ruffians stampeded down the street. They seized him, while shouting, "Here's one of those three-hundred-dollar fellows!" Recounting the incident in a letter to her cousin Nancy Smith, Elizabeth described how Neil, quick-witted, steered the leaders to a saloon where he treated them to drinks and joined them in giving three cheers for "Jeff Davis," the president of the Confederacy.

"Thus," Elizabeth wrote, "he undoubtedly saved his life by deception, though it would have been far nobler to have died in defiance of the tyranny of mob law. . . . You may imagine what I suffered in seeing him dragged off." Taking her other children and servant to the top floor, she opened the skylight and left them with instructions in case of an attack to run out on the roof into a neighboring house. Then she "prepared a speech, determined, if necessary, to go down at once, open the door and make an appeal to them as Americans and citizens of the republic."

When a squad of police and two companies of soldiers arrived, Elizabeth gathered up her children and servants and fled to the safety of her mother's home in Johnstown. As for Susan, she was on her way to work when she discovered that the mob had shut down all the means of transportation. Making her way by ferry across the East River, she sought refuge at her cousin's house in Flushing, Queens, only to discover that there was trouble there too. "These are terrible times," she wrote home. "We all arose and dressed in the middle of the night, but it was finally gotten under control."

### "We Will Have a Room Ready for You"

Susan and Elizabeth soon returned to work circulating petitions. The first batch was presented to Congress in February 1864. Two free black men carried the large bundle of rolled-up petitions into the Senate, where Senator Charles Sumner presented them to his colleagues. "These petitions are signed by 100,000 men and women, who . . . ask nothing less than universal emancipation," he said. Repeatedly he requested additional petitions with signatures to show his colleagues that there was enormous public support for passage of the amendment abolishing slavery. By August 1864, the league had sent petitions with over three hundred thousand signatures, two-thirds of them from women. It was the first grassroots campaign in America on behalf of a constitutional amendment.

The Civil War ended in April 1865 with a Union victory. That same year the Thirteenth Amendment, which abolished slavery, was added to the Constitution. The Women's Loyal National League was widely praised for its contributions. Although satisfied with her efforts, Susan still believed it had been a disastrous mistake to suspend the campaign for woman's rights during the long war. Elizabeth still believed that women would be rewarded for their work and granted suffrage.

With the work of the Loyal League finished, Susan accepted her brother Daniel's invitation to visit him and his new wife,

Anna, in Leavenworth, Kansas. During Susan's absence, Elizabeth moved her family into a new house in New York City. "We will have a room ready for you," she wrote to Susan. "I long to put my arms about you once more and hear you scold me for all my sins and shortcomings. . . . Oh, Susan, you are very dear to me. I should miss you more than any other living being on this earth. You are entwined with much of my happy and eventful past, and all my future plans are based on you as coadjutor. Yes, our work is one, we are one in aim and sympathy, and should be together. Come home."

Susan was not inclined to leave Kansas. The change had refreshed her, although she worried about being seduced by the pleasures of long carriage rides in the prairies with Anna. She did, however, miss Elizabeth. "How I wish you were here & free with me to travel & see & be seen," she wrote to her.

## *"Woman's Cause Is in Deep Water"*

The post–Civil War period, known as Reconstruction, was tumultuous. The assassination of President Lincoln five days after the Union victory left a tragic vacuum of political leadership. Congress was controlled by the Republican Party, which was controlled by former abolitionists known as Radical Republicans. Determined to stay in power, the Radical Republicans wanted to secure the votes of former male slaves by enfranchising them. They did not, however, intend to fight for woman suffrage. That issue, they said, was too controversial. It would split the Republican Party and jeopardize the chance of winning black male suffrage. The question was how to enfranchise black men without opening the door to black or white women.

The answer lay in the wording of the proposed Fourteenth Amendment to the Constitution, which was intended to make freed slaves citizens. The first section established that anyone "born or naturalized in the United States" is a citizen. The second section defined a citizen as "male," thus for the first time interjecting gender into the Constitution. When Elizabeth heard about the amendment, she was outraged. "If that word 'male' be inserted as now proposed . . . it will take us a century at least to get it out again," she wrote to Gerrit Smith. "Oh! my cousin! Heal my bleeding heart with one trumpet note of manly indignation."

He refused. As did Wendell Phillips, the newly elected president of the American Anti-Slavery Society (AASS), who declared it was now "the Negro's hour," a phrase he coined for the agenda of first enfranchising black men. In a letter to Elizabeth, he wrote, "I think such a mixture would lose for the Negro far more than we should gain for the woman."

"My question is this," she fired back. "Do you believe the African race is composed entirely of males?"

In a letter to Susan, she wrote, "Woman's cause is in deep water. . . . Come back and help. . . . I seem to stand alone."

After eight months in Kansas, Susan returned and moved into a room in Elizabeth's house. Henry was there now too, plus all seven children, who ranged in age from twenty-three to six, and Amelia Willard. Henry practiced law. Neil helped him. Kit and Gat attended Columbia University Law School; Theo attended the College of New York City; Maggie and Hattie went to a boarding school; and Bob attended a public school. Elizabeth's sister Tryphena and her husband, Edward Bayard, lived nearby. Her sister Harriet, who was a widow, lived with them. The youngest sister, Catharine, lived on Long Island but frequently stayed at Tryphena's house.

Stout and rotund, Elizabeth was fifty years old. Her hair was now an eye-catching brilliant white color that she carefully arranged in a crown of curls. Tall and lean, Susan was a few months shy of forty-six years old. Her straight dark-brown hair was parted in the middle, sides swept over her ears, and gathered in a bun on the back of her head. Together the seasoned warriors revived the fight for woman suffrage.

To their old friends and allies, Elizabeth wrote letters and articles. Susan traveled to their homes. They started a petition campaign for a woman suffrage amendment to the Constitution. When petitions with ten thousand signatures were presented to Congress, a senator warned his colleagues that Elizabeth and Susan "have their banner flung out to the winds. They are after you; and their cry is for justice."

### "The Gate Is Shut"

On May 10, 1866, Susan and Elizabeth convened the Eleventh National Woman's Rights Convention in New York City, the first woman's rights convention to be held after the Civil War. A resolution was passed to create a new organization—the American Equal Rights Association (AERA)—to demand universal suffrage. "We can no longer . . . work in two separate movements," Susan declared, "to get the ballot for the two disfranchised classes—the negro and woman—since to do so must be at double cost of time, energy and money." Robert Purvis, who was of mixed race and had helped many slaves escape during the 1850s, supported universal suffrage. He said, according to Susan, that he and his son should not be enfranchised before his daughter because she "bore the double disability of sex and color." Although Wendell gave an eloquent speech at the convention, Elizabeth and Susan noted how he adroitly skirted the issue of woman suffrage.

Before long it became clear that other friends and allies were aligning themselves with the effort to first enfranchise black men. Elizabeth's letters to the *National Anti-Slavery Standard*, the official paper of the AASS, were no longer being published. Susan was informed that she would now have to pay "full advertising rates" to publish notices of woman's rights meetings. "The gate is shut, wholly," she said.

Undeterred, Susan and Elizabeth persevered. They wrote articles and letters, distributed tracts, organized meetings, and circulated petitions asking Congress to "extend the right of suffrage to woman." In response to a woman who refused to sign a petition, Elizabeth replied that her action "would have been a wet blanket to Susan and me were we not sure that we are right. . . . When your granddaughters hear that . . . you made no protest, they will blush for their ancestry."

Lucretia and James Mott initially refused to sign the petition because they felt it was "emphatically the negro's hour." Elizabeth changed their minds by persuasively putting forth her reasons—Congress was still debating the Fourteenth Amendment, the New York State Constitution was going to be revised, and the "negro's hour was decidedly the fitting time for woman to slip in." Explaining their change of mind in a letter to Wendell, Lucretia asked him to support woman suffrage in this "perilous hour."

He refused.

### "It Was a Blunder"

In August 1866, Elizabeth made a bold decision. She put herself on the ballot as a candidate to represent the Eighth Congressional District in New York City; the Constitution, she said, did not prevent women from being elected to an office.

Running as an independent, she proclaimed, "I would gladly have a voice and vote in . . . Congress to demand universal suffrage. . . . On no principle of justice or safety can the women of the nation be ignored."

In October, her cousin Libby invited her to Peterboro, New York, for a visit. Elizabeth reluctantly refused because, she pointed out, in addition to campaigning, she "must buy butter and meat, hear youngsters spell and multiply. . . . Then comes Susan, with the nation on her soul, asking for speeches, resolutions, calls, attendance at conventions. So you now see why I cannot accept your invitation."

Twenty-four people cast their vote for Elizabeth in the November election. Having proven her point that even though women were denied the right to vote, they could still run for a political office, her only regret was that she had not gotten photographs of her "two dozen unknown friends."

By the end of 1866, Congress had passed the Fourteenth Amendment, in which the word *male* appears three times. (Two years later, it was ratified by the states and added to the Constitution.) Clearly disabused of her belief that women would be rewarded for focusing on the war effort, Elizabeth conceded that it had been a mistake to suspend the fight for woman's rights during the Civil War.

"I was convinced at the time that it was the true policy," she reflected in her autobiography, "I am now equally sure it was a blunder."

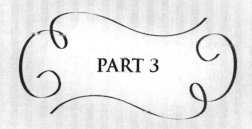

PART 3

## 14

# "KEEP THE THING STIRRING"

## TWO CAMPAIGNS
### 1867

ELIZABETH AND SUSAN THREW THEMSELVES into two state battles for woman suffrage in 1867; both fights were over whether or not to take the words *white* and *male* as qualification for voting out of the state constitution. In New York the issue was before a constitutional convention, which would issue a report in June. In Kansas the voters would decide in a referendum in November.

Elizabeth fired the first salvo in January when she argued before a committee of New York State legislators that women should be appointed delegates to the constitutional convention. Although she reported that Susan approved of her speech, the committee appointed only men. Undaunted, she and Susan and their band of coworkers resolutely lobbied committee members, circulated petitions, and held meetings to rally public support.

In the spring, a request arrived from Samuel Wood, a Kansas state senator, urging Susan to send her strongest speakers to canvass the state in support of the woman suffrage referendum. Unwilling to remove either herself or Elizabeth from the New York campaign, Susan asked Lucy Stone, who had returned to the fight after a twelve-year hiatus to tend to her family, and her husband, Henry Blackwell, to go.

### "There Is a Great Stir"

In May, Elizabeth and Susan attended the American Equal Rights Association meeting in New York City. Sojourner Truth, who was Elizabeth's house guest, spoke. Once a slave named Isabella Baumfree, she had renamed herself and become an outspoken abolitionist and woman's rights advocate. "There is a great stir about colored men getting their rights, but not a word about the colored women theirs, you see the colored men will be masters over the women," Sojourner proclaimed. "I suppose I am about the only colored woman that goes about to speak for the rights of colored women. I want to keep the thing stirring, now that the ice is cracked."

A resolution for universal suffrage was unanimously passed that declared "Women and colored men are loyal, liberty-loving citizens, and we can not believe that sex or complexion should be any grounds for civil or political degradation." From Kansas, Sam Wood sent a telegram with a message that heartened the audience: "With the help of God and Lucy Stone, we shall carry Kansas!"

Lucy, however, was not as confident, as she sensed the lack of support for woman suffrage from Republicans, the dominant political party in Kansas. She was also alarmed by the lack of support in the widely read, highly influential newspaper, the *New York Tribune*, edited by Horace Greeley, a longtime friend and ally. "I could not sleep the other night, just thinking about it," she wrote to Susan.

Lucy and Henry left Kansas after two months; their coworker Olympia Brown and the popular Hutchinson Family Singers went in their stead. Upon her return, Lucy went to New York City to confront Horace. After teasing her about crying over his lack of support, he agreed to give her "a finger's length" of space in his newspaper to write anything she liked. He also wrote a semipositive editorial about the Kansas campaign for woman suffrage.

## *"Tabooed in the Future"*

On June 27, Elizabeth and Susan testified in Albany before the committee that would recommend whether or not to strike the word *male* out of the New York State Constitution. The chairman was Horace Greeley, who now appeared to favor enfranchising black men before women. "The best women I know," he repeatedly said, "do not want the vote."

He asked Susan, "Miss Anthony, you know the ballot and the bullet go together. If you vote are you ready to fight?"

"Yes, Mr. Greeley, just as you fought in the late war—at the point of a goose-quill!" Susan's quip elicited laughter at Horace's expense.

He was infuriated by what happened next. Because there were no women delegates, Susan and Elizabeth had asked a sympathetic male delegate to present the woman suffrage petitions with 28,000 signatures. Horace did not know that Elizabeth and Susan had asked his wife to sign and circulate a petition. He found out when the man stood up and said, "Mr. Chairman, I hold in my hand a petition signed by Mrs. Horace Greeley and 300 other women of Westchester asking that the word 'male' be stricken from the constitution."

In retaliation, Horace successfully pressured delegates to make it possible for black men to vote, but not women. Several weeks after the convention, Elizabeth and Susan encountered Horace at a social event. Confronting them, he denounced them as the "most maneuvering politicians in the State of New York." Then he informed them that he had "given strict orders at the *Tribune* office that you and your cause are to be tabooed in the future." Furthermore, if mention of Elizabeth in a news item was unavoidable, she would be referred to as "Mrs. Henry B. Stanton."

In recounting the incident in a letter to a friend, Elizabeth wrote, "Of course this will not deter me from speaking my mind in the future as in the past, though I am sorry for our cause. . . . This may do something to retard our final triumph, but it will take more than Horace Greeley and the *New York Tribune* to prevent the success of the movement. . . . So, more valiant than ever, I am as always, Your old friend and co-worker, 'Mrs. Henry B. Stanton!'"

After the defeat in New York, Susan and Elizabeth were free to campaign in Kansas. But first Susan had to raise money. She solicited funds from supporters, and at the height of a hot, sticky summer in New York City, she trekked along Broadway selling advertisements for suffrage publications. In a letter to Martha Wright, Susan expressed her feelings of desperation about "so much waiting to be done, and not a penny but in hope and trust." But she soldiered on because "we must not lose Kansas now, at least not from lack of work done according to our best ability."

## "We Have Not Slept a Wink"

On August 28, Elizabeth and Susan boarded the train for Kansas; the fifteen-hundred-mile trip would require them to change trains several times.

Kansas was frontier country. The state capitol was still being built in Topeka (construction took thirty-seven years). There were sporadic conflicts between federal troops and Native American tribes. White settlers lived in primitive cabins in sparsely settled areas. Roads were faintly outlined tracks across prairies. Telegraph and postal service was unreliable. Towns were likely to have more saloons than stores, more cowboys than farmers, more outlaws than teachers.

Helen Ekin Starrett, who was awaiting their arrival, later wrote, "All were prepared beforehand to do Mrs. Stanton homage for her talents and fame." However, many people were prejudiced against Susan. Elizabeth's appearance—her short roly-poly shape, sparkling blue eyes, rosy cheeks, and clouds of the whitest of white hair carefully arranged around her head—disarmed many people. Her quick wit, sunny personality, and the fact that she had raised seven children made her very appealing.

That was not the case for Susan, with her tall, lean shape, angular features, slightly askew eye, and stern demeanor. Her reputation also suffered because she bore the brunt of hostile remarks in unfriendly newspapers. Getting to personally know Susan, however, converted most people, as it did Helen Starrett, who was charmed by her "genial manner and frank, kindly face" and soon considered her a "beloved and helpful friend."

Susan and Elizabeth arrived in Atchison, Kansas, in early September and spent the first two weeks campaigning with Sam Wood under rugged conditions. The worst were the infestations of insects, including chinch bugs. "We have not slept a wink for several nights, but even in broad daylight our tormentors are so active that it is impossible," Susan reported in a letter home. "We find them in our bonnets, and this morning I think we picked a thousand out of the ruffles of our dresses. I can assure you that my avoirdupois [weight] is rapidly reduced."

Shortly after their arrival, the Republican Party met in Lawrence, Kansas, and passed a resolution that they were "unqualifiedly opposed to the dogma of 'Female Suffrage.'" An Anti-Female Suffrage Committee was appointed to ensure defeat in November. In light of this alarming development, Susan and Elizabeth decided that they should divide their duties. Susan set up headquarters in Lawrence, where she could distribute suffrage tracts and coordinate the activities of local women who supported suffrage.

Elizabeth resolutely set off on a speaking tour accompanied by Charles Robinson, an antislavery man who had founded Lawrence in 1854 and had been elected the first governor of Kansas. Two mules pulled the ex-governor's open carriage, packed with a "bushel of tracts, two valises, a pail for watering the mules, and a basket of apples," as well as other food that they bought along the way: dried herring and slippery elm, pieces of dried inner bark from the slippery elm tree, which they could chew or use to make gruel, tea, or a poultice.

In her autobiography, Elizabeth described how they went to the "very verge of civilization." They spoke in the morning and afternoon, and at night by candlelight. They found themselves in small log cabins; in large mills and barns; in unfinished schoolhouses, churches, and hotels; and in the open air. Along the way, they were often lost. To find their way on moonless nights, Charles walked ahead with his coat off so Elizabeth could see his white shirt and drive slowly behind him. For food, she recalled, "We frequently sat down at a table with bacon floating in grease, coffee without milk sweetened with sorghum, and bread or hot biscuit, green with soda, while vegetables and fruit were seldom seen."

One night to escape from bedbugs, Elizabeth decided to sleep outside in the carriage. She had just fallen asleep when "a chorus of pronounced grunts and a spasmodic shaking of the carriage" jarred her awake to discover that the carriage was surrounded by long-nosed, black, flea-infested pigs who were using the iron steps of the carriage as scratching posts. "I had a sad night of it," she recalled, "and never tried the carriage again, though I had many equally miserable experiences within four walls." That included the night she felt a mouse scamper across her face and discovered a mouse nest in her bed. "Fortunately," she wrote, "I was very tired and soon fell asleep. What the mice did the remainder of the night I never knew, so deep were my slumbers. But, as my features were intact, and my facial expression as benign as usual the next morning, I inferred that their gambols had been most innocently and decorously conducted."

Elizabeth never regretted the discomforts of the campaign. "I was glad of the experience," she wrote. "It gave me added self-respect to know that I could endure such hardships and fatigue with a great degree of cheerfulness."

### *"To Be Sure Our Friends, on All Sides, Fell Off"*

In October, Susan and Elizabeth made a fateful decision. They accepted George Francis Train's offer to campaign for woman suffrage. A wealthy, flamboyant entrepreneur, he was a crowd-pleasing speaker who had a gift for mimicry and repartee. Because he was a Copperhead, or a proslavery Democrat, they had been reluctant to associate with him. But as Republicans and abolitionists abandoned woman suffrage, Elizabeth and Susan, along with Sam Wood, Charles Robinson, and two local women, sent a telegram to George, who was in Omaha, Nebraska, that read "Come to Kansas and stump the State for equal rights and female suffrage."

When Lucy found out, she was appalled. George Train, she wrote, was "a lunatic, wild and ranting." In defending their decision, Elizabeth pointed out that Republicans and abolitionists did not "shut out all persons opposed to woman suffrage." Therefore she asked why should they not "accept all in favor of woman suffrage . . . even though they be rabid proslavery Democrats?"

He arrived in time to campaign with Susan for the last two and a half weeks before the vote. Their speaking tour took them throughout Kansas from Lawrence to Olathe, Paola, Ottawa, Mound City, Fort Scott, Humboldt, LeRoy, Burlington, Emporia, Junction City, Manhattan, Wyandotte, Topeka, and back to Leavenworth. On election day, Susan, Elizabeth, and the Hutchinson Family Singers rode in an open carriage to all the polling places in Leavenworth, where they gave speeches and the Hutchinson family sang suffrage songs, including one John had written, titled "Kansas Suffrage Song," with the verse:

*We frankly say to fathers, brothers,*
*Husbands, too, and several others,*
*We're bound to win our right of voting.*
*Don't you hear the music floating?*

Both referendums were overwhelmingly defeated. Out of thirty thousand votes, 10,502 white men voted for black male suffrage, 9,091 voted for woman suffrage. Elizabeth later wrote that she believed both propositions would have passed except for the Republicans' "narrow policy, playing off one against the other." Susan heralded the 9,070 votes as the "first ever cast in the United States for the enfranchisement of women."

George offered two more opportunities to Elizabeth and Susan, one irresistible, the other a dream come true. The first was a woman suffrage lecture tour for the three of them that he would finance. The second was his promise to underwrite their own weekly woman suffrage newspaper to be called the *Revolution*. Elizabeth initially wavered because of their friends' protests, but then sided with Susan: "I take my beloved Susan's judgment against the world," she once wrote. "After we discuss any point and fully agree, our faith in our united judgment is immovable, and no amount of ridicule and opposition has the slightest influence."

The lecture tour was a luxurious experience for Susan and Elizabeth—the best rooms in the best hotels, fine food, flowers—and it garnered a great deal of publicity. "The agitation was widespread, and of great value," Elizabeth later recalled. "To be sure our friends, on all sides, fell off, and those especially who wished us to be silent on the question of woman's rights, declared 'the cause too sacred to be advocated by such a charlatan as George Francis Train.' We thought otherwise." She and Susan had "solemnly vowed that there should never be another season of silence until woman had the same rights everywhere on this green earth, as man."

## 15

# "Male Versus Female"

## DIVISION IN THE RANKS
## 1868–1870

Trunk to his word, George Francis Train provided the money to start publishing the *Revolution*. Susan was the business manager. Elizabeth and Parker Pillsbury, a social reformer, orator, and writer, were the editors. The first edition was published on January 8, 1868. In an editorial, Elizabeth wrote that it would be "charged to the muzzle with literary nitro-glycerine." Week after week, it was, as Elizabeth published uncensored articles and editorials on anything and everything that pertained to women— divorce reform, child rearing, unfair working conditions, equal education, and woman suffrage. Parker covered political events. Together, Susan said, Elizabeth and Parker "can make the pages burn and freeze—laugh and cry."

Their old friends were beside themselves. In a letter to Susan, William Lloyd Garrison, the pioneering abolitionist, condemned George as a "crack-brained harlequin." The public response was mixed. An editorial in the *Cincinnati Enquirer* declared it "spicy, readable and revolutionary." It was "plucky, keen, and wide awake," pronounced the *Home Journal*, a society newspaper. The editor of the *New York Sunday Times,* however, expressed the opinion that Elizabeth should tend to her "domestic duties" and that Susan needed a "good husband and a pretty baby."

As for Elizabeth and Susan, the *Revolution* was a powerful mouthpiece for spreading their ideas and mobilizing supporters. To cover operating expenses, Susan hustled after subscribers from the president of the United States to supporters in California. She solicited advertisers, but only for products that she and Elizabeth considered reputable.

Adept in writing satire, sarcasm, and ridicule, Elizabeth employed them in her articles and editorials. She spared no one—not her cousin Gerrit when he refused to sign one of their petitions or Wendell for refusing to back universal suffrage. Although Gerrit took her attack in stride, Wendell did not. In a letter to a friend, Elizabeth recounted an unpleasant encounter with him at an event in Boston: "In quite a large circle of my friends, [he] refused to shake hands with me, rebuffing my advance with the rather surly remark, 'Mrs. Stanton is no friend of mine.'" Concluding that he could not stand her satire of him, although he did not hesitate to use it himself, she wrote, "Seeing that he feels it, I will give him some more!"

The breach with their friends and allies widened as Elizabeth, with Susan's support, insisted on tackling taboo subjects such as liberalizing divorce laws and dress reform. Having given up on bloomers, she now proposed that women wear men's clothing for three reasons: convenience, freedom from lewd remarks, and equal wages for women who were dressed like men who were doing the same job.

Elizabeth and Susan also took on controversial causes that their old friends feared would sully the woman's movement, such as the case of twenty-year-old Hester Vaughn. Abandoned by her husband, Hester was working as a servant when she was impregnated and deserted by another man. On her own in the middle of the winter, she found refuge in an unheated room, where she gave birth. By the time they were discovered, the baby was dead and Hester nearly dead. The *Revolution* and the Working Woman's Association, a group Susan formed of typesetters and clerks, rallied support to her side. They sent Dr. Clemence Lozier, a staunch woman's rights activist, to investigate, published demands for a new trial, and held a huge meeting in New York City.

In speeches and articles, Elizabeth railed against the unequal moral code that found Hester guilty of infanticide, but not her seducer and the legal system that prevented women from serving as lawyers, judges, and members of the jury. Elizabeth and her cousin Libby visited Hester in prison. Then they personally presented their plea for clemency to the governor of Pennsylvania, who finally agreed to release Hester.

### *"Propulsive Force"*

After the Fourteenth Amendment, which defined a citizen as "male," was ratified in July 1868, Elizabeth and Susan issued a call for a National Woman Suffrage Convention, the first to be held in Washington, DC, in order to lobby legislators. On January 19 and 20, 1869, people from twenty states gathered together, a sign of the growth of the woman's movement. A number of senators and representatives spoke, raising the hope that perhaps Congress would pass a woman suffrage amendment.

A prominent journalist, Grace Greenwood, the pseudonym of Sara Jane Lippincott, covered the convention. She described

Susan as giving a speech in "her usual pungent, vehement style, hitting the nail on the head every time, and driving it in up to the head." Elizabeth's speeches were "models of composition— clear, compact, elegant, and logical. . . . There is no denying or dodging her conclusions." Elizabeth, Grace concluded, was the "swift, keen intelligence" of the movement, and Susan "its propulsive force," while Lucretia Mott was its "soul."

### *"It Will Be Male Versus Female, the Land Over"*

In the wake of losing the Civil War, Southern legislatures passed Black Codes, or laws that limited the freedom of black people and undermined the Fourteenth Amendment. The Klu Klux Klan, a terrorist group, was organized by former Confederate soldiers who were committed to perpetuating white supremacy. Concealing themselves in white—robes, masks, and tall, cone-shaped hats—the Klan terrorized and murdered former slaves, in particular black men who voted for candidates who were Republicans, the political party that had passed the Thirteenth Amendment prohibiting slavery.

In an effort to protect black male voters, the Republican-led Congress passed the Fifteenth Amendment in February 1869, which prohibited the government of the United States or of any individual state from denying a citizen the right to vote "on account of race, color, or previous condition of servitude." Noting that the word *sex* was omitted, Elizabeth and Susan were outraged. "Woman will then know with what power she has to contend. It will be male versus female, the land over," Elizabeth wrote in the *Revolution*. She railed against establishing an "aristocracy of sex." Her rhetoric became increasingly anti-immigrant and black men. Susan protested that the amendment would "put two million more men in position of tyrants."

Lucy Stone, who was already at odds with Elizabeth and Susan over their alliance with George Train and the *Revolution*, vehemently disagreed with them about the Fifteenth Amendment. "There are two great oceans [of wrongs]," she said, and she would be thankful if "*any* body can get out of the terrible pit. . . . I thank God for the Fifteenth Amendment." In Boston, Massachusetts, where she lived, Lucy threw herself into organizing suffrage workers to wrest control of the movement from Elizabeth and Susan.

Fired up, Elizabeth and Susan headed west to rally supporters in Ohio, Illinois, Indiana, Missouri, and Wisconsin. They traveled from Chicago to St. Louis on a train with the new Pullman sleeper cars. Delightedly, Elizabeth described the experience as "like magic to eat, sleep, read the morning papers, and talk with one's friends in bedroom, dining room, and parlor, dashing over the prairies at the rate of thirty miles an hour."

## *"Division in the Ranks"*

In the midst of the fight over the Fifteenth Amendment, Representative George Washington Julian introduced a joint resolution in Congress proposing the Sixteenth Amendment, a woman suffrage amendment. Elated, Elizabeth wrote in the *Revolution* that March 15, 1869, the day he introduced the resolution, "will be held memorable in all coming time." Hoping to recruit allies to work for passage of the amendment, she and Susan prepared for the next meeting of the American Equal Rights Association (AERA). Adopting a conciliatory tone to smooth hurt feelings and repair the breach, they sent out hundreds of letters. "I wish so much all petty jealousies could be laid aside, for all that our cause needs now for a speedy success is union and magnanimity," Elizabeth wrote to one former ally. In the May issue of the

*Revolution,* they announced the dissolution of their relationship with George Francis Train. In her editorial, Elizabeth explained, "Feeling that he has been a source of grief to our numerous friends . . . he magnanimously retires."

The well-attended AERA meeting opened on May 12, 1869, in Steinway Hall in New York City, with Elizabeth presiding. All went well until a debate broke out over whether or not Elizabeth and Susan should resign from the association because of their position on the Fifteenth Amendment. Although they remained, it was clear that there would be no reconciliation.

In response to the contentious meeting, Elizabeth and Susan invited a select group of women to a reception at the office of the *Revolution.* There they formed a new organization—the National Woman Suffrage Association (NWSA). Elizabeth was elected president. This news prompted Lucy to put out a feeler for forming a separate national organization for people "who cannot use the methods, and means, which Mrs. Stanton and Susan use." Newspapers began to speculate about "division in the ranks of the strong-minded" women. Addressing an editorial to the "Boston malcontents," Elizabeth offered to resign as president of the NWSA if that would reunite them.

Then Isabella Beecher Hooker entered the fray. The half sister of Henry Ward Beecher, the prominent preacher, and Harriet Beecher Stowe, the best-selling author of *Uncle Tom's Cabin,* Isabella had been prejudiced against Elizabeth and Susan until they spent time together and she was smitten by them. Attempting to broker a rapprochement, she organized a reconciliation convention and sent out a list of instructions on how to dress and behave.

"I did my best to obey orders," Elizabeth later recalled, "and appeared in a black velvet dress with real lace, and the most inoffensive speech I could produce; all those passages that would shock the most conservative were ruled out, while pathetic and aesthetic passages were substituted in their place. From what my friends said, I believed I succeeded in charming everyone but myself and Susan who said it was the weakest speech I ever made. I told her that was what it was intended to be."

Despite Isabella's efforts, the tension continued unabated. Lucretia tried to ameliorate the situation; she traveled to New York and Boston to plead with both sides to "merge their interest in one common cause." But to no avail.

On November 24, 1869, Lucy and her allies gathered in Cleveland, Ohio, to form the American Woman Suffrage Association (AWSA). Elizabeth did not attend. Having recently signed up as a speaker with the New York Lyceum Bureau, she was on a lecture tour. Susan, however, was there. Henry Ward Beecher was elected the president. The establishment of a new newspaper, the *Woman's Journal*, was announced. The primary purpose of the organization was stated: to conduct state-by-state campaigns, contrary to NWSA's focus on passage of the Sixteenth Amendment, with which every state would have to comply. A letter from William Lloyd Garrison was read that included a thinly veiled attack on Susan and Elizabeth.

Finally Susan asked to speak. The new organization, she said, was a sign of the growing strength of the woman's movement. "So, I say to you to-night: don't be scared. Our situation is most hopeful and promising. These independent and separate movements show that we are alive." Criticizing the Fifteenth Amendment, not because it enfranchised black men, but because it ignored women, she urged everyone to work for passage of the Sixteenth Amendment. Reading newspaper accounts of Susan's speech, Elizabeth applauded her spunk and fortitude for boldly speaking up at their former friends' rival convention. In the *Revolution*, she wrote that they "deplored" the division in their ranks. The "personal bickerings" distracted the old friends from the real enemy of woman's rights: "prejudice, custom, unjust laws, and false public sentiment."

## *"No Power in Heaven, Hell or Earth"*

The years of attacks by their enemies and friends had taken a toll on Elizabeth and Susan. In a letter to Susan dated December 28, 1869, Elizabeth wrote, "You and I know the conflict of the last twenty years; the ridicule, persecution, denunciation, detraction, the unmixed bitterness of our cup for the past two, when even friends have crucified us." Elizabeth, who was on her lecture tour in St. Louis, Missouri, also expressed her opinion about two looming issues in their relationship: the fate of the *Revolution* and her increasing reluctance to attend conventions.

Financially, the *Revolution* was in trouble. Although it had attracted three thousand paying subscribers, not enough businesses were willing to spend money on advertisements. Susan appealed to her friends and family. "My paper must not, shall not go down," she wrote to her cousin Anson Lapham. "I know you will save me from giving the world a chance to say, 'There is a woman's rights failure; even the best of women can't manage business.'" He sent money, as did her sister Mary. A friend sent five hundred dollars.

Isabella persuaded her half sister Harriet to serialize her forthcoming novel in the *Revolution*, a surefire way to attract subscribers and advertisers. They, however, had a condition: Susan and Elizabeth must change the name of the *Revolution* to "The True Republic, or something equally satisfactory to us." Susan sought Elizabeth's opinion.

"My Dear Susan," Elizabeth replied, "As to changing the name of the *Revolution,* I should consider it a great mistake. . . . Establishing woman on her rightful throne is the greatest revolution the world has ever known or ever will know. To bring it about is no child's play. . . . A journal called the *Rosebud* might answer for those who come with kid gloves and perfumes . . . but for us . . . there is no name like the *Revolution.*" Susan agreed. Isabella and Harriet withdrew their offer. Susan continued her increasingly futile search for money to save the *Revolution.*

As for Susan's insistence that Elizabeth preside over the next annual convention, Elizabeth reminded her that she hated conventions because she did not like to "manage other people" or to have other people "manage" her. Besides, she wrote, she would do more good on her lecture tour talking to Western women than to Washington politicians. She offered to pay someone else to take her place at the convention. "But of course," she added, "I stand by you to the end. I would not see you crushed by rivals even if to prevent it required my being cut into inch bits. . . . No power in heaven, hell or earth can separate us, for our hearts are eternally wedded together. Ever yours, and here I mean *ever.*"

Would Elizabeth's declaration of loyalty include presiding over one more convention? For now, it did.

## *"Already Free"*

The second annual National Woman Suffrage Convention in Washington, DC, opened on January 19, 1870. It was scheduled to last for two days, but the enthusiastic participants continued meeting for a third day. Letters from prominent people were read. Politicians, judges, ministers, and suffrage workers gave speeches. At a follow-up meeting before a joint congressional committee, Elizabeth boldly argued that women already had the vote under the recently ratified Fourteenth Amendment, a new legal theory that had been first articulated by Francis Minor, a lawyer in St. Louis, and his wife, Virginia, president of the Woman Suffrage Association of Missouri. Since the amendment established that "All persons . . . are citizens of the United States," the Minors reasoned that women are persons, therefore they are citizens, and the right to vote is inherent in citizenship.

The Minors' proposition, which became known as the New Departure, seemed like a promising path to securing the vote. Susan and Elizabeth enthusiastically promoted it, along with the stirring refrain "Already Free."

# 16

## "THE CROWNING INSULT"

### ANOTHER BATTLE
### 1870–1871

FOR SEVERAL MONTHS, A SENSATIONAL TRIAL had been going on in New York City. Throughout America, people were devouring every shocking and scandalous detail. Daniel McFarland, an alcoholic and abusive man, had been married to Abby Sage. Together they had two sons. A successful actor, Abby had financially supported the family. Finally she divorced Daniel and entered into a new relationship with Albert D. Richardson, a prominent reporter for Horace Greeley's *New York Tribune*. One day, Daniel walked into Albert's office and shot him. As Albert lay dying, he and Abby were married in a ceremony performed by Henry Ward Beecher and attended by Horace and other prominent people.

Upon Albert's death, Daniel was arrested. During his trial, the press coverage portrayed Abby as a wanton woman and Daniel as a sympathetic figure. In mid-May, he was acquitted on the grounds of insanity, set free, and given custody of one of his and Abby's sons. Many people, because she had worked as an unpaid editor or because she was helping support two households, one in New York City, where Henry spent most of his time, and the other a spacious house she had recently bought in Tenafly, New Jersey, a town not far from New York City. She also paid school and college tuitions for her children. Whatever Elizabeth's reasons, Susan shouldered the debt and eventually paid back every cent.

Susan spent the summer on a lecture tour in the West. Elizabeth stayed in Tenafly, reading, writing, and tending to her family. "I never want to go to another convention," she wrote Isabella. If she did, it would be only because she was worried about "outside influences" or if Susan made her. "No other mortal," she wrote, "has the faculty of pulling me out of my retreat."

The current state of the suffrage movement, Susan wrote to a friend in England, was "at a dead-lock." The Republicans—a "purse-proud, corrupt, cowardly party: not that I expect from the Democrats anything better"—who controlled Congress were afraid to support the Sixteenth Amendment, lest they be voted out of office in the presidential election of 1872. Even worse, she continued, was Elizabeth's reluctance to attend conventions and the loss of the *Revolution*. "We, E.C.S. and S.B.A.," she wrote, "have let slip from our hands all control of organizations and newspapers." It would take "some terrific shock to startle the women of this nation into a self-respect . . . [and] force them to break their yoke of bondage."

Clearly concerned about Susan's spirits, Elizabeth sent her a letter dated June 27, 1870: "Dearest Susan, Do not feel depressed, my dear friend. What is good in us is immortal. . . . We shall not have suffered in vain. How I long to see my blessed Susan!"

particularly women, were outraged. Seizing on the verdict as a "golden opportunity" to educate women about their situation under the law, Susan and Elizabeth took a bold step—they arranged two women-only meetings to protest the verdict, the press treatment of Abby, and the law that gave custody of a child to a man who was a murderer. Thousands of indignant women attended each meeting and enthusiastically applauded for Susan and Elizabeth.

First, Susan spoke, then she introduced Elizabeth, who was "robed in quiet black, with an elegant lace shawl over her shoulders and her beautiful white hair ornamented with a ribbon." In her speech, Elizabeth critiqued the double moral standard, the all-male justice system, biased laws, and biased press coverage. As usual, Elizabeth and Susan were attacked by th press for discussing such unladylike subjects. They had e pected that response; what they had not expected was t outpouring of similar stories from so many women.

### *"My Own Death-Warrant"*

On May 18, Susan finally accepted the inevitable—she c no longer pay for the *Revolution*. In fact, there was a debt o thousand dollars. Four days later, she formally transferre beloved newspaper to Laura Curtis Bullard for the sum o dollar. "It was like signing my own death-warrant," she wr her diary.

"Our *Revolution* no more!" Elizabeth wrote to her. "Th sadness, though relief in the fact." Susan, who was the b manager, however, felt only sadness, but she determin out on a lecture tour to earn money and pay off t Elizabeth felt no responsibility to help her financially,

## *"Between Two Fires"*

In late September, Susan interrupted her lecture tour in response to Elizabeth's pleas for her to help Paulina Wright Davis plan a convention in New York City to mark the twentieth anniversary of the first national woman's rights convention that had been held in 1850 in Worcester, Massachusetts. Although Paulina had ably planned the first one, she was struggling to finalize the arrangements for this one.

On October 1, Susan arrived in Tenafly on the four P.M. train. "Met Mrs. S & Hattie driving out," she wrote in her diary, "got in & rode an hour with them—Henry," she noted, had "gone to Washington." (The seven children now ranged in age from twenty-eight to eleven years old. Neil lived in Louisiana, Kit practiced law and lived with his father in New York City, Gat lived on a farm in Iowa, Maggie and Theo were away at school, and Hattie and Bob lived in Tenafly.)

For three weeks, Susan traveled back and forth between Tenafly and New York City by train and ferry to plan the convention. Some days she stayed in Tenafly and worked with Elizabeth: "Took walk at dusk—the day perfectly charming. . . . Wrote all day on the government branch of true republic took ride at dusk Bob & Hattie drivers—Heavy rain all night. . . . Writing writing beautiful day. . . . Mrs S & self wrote & worked up to 3 P.M. then dinner & she started for Washington at 5 P.M [to give a speech on the next day]. . . . Hattie & self took a walk—then went to my room & to bed—perfectly tired out."

The convention was a grand success. Lucretia, Sarah Pugh, Elizabeth, Olympia Brown, and more than two hundred people attended, including Sarah J. Smith Tompkins, the first black woman to be appointed a school principal in New York

City. Shortly afterward, both Elizabeth and Susan left on their lecture tours.

From Chicago, Elizabeth wrote a letter to Amelia Willard, her longtime housekeeper. "I send you a splendid recipe for corn muffins. Try it so that you can give me some when I return. I hope to see you in two weeks." She described her tour in Iowa; her son Gat, who lived there, traveled with her. "What times we have had," she wrote, "what detestable tea, coffee, what forlorn rooms and dirty beds." Finally they arrived in Chicago and reveled in their stay at the elegant Sherman House, where they had "nice room, clean beds and something good to eat."

Susan, who was at a woman suffrage convention in Detroit, Michigan, received a telegram that her nephew Thomas, Guelma's son, was dying, just five years after his sister Ann Eliza had died at the age of twenty-three. "I loved her merry laugh," Susan wrote at the time, "her bright, joyous presence." Now, twenty-one-year-old Thomas was dying; she hastened to his bedside. Once again she was reminded of "the brittleness of life's threads."

In December, Isabella wrote to Elizabeth and Susan and proposed taking charge of the annual National Woman Suffrage Convention in Washington, DC. She would make all the arrangements, pay all the expenses, and preside. The convention would focus on the Sixteenth Amendment; no controversial issue would be discussed, such as divorce or the rights of working women. Given her distaste for conventions, Elizabeth was agreeable, but she was annoyed when Isabella asked her to stay away. In a letter to Martha Wright, she wrote, "I think her letter quite blunt and egotistic and somehow it hurts my self-respect."

Susan, however, "declined to be snubbed, subdued or displaced" and was furious with Elizabeth. Isabella was a newcomer to the woman's movement, while Elizabeth was a pioneer. Therefore, Susan wrote, it was "suicidal" for Elizabeth to drop out: "O, how I have agonized over my utter failure to make you feel and see the importance of standing fast and holding the helm of our good ship to the end of the storm. . . . How you can excuse yourself, is more than I can understand."

Elizabeth sent Susan's letter to Martha with this comment, "'You see I am between two fires all the time. Some, determined to throw me overboard, & Susan equally determined that I shall stand at the mast head, no matter how pitiless the storm."

Organizing the convention proved too much for Isabella, and she begged for help. Elizabeth refused (she sent one hundred dollars and a letter to be read at the event), but Susan responded in person. Shortly after she arrived in Washington, she read a surprising announcement in a newspaper: Victoria Woodhull, a brand-new advocate for woman suffrage, was going to address a joint congressional committee on the day the convention was scheduled to begin.

Brazen and controversial, Victoria and her sister Tennessee Claflin, who had grown up in poverty, had recently become the first women stockbrokers on Wall Street. Skilled at enlisting the help of powerful men, they had made a fortune that they used to start *Woodhull and Claflin's Weekly*, a newspaper in which they promulgated shocking ideas: sex education, spiritualism (the belief that living people can communicate with the spirits of the dead), legalized prostitution (allegedly Tennessee was a prostitute), women serving in the military, vegetarianism, free love, and woman suffrage.

Victoria had persuaded a representative to Congress to

present a written memorial asking for passage of a declaratory act that would enforce woman's right to vote under the Fourteenth Amendment. Her memorial had been referred to the joint committee that she was scheduled to address. Susan and Elizabeth knew of her and about her memorial, but they had not met her. Clearly the time had come. Susan, Isabella, and Albert Gallatin Riddle, a strong woman suffrage advocate (and the male escort they needed to gain entrance to the meeting room), went to hear her.

Unlike her flamboyant reputation, Victoria appeared to be modest and serious. She echoed the Minors' argument, known as the New Departure, that women had the right to vote under the Fourteenth Amendment because they were citizens. The Fifteenth Amendment, Victoria also argued, which included the clause that the right to vote could not be denied "on account of race," also gave women the right to vote, because "women, black and white, belong to races." After she spoke, Susan told the committee members to listen to this "new, fresh" voice and "grant our appeal, so I can lay off my armor, for I am tired of fighting." She invited Victoria to the woman suffrage convention that was opening that afternoon.

Victoria came with her sister Tennessee. "Two New York sensations . . . ," a newspaper reporter described them, "both in dark dresses, with blue neckties, short, curly brown hair, and knobby Alpine hats, the very picture of the advanced ideas they are advocating." Repeating her woman suffrage speech, Victoria was well received. However, word of her appearance set off a firestorm of protests by people who insisted that her reputation as an advocate of "free love" would taint the woman suffrage movement.

Following the events in the newspapers, Elizabeth had two responses: In a letter to Susan, she warned her, "Do not have another Train affair with Mrs. Woodhull." In response to men who objected to Victoria's presence on the convention platform, she wrote, "When men who make laws for us in Washington can stand forth and declare themselves pure and unspotted . . . then we will demand that every woman who makes a constitutional argument on our platform shall be as chaste."

### *"We Will Win the Battle Yet"*

It appeared that Congress would soon pass the declaratory act that would enable women to vote. Although a small group of women had recently presented an antisuffrage petition to the Senate, more than 80,000 women signed a prosuffrage statement. Women who were connected to prominent men expressed their support, including Julia Dent Grant, the wife of President Ulysses Grant. Some newspaper editors endorsed the idea. Republican politicians who controlled Congress now seemed to support it, as did influential constitutional lawyers.

"I feel new life," Susan wrote to an advocate, "now hope that our battle is to be short, sharp & decisive under this 14th & 15th amendment claim—it is unanswerable."

The next crucial step was for the joint judiciary committee to make a favorable report to Congress. But on January 30, 1871, the committee issued a negative report: Congress did not have the power to act because women were not citizens, they were only "members of the state." Therefore it was up to each state to decide whether or not to enfranchise women.

That report, Elizabeth wrote to Susan, was "the crowning

insult." She reminded Susan of the speech she had given decrying the "aristocracy of sex" that the Fifteenth Amendment had established. "That night in Washington when you said you had never before seen me so on the rampage," she wrote, "I had a vivid intuition of the dark clouds hanging over us; and now they are breaking."

Outraged by the "open declaration" that women were "not citizens," Elizabeth exhorted Susan into action: "So go ahead and 'deal damnation round the land with a high hand,' as the *Tribune* says you do; only don't run in debt in order to do it." Then perhaps recognizing that she, too, needed to return to the fray, she used a plural pronoun in her last sentence: "We will win this battle yet, Susan!" and signed it "With love unchanged, undimmed by time and friction."

In May, Elizabeth joined Susan at the annual state woman suffrage convention in New York City. Lucretia came, she explained in a letter to her sister Martha, despite her "feeble health, to identify" herself with the New York branch of the suffrage movement. The Boston group had offended her sensibilities by recently passing resolutions that unfairly linked the New York group with "the doctrine of Free Love."

Seeking to bolster Victoria's standing, Elizabeth seated her between herself and the venerable Lucretia. That did not stop the press, in particular Horace Greeley, from trumpeting her notoriety in their newspapers and dubbing the convention "The Woodhull Convention." Victoria gave a defiant speech: "We mean treason, we mean secession. We are plotting revolution; we will overthrow this bogus republic and plant a government of righteousness in its stead."

Thrilled by Victoria's fiery rhetoric, Elizabeth declared that she was "a grand, brave woman, radical alike in political, religious, and social principles." Susan, however, was becoming wary of Victoria. She suspected that Victoria had attached herself to the suffrage movement in order to advance a personal ambition that she had recently revealed—to run for president of the United States.

## 17

# "I HAVE BEEN & GONE & DONE IT!"

### TAKING A STAND
### 1871–1872

DESPITE THEIR SIMMERING DISAGREEMENT over Victoria Woodhull, Susan and Elizabeth decided to do a joint lecture tour that would take them across the country to California. They traveled in style on the new transcontinental railroad. "We have a drawing-room all to ourselves," Susan wrote in a letter to her sisters, "and here we are just as cozy and happy as lovers." The sight out their window of slow-moving prairie schooners carrying pioneers westward or a "lone cabin-light on the endless prairie" prompted Elizabeth to reflect that there is "real bliss, if only the two are perfect equals, two loving people, neither assuming to control the other." Susan agreed: "Yes, after all, life is about one and the same things, whether in a prairie schooner and sod cabin, or the Fifth Avenue palace. Love for and faith in each other. . . . It is not the outside things which make life, but the inner, the spirit of love."

Along the way, they stopped to give suffrage speeches, including one to "women alone." The idea of addressing women separately was hers, Elizabeth explained in a letter to her cousin Libby. "What radical thoughts I then and there put into their heads . . . these thoughts are permanently lodged there! That is all I ask."

In Denver, Colorado, the governor and his wife welcomed them. Large audiences heard them speak. The press was uncharacteristically positive. A reporter for the *Denver News* acknowledged that the "press sneers at Miss Anthony, men tell her she is out of her proper sphere, people call her a scold, good women call her masculine, a monstrosity in petticoats." But after hearing her speak, he concluded that "if one-half of her sex possessed one-half of her acquirements, her intellectual culture, her self-reliance and independence of character, the world would be the better for it."

They were invited to speak at a newly established colony in Colorado named Greeley, after Horace Greeley, who had provided the money for the founder Nathan Cook Meeker, a former reporter for Horace's newspaper. Nathan's son Ralph described their visit in a letter to the *Tribune*: "Mrs. Stanton and Miss Anthony were the guests of my father and mother here in our rough adobe house. They melted into the family life like sunshine, and soon seemed like friends who had lived here for years." Although most of the residents, he noted, had adopted Horace's antisuffrage stance, they were receptive to what Elizabeth and Susan had to say.

Their arrival in San Francisco, during the dry and dusty season in mid-July, prompted great fanfare. A suite for them in the elegant Grand Hotel was filled with flowers and food. They were taken on sailing excursions in the harbor and for drives to the seashore and along the coast. Elizabeth noted the windmills for pumping water that were everywhere, "a very pretty feature in the landscape." Huge audiences of admirers,

143 ∿

detractors, curiosity seekers, and suffrage advocates, whom Elizabeth dubbed their "suffrage children," flocked to their lectures.

Soon, however, they ran afoul of public opinion by getting involved in the case of Laura D. Fair who had murdered her lover, A. P. Crittenden, a prominent judge with a wife and children, after he dropped her. Laura had been tried and sentenced to be hanged. Wanting to hear Laura's side of the story, Elizabeth and Susan visited her in jail, an act for which they were soundly criticized in local newspapers. The attacks escalated after Susan gave a speech in which she appeared to sympathize with Laura's plight because a married man had apparently used her and then jilted her. Other newspapers across America picked up the story. Although Elizabeth received some of the vitriol, Susan bore the brunt. "Never in all my hard experience," she wrote in her diary, "have I been under such fire." In another entry, she wrote, "I never before was so cut down."

Faced with such a furor, Susan and Elizabeth took a break. By train and private carriage, the intrepid companions traveled to see the wonders of California—the geysers and mountain ranges, which Elizabeth described as "piled one above another, until they seemed to make a giant pathway from earth to heaven." Their trip included a visit to Yosemite Valley, a remote, rugged area of spectacular natural beauty. A long, steep, narrow trail led down the mountain into the valley.

Wearing linen bloomers for the descent on horseback, Elizabeth and Susan met their guides on a very hot and dusty day. Susan mounted her horse. But Elizabeth set off on foot. (Their accounts of why she walked differ: Susan wrote that Elizabeth was too "fat" to get into the saddle; Elizabeth reported that the horse's back was so broad she could not reach the stirrups, thus as the horse started the descent, she felt as if she was going to pitch forward out of the saddle over the horse's head.)

Elizabeth slowly made her way down, alternating between walking and sliding, catching hold of rocks and twigs to steady herself, while she and her guide, who was leading her horse, argued about whether it was better to "trust one's own legs, or, the horse." Four hours later, she arrived in the valley "covered with dust, dripping with perspiration," her clothes in "tatters." After dispatching the guide to find their host, Mr. Hutchins, and tell him "to send a wheelbarrow, or four men with a blanket to transport" her to the hotel, she lay down on the grass and "fell asleep, perfectly exhausted."

Fortunately the first carriage had just been delivered to the valley that day, and finally Elizabeth arrived at the hotel. Susan, Elizabeth recalled, met her on the steps of the hotel and "laughed immoderately at my helpless plight." Elizabeth, Susan later recalled, appeared to be "pretty nearly jelly."

A hot bath and long night's sleep restored Elizabeth, and she and Susan spent several days exploring the "glory and grandeur" of Yosemite. They spent a day at the nearby Calaveras Grove, a stand of giant sequoia trees. Many of the trees had been given the names of distinguished men. As for unnamed trees, Elizabeth and Susan tacked on cards (with their guide's permission) with the names of distinguished women, including Lucretia Mott and Lucy Stone.

On August 22, 1871, Elizabeth boarded the train headed East. She stopped in Johnstown, New York, to visit her mother, who was eighty-six years old and ailing. A week later her mother died, and Elizabeth returned for the funeral. Her mother, she said, was a "grand brave woman."

## "Want to Tell You"

Since Susan was not welcome to lecture in California, she accepted an invitation from Abigail Scott Duniway, a suffrage advocate and editor of a weekly newspaper, the *New Northwest*, to speak in Oregon and Washington Territory. Boarding a ship in San Francisco bound for Portland, Susan endured seven miserable days of stormy seas. On the second day, she noted in her diary, "Strong gale and rough seas. Tried to dress—no use—back to my berth and there I lay all day. Everybody groaning, babies crying, mothers scolding, the men making quite as much fuss as the women." Finally, on the seventh day, she wrote, "I felt well enough to discuss the woman question with several of the passengers. Arrived at Portland at 10 P.M., glad indeed to touch foot on land again."

Still shaken by the fury unleashed against her in San Francisco, Susan was apprehensive the first time she spoke in Portland. But it went well. "The first fire is passed. . . . The wet blanket is now somewhat off," she wrote to Elizabeth. "I want to tell you," she continued, "that with my gray silk I wore a pink bow at my throat and a narrow pink ribbon in my hair!" She spent the rest of the year lecturing in the Northwest. "I miss Mrs. Stanton," she wrote in a letter to her family in Rochester. "Still I can not but enjoy the feeling that the people call on me." She welcomed the opportunity to answer questions and "sharpen her wit," instead of sitting silently and listening to Mrs. Stanton's "brilliant scintillations as they emanate from her never-exhausted magazine. . . . Whoever goes into a parlor or before an audience with that woman does it at the cost of a fearful overshadowing." She had "cheerfully" paid that price because she "felt that our cause was most profited by her being seen and heard, and my best work was making the way clear for her."

Everywhere she went, Susan promulgated the New Departure, the argument that women already had the right to vote under the Fourteenth and Fifteenth amendments. She exhorted women to "seize their rights to go to the polls and vote" in the upcoming presidential election. Determined to continue holding annual National Woman Suffrage Conventions in Washington, DC, but aware of Elizabeth's antipathy for conventions, Susan wrote to her, "Remember that you—E.C.S.—are President . . . and that is your immediate duty as such—to issue the call forthwith, at once—without delay . . . [a] good, strong, singing bugle blast—inviting every earnest worker & speaker to come."

Her intent, Susan wrote, was to "fire your soul to the importance of seizing the helm of our ship again . . . & keep the ship from running on shoals and quicksand."

In her last diary entry for 1871, Susan wrote, "Thus closes 1871, a year full of hard work, six months east, six months west of the Rocky Mountains; 171 lectures, 13,000 miles of travel; gross receipts, $4,318, paid on debts $2,271. Nothing ahead but to plod on."

Elizabeth wrote the call, and Susan returned in time to join her at the convention in Washington. A resolution was adopted demanding that Congress pass a declaratory act to clearly state that women had the right to vote under the Fourteenth and Fifteenth amendments. Another resolution urged women to act as if they had the right to and go to the polls on election day. Once again Elizabeth and Susan addressed a congressional committee. Once again the committee issued a negative report on the question of woman's right to vote. Susan returned to the lecture tour. Elizabeth canceled her engagement and stayed in Tenafly to tend to Hattie, who was ill.

While at home, Elizabeth packed up a big bundle of colorful rags and clothing her children had outgrown and sent them to Lucretia, who loved to make rag carpets. A delighted Lucretia replied with a description of her pleasure at "looking over each piece, opening every pinned up bundle, amazed that thou had collected so much."

### "A Sad Day for Me"

In the spring, Elizabeth got embroiled in Victoria Woodhull's scheme to launch a new political party. A presidential election would be held in November, and Victoria, who had announced herself as a candidate, needed a party to nominate her. Susan was adamantly opposed to the idea of forming a new party. "All our time and words in that direction are simply thrown away," she wrote to Elizabeth. Furthermore, she warned her, "my name must not be used to call any such meeting." Nevertheless, in April, Susan's name appeared on a call published in *Woodhull and Claflin's Weekly* to form a new party at the annual May meeting of the National Woman Suffrage Association (NWSA), at Steinway Hall in New York City. Elizabeth's name was there too, along with Isabella's and Matilda Joslyn Gage's.

It was by chance that Susan saw the announcement; a gentleman had handed her a copy of a newspaper to read while she was waiting in a small train station in Illinois. Furious, she sent a telegraph with instructions to remove her name and headed back East. Arriving at Elizabeth's home, she had it out with her but could not shake Elizabeth's enthusiasm for Victoria and a new party.

Calling Susan "narrow, bigoted and headstrong," Elizabeth refused to serve as president of the NWSA; instead, Susan was elected. In the evening of the first day of the annual meeting,

Victoria appeared and started to speak. Susan declared the meeting adjourned and ordered the janitor to turn off the gas lights.

The next day, thwarted in her attempt to appropriate the NWSA, Victoria and her supporters met at Apollo Hall. During a raucous meeting, she was nominated for president of the United States. Frederick Douglass, who was not there, was nominated for vice president. (He refused the nomination.)

Abandoned by Elizabeth, Susan presided over the last day of the convention. Demoralized but relieved that she had kept NWSA out of Victoria's clutches, Susan wrote in her diary, "A sad day for me; all came near being lost. Our ship was so nearly stranded by leaving the helm to others, that we rescued it only by hair's breadth. . . . I never was so hurt by the folly of Stanton."

In the aftermath, Elizabeth distanced herself from Victoria, although she continued to admire her outspokenness. Susan forgave her "oldest and longest tried woman friend, ECS."

## "Never So Blue in My Life"

That summer, political parties met to nominate presidential candidates. President Ulysses Grant's corrupt administration had split the Republican Party. One faction, called the liberal Republicans, met in Cincinnati, Ohio, and nominated Horace Greeley. The regular Republican Party met in Philadelphia and nominated Grant for a second term. The Democrats met in Baltimore and also nominated Greeley. Susan and Isabella lobbied all three parties to recognize woman suffrage in their platform.

Only the regular Republicans included a statement in their platform affirming that women's demand for "equal rights should be treated with respectful consideration." Susan was triumphant; finally a major political party had acknowledged women in its official party platform. Admittedly she recognized the "meagerness" of the statement and "the timidity of politicians"; nevertheless, she promised to work for the Republican Party.

Elizabeth was not elated; the statement was but "a splinter." Feeling "intensely bitter," she wrote to Susan, "I do not feel jubilant over the situation; in fact I never was so blue in my life. . . . Dear friend, you ask me what I see. I am under a cloud and see nothing." Despite her gloomy mood, Elizabeth joined Susan at some campaign events, but only because she could not abide the thought of Horace Greeley winning the election.

Shortly after losing the election to Grant, Horace died. Writing to Susan, Elizabeth remarked that she was "dreadfully shocked" but noted that he was "one of woman's worst enemies." His departure, she prophesized, would smooth the path to enfranchisement. "Here, as in many other cases," she wrote, "you and I have made enemies of old friends because we stood up first and always for woman's cause and would not agree to have it take second place. Expediency does not belong to our vocabulary."

### "Register Now!"

For several years, scores of women had gone to local polling places to assert what they believed was their constitutional right to vote. Mary Ann Shadd Cary, a black journalist, had been allowed to register in Washington, DC, but not to vote. Sojourner Truth had tried to vote in Battle Creek, Michigan. Through a blizzard and past a crowd of jeering men in New Hyde Park, New York, Sarah Grimké and her sister Angelina had led forty women to dispose of ballots in a special box. In

Vineland, New Jersey, activists had set up a box at the polling place in which 172 women, both black and white, had placed their ballots. In 1871, Nanette Gardner's vote for a state official was actually counted in Detroit, Michigan.

Susan had wanted to vote too, but she was never at her home in Rochester, New York, long enough to meet the requirement that voters had to be in residence for thirty days before the election. Finally, in the fall of 1872, she was, but first she needed to register.

Four days before the election, she read a notice in the newspaper:

> **Now register! Today and tomorrow are the only remaining opportunities. If you were not permitted to vote, you would fight for the right, undergo all privations for it, face death for it. . . . Register now!**

Taking the notice at face value, Susan and her three sisters— Guelma, Hannah, and Mary—went to the registry office in the eighth ward, located in a barber shop. The inspectors reluctantly entered their names as voters, but only after Susan read aloud the Fourteenth Amendment. At Susan's request, more women showed up and were registered in the eighth ward. By the next day, many more women had registered in other wards in the city. Two of the three local newspapers noted the event, but refrained from editorializing. The third newspaper condemned the action and insisted that any inspector who accepts a woman's vote on election day "should be prosecuted to the full extent of the law."

Before taking the next step—voting on November 5, 1872— Susan sought legal advice. Numerous lawyers turned her away. Finally, Henry R. Selden, a prominent lawyer and former judge, agreed to study the documents she had compiled that supported the argument that women had a constitutional right to vote. Convinced, after a thorough review, that her claim was valid, he told her, "I will protect you in that right to the best of my ability."

On election day, Susan, her sisters Guelma, Hannah, and Mary, and several other women, who lived in the eighth ward in Rochester, voted. (The women who had registered in other wards stayed home, apparently intimidated by the threat of being arrested.) "Well," she wrote to Elizabeth, "I have been & gone & done it!! Positively voted." Newspapers across the country carried the story, most of them calling for punishment of the women, especially of Susan. Two weeks later, she was arrested.

The United States deputy marshal refused Susan's suggestion that he handcuff her. He did, however, allow her to change her dress before escorting her to court to be arraigned on the criminal charge of voting "without having a lawful right to vote." After a series of hearings, her trial was scheduled for June 17, 1873.

# 18

## "Our Friendship Is
## Too Long Standing"

### GAINS AND LOSSES
### 1873–1879

Susan's upcoming trial attracted a great deal of attention. The pros and cons were discussed in the pages of private letters and newspapers and wherever people met. Susan undertook an exhausting tour throughout Monroe County, where her trial would be held, to lecture on the question "Is it a Crime for a Citizen of the United States to Vote?" She buttressed her argument with quotations from the Declaration of Independence, the Constitution, Supreme Court decisions, and the writings of James Madison and Thomas Paine. Acknowledging the effectiveness of her persuasive speech, the U.S. District Attorney concluded he could "hardly find twelve men so ignorant on the citizen's rights— as to agree on a verdict of Guilty." Therefore, he asked Judge Ward Hunt, a recently appointed judge who would preside over the trial, to move it to the village of Canandaigua, the county seat in Ontario County.

The trial was a sham. Judge Hunt was, in Susan's words, "a small-brained, pale-faced, prim-looking man, enveloped in a faultless black suit and a snowy white tie." He refused to allow her to testify because she was "not a competent witness." He preempted the jurors' role by ordering them to "find a verdict of guilty." That night in her diary, Susan fumed against "the greatest judicial outrage history has ever recorded!" The next day she returned to court to be sentenced.

"Has the prisoner anything to say why sentence shall not be pronounced?" Judge Hunt asked.

"Yes, your honor," she replied, rising to her feet. "I have many things to say; for in your ordered verdict of guilty, you have trampled under foot every vital principle of our government. My natural rights, my civil rights, my political rights, my judicial rights, are all alike ignored. Robbed of the fundamental privilege of citizenship, I am degraded from the status of a citizen to that of a subject; and not only myself individually, but all of my sex, are, by your honor's verdict, doomed to political subjection under this, so-called, form of government."

The judge tried to silence her, but Susan was unstoppable. He tried again and again, six times in all. Finally, she sat down. Ordering her to rise to be sentenced, the judge fined her one hundred dollars and court costs.

Stating that she would never pay a dollar of the "unjust penalty," Susan declared that she would continue to "educate all women to do precisely as I have done, rebel against your manmade, unjust, unconstitutional forms of law, that tax, fine, imprison and hang women, while they deny them the right of representation in the government." To that end, she had thousands of copies of the trial proceedings printed and distributed.

Under the law, the judge should have sent Susan to jail until she paid her fine. Then she would have had the right to appeal to a higher court. Determined to forestall that, he announced, "Madam, the Court will not order you committed until the fine is paid."

The judge's conduct was thoroughly denounced even in antisuffrage newspapers. Public opinion was mixed; Susan was cast as a hero, a martyr, a criminal, a threat to an orderly society. Matilda Joslyn Gage, who had attended the trial, was outraged. Elizabeth was not. In explaining her lack of indignation to Matilda, she wrote, "My continuous wrath against the whole dynasty of tyrants has not left one stagnant drop of blood in my veins to rouse for any single act of insult." She did, however, publish an article about the case in the *New York Times.* "It is as you say," she wrote to Susan, "terribly humiliating to be asking these supercilious boys to consider our right" and signed it "Your rebellious friend, E.C.S."

Although the judge had thwarted Susan's plan to appeal to a higher court, another important case—*Minor v. Happersett*—would make its way to the Supreme Court of the United States. Like Susan, Virginia Minor went to vote in St. Louis, in 1872. (She and her husband, Francis, had introduced the New Departure, the legal argument that the Fourteenth Amendment gave women the right to vote.) But when Reese Happersett, the registrar, refused to register her, she filed a lawsuit against him. In 1875, the Supreme Court ruled against her in a unanimous opinion that although women were citizens, the "Constitution of the United States does not confer the right of suffrage upon anyone." The power to determine who could vote belonged to the states, the justices asserted, thus pronouncing a death sentence on the New Departure strategy. Resolute in the face of defeat, Susan and Elizabeth and their coworkers redoubled their efforts in support of a Sixteenth

Amendment to the Constitution that would prohibit states from denying women the right to vote.

But then Victoria Woodhull detonated a powder keg that set off what Elizabeth later described as a "great social earthquake." In the pages of her newspaper, Victoria published an exposé of an affair between Henry Ward Beecher, a powerful clergyman, and Elizabeth "Lib" Tilton, a member of his congregation and the wife of Theodore Tilton, who was also a member. Beecher had been president of AWSA, the rival woman suffrage organization established by Lucy Stone. Victoria named Elizabeth as one of her sources for the scandalous story.

Lib had confided in Susan, who told Elizabeth, expecting her to remain silent. However, the story spread—Lib's mother publicized it to defend Lib against Henry Beecher's claim that she had seduced him. Theodore (who had just ended his own dalliance with another woman) told his version to Elizabeth, and they both told Victoria. Victoria published the graphic details to expose Henry's hypocrisy because he had been publicly criticizing her for her advocacy of "free love." Shortly after she published the scandalous story, Victoria was arrested and sent to jail under a federal law that made it illegal to send obscene material through the United States Postal Service.

Then a reporter wrote a newspaper article in which Elizabeth denied Victoria's version. Susan accused Elizabeth of abandoning a woman to save a man's reputation. Indignant that Susan would believe a reporter rather than trust her, "a friend of twenty years' knowledge," Elizabeth explained, "I simply said I never used the language Victoria put in my mouth." The words she used were "clothed in refined language at least however disgusting the subject."

Theodore filed a lawsuit against Henry; a sensational trial

ensued that lasted three months and ended in a hung jury. In the aftermath, Theodore divorced Lib and went to live in Paris. Lib disappeared from public scrutiny. Victoria moved to England, where she married a wealthy man and renounced free love. Henry, backed by powerful and rich members of his church, maintained his prominent position.

The press had a heyday. Susan was hounded to reveal what she knew. Reporters stalked her. Passengers on trains queried her. She kept silent; to speak, she believed, would incriminate Lib. Elizabeth agreed but felt compelled to protest the hypocrisy and injustice in her speeches and articles, especially since part of Henry's strategy was to intimidate and discredit anyone who might testify against him. To that end, he and his lawyers spewed vitriol against Lib, Victoria, Elizabeth, Susan, and Isabella Beecher Hooker, his half sister, who had urged him to confess. He smeared woman suffrage activists as "insane" and "human hyenas" and "free lovers."

Susan supported Elizabeth's outspokenness, until she repeated information to a reporter that Susan had warned her to keep confidential. Infuriated, Susan wrote her a scathing letter. "Offended, Susan," Elizabeth responded, "come right down and pull my ears. I shall not attempt a defense." But, she explained, she could not keep silent in the face of the "terrible onslaught on the suffrage movement. . . . We must not let the cause of woman go down."

### *"We Ask Justice"*

The United States celebrated its centennial in 1876. Patriotic events were scheduled to run from January through June, culminating with a gala event on the Fourth of July in Philadelphia. Noting that the Centennial Celebration committee neglected to plan events that honored women's contributions, or even to include women participants at the gala celebration, the National Woman Suffrage Association (NWSA) passed a resolution pointing out that "one-half of the citizens of this nation, after a century of boasted liberty, are still political slaves," and demanding "justice for the women of this land."

In late May, Susan and Matilda set up the NWSA's Centennial headquarters near Independence Square in Philadelphia. Elizabeth "found them pleasantly situated" when she arrived in mid-June after finishing her lecture tour. Writing in her diary, Susan noted that she was "glad enough to see her & feel her strength."

Together Elizabeth, Susan, and Matilda wrote a "Woman's Declaration of Rights" that would be read during the main event. But they were refused a seat on the platform; finally they managed to secure five tickets in the audience. July 4 was recorded as one of the most oppressively hot days in an already extremely hot summer. Waiting until the Declaration of Independence had been read, Susan and the others then rose to their feet, walked to the platform, and presented their Declaration to Thomas W. Ferry, the vice president of the United States.

Then they went to a platform in front of Independence Hall, where Lucretia Mott presided over a five-hour-long ceremony. Elizabeth and other women spoke. The Hutchinsons sang. Susan read the Woman's Declaration aloud while Matilda held an umbrella over her head to protect her from the broiling sun. People applauded as Susan ended with the words: "We ask justice, we ask equality, we ask that all the civil and political rights that belong to citizens of the United States, be guaranteed to us and our daughters forever."

## *"I Am Immersed to My Ears"*

Ever since the mid-1850s, Elizabeth had planned to write a history of the woman's movement. Lucretia had encouraged her, but she had never found the time to focus on it. Now together, she and Susan, undoubtedly fired up by the invisibility of women in the hoopla over the Centennial, decided the time had come. Their idea was to solicit material from advocates throughout America, including firsthand accounts, speeches, letters, biographical sketches, reports from conventions, portraits, newspaper articles, and legal documents. They enlisted Matilda to help them compile, edit, and write the *History of Woman Suffrage*.

For years, Susan had filled trunks and boxes with letters, documents, articles, tracts, books, posters, cartoons, advertisements, petitions, resolutions, diaries. Some were pasted in scrapbooks that her father had urged her to make. Others were loose. She had everything shipped to Elizabeth's house. Optimistically they thought they could finish the book in four months and blocked out four months of working time—August through November. Writing to a friend, Susan reported that they were "working for dear life" in Elizabeth's "delightfully quiet & pleasant home" in Tenafly, New Jersey.

They kept at it for months, interspersed with the comings and goings of Elizabeth's college-age children—Theo, Maggie, Hattie, and Bob. (Neil, Kit, and Gat lived elsewhere.) Occasionally Henry would come to Tenafly, but he spent most of his time in New York City, where he practiced law. Amelia Willard was still a mainstay in the household. They had a horse, named Jule after George Julian, the prosuffrage representative in Congress; chickens; and Bruno, an immense Saint Bernard dog who, according to Elizabeth, had a "wonderful

159

head" and a "beautiful coat of long hair." Around his neck he wore a "bright brass collar."

Susan and Elizabeth had met when Theo was several months old, and Susan was like another parent to him and his younger siblings. Writing to Susan about the children or forwarding their letters, Elizabeth typically referred to them as "*our* children." In one letter, Elizabeth wrote, "There is no doubt you have had a part in making them what they are. There is a depth and earnestness in these younger ones and a love for you that delight my heart."

Elizabeth's daughter Maggie later described how they sat across from each other at a large desk "with innumerable drawers and doors" that stood in the center of a sunny room with a large bay window, hardwood floors, and a fireplace. They each had an "ink stand, bottle of mucilage, and array of pens, pencils, knives, brushes, etc."

They were "fresh and amiable" in the mornings, Maggie recalled. "They write page after page with alacrity, they laugh and talk, poke the fire by turn, and admire the flowers on their desk . . . suddenly . . . from the adjoining room I hear a hot dispute about something. . . . Sometimes these disputes run so high that down go the pens, one sails out of one door and one out the other, walking in opposite directions around the estate, and just as I have made up my mind that this beautiful friendship . . . has at last terminated, I see them walking down the hill, arm in arm. . . . When they return they go straight to work. . . . They never explain, nor apologize, nor shed tears, nor make up, as other people do."

The project turned out to be bigger than either of them imagined. Soon the mass of material overwhelmed them. "I am immersed to my ears and feel almost discouraged," Susan wrote in her diary. "The prospect of ever getting out a satisfactory history grows less each day."

## *"I Should Feel Desolate Indeed"*

In late January 1877, Susan and Elizabeth left for their separate lecture tours. Susan's lasted nine months and took her to Iowa, Wisconsin, Kansas, Nebraska, and Missouri. She went to Colorado when she heard that there was going to be a woman suffrage referendum there in October. Throughout the sparsely settled state, she traveled by stagecoaches and wagons over high mountains, through deep canyons, and across arid plains. Occasionally she found a clean place to sleep and eatable food. Writing to her, Elizabeth cautioned, "Do be careful, dear Susan, you can not stand what you once did. I should feel desolate indeed with you gone." On election day, the male voters rejected woman suffrage.

Elizabeth spent five months on the circuit. "I sit today in a forlorn old hotel, poor bed and worse fare, and yet I am comfortable. These trips have taught me one thing in regard to myself and that is that I can be happy under most conditions," she wrote to Hattie, a senior at Vassar College. In a letter to Maggie she wrote, "You would laugh to see how everywhere the girls flock round me for a kiss, a curl, an autograph." She admitted to being lonely and fatigued, but it was worth it because she was "doing an immense amount of good in rousing women to thought and inspiring them with new hope and self-respect."

At the end of the 1870s, Susan and Elizabeth could count gains and losses. Many states had changed laws that discriminated against women. Schools, colleges, universities, and trade schools were opening their doors. Women were filling jobs in government, factories, and businesses. In the early 1830s, Harriet Martineau, a prominent English journalist, had toured America and found women employed in seven occupations: milliner, dressmaker, tailoress, seamstress, factory worker, teacher of young children, and domestic servant. In 1880, the census found women engaged in 350 occupations.

Women had won the right to vote in municipal elections, or local affairs, known as partial suffrage in Kansas, school suffrage in Massachusetts, and full suffrage in the territories of Wyoming and Utah. A resolution to pass a woman suffrage amendment to the Constitution had been introduced. Although most newspapers were antisuffrage, some press coverage was respectful, even laudatory. Of course, there were many mudslinging reporters who described advocates as "withered beldames" (or ugly old women) or "cats on the back roof" and advised them to "go home."

A network of suffrage organizations existed across the country; new recruits joined in record numbers. A woman in St. Paul, Minnesota, confessed to Susan that for ten years she had swallowed the "newspaper ridicule" of her. However, she wrote in a letter, "Your lecture tonight has been a revelation to me. I wanted to come and touch your hand, but I felt too guilty. Henceforth I am the avowed defender of woman suffrage."

Their losses included the demise of the *Revolution*; failure to secure full woman suffrage in Kansas and New York, or passage of the Sixteenth Amendment to the Constitution; breaches with some of their friends and allies; the deaths of others, including Gerrit Smith and Martha Wright; and setbacks dealt by the courts in the *United States v. Susan B. Anthony* and *Minor v. Happersett*.

At times, their relationship had been tested. But, as Elizabeth once wrote, "Our friendship is of too long standing and has too deep roots to be easily shattered. . . . Nothing that Susan could say or do could break my friendship with her; and I know nothing could uproot her affection for me."

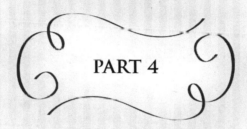

PART 4

# 19

# "WE STOOD APPALLED"

## MONUMENTAL PROJECT
## 1880–1883

ELIZABETH ENDED HER LECTURE TOUR on the verge of pneumonia. While she recuperated at home, Susan continued her peripatetic lifestyle. It was a presidential election year, and she envisioned a multipronged campaign—thousands of women attending mass meetings, signing petitions, and sending postal cards (a new product that sold for a penny)—to force the political parties to endorse the Sixteenth Amendment. She outlined her plans to Sara Spencer, the secretary of the National Woman Suffrage Association (NWSA, the organization Susan and Elizabeth founded in 1869), including "the rousingest rally cry ever put on paper." Susan asked Sara to write to Elizabeth and "fire her soul and brain, and get her to work on resolutions, platform and address." Since Elizabeth "has been to the dinner-table," Susan assured Sara, "I infer she is well enough to begin to work up the thunder and lightning."

Elizabeth and thousands of women vigorously executed Susan's plan. But their efforts "had not the slightest influence" on either major political party; the Republican and Democratic platforms "contained not the slightest reference to the claims of women or, in fact, to their existence." Refusing to campaign for politicians who stood with "their heel on the neck of woman," Susan and Elizabeth returned to their monumental project—the *History of Woman Suffrage*. Elizabeth later described how they had turned the "large room with a bay-window" into a "literary workshop" where the sun poured in on them from all sides. A "bright wood fire" burned in the fireplace; a "bouquet of nasturtiums" stood on the table with a dish of grapes and pears. Day in and day out, she wrote, they worked, "laughing, talking squabbling."

On election day, November 2, the Republican carriage, decorated with flags and evergreens, stopped at Elizabeth's house to take male voters to the polls. She announced that she would "go down and do the voting." She owned the house and paid the taxes—besides, none of the males were at home. Accompanied by Susan, she boarded the carriage and was driven to the polling place. "The inspectors were thunderstruck," she wrote in her autobiography. Apparently afraid that she was going to seize the ballot box, the inspector grasped it, covering the opening with one hand. "Oh, no, madam!" he sputtered. "Men only are allowed to vote. . . . I cannot accept your ballot." Placing her ballot on his hand, Elizabeth replied that she "had the same right to vote that any man present had."

November 12, a "bright sunny day," was Elizabeth's sixty-fifth birthday. Susan was away for several days, and her family was scattered—Hattie in France; Theo in Germany; Maggie, Gat, and Neil in Iowa; Bob away at college in New York. Kit and Henry were in New York City. It was the day she began keeping a diary: "My philosophy," she noted, "is to live one day at a time, neither to waste my force in apprehension of evils to come, nor regrets for the blunders of the past." The next day, she read in the newspaper that her "much loved friend Lucretia Mott" had died. Remembering Lucretia's "repose, self-control, and beautiful spirit," Elizabeth "vowed," as she had many times before, to "try to imitate her noble example."

On November 20, Elizabeth noted in her diary that Susan and Matilda had arrived to work on volume one of the *History of Woman Suffrage*. Although they "stood appalled before the mass of material," they worked steadily, often until midnight, all through the winter. Periodically Matilda returned to her home in Fayetteville, New York. Susan complained in a letter to a friend, "I am just sick to death of it. I had rather . . . *make* history than write it." But Elizabeth happily immersed herself in the work. "We are getting on finely with our *History*," she noted in her diary.

Friends pitched in to help. Although she was bedridden and over seventy years old, Clarina Howard Nichols wrote some reports and sent them to Elizabeth. Finally, in early spring, the book was finished. "I welcomed it with the same feeling of love and tenderness as I did for my firstborn," Elizabeth confided in her diary. Heartened by excellent reviews, they started on volume two.

Susan and Elizabeth interspersed their work with attending a series of conventions in the New England states, starting in Boston, the headquarters of the American Woman Suffrage Association (AWSA), their rival organization. A new recruit, Rachel Foster, made all the arrangements. Writing to her, Susan confessed, "It is such a relief to roll off part of the burden on stronger, younger shoulders."

They were welcomed by the governor of Massachusetts and

the mayor of Boston. Although Lucy Stone wrote positively about their arrival in the *Woman's Journal*, there was no effort toward reconciling the two factions. Indeed, Susan enlisted Harriet Robinson, who had recently split with Lucy, to secretly recruit AWSA members to the NWSA. She advised her on "a little stratagem. . . . "Keep cool—keep quiet—as military men say—'lay low—and work on'—move on to the taking of the fort."

Elizabeth, however, felt that "union of the suffrage forces would be a move in the right direction." Regardless of what happened, she wrote to Isabella, "Our cause is too great to be hurt permanently by what any one individual or group of individuals may do." People had said that she had "injured the suffrage movement beyond redemption; but it still lives. Train killed it. Victoria Woodhull killed it, the *Revolution* killed it. . . . But every time it is stricken to earth it comes up again with fresh power."

### *"This Slightest Recognition"*

In July, Elizabeth admonished Susan to "leave these state conventions alone . . . at least until we can finish the *History*." Susan heeded her, and soon they were back in their old routine; then Elizabeth was stricken with malaria. Her family attributed her illness to the strain of writing the book. Susan vehemently disagreed. "It is so easy to charge every ill to her labors for suffrage, while she knows and I know that it is her work for women which has kept her young and fresh and happy all these years."

During her illness, Elizabeth told Susan that she was more afraid that "she never should finish the *History* than from the thought of parting with all her friends." In October, she had recovered and Susan returned to Tenafly for several months. Her last diary entry for 1881 read, "The year closes down on a wilderness of work, a swamp of letters and papers almost hopeless."

Early in January 1882, Susan received a "most surprising letter" from Wendell Phillips. Eliza Eddy, a longtime supporter, had instructed him to make her will and divide a portion of her estate between Susan and Lucy "to use for the advancement of the woman's cause." Personally, Susan lived at a subsistence level; the money she earned by lecturing and selling tracts, or that Lucretia and others donated, or that working women squeezed out of their meager salaries to give her, she spent "for the cause." Her share of Eliza's bequest was about $24,000, more money than she had ever had. It was a timely inheritance, and Susan would use it to cover the costs of publishing the future volumes of the *History* and to widely distribute free copies.

They interrupted their work to attend the annual National Woman Suffrage Convention in Washington. After years of intense lobbying, petitioning, and speaking, they achieved a tiny victory: the Senate finally agreed to appoint seven senators to a select committee on woman suffrage. But even this small step roused the ire of politicians opposed to woman suffrage: Senator George Graham Vest of Missouri denounced the decision as "mischief to the institutions and to the society of the whole country." Senator John Tyler Morgan of Alabama predicted that the result would be "disbanded families."

Addressing the committee members, Elizabeth said that their appointment "thrilled the hearts" of their "countrywomen." They were "grateful for even this slight recognition." Susan celebrated the achievement in her diary: "If the best of worldly goods had come to me personally, I could not feel more joyous and blest." They gave each man a copy of the *History of Woman Suffrage.*

Surely, they must have thought that victory was possible in their lifetime.

### *"A Heavily Veiled Woman"*

Hattie, who had been traveling and studying in Europe, was summoned home to help finish volume two. Elizabeth was running out of energy. Susan was restless. She chafed at her confinement. "O, how I long to be in the midst of the fray," she confided in her diary. "I shall feel like an uncaged lion when this book is off my hands."

Their work was complicated by the fact that the volume they were working on covered the period of the split into two rival organizations. Lucy Stone, who founded the AWSA, had summarily rejected Elizabeth's requests for material. She had too much to do, plus no one should write the history "while the war goes on." Hattie took on the task because she thought it would "do credit" to her mother and Susan if "they rose above the roar of battle and gave space for a record of the work of their antagonists." Elizabeth agreed, although "at no point," she said, could Hattie consult her. Susan paid Hattie one hundred dollars.

The work on volume two was done by mid-May, and Elizabeth and Hattie left on a ship bound for Europe. With them they took a box of volume one of the *History,* piles of baggage, and a baby carriage for Elizabeth Cady Stanton II, known as Lizette, the child of Theodore and his wife Marguerite Berry. After spending time with them at their home in France, Elizabeth moved with Hattie to a convent near the University of Toulouse, where Hattie attended classes. Within a few months, however, Hattie decided to marry a "tall, dark Englishman," named William Henry Blatch, Jr., known as Harry.

After Hattie's wedding in England, Elizabeth, whose reputation was well known there, attended a woman's rights meeting in Glasgow, Scotland. She spent several weeks in London, renewing friendships with leading reformers and intellectuals. On a day when "one of the blackest and most dense fogs" shrouded London, she was visited by a heavily veiled woman. When she "threw off her concealment," Elizabeth wrote in her diary, "there stood Victoria Woodhull." Now the wife of a prominent Englishman, she took Elizabeth to her "beautiful home." Victoria had endured "great suffering," Elizabeth wrote in her diary. "May the good angels watch and guard her."

## *"She Is Not to Be There"*

During Elizabeth's absence, Susan kept up her ceaseless fight for woman suffrage. The struggle had been going on for years in Nebraska, spearheaded by Clara Bewick Colby and Lucy and Erasmus Correll. Finally in 1882, a referendum would take place in November. Susan was summoned to campaign. En route to Nebraska by train, she wrote a letter to an old friend and coworker that reflected both her longing for Elizabeth and her awareness that she was no longer young: "Only think, I shall not have a white-haired woman on the platform with me. . . . Mrs. Stanton's presence has ever made me feel that we should get the true and brave words spoken. Now that she is not to be there, I can not quite feel certain that our younger sisters will be equal to the emergency, yet they are each and all valiant, earnest and talented, and will soon be left to manage the ship without even me."

Seven thousand people showed up to hear her speak in the

newly built Boyd's Opera House in Omaha, Nebraska. Another huge crowd listened to her in Lincoln, Nebraska. The press coverage was generally fair, although there were the usual nasty articles, including one with the headline "Mad Anthony's Raid." Despite a massive effort by prosuffrage forces, male voters soundly defeated the referendum. Celebrating the outcome, antisuffrage students at the state university conducted a mock funeral procession with an effigy of Susan placed in the coffin. Midway into the torchlit spectacle, prosuffrage students commandeered the effigy and spirited it out of sight.

Susan celebrated her sixty-third birthday on February 15, 1883. A reporter described her as having "an extra wrinkle in her face, a little more silver in her hair, but her blue eyes are just as bright . . . her step as active as when she was forty. . . . her face is wonderfully intellectual, and she moves about like the woman of purpose she is."

Suffrage advocates across America marked the day. Groups and individuals sent her letters, telegrams, flowers, and gifts, including a man who sent her one hundred dollars. Use it to buy a shawl, he wrote in a note, adding, "I don't believe in woman suffrage, but I do believe in Susan B. Anthony."

Susan attended an event in Philadelphia presided over by an old friend, Robert Purvis. He read resolutions that honored her and spoke about the "stormy periods of persecution and outrage" that she had weathered in the fight to end slavery and then to gain "woman's emancipation from civil and political debasement." Susan replied that she had "been only one of many men and women who have labored side by side in this cause." She singled out Lucretia and Elizabeth, who had led her "to consider and accept the then new doctrine" of woman's rights. "Alone I should have been as a mere straw in the wind," she said.

She capped off the celebrations by sailing for Europe at the end of February. Despite the cold weather, a crowd stood on the wharf to bid her farewell. Wearing a black velvet bonnet, velvet-trimmed black silk dress, and a beaver-lined black cloak, she waved farewell. Elizabeth had been urging her to come, as had her friends, who thought it was time she had a vacation. She finally agreed when Rachel Foster offered to make the arrangements and accompany her.

After twelve days at sea, they disembarked at Liverpool, England, and took the train to London, where Elizabeth was waiting on "the tiptoe of expectation." Writing to her sister, Susan reported that "Mrs. Stanton was at the station, her face beaming and her white curls as lovely as ever."

### *"More Worlds to Conquer"*

Susan spent nine months in Europe. With Rachel she traveled throughout Italy, Switzerland, Germany, and France. She spent a great deal of time with Elizabeth in London and Basingstoke, where Hattie, who was pregnant, lived with her husband. Together they visited prominent reformers, woman suffrage activists, religious and political leaders, and attended woman suffrage meetings. In June she and Elizabeth were invited to speak on the American woman's movement. Hattie divvied up the topics: Elizabeth discussed the educational, social, and religious aspects, and Susan covered employment and the legal and political situation. "Our friends said we spoke well; but we were not at all satisfied with ourselves," Elizabeth wrote in her diary. "Well, the ordeal is over and everybody is delighted," Susan wrote in her diary. "Even the timid ones expressed great

satisfaction. Mrs. Stanton gave them the rankest radical sentiments, but all so cushioned they didn't hurt."

Hattie's baby Nora was born in September. "The first bugle
blast of the event was at dinner and in six hours all was over,"
Elizabeth wrote to her cousin Libby. A week later, she wrote in
her diary, "As I sit beside Hattie with the baby in my arms, and
realize that three generations of us are together, I appreciate
more than ever what each generation can do for the next one,
by making the most of itself."

Elizabeth had been abroad for a year and a half. Now Susan
convinced her that they had "more worlds to conquer." It was
time for her to return; together they would plan an international meeting of women in Washington. "I prefer a tyrant of
my own sex," Elizabeth once wrote, "so I shall not deny the
patent fact of my subjection; for I do believe that I have developed into much more of a woman under her jurisdiction . . .
than if left to myself reading novels in an easy chair, lost in
sweet reveries of the golden age to come without any effort of
my own."

Her last day with Hattie and Nora was her birthday, November 12. "When Hattie and I parted," she wrote in her diary,
"we stood mute, without a tear, hand in hand, gazing into each
other's eyes. My legs trembled so that I could scarcely walk to
the carriage. The blessed baby was sleeping, one little arm over
her head."

While they were at sea, the governor of the Territory of
Washington signed a bill granting women in the Territory the
right to hold office and vote.

## 20

# "Brace Up and Get Ready"

### SETBACKS
### 1884–1889

Y EARS OF INTRACTABLE RESISTANCE TO THEIR CAUSE
finally impelled Susan to curb Elizabeth's penchant
for getting involved in tangential issues, such as Frederick
Douglass's recent marriage to Helen Pitts, a white woman.
Their "amalgamation of different races," as it was called at
the time, set off a firestorm of criticism. When Elizabeth
had heard the news, she proposed that they write a letter
of congratulations to Frederick and Helen and send it to
the press. Also, they should invite their old friend Frederick to speak at the upcoming convention. No, Susan, replied. As leaders of the movement, neither she nor Elizabeth
had the right to "complicate or compromise" their arduous
battle to enfranchise women. The "question of intermarriage of the races," she pointed out, affected "women and
men alike"; therefore, opposition to intermarriage was not
an example of "invidious discrimination" against women,
which, of course, they would protest. "Your sympathy has
run away with your judgment," Susan wrote in a letter
that she closed with "Lovingly and fearfully yours." She

prevailed; Elizabeth limited her actions to writing a private letter to Frederick and Helen.

### *"Keep the Pot Aboiling"*

In early spring, Elizabeth rented out the Tenafly house, perhaps
to generate income. She returned to Johnstown, New York, and
lived with her sisters in their old family home. Susan arrived to
resume work on volume three of the *History of Woman Suffrage*
and rented a sunny room, called the "Parlor Chamber" in Mrs.
Henry's Boarding House, a block away from Elizabeth.

They worked all day sorting through the "number of appall-
ing boxes of papers"—reports, clippings, personal accounts, and
autobiographical sketches that they had requested from activists. In the evening, Elizabeth noted in her diary, they would
"take a walk, then chat for a while, look over the daily [news]
papers, drink a glass of lemonade or eat an orange, and then we
part for the night." Susan went to bed early, while Elizabeth
stayed up for a couple more hours, "reading and thinking about
the great world."

Since it had always been their rule "to keep the pot aboil-
ing," Susan and Elizabeth took time away from the *History* to
hold a convention in the old courthouse, where Elizabeth's
father had argued many cases. Their agenda was "stirring the
women up to vote" in the upcoming school election, the right
they had recently won in New York. On election day, they
went to the polls and voted. In Johnstown, one woman was
elected to the school board. Two women were elected in nearby
Gloversville. The results delighted Elizabeth and Susan, although their pleasure was tempered by the defeat of a woman
suffrage referendum in Oregon.

In the spring, Elizabeth returned to Tenafly. In July, Susan came to continue the work on volume three of the *History*. "I really think of you with pity these hot midsummer days," a friend wrote to Elizabeth, "under the lash of blessed Susan's relentless energy." But, she acknowledged, Susan was just as hard on herself.

Deciphering illegible accounts and reports from coworkers "was enough to destroy our old eyes," Elizabeth complained, but they kept at it. As always, they shared pleasurable times. "Susan and I take moonlight walks now and then," Elizabeth wrote in her diary. "When weary, we sit on the benches which I have had scattered along the hillside road, and we gaze at the moon, which I enjoy more than walking." Occasionally they rode in the phaeton, a low-slung carriage, a gift from her son Neil. Having sold her reliable horse, Jule, they had to depend on whatever horse the livery had in the stable. It took both of them to keep the horse moving—Susan using the whip, and Elizabeth jerking the reins and calling out "get up." Invariably, they would become engrossed in a conversation and forget the horse, who would "soon come to a dead standstill."

Elizabeth celebrated her seventieth birthday on November 12 and was showered with telegrams and letters from across America; cablegrams from England, France, and Germany; express packages with gifts of books, pictures, silverware, mosaics, and Indian blankets; and baskets of fruit and bouquets of flowers. That day she and Susan attended a large reception at Dr. Clemence Lozier's home, where Elizabeth had been asked to speak on "The Pleasures of Old Age." It took her a "week to think up all of the pleasures," she noted in her diary. A letter from Hattie was read aloud: "Kiss dear Susan and let her kiss you for me. . . . I throw up my cap and cry hurrah for you two grand old warriors!"

On December 31, Elizabeth wrote in her diary, "We have finally penned the last page" of the *History of Woman Suffrage*. It was a monumental accomplishment—ten years of "arduous toil," three volumes, more than three thousand pages illustrated with fine steel engravings of many coworkers. Their reward for their "arduous toil" was their certainty that present and future women would be inspired to action by reading it. "Lifting woman into her proper place in the scale of being," Elizabeth wrote, "is the mightiest revolution the world has yet known, and it may be that more than half a century is needed to accomplish this."

### "When the News Comes"

With the *History* finished, Elizabeth decided to return to England. First, however, she attempted to mend the breach with Lucy Stone by asking Antoinette Brown Blackwell, her friend and Lucy's sister-in-law, to arrange a meeting with the four of them—Antoinette, Lucy, Susan, and Elizabeth.

"As to meeting with Mrs. Stanton," Lucy replied, "it is out of the question with me" because she had heard that Elizabeth had written a letter in which she characterized Lucy as "the biggest liar and hypocrite she had ever seen." Susan had already complicated the situation by recently rejecting Lucy's invitation to get together during one of Susan's trips to Boston. All in all, Lucy replied that she was "too busy with the work that remains, to take time to mend broken cisterns."

In late October, Elizabeth left for England. One morning in January 1887, she was eating breakfast in her room at her daughter's home in Basingstoke, England, when Hattie entered and handed her a cablegram from New York with the news that Henry Stanton had died. "Death!" she wrote in her diary. "We all think we are prepared to hear of the passing away of the aged. But when the news comes, the heart and pulses all seem to stand still." After forty-six years of marriage, Henry, she wrote, now "leads the way to another sphere." What that was, no one knew; she and Hattie "sat together and talked all day long of the mysteries of life and death, speculating on what lies beyond."

Some years earlier, Elizabeth had sought to reassure Isabella Beecher Hooker about her marriage because, she wrote, "I fear from our conversation you may imagine my domestic relations not altogether happy." They are, she asserted, "far more so than 99/100 of married people. . . . Mr. Stanton . . . is a very cheerful sunny genial man, hence we can laugh together. . . . He loves music so do I, he loves oratory so do I . . . but," she acknowledged, "our theology is as wide apart as the north and south pole. . . . My views trouble him. I accept his philosophically. . . . If he could do the same we should be nearer and dearer I have no doubt."

A few days later in Washington, DC, Susan presided over the Nineteenth National Woman Suffrage Convention. A resolution was passed extending sympathy to "our beloved president, in the recent death of her husband, Henry B. Stanton." Susan read Elizabeth's annual letter: "For half a century we have tried appeals, petitions, arguments. . . . Be assured that the next generation will not argue the question of woman's rights with the infinite patience we have had for half a century."

On the second day came word that finally the full Senate had voted on the Sixteenth Amendment, which read, "The right of citizens of the United States to vote shall not be denied or abridged by any State on account of sex." Many women observed the debate from the Senate gallery. (Susan remained to preside at the convention.) One senator presented a prosuffrage petition from the Woman's Christian Temperance Union, an organization of 200,000 members. Another introduced an antisuffrage document from two hundred men, including the president of Harvard University. That document and the claim that granting woman suffrage would "unsex our mothers, wives, and sisters" prevailed; the amendment was defeated.

Noting, however, that sixteen of the senators had voted for the amendment, convention delegates passed a resolution: "That we rejoice in this evidence that our demand is forcing itself upon the attention and action of Congress, and that when a new Congress shall have assembled, with new men and new ideas, we may hope to change this minority into a majority."

But soon all-male courts, legislators, and voters delivered a series of setbacks to the cause. In February, the Territorial Supreme Court of Washington repealed the woman suffrage that had been won four years earlier. In March, the U.S. Congress passed a bill outlawing polygamy and disenfranchising women, who had been voting since 1870, in the Territory of Utah. In April, male voters in Rhode Island resoundingly rejected a woman suffrage referendum.

In the wake of these defeats, Susan turned her attention to planning for the upcoming eight-day meeting of the International Council of Women (ICW) that she and Elizabeth had set in motion during their time together in Europe. It was a massive undertaking. "Oh dear—how I wish I had Mrs. Stanton here—and I could galvanize her to make beautiful my crude glimmering of ideas," she wrote to her niece. She sent a draft of the sixteen-page program to Elizabeth, who deemed it too verbose. "Put every sentence through your metaphysical, rhetorical & common sense tweezer," she exhorted Susan.

### *"Full of Fight and Fire"*

Elizabeth reveled in her time abroad. She read voraciously—books by British thinker John Stuart Mill, German novelist Jean Paul Richter, and Russian novelist Leo Tolstoy, and essays by the English writer George Eliot—and commented on them in her diary. She did not like Tolstoy's *Anna Karenina* because "all the women are disappointed and unhappy; and well they may be, as they are made to look to men, and not to themselves, for their chief joy."

She corresponded regularly with Susan, who was juggling attending state conventions and planning the upcoming ICW meeting. In January 1888, Elizabeth wrote to Susan, "We have jogged along pretty well for forty years or more. Perhaps mid the wreck of thrones and the undoing of so many friendships, sects, parties and families, you and I deserve some credit for sticking together through all adverse winds, with so few ripples on the surface. When I get back to America I intend to cling to you closer than ever. I am thoroughly rested now and full of fight and fire, ready to travel and speak from Maine to Florida. Tell our suffrage daughters to brace up and get ready for a long pull, a strong pull, and a pull all together when I come back."

Every day, she noted in her diary, she received letters from "the faithful," perhaps writing at Susan's behest, urging her to return for the ICW and the celebration of the fortieth anniversary of the Seneca Falls convention that she had initiated. Elizabeth did not like ocean travel in the stormy winter weather, "but for blessed Susan's sake," she wrote in her diary, "I suppose I must go." Then she changed her mind.

Susan was outraged when she received Elizabeth's letter. "I am ablaze and dare not write tonight," she wrote in her diary.

The next day, she sent Elizabeth a fierce letter that "will start every white hair on her head." The "terrible" charges she leveled against Elizabeth in her letter made Susan's "own heart ache all night, awake or asleep." Ten days passed; then, finally, a cablegram from Elizabeth arrived with three words—"I am coming." Susan was "so relieved" she felt like she was "treading on air."

Although Susan was glad to see Elizabeth, she was not pleased that she came unprepared to speak and told her she had to produce two speeches—one for the congressional suffrage committees, the other for the opening of the ICW. To that end, Susan later recalled, she "shut" Elizabeth in a room with "pen and pencil, kept a guard at the door, permitted no one to see her" until she produced her "usual magnificent address." Elizabeth's recollection of the incident was more benign: Yes, Susan had "ordered" her "to remain conscientiously" in her room and write the speeches. However, she was "permitted" to take carriage rides for an hour or two every day. And there was no guard at her door.

### "We the People"

The ICW opened on March 25, 1888, in the Albaugh's Opera House, a spacious and elegant auditorium decorated with evergreens and flowers. A large portrait of Lucretia Mott surrounded by smilax and lilies of the valley stood on the platform where Susan, Elizabeth, and other dignitaries sat on elegant sofas and chairs. Soft music played while the hall filled with delegates from every state and territory in the United States and from seven countries—England, France, Norway, Denmark, Finland, India, and Canada. Fifty-three different women's organizations, from religious to literary to political, sent representatives. For eight days, women and men packed the hall in what Elizabeth called a "splendid agitation." Susan presided. When she introduced Elizabeth to deliver her keynote speech, the audience stood, clapping, cheering, and waving their handkerchiefs, a gesture of affection and respect.

Susan was in high spirits; reporters described her as "gay-hearted, good-natured." Audiences loved her for her "brightness and wit." The press appreciated her "frank, plain, open, business-like way of doing everything connected with the council." If a speaker went on too long, Susan gave them a series of warnings. First she said, "Your time's about up, my dear." Next it was, "I guess you'll have to stop now; it's more than ten minutes." Then she tugged on the speaker's skirt; finally, she would rise and go stand beside the speaker, an action that inevitably got results.

The event culminated in hearings before the congressional committees on woman suffrage where Elizabeth masterfully articulated how denying woman suffrage violated the Constitution that the legislators had sworn to uphold. "Even the preamble of the Constitution is an argument for self-government—'We, the people,'" she pointed out. There is a provision—Article 1, Section 9, Clause 9—that prohibited the United States from granting titles of nobility, yet, Elizabeth charged, "You have granted titles of nobility to every male voter, making all men rulers . . . over all women." If the legislators did not "settle this question by wise legislation," Elizabeth predicted that "it will eventually be settled by violence."

After the convention, Elizabeth, who was homeless because she had sold her house in Tenafly, set off to visit her family and friends. She spent her seventy-third birthday with her son Gat and his wife, who lived on a farm in Iowa. That winter she spent at Maggie's home in Omaha, Nebraska, where she

185 ∾

delighted in taking a daily ride on a cable car that ran for nine miles "up hill and down" for a fare of fifteen cents. Neil, who also lived in Omaha, escorted her. Regardless of the weather, Elizabeth took an outside seat; Neil always sat inside with passengers who commented on the "queer old lady who rode outside in all kinds of wintry weather."

In late spring, Elizabeth relocated herself to Hempstead, Long Island, at the home of Gat and his wife, who had recently moved there from Iowa. Because she considered it her "mission to 'stir up'" conventional ideas, she agreed to speak to a group of literary and musical women who were staying at an elegant hotel in Coney Island, a nearby summer resort. "I said a good many radical things," she wrote in her diary, "but being well sugar-coated their deglutition was easy." While there, she attended several concerts. "And such music!" she wrote. "I was in the seventh heaven."

Susan, who had been lecturing and attending state suffrage conventions, came to speak to the club in August, and she and Elizabeth spent several days together. Before parting, they wrote the call for the upcoming convention of the National American Woman Suffrage Association (NAWSA), the new organization formed by the merger of the old rivals, the NWSA and AWSA. After years apart and two years of intense negotiations, the breach had finally been closed.

## 21

# "Under Your Thumb"

A MOUNTAIN OF WORK
1890–1895

ELIZABETH WAS OVERWHELMED BY THE DEMANDS facing her in early 1890: appearances before congressional committees, Susan's seventieth birthday celebration, and the first convention of the NAWSA, the united suffrage association. She was "tempted to escape from all the excitement" and go with her daughter Hattie, who was returning in February to England, after having spent several months in the United States. That idea prompted a "stormy correspondence" with Susan. Finally, Elizabeth capitulated. In a diary entry dated January 2, she wrote, "Susan commands me to come, and so I have finally written her: 'You will have me under your thumb the first of February."

Susan made good use of the time; on February 8, Elizabeth appeared before a congressional committee. After she spoke, Senator Zebulon Vance, the chairman, asked her:

"Would women be willing to go to war if they had the ballot?"

"We would decide first whether there should be war," Elizabeth replied. "You may be sure, Senator, that the influence of women will be against armed conflicts."

She went on to say that if there were a war, women would "do their share of work"; however, they [like men who served] would be "paid for their services and pensioned at the close of the war."

A week later, on the fifteenth, Susan turned seventy. Two hundred women and men feted her at a grand banquet in Washington, DC. The dining room at the Riggs House was festooned with tropical flowers, foliage, and American flags. Gifts were piled high on a table. Seventy pink carnations were presented to her. Toasts were made. Poems, telegrams, cablegrams, and letters were read, including one from Lucy Stone signed "I am very truly your co-worker."

Elizabeth gave the main address on the friendships of women: "If there is one part of my life which gives me more intense satisfaction than another, it is my friendship . . . with Susan B. Anthony." In response, Susan said, "I never could have done my work if I had not had this woman at my right hand."

Two days later, the executive committees of the rival suffrage organizations met to formalize their union and to elect officers for the NAWSA. Lucy's proposal that she and Elizabeth and Susan refuse to be elected president had been rejected by members who rallied around Susan. In a dramatic speech, Susan implored her supporters to vote for Elizabeth. The NWSA, she said, had stood for the "utmost liberty," for the "grand principle" of welcoming "representatives of all creeds and no creeds—Jew or Christian, Protestant or Catholic, Gentile or Mormon, pagan or atheists." If you embrace that idea, she said, "vote for Mrs. Stanton." And they did.

## *"All Hail and Congratulations"*

As the newly elected president of the NAWSA, Elizabeth gave the opening address at the historic convention. Scheduled to leave the next day for England, she told her audience that she considered it a "greater honor to go to England as the president of this association" than to go as an ambassador sent by the government. After her speech, she introduced Hattie, who said a few words. As they left the platform together, the audience erupted with cheers, applause, and a flurry of waving handkerchiefs. "Needless to say," Elizabeth wrote in her diary, "I was deeply touched by this hearty demonstration." That night Susan wrote in her diary that Hattie "showed herself worthy of her mother and her mother's life-long friend and co-worker. It was a proud moment for me."

Susan reigned over the rest of the convention. "'Saint Susan,' as her followers love to call her . . . was the life and soul of the meeting," wrote one reporter. A month later, she sat in the gallery of the House of Representatives and witnessed legislators debate about whether or not to admit the Territory of Wyoming into the Union as a state with woman suffrage in its constitution. Representative Joseph Washington from Tennessee was "unalterably opposed" because woman suffrage would "only end in unsexing and degrading the womanhood of America." After haggling for three days, the representatives voted, and Susan finally had the "inexpressible pleasure" of seeing the prosuffrage representatives prevail.

Next was the fight in the Senate. Senator John Reagan of Texas warned that woman suffrage in Wyoming would "make men of women." George Vest of Missouri declared it "a calamity . . . an absolute crime." Nonsense, replied the Wyoming legislators, who unequivocally declared in a telegram that they would "remain out of the Union a hundred years rather than come in without woman suffrage." That tipped the balance, and a majority of senators voted to admit Wyoming with woman suffrage intact.

By the time President William Henry Harrison signed the bill, Susan was in South Dakota campaigning in favor of an upcoming referendum on woman suffrage. She had just finished speaking when someone handed her a telegram with the news, and she read it to the crowd, who responded with mighty cheers. When the news reached Elizabeth in England, she wrote in her diary, "I cannot express the joy that this victory has brought to my soul." Forty-two years had passed since she had insisted on demanding woman suffrage at the Seneca Falls convention.

Local suffrage workers in South Dakota had pleaded for Susan to come and campaign. They were "very sanguine" for victory; she, however, was not, having had her "hopes dashed to the earth" in seven other state campaigns. Nevertheless, she went because, she said, "I shall not be cast down, even if voted down." It was a grueling experience—long rides in freight cars and in stagecoaches that creaked with every turn of the wheel over deeply rutted dirt roads, nights spent in primitive sod houses, meals that sometimes consisted of "sour bread, muddy coffee and stewed green grapes." The weather fluctuated from broiling heat to cold winds. Storms, including cyclones, were commonplace.

The referendum was defeated. When Susan returned to her sister Mary's house in Rochester, Mary remarked that it was the first time she realized that Susan was indeed seventy years old. Susan started to think that perhaps it was time to settle down and turn over some of the fieldwork to the eager young women who had joined the cause. Elizabeth supported the idea: "My advice to you, Susan, is to keep some spot you can call your own; where you can live and die in peace and be cremated in your own oven if you desire." Susan decided to move in with Mary.

For years, Mary, a retired school principal, and their mother Lucy had lived in the two-story house and kept a room for Susan, who visited when she could. After Lucy's death, Mary had rented out the first floor and lived on the second, with a room set aside for Susan. A devoted sister and suffrage worker, Mary welcomed Susan's decision; the renters moved out, and an army of carpenters, wallpaper hangers, and painters renovated the entire house. Susan's office was on the second floor, where framed photographs of her coworkers stood on her desk and hung on the wall. Elizabeth's picture was front and center. In June, when Susan officially moved in, three hundred people attended the housewarming party.

## "Might Have a Home Together"

At the same time that Susan "anchored" herself to one spot, Elizabeth, after eighteen months in Europe, decided to return to America. There had been so many changes during her absence. Her son Neil had died at the age of forty-eight. Her sister Tryphena was dead. Maggie's husband had died.

She left on August 23, 1891. Her last days were "filled with sadness" as she prepared to leave "those so dear to me," especially her granddaughters. Theodore and Hattie accompanied her to the ship. "It was very hard for us to say the last farewell," she recalled in her autobiography, "but we all tried to be as brave as possible." The question was: Where would she settle when she arrived?

Susan hoped that "they might have a home together and finish their lifework." Elizabeth's children thought otherwise. Instead they insisted that their mother share an apartment with two of her offspring who lived in New York City—Maggie, now studying physical education at Teachers College, Columbia University, and Robert, a lawyer and a bachelor. That possibility, Susan wrote in a heartfelt letter to Elizabeth, set off an "inner wail" in her "soul" because it meant that she could not "carry out the dream" of her life, which was to help Elizabeth collect and "carefully dissect" all her speeches and articles and publish her "best utterances" into a single volume.

Elizabeth's children prevailed. In early September, she, along with Maggie and Robert, moved into an eight-room penthouse, which Elizabeth dubbed her "eyrie." But by the end of the month, she was in Rochester. Susan had "summoned" her to pose for Adelaide Johnson, a sculptor who had already carved marble busts of Susan and Lucretia, which were to be displayed in the Women's Building at the upcoming World's Columbian Exposition, a spectacular event to celebrate the four hundredth anniversary of the arrival of Christopher Columbus. For four to five hours a day, Elizabeth sat still while Adelaide shaped a "huge mass of clay" into her "familiar facial outlines." Because Adelaide indulged her penchant for napping, Elizabeth reciprocated by "summoning up, when awake, the most intelligent and radiant expression that I could command."

In November, Elizabeth returned to New York City and celebrated her seventy-sixth birthday with her family. Both she and Susan were ready to slow down, but in stark contrast to the days when they were reviled, they were now revered and besieged with requests to speak. "I felt that my threescore and ten and two years added ought to excuse me," Susan wrote to suffrage workers in Kansas who were begging her to attend their convention. Finally, overwhelmed by their pleas, she wrote, "I will say yes, tuck on my coat and mittens," and come. Elizabeth addressed many local groups and wrote newspaper and magazine articles. For the upcoming NAWSA convention in Washington, DC, she wrote "The Solitude of Self," a speech many people considered a masterpiece (and still do today). Elizabeth wrote that she was also inclined "to think" it the "best thing" she had ever written, at least, she added, in her "declining years."

## *"That Day Is Passed for Me"*

The convention opened on January 16, 1892, and as the time drew near, Elizabeth informed Susan that Maggie and Robert were urging her to rest, to skip the convention; Susan would have to come and personally escort her to Washington, which is, of course, exactly what Susan did.

Elizabeth delivered her speech to the House and Senate judiciary committees and at the convention. "The point I wish plainly to bring before you on this occasion," she said, "is the individuality of each human soul. . . . Who, I ask you, can take, dare take, on himself, the rights, the duties, the responsibilities of another human soul?" The House committee had ten thousand copies of her speech printed and distributed throughout the country. Susan got a copy to give Elizabeth and wrote on it, "To Elizabeth Cady Stanton—This is pronounced the strongest and most unanswerable argument and appeal ever made by mortal pen or tongue for the full freedom and franchise of women."

It was Elizabeth's last convention. Although she was in good health, her age and her excessive weight made it difficult for her to "clamber up and down platforms, mount long staircases into halls and hotels, be squeezed in the crush at receptions, and do all the other things public life involves." In reflecting, she wrote, "That day is passed for me." Susan was elected to take her place as president of NAWSA. Anna Howard Shaw, a close ally of Susan and Elizabeth, was elected to take Susan's position as vice president at large. Elizabeth and Lucy Stone were made honorary presidents. (Lucy Stone died the following year.)

Elizabeth vowed to turn her attention to "general reading and thinking, to music, poetry, and novels." Soon, however, she found herself "wheedled into" accepting speaking engagements. Then there were Susan's demands; it was a presidential election year, and she needed speeches to deliver at the political conventions. "Susan is still on the war-path," Elizabeth noted in her diary. "All through this hot weather she has been following the political conventions. I wrote the addresses to all, and she read them." But to no avail. As they had in years past, the major political parties—Republicans and Democrats— ignored their appeals. In November, Grover Cleveland, a Democrat who was staunchly opposed to woman suffrage, was elected president.

Although the political system remained impervious to women's demands, a sea change had occurred in other arenas.

Colleges and universities had opened their doors (women comprised 40 percent of the total of college graduates), and employment opportunities had expanded to include clerical jobs and professional positions as doctors and lawyers. A new image of women was emerging in the popular culture—the New Woman, who challenged the traditional notion of a "separate sphere" for a "true woman," who exemplified religious piety, sexual purity, wifely submission, and motherly domesticity. A New Woman was bold; she believed she had choices—an education, a paid position, marriage, motherhood, public service. These women and sympathetic men were enthusiastic suffrage workers. They joined organizations and attended conventions. The "whole matter" of woman's rights, Susan told a reporter in 1892, was no longer "regarded with such horror and aversion" as it once was. As for Susan and Elizabeth, they had gone from being ridiculed to being lionized, with their friendship intact.

### *"She Came to Stir Me Up"*

A mountain of work awaited Susan in 1893, and she confided in her diary that she was "simply overwhelmed." The World's Columbian Exposition was set to open in Chicago, Illinois, where more than two hundred structures were built on the six-hundred-acre fairground. Exhibits from around the world included an eleven-ton cheese and a seventy-foot-high tower of electric lightbulbs. An amusement park featured the world's first Ferris wheel, a 250-foot-high steel structure with thirty-six cars that could hold sixty people (fully loaded, it carried 2,160 people). William "Buffalo Bill" Cody set up his Wild West show, an extravaganza with horsemen from different cultures—Turks, Gauchos, Arabs; performers such as Annie Oakley; an appearance by Sitting Bull and a band of braves; and Buffalo Bill's reenactments of his feats as a Pony Express rider.

Susan arranged for a series of congresses, or conferences, on a range of topics, to be held during the Exposition. In need of speeches, she spent a week with Elizabeth. "She came to stir me up to write papers for every Congress at the Exposition, which I did," Elizabeth noted in her diary.

They also weighed in on the controversial issue of whether or not the Fair should remain open on Sundays. Vocal religious leaders opposed the idea. Elizabeth and Susan argued it should be open for the enjoyment of people who work six days a week, as most did at that time. Elizabeth wrote articles and distributed leaflets. In a wrangle with a clergyman, Susan said she would allow a young man to go to Buffalo Bill's Wild West Show instead of church because "he'd learn more from Buffalo Bill than from listening to an intolerant sermon."

At Buffalo Bill's invitation, she attended a show. Riding his majestic horse up to her box, he swept off his cowboy hat and bowed to her while his horse reared up on its hind legs. Not to be outdone, Susan stood and bowed in return. The crowd loved it!

That fall in Colorado male voters were going to vote on a woman suffrage amendment. Carrie Chapman Catt, one of the new generation of suffrage workers, orchestrated a campaign that resulted in a resounding victory. "Now we have full suffrage in two states. My soul rejoices," Elizabeth noted in her diary. "But how slowly the world moves." Susan pronounced herself "the happiest woman in America."

In November, Susan went to New York City to celebrate Elizabeth's seventy-eighth birthday and make plans for the upcoming campaigns in two states—New York and Kansas, the same states for which they had waged hard-fought but unsuccessful campaigns in 1867. In New York, wealthy women, for the first time, actively advocated for suffrage, a development one newspaper called "an insurrection." Another first was the emergence of groups called "Remonstrants" and "Antis" comprised of women who opposed suffrage. Their claims ranged from the assertion that only an "insignificant minority" of women wanted to vote to the statement that a woman was "unfitted for the ballot because she was influenced by pity, passion and prejudice rather than by judgment."

"I seem to thrive on all this excitement," Elizabeth wrote in her diary. When Hattie arrived from England for a three-week visit in the "white heat" of the battle, she was "immediately pressed into service." By the time she left, Elizabeth noted, they had "scarcely seen each other."

But once again the "great battles" ended in failure. "I feel sad and disappointed at such contemptuous treatment," Elizabeth confided in her diary. "It is very humiliating for women . . . to have their sacred rights at the mercy of a masculine oligarchy."

California was the next battleground. A vote on a woman suffrage amendment was scheduled for the following year, and suffrage workers begged Susan to come to kick off their campaign. Before heading west, she spent a few weeks in Rochester, where she went to an antilynching lecture given by Ida B. Wells, a fearless black journalist. Ida was repeatedly and rudely interrupted by a man who identified himself as a Texan studying at the local theological seminary. Finally, he shouted, "If the negroes don't like it in the South, why don't they leave and go North?"

Jumping to her feet, Susan said, "I will tell you why; it is because they are treated no better in the North than they are in the South." Then she backed up her statement with a list of examples. After the lecture, Susan invited Ida to stay at her house. The next day, Susan instructed her stenographer to assist Ida with her correspondences. When the stenographer said she would not work for a black woman, Susan fired her.

## "No Limit, if Dead"

Anna Howard Shaw accompanied Susan to California. Suffrage workers in cities along the railroad route begged her to stop and spend time with them. Leaving on April 27, 1895, Susan was heralded by admirers in Warren, Ohio; Indianapolis, Indiana; Chicago, Illinois; St. Louis, Missouri; Denver, Colorado; Cheyenne, Wyoming; Salt Lake City, Utah; Reno, Nevada. On May 20, she was led into the Golden Gate Hall in San Francisco, onto a stage decorated with bamboo, palms, and all kinds of tropical foliage. There she was seated under a canopy of roses in a chair decorated with an array of fragrant flowers—lilies, roses, carnations, sweet peas. Then woman after woman came to her with more flowers until she was "literally buried under an avalanche of the choicest blossoms." While in California, she returned to Yosemite, at the age of seventy-five, riding into the valley on the back of a mule. In the Mariposa Big Tree Grove, a park commissioner officially named one of the trees "Susan B. Anthony."

After six weeks, Susan and Anna headed home, making stops along the way. In Chicago, a reporter who had interviewed Susan when she attended the World's Fair in 1893 described her as "thinner and more spiritual-looking . . . her transparent hands grasping the arms of her chair, her thin, hatchet face and white hair, with only her keen eyes flashing light and fire. . . . She recalls facts, figures, names and dates with unerring accuracy."

In July, Susan collapsed while giving a speech in Lakeside, Ohio. Word spread that she would not survive the night. A newspaper editor in Chicago sent instructions to a reporter on the scene to write "5,000 words if still living; no limit, if dead." Louisa Southworth, a longtime close friend to her and to Elizabeth, took Susan to her summer home to recover. "I never realized how desolate the world would be to me without you until I heard of your sudden illness," Elizabeth wrote to her. "Let me urge you with all the strength I have, and all the love I bear you, to stay at home and rest and save your precious self."

Susan's diary remained blank for many days, until finally she wrote, "On the mend." In November, she went to New York City for Elizabeth's eightieth birthday party, an extravaganza staged at the Metropolitan Opera House by the National Woman's Council, an organization that represented diverse groups of women and their interests, instead of focusing only on suffrage. This disappointed some suffrage workers but delighted Susan. From the beginning, she pointed out, Elizabeth had promulgated an array of ideas and issues. "Surely," she said, "for all classes of women, liberal, orthodox, Jewish, Mormon, suffrage and anti-suffrage, native and foreign, black and white—to unite in paying a tribute of respect to the greatest woman reformer, philosopher and statesman of the century will be the realization of Mrs. Stanton's most optimistic dream."

More than three thousand people packed the opulent opera house. Elizabeth was enthroned in a large red armchair bedecked with flowers under an arch of white carnations with *Stanton* spelled out in red carnations. Susan sat beside her and opened the event by paying tribute to the "pioneers"—Lucretia Mott, Martha Wright, Frederick Douglass—and reading some of the hundreds of congratulatory messages, including an eloquent one from Theodore Tilton, who was still living in Paris. "At the present day, every woman who seeks the legal custody of her children, or the legal control of her property; every woman who finds the doors of a college or a university opening to her; every woman who administers a post-office or a public library; every woman who enters upon a career of medicine, law or theology; every woman who teaches a school, or tills a farm, or keeps a shop; every one who drives a horse, rides a bicycle, skates at a rink, swims at a summer resort, plays golf or tennis in a public park, or even snaps a kodak [camera]; every such woman, I say, owes her liberty largely to yourself and to your earliest and bravest co-workers in the cause of woman's emancipation. So I send my greetings not to you alone, but also to the small remainder now living of your original bevy of noble assistants, among whom—first, last and always—has been and still continues to be your fit mate, chief counselor and executive right hand, Susan B. Anthony."

Elizabeth expressed her profound appreciation. Then telling the great audience that she was no longer "able to stand very long, nor talk loud enough," she said that she had asked Helen Potter, a young suffrage worker, to deliver her address. As always Elizabeth's intent was to stir up people. "Do all you can, *no matter what*, to get people to think," she had once written. This time she critiqued the restraints placed on women, particularly by religious institutions.

Susan had tried to get her to tone down her criticism because, she said, slowly but surely churches were adopting more liberal positions. But Elizabeth had refused to back down; it was imperative for women to question religious literature, such as the Bible, that was used to justify the elevation of men over women. However, she also made a point of acknowledging the men in the audience who "may feel that the new woman will crowd them entirely off the planet." Reassuring them, she said "they need not despair" because they will be looked after as long as they have mothers, sisters, wives, daughters, and sweethearts.

Shortly after the celebration, Elizabeth published *The Woman's Bible,* a book she had started working on while she was in England. "Church and state, priest and legislators, all political parties and religious denominations," she wrote in the introduction, "have alike taught that woman was made after man, of man, and for man, an inferior being, subject to man." She challenged this idea by scrutinizing and reinterpreting the parts in the Bible that referred to women. She had tried to enlist women to work on the project. Some initially agreed, but then backed out. Others helped her, including Clara Bewick Colby, Matilda Joslyn Gage, and the Reverend Olympia Brown. Susan refused, although she defended Elizabeth's right to write her commentaries on scriptures: "Women have just as good a right to interpret and twist the Bible to their own advantage as men have always twisted it and turned it to theirs," she told a newspaper reporter. But, as a strategy for achieving suffrage, she thought that it was foolhardy to stir up a controversy over orthodox religious beliefs.

As a Quaker, Susan belonged to a liberal religion that had always allowed women to preach and participate in governance. The Bible was a historical document, not the infallible word of God. She maintained that once women were enfranchised, conservative churches and clergymen would adopt more liberal interpretations. "Get political rights first and religious bigotry will melt like dew before the morning sun," she wrote to Elizabeth. Elizabeth vehemently disagreed. Women, she said, had to first free their minds.

## 22

# "To Stir You and Others Up"

### FREE EXPRESSION
### 1896–1900

As Susan feared, *The Woman's Bible* ignited a firestorm of criticism. "I could cry a heap every time I read or think [about it]," she wrote to Clara Bewick Colby. As for Elizabeth herself, Susan admitted to Clara, "She thinks I have gone over to the enemy—so counts my judgment worth nothing more than that of any other narrow-souled body." But ever loyal, Susan concluded, "I shall love and honor her to the end—whether or not her *Bible* pleases me or not. So I hope she will do for me."

Susan's loyalty was sorely tested in January 1896 at the annual NAWSA Convention. Women who were "especially near and dear to her" introduced a resolution disavowing the "so-called Woman's Bible." Outraged, Susan expressed her indignation at their repudiation of "the right of individual opinion for every member."

Throughout the long fight for woman's rights—begun before many of the new members were born—she and Elizabeth had fought for that principle. "When our platform becomes too narrow for people of all creeds and of no creeds, I myself can not stand upon it," she declared. "You would better not begin resolving against individual action or you will find no limit. This year it is Mrs. Stanton; next year it may be I or one of yourselves, who will be the victim." She warned delegates that a vote for the resolution was a "vote of censure upon a woman who is without a peer in intellectual and statesmanlike ability; one who has stood for half a century the acknowledged leader of progressive thought and demand in regard to all matters pertaining to the absolute freedom of women." By a vote of fifty-three to forty-one, the resolution passed. Susan was disconsolate.

After the convention, she visited Elizabeth, who was "thoroughly indignant over the petty action of the convention" and insistent that they both resign their positions, Susan as president and Elizabeth as honorary president. Returning home, Susan spent "three weeks of agony of soul, with scarcely a night of sleep." Her sister Mary, who had voted against the resolution, felt that for her own sake Susan should resign, however, for the good of the organization she should remain.

Still "sick at heart," Susan finally made her decision. Informing Elizabeth, she wrote, "No, my dear, instead of my resigning and leaving those half-fledged chickens without any mother, I think it my duty and the duty of yourself and all the liberals to be at the next convention and try to reverse this miserable, narrow action." Respecting Susan's reasoning, Elizabeth agreed not to resign her position. (The action was never reversed.)

Their friendship survived the trauma; their bond was indissoluble, their loyalty transcendent.

## "Is It Not Time?"

Two states were holding elections on woman suffrage amendments in 1896—Idaho and California. "Won't it be a magnificent feather in our cap if we get both California and Idaho into the fold this year?" Susan wrote to Carrie Chapman Catt, who was working on the Idaho campaign. Susan had returned to California, having succumbed to repeated pleas from advocates to come.

"O, that I had you by my side," she wrote to Elizabeth, "what a team we would make!" Every day she sent her newspapers with reports of the campaign.

"I feel at times as if I should fly to your help," Elizabeth replied.

But, of course, she could not; her great weight limited her mobility, and she was losing her eyesight. "A great loss," she confided to her diary, "for me whose chief pleasure is reading." To compensate, she hired a young woman to read to her: "I like to sandwich the solid [nonfiction books] with the light [novels]."

Fortunately she could see enough to write. As usual, she was juggling multiple projects—an article supporting women's right to ride bicycles, the new craze; volume two of *The Woman's Bible*; and her autobiography. For the latter, she playfully asked Susan to reveal a romance from her younger days so that she could "weave a sentimental chapter entitled, for instance, 'The Romance of Susan B. Anthony's Younger Days.' How all the daily papers would jump at that!"

Victory seemed possible in California, until ten days before the election, when the Liquor Dealers' League launched a scare campaign that women voters would pass laws banning the sale of beer and whiskey. That shifted the momentum, and the amendment was defeated; the loss was tempered by the news of a victory in Idaho. Susan returned to Rochester and began planning for the upcoming NAWSA Convention to be held in Des Moines, Iowa. As always, she expected Elizabeth to produce "an argument, strong resolution, and tributes to those of our band who have died during the present year."

In her diary, Elizabeth complained, "One would think I were a machine; that all I had to do was to turn a crank and thoughts on any theme would bubble up like water." To Susan, she wrote, "Dear Susan, is it not time that some of our younger coadjutors do the bubbling? The fact is that I am tired bubbling on one subject." But, as usual, Elizabeth wrote what Susan requested for the convention.

In late January 1897, Susan boarded a train for Des Moines on a day when snow was piled high and the temperature was fifteen degrees below zero. The weather was even worse in Iowa—a heavy blizzard and twenty-four degrees below zero. Braving those conditions, sixty-three delegates from twenty states attended the convention. Susan presided. "It is not difficult for one who saw Miss Anthony for the first time to understand why she is so well beloved by her associates," a reporter wrote. She was the "most earnest worker of them all . . . their leader . . . counsellor and friend . . . [who was] not to be daunted by any obstacle."

Susan told the gathering that "the year 1896 witnessed greater successes than any" since the first convention in Seneca Falls, New York, in 1848. Utah had become a state with woman suffrage in its constitution. Male voters in Idaho had voted for a woman suffrage amendment to the state constitution. Equally important, she said, when opponents challenged that victory, the three male justices on the Idaho Supreme Court unanimously ruled in favor of the amendment. This, Susan said, was "the first time in the history of judicial decisions upon the enlargement of woman's rights, civil and political, that a court had issued a favorable ruling." To educate younger suffrage workers, Susan reviewed the long history of judicial decisions that had restricted woman's progress, including the Supreme Court ruling in *Myra Bradwell v. Illinois*, in which the court upheld a decision by the Illinois Supreme Court that denied a woman the right to practice law. In explaining his vote, Justice Joseph P. Bradley wrote that women's "natural and proper timidity and delicacy" makes them "unfit" for "many of the occupations of civil life. . . . The paramount destiny and mission of women are to fulfill the noble and benign office of wife and mother. This is the law of the Creator."

## "Tired of Begging"

That spring both Susan and Elizabeth were immersed in writing projects. In Rochester, the attic in Susan's house was lined with boxes, bags, and trunks of material—reports, receipts, memorabilia, diaries, notebooks, legal papers, handbills, leaflets, petitions. Bundles of documents, newspapers, magazines, scrapbooks, and letters were stored on shelves. There, with the help of two young women, Susan and Ida Husted Harper, a journalist who was writing Susan's biography, worked together sorting through and organizing the records of Susan's extraordinary life and the fight for woman's rights.

Elizabeth could still write, but she could not read what she had written—someone else did that for her. Undaunted, she was hard at work finishing volume two of *The Woman's Bible* and her autobiography.

Periodically Susan took a break to give a speech. In late March, she reluctantly agreed to testify on behalf of a woman suffrage amendment before a committee of the New York State Legislature. Never again, she declared afterward, "would she stoop to plead her cause before one of these committees," which were now populated by the sons and grandsons of men she and Elizabeth had appealed to in previous years. She "was tired of begging for liberty from men not half her age and with not a hundredth part of her knowledge of State and national affairs."

In June, Susan and Ida went to Auburn, New York, to spend a few days with Elizabeth and Maggie, who were staying with Eliza Wright Osborne, the daughter of their old friend Martha Wright. During the day, they took long carriage rides, walked through the lovely gardens around Eliza's elegant home, and entertained friends who lived nearby. In the evening, Ida read them sections from Susan's biography. Then sitting side-by-side, Susan and Elizabeth would reminisce.

"It was a rare and sacred occasion," Ida later wrote, "and those who were present ever will cherish the memory of those two grand pioneers . . . both having given to the world fifty years of unremitting service, and yet both as strong in mind, keen in satire, as brimming with cheerfulness, as in those early days when they set about to revolutionize the prejudice and customs of the ages."

From Eliza's, Elizabeth and Maggie moved on to spend the rest of the summer with cousin Libby, who lived in Lochland, her mansion in nearby Geneva, New York. While there, Elizabeth noted in her diary that she gave several speeches. "The first one," she wrote, "at a great picnic" attended by a thousand people, where she "held forth for an hour and a half." Satisfied with reports that everyone could hear her, she wrote, "Though my eyes may be failing, my voice seems to hold its own."

## *"My Steadfast Friend"*

That fall, Susan began reminding Elizabeth that the next convention in 1898 marked the fiftieth anniversary of the first woman's rights convention at Seneca Falls, of which she was "the prime mover and the soul, young as you were." For the occasion, Susan told her to write four papers—two for congressional committees, one for the opening of the convention, another for the closing ceremony. "Now, my dear," Susan assured her, "this is positively the last time I am ever going to put you on the rack and torture you to make the speech or speeches of your life."

"I cannot go on to Washington, as Susan urges," Elizabeth wrote in her diary. "I am really getting too old for such things— nor can I write four papers."

But she could write two. In one titled "The Significance and History of the Ballot," she proposed that Congress pass a law for "educated suffrage," the requirement that voters be able to read and write English. This was a dramatic shift from the "universal suffrage" that she and Susan had always advocated and that Susan still did. Elizabeth, however, now adopted "educated suffrage" as a tactic that would address the commonly expressed opinion that women were "too ignorant" to be allowed to vote. It would also deal with the huge influx of immigrant men, whom she viewed as uneducated and easily bribed by antisuffrage groups to vote against woman suffrage. Susan, of course, had the power to refuse to read Elizabeth's speech, but, as always committed to the free expression of ideas, she did not.

In her last diary entry for 1897, Elizabeth noted that both volume two of *The Woman's Bible* and her autobiography, *Eighty Years & More: Reminiscences 1815–1897*, were in print: "I am as much relieved as if I had given birth to twins." She dedicated *Eighty Years* to Susan, "my steadfast friend for half a century." Writing to Susan, she said, "The current of our lives has run in the same channel so long it cannot be separated, and my book is as much your story, as I doubt not, yours is mine."

By the end of January 1898, Elizabeth had "practically finished" her two papers, but she was still fending off Susan, who was "urging" her to attend. "I shall not go," Elizabeth wrote in her diary, "as my eyes grow dimmer and dimmer and my legs weaker and weaker." Happily, she noted, "My brain seems as strong as ever."

A few weeks later, on her way to the convention, Susan stopped to visit Elizabeth to pick up her papers and, perhaps, personally escort her. But Elizabeth refused; Susan would have to celebrate the fiftieth anniversary of Seneca Falls without her.

The convention opened on February 13. A small, round mahogany table stood in the center of the stage. Two flags were draped over it—the American flag and the silk suffrage flag with four golden stars representing the states with full woman suffrage: Wyoming, Utah, Colorado, and Washington. It was the table at which Elizabeth had written the "Declaration of Rights and Sentiments." Originally the table had stood in Mary Ann M'Clintock's house; she passed it on to Elizabeth, who gave it to Susan as a house-warming gift when she settled down in Rochester.

It was Susan's idea to bring the historic table to the convention. She also had copies of the Declaration distributed to the delegates. "You will notice," she told them in her presidential address, "that those demands which were ridiculed and denounced from one end of the country to the other, all have now been conceded but the suffrage, and that in four States."

Susan presided over the six-day convention wearing a red shawl that had become her trademark. "Spring is not heralded in Washington by the approach of the robin red-breast but by the appearance of Miss Anthony's red shawl," a newspaper reporter noted. When she suddenly appeared at a session wearing a white shawl, reporters who were sitting at the press table sent her a note: "No red shawl, no report." Reading it out loud, she laughingly replied that she would fetch it from her hotel.

### *"Wake Up and Raise Your Voices"*

As they had many times before, a distinguished group of women testified before two congressional committees, which received them politely but ignored their requests to recommend passage of the Sixteenth Amendment. Elizabeth's daughter Hattie was one of the women. Hattie and thirteen-year-old Nora now spent seven months of the school year in New York City. They lived with Elizabeth, Bob, and Maggie in their new spacious apartment on West Ninety-fourth Street. Nora rode the trolley to the Horace Mann School, a coeducational, experimental school, which was part of Teachers College, Columbia University. She called Elizabeth "her Queenmother" and embraced her as the "guide and philosopher" who taught her "the facts of life," including the "history of woman and of her long subjection."

Foreign affairs dominated the news in 1898 as the United States government sought to increase its influence through a policy of expansionism, a course that Elizabeth supported and Susan opposed. Before the year ended, the government had annexed Hawaii as the Territory of Hawaii. It had fought and won a short war, the Spanish-American War, and gained control over Puerto Rico, Guam, and the Philippine Islands. Cuba won its independence, although within a few years the United States gained a measure of legal control over Cuba. Ever vigilant about woman's rights, Susan and Elizabeth were outraged when Congress proposed to restrict the vote to men in these new areas. "I really believe I shall explode," Susan wrote to Clara Bewick Colby, "if some of you young women don't wake up and raise your voices in protest . . . I wonder if when I am under the sod—or cremated and floating in the air—I shall have to stir you and others up. How can you not be all on fire?"

## *"Her Time May Be Shorter"*

In June, Susan was bound for London to attend the International Council of Women meeting, the organization she and Elizabeth had first convened in 1888. She spent several days in New York saying good-bye to Elizabeth. Earlier in the year, Elizabeth had been very ill until she had summoned Dr. Caroline Cabot, who prescribed the following regime: drink beef tea, glycerine, and whisky; inhale pine steam; take two kinds of pills throughout the day; and soak in a very hot bath. The next day, Elizabeth reported in her diary, "I am as agile as a grasshopper."

Susan returned in August and spent a week with Elizabeth and her cousin Libby in Geneva, New York. Afterward, Susan confided in a letter to Clara, "Though she may outlive me by years . . . her time may be shorter than mine."

Elizabeth was also thinking about mortality. Her sisters were in "failing health." In her diary, she quoted the words of the old hymn describing heaven as the "land of pure delight, where saints immortal reign." However, she wrote, "I must confess that I am in no hurry to go there. Life has been, and still is, very sweet to me, and there are many things I desire to do before I take final leave of this planet."

On her eighty-fourth birthday on November 12, 1899, Elizabeth noted that she received "a warm telegram from my dear Susan, and a resolution of 'respect and gratitude' from the Federation of Women's Clubs." She was in good health. Although her mobility was limited by her bulk and her sight grew dimmer, she noted that her "intellectual vision grows clearer." Recently a doctor had told her she had cataracts on both eyes. Hattie accompanied her to the doctor's office and later reported, "She accepted his diagnosis without a word. When we were seated in our carriage, I laid my hand on hers. She said, as if to herself, 'And both eyes.' She never referred to the matter again." In her diary, however, Elizabeth noted in a later entry that her friends in England had told her Queen Victoria had a cataract but refused to let surgeons remove it: "I suppose she feels just as I do—that so long as one can see fairly well, it is better to wait."

# 23

# "Oh, This Awful Hush"

## THE END
## 1900–1906

At the close of the nineteenth century, Susan decided to put the NAWSA into younger hands. She planned to announce her resignation at the annual convention that was scheduled to meet in Washington, DC, February 8 through 14, 1900. On the fifteenth, she would turn eighty years old. She asked Elizabeth what she thought "ought to be done" at the upcoming meeting.

Elizabeth's to-do list had five items: one dealt with the male oligarchy that was established in Hawaii; two focused on discrimination against working women. In another, she urged a return to the principle that she and Susan held dear: a broad-based association—"At the inauguration of our movement," she explained, "we numbered in our Declaration of Rights eighteen grievances covering the whole range of human experiences. On none of these did we talk with bated breath. . . . In response to our radicalism, the bulwarks of the enemy fell as never since. . . . But at present our association has so narrowed its platform for reasons of policy and propriety that our conventions have ceased to point the way." Finally, she said that annual conventions should be held in Washington in order to "examine intelligently the bills before Congress which nearly or remotely affect the women of the nation."

Susan embraced all of Elizabeth's ideas, except one; the time had passed for the association to reclaim its broad-based heritage. Most of the younger members shunned radicalism; their lives were so different from Elizabeth's and Susan's. "The hardships of the last half-century are forgotten," Susan explained. Elizabeth concurred. Many women, she observed, "seem to know nothing of the . . . progressive steps made by their own sex in the last fifty years."

The convention was fraught with emotion as Susan relinquished her role. "I am not retiring now because I feel unable, mentally or physically, to do the necessary work," she told the delegates, "but because I want to see . . . you all at work while I am alive, so I can scold you if you do not do it well." Carrie Chapman Catt, Susan's choice, was selected to succeed her. Susan was elected an honorary president, a position Elizabeth still held. "You have moved me up higher," Susan told the delegates. "I always did stand by Elizabeth Cady Stanton . . . and I am glad to be there again."

### "Your Lives Have Proved"

A gala event was held to celebrate Susan's birthday. Her old friend John Hutchinson, who had been singing protest songs for fifty years, sang. Frederick Douglass's grandson Joseph played a violin solo. Coralie Franklin Cook, a professor at Howard University and founder of the Colored Women's League, spoke, as did representatives from the suffrage states. Eighty children, one by one, laid a single rose on her lap.

Elizabeth was unable to attend, but Hattie came and conveyed her mother's birthday greetings. Then she gave a tribute to Susan and Elizabeth: "The friendship of you two women will remain a precious memory in the world's history, unforgotten and unforgettable. Your lives have proved not only that women can work strenuously together without jealousy, but that they can be friends in times of sunshine and peace, of stress and storm."

Now Susan had time to undertake a project she dreaded but was determined to complete—volume four of the *History of Woman Suffrage.* She recruited Ida Husted Harper, who had written her biography, as a coeditor. Elizabeth reviewed material and wrote a steady stream of letters. "As I was wide awake last night for hours when I should have been asleep, I spent the time in thinking of you and your work," she typically wrote before going on for pages offering cogent suggestions and advice.

In September, Susan discovered that the University of Rochester was about to back out of its promise to admit female students. Two years earlier, when she and Elizabeth had raised the issue, the school finally agreed to open its doors, but for a price—$50,000 to pay for new facilities.

### *"Let the Girls In"*

A committee of local women managed to raise $42,000, but that was it. However, they did not notify Susan about the shortfall until the evening before the deadline day. Having long dreamed of opening the doors of the university, Susan propelled herself into action. Mary planned to donate $2,000 once the school was coeducational. "Give it now," Susan insisted. "Don't wait or the girls may never be admitted."

Then she went out on a particularly hot day to canvass business owners, rich people, office workers, everyone she knew. By late afternoon, she appeared before the trustees with pledges worth $8,000, but the officials rejected one pledge of $2,000 because the man was very ill and might die before he paid. Temporarily foiled but as determined as ever, Susan pledged her life insurance to make up the difference. "They let the girls in," she wrote that night in her diary.

News of her triumph spread. The headline across two columns in the newspaper read, "Opens Its Doors to Young Women. Rochester University Henceforth a Coeducational Institution." The subheading was "Last $8,000 Needed for the $50,000 Endowment Fund Raised by Susan B. Anthony Yesterday. What Seemed a Hopeless Task Accomplished by her Energy and Courage."

Susan's heroic effort was costly. Two days later, she had a stroke. For a week, she could not speak. For a month, she needed constant care. Elizabeth wrote to Mary to keep Susan at home: "There is no necessity for her gallivanting off to the ends of the earth." Mary assured her that Susan "would stay at home & rest." That, Elizabeth replied, was "a rational idea, we all sing in chorus 'A-MEN!'"

In early October, Susan was finally able to go for a carriage ride and asked to be driven through the campus. That night, she wrote in her diary, "I thought with joy, 'These are no longer forbidden grounds to the girls of our city.'" But she worried, "Will the vows made to them be kept? Will they have an equal chance? All promises well but the fulfillment is yet to be seen."

She recovered her mental acuity and speech, but not her extraordinary stamina and resilience. That was gone, her doctor said, and warned her that she could have another stroke at any time. She should rest, get fresh air, avoid extremes in temperatures and large crowds. His advice sounded worse than death to Susan; she preferred to "die in the harness" doing her life's work. Mary understood and accepted Susan's decision to attend the Woman Suffrage Bazaar in New York City.

A huge fund-raising event at Madison Square Garden, the bazaar ran from December 3 through 8, 1900. Sale items were displayed in decorated booths—pecans from Louisana, cradles made of hundred-year-old mahogany from Maryland, and buckeye nuts from Ohio that were advertised as "a sure cure for rheumatism. Carry one in your pocket." A peace pageant was held one evening. Dressed in costumes from many countries, participants carrying olive branches marched around the hall, then laid the branches at the feet of the Goddess of Liberty, played by Alva Halstead of Brooklyn, New York.

Susan spent the week there. It was everything the doctor warned against—chilly, crowded, stuffy, overstimulating—but she appeared herself to the hundreds of people who lined up to shake her hand. Elizabeth had wanted to go, too, but Maggie and Bob had "persuaded not to do so." She spent her days "writing articles, long and short . . . in a word," she noted in her diary, "I am always busy, which is perhaps the chief reason why I am always well."

## *"Think of It!"*

The next annual NAWSA Convention opened on May 30, 1901, in Minneapolis, Minnesota. Susan was there. As always, she had tried to get Elizabeth to come. Elizabeth replied that she thought they "had earned the right to sit in our rocking-chairs and think and write." In her diary, she added, "But it

occurred to me later that that would be purgatory for Susan!"
Elizabeth did, however, write an address, titled "The Duty of
Church to Women at This Hour," to be read at the convention,
which Susan knew would undoubtedly offend conservative delegates. Nevertheless, her loyalty to Elizabeth "was so strong . . .
and the memory of her great service to the cause of woman was
so faithful, that, in the face of much opposition, she had the address in full presented to the convention." Another pioneer, their
old friend Olympia Brown, read it.

Susan spent the summer resting and attending a few events. In
the fall, she spent several weeks with Sarah J. Eddy, whose grandfather, Francis Jackson, and mother, Eliza Jackson Eddy, had once
willed generous sums of money for Susan to use for the cause. An
accomplished artist, Sarah had been wanting to paint Susan's portrait. They got together at Sarah's summer home in Bristol Ferry,
Rhode Island, overlooking Narragansett Bay. Susan reveled in the
beauty of her surroundings—"magnificent view, ocean and islands, hills and autumn foliage." Sarah completed two paintings: a
bust portrait and a full-length profile of Susan with a group of
children presenting her with roses, as they had at her eightieth
birthday celebration.

Elizabeth spent several months with her family at Warden-
clyffe, Long Island, near where the famed inventor Nikola Tesla
had just built a laboratory and transmitting tower. "He said to
me the other day: 'It is possible to telegraph to all parts of the
earth without wires.' Think of it! Where will the wonders of
science end?" Elizabeth wrote in her diary.

## "Shall I See You Again?"

The two old friends rarely saw each other, but they regularly
corresponded. Elizabeth remained a prolific writer. Susan

continued to attend suffrage events. In February 1902, she started out in a fierce blizzard for the annual convention of the NAWSA in Washington, DC. After waiting at the station for two hours, she boarded a train that "crept along with a snow plow in front" of it. The NAWSA was also hosting the first meeting of the International Woman Suffrage Conference. A thousand people from around the world attended—the United States, Russia, Chile, Norway, Australia, Sweden, Germany, and England. Elizabeth sent a paper on "Educated Suffrage." As always, even though she did not agree with her position, Susan insisted on having it read by Clara Bewick Colby.

In May, Susan spent a week with Elizabeth, who insisted that she stay at her apartment in a room that had been vacated by someone in the family. It was good to be there, Susan wrote in her diary, "though Mrs. Stanton does not feel quite as she used to. We have grown a little apart since not so closely associated as of old." The issue between them was Elizabeth's attitude toward religion. "She thinks the Church is now the enemy to fight," Susan wrote, "and feels worried that I stay back with children—as she says—instead of going ahead with her." In June, she spent another day with Elizabeth. Elizabeth's "wonderful brain was still strong," but her heart was not. Susan said goodbye with tears in her eyes.

"Shall I see you again?" she asked her beloved friend.

"Oh, yes," Elizabeth replied. "If not here, then in the hereafter, if there is one, and if there isn't we shall never know it."

That fall Hattie wrote to Susan urging her to come for Elizabeth's eighty-seventh birthday because she was "sure there won't be another." Susan had already planned to come, and in anticipation, she wrote a letter to Elizabeth.

*It is fifty-one years since we first met and we have been busy through every one of them, stirring up the world to recognize the rights of women. . . . We little dreamed when we began this contest . . . that half a century later we would be compelled to leave the finish of the battle to another generation of women. But our hearts are filled with joy to know that they enter upon this task equipped with a college education, with business experience, with the freely admitted right to speak in public—all of which were denied to women fifty years ago. . . . These strong, courageous, capable, young women will take our place and complete our work. There is an army of them where we were but a handful.*

Two weeks before Elizabeth's birthday, Hattie sent a telegram to Susan with this news: "Mother passed away at three o'clock." Susan was devastated. For hours she sat alone in her study, where Elizabeth's picture hung on the wall. In the evening, Mary coaxed her downstairs to eat some supper. A reporter was waiting to get her reaction. She spoke to him of their "unbroken friendship" and how they "never believed any talk of disloyalty of one to the other." That although they "did not agree on every point," they always agreed "on the central point of woman suffrage." The best parts of their lives together, she said, were "the days when the struggle was the hardest and the fight the thickest; when the whole world was against us and we had to stand the closer to each other; when I would go to her home and help with the children and the housekeeping through the day and then we would sit up far into the night preparing our ammunition and getting ready to move on the enemy."

Susan left the next day to attend Elizabeth's funeral. It was a private event in her apartment. "Oh, this awful hush," Susan wrote to Ida Harper. "It seems impossible that voice is stilled which I have loved to hear for fifty years. Always I have felt that I must have Mrs. Stanton's opinion of things before I knew where I stood myself. I am all at sea—but the laws of nature are still going on. . . . What a world it is, it goes on and on just the same no matter who lives or who dies!"

During the week that Elizabeth would have turned eighty-seven, Susan was in Auburn, New York, with Eliza Wright Osborne, the niece of Lucretia Mott and daughter of Martha Wright. Elizabeth's cousin Libby and a few other friends joined her to share their memories.

## "Press Forward"

A few days before Elizabeth died, she had written a letter to President Theodore Roosevelt asking him to advocate for woman suffrage. Susan followed up on Elizabeth's appeal. "Dear Mr. Roosevelt, let us not watch and wait in vain." But, like all the presidents before him and most elected officials, Roosevelt did nothing. At the NAWSA Convention in 1903 in New Orleans, Louisiana, Susan repeated Elizabeth's exhortation: "The pioneers have brought you within sight of the promised land. . . . Go ahead; press forward!"

The following year, the NAWSA Convention met in Washington, DC, and, as she had since 1869, Susan testified before a congressional committee. "We have waited," she reminded them. "How long will this injustice, this outrage, continue?" In May, at the age of eighty-four, she went to Berlin, Germany, to attend the International Council of Women. In 1905, the NAWSA Convention was scheduled to be held in Portland, Oregon. Refusing to worry about her health, Susan decided to attend. "Why not this one?" she replied to a concerned friend. Mary went with her. They met up in Chicago with a hundred delegates and traveled across the country in special train cars.

In Portland, Susan was given a hotel room with a spectacular view of Mt. Hood, a sight that thrilled her. During her stay, she participated in the dedication of a bronze statue of Sacajawea. Created by Alice Cooper, it was the first statue erected of a woman "because of deeds of daring." Susan told the audience, "Let men remember the part that women" have played and vote for woman suffrage.

In 1906, the NAWSA Convention was held in Baltimore, Maryland. Susan arrived with a bad cold and struggled to attend the meetings. At the final gathering, she told the delegates, "The fight must not cease; you must see that it does not stop." A few days later, a birthday celebration was held for her in Washington, DC. When a letter was read from President Theodore Roosevelt congratulating her on her eighty-sixth birthday, she exclaimed, "I would rather have President Roosevelt say one word to Congress in favor of amending the Constitution to give women the suffrage than to praise me endlessly!"

Susan was exhausted, but she rallied to express her gratitude for the celebration. "There have been others also just as true and devoted to the cause—I wish I could name every one—but with such women consecrating their lives—failure is impossible."

Those words—"failure is impossible"—were the last words Susan B. Anthony spoke in public. On March 13, 1906, she died at home in Rochester, New York. The next day, Elizabeth's daughter Maggie wrote to Mary, "So dear Susan has gone and left you! I wonder if she and mother are walking hand in hand in the great beyond? A long time ago a sculptor here in New York made a cast of mother's and Susan's hands clasped. I got it out yesterday, threw a yellow silk kerchief over a pillow and laid the hands thereon. Then I got out numerous pictures that I have and placed them around. . . . In front of this group I stood a vase of yellow flowers. I quite felt with all these pictures and with the clasped hands that both mother's and Susan's souls were with me in my little home."

# Epilogue

SUSAN WAS RIGHT ABOUT FAILURE BEING IMPOSSIBLE, but it took another fourteen years before a woman suffrage amendment was added to the Constitution of the United States, on August 26, 1920. By then three other amendments had been ratified, and so the Sixteenth Amendment that Elizabeth and Susan fought for ended up being the Nineteenth Amendment. It reads "The right of citizens of the United States to vote shall not be denied or abridged by the United States or by any State on account of sex."

A year later, on Susan's birthday, February 15, 1921, an unveiling ceremony was held in the United States Capitol Rotunda for the *Portrait Monument to Lucretia Mott, Elizabeth Cady Stanton, and Susan B. Anthony,* sculpted by Adelaide Johnson (the sculptor Elizabeth and Susan posed for in Rochester in the 1890s). Carved from an eight-ton block of marble from Carrara, Italy, the massive monument was quickly relegated to the Crypt, a much less visible space, where tour guides dubbed it "Three ladies in a tub." In 1997, after a passionate grassroots effort, the monument was relocated to the Rotunda.

# CHRONOLOGY

1815      Elizabeth Cady is born in Johnstown, New York, November 12.

1820      Susan Brownell Anthony is born in Adams, Massachusetts, February 15.

1833      Elizabeth graduates from the Troy Female Seminary.

1839      Susan becomes a teacher in New Rochelle, New York.

1840      Elizabeth marries Henry Stanton. They travel to London, England, for the World's Anti-Slavery Convention, where she meets Lucretia Mott.

1842      Elizabeth gives birth to her first child.

1846–49  Susan teaches in Canajoharie, New York, where she joins the Daughters of Temperance.

1848      Elizabeth, along with Lucretia Mott, Martha Coffin Wright, Mary Ann M'Clintock, and Jane Hunt, organize the first woman's rights convention, which takes place on July 19–20 in Seneca Falls, New York. Elizabeth authors the Declaration of Sentiments. A second woman's rights convention is held in Rochester, New York, on August 2, which Susan's parents and sister Mary attend.

1851      Amelia Bloomer introduces Elizabeth and Susan in Seneca Falls, New York.

1852      Susan and Elizabeth found the Women's New York State Temperance Society. Elizabeth is elected the president. The following year, they leave the organization. Susan attends her first woman's rights convention.

1854    Susan campaigns for woman's rights throughout New York.
Elizabeth gives her "Address to the Legislature of New York." Susan has fifty thousand copies printed for distribution.

1856    Susan becomes an agent of the American Anti-Slavery Society.

1859    Elizabeth gives birth to her seventh and last child. She has five sons and two daughters, all of whom live to be adults, an unusual occurrence at that time.

1860    Susan and other woman's rights activists lobby the New York Legislature, which passes the Married Women's Property Act.
Elizabeth addresses joint committees of the New York Legislature.

1861    Susan and Elizabeth undertake a "No Compromise with Slaveholders" lecture tour.
The Civil War begins.

1863    Elizabeth and Susan organize the Women's Loyal National League to agitate for the end of slavery.

1866    Elizabeth and Susan help found the American Equal Rights Association, which advocates for universal suffrage.
Elizabeth is a self-nominated candidate for Congress.

1867    Elizabeth and Susan campaign for woman suffrage in New York and Kansas; both campaigns fail.

1868    Susan and Elizabeth begin publishing the *Revolution.*
Elizabeth and Susan split with some of their friends and allies over the Fourteenth Amendment.

1869    Elizabeth and Susan found the National Woman Suffrage Association (NWSA) to fight for a woman suffrage amendment, the Sixteenth, to the United States Constitution.

Lucy Stone founds the rival American Woman Suffrage Association (AWSA) to focus on state-by-state campaigns to win woman suffrage.

Elizabeth begins crisscrossing the country on lecture tours.

Women win suffrage in the Wyoming Territory.

1870    Susan sells the *Revolution* for one dollar and joins the lecture circuit.

Women win suffrage in the Utah Territory. The right is lost in 1887 and restored in 1896.

1871    Elizabeth and Susan travel together to California on a lecture tour.

1872    Susan registers to vote on the grounds of the Fourteenth and Fifteenth amendments. She is arrested and charged with "unlawfully" voting.

1873    Susan is tried and found guilty of illegal voting.

1875    The United States Supreme Court rules in *Minor v. Happersett* that the United States Constitution does not give women the right to vote.

1880    Elizabeth and Susan retire from the lecture circuit and focus on writing their *History of Woman Suffrage*, along with Matilda Joslyn Gage.

1881    *History of Woman Suffrage*, volume I, is published. Volumes II and III will follow in 1882 and 1886.

1882    Elizabeth goes to Europe to visit two of her children and her first grandchild. While there, she connects with woman's rights advocates.

1883    Susan goes to Europe and spends time with Elizabeth. They initiate an international dialogue about woman's rights. Together, they return to the United States.

1887    The first vote on a woman suffrage amendment, the Sixteenth, is held in the United States Senate. It loses 34 to 16.

1888    Susan presides over and Elizabeth addresses the first meeting of the International Council of Women (ICW) in Washington, DC.

1890    The NWSA and the AWSA merge into the National American Woman Suffrage Association (NAWSA). Elizabeth is voted the president, after Susan's impassioned plea.
Wyoming becomes a state with woman suffrage in its constitution.
A gala celebration is held for Susan's seventieth birthday.

1891    Susan decides to settle down with her sister Mary in Rochester, New York. Elizabeth moves in with two of her children in New York City.

1892    Elizabeth gives a speech that becomes famous, "The Solitude of Self," before congressional committees and the NAWSA Convention. She resigns as president and is made an honorary president of the organization. Susan is elected president.

1893    Woman suffrage is approved in Colorado.
Marble busts of Elizabeth, Susan, and Lucretia Mott by sculptor Adelaide Johnson are on display at the World's Columbian Exposition in Chicago, Illinois.

1894    Elizabeth and Susan work on the New York woman suffrage campaign; Susan helps in the Kansas campaign; both campaigns fail.

1895    Susan campaigns for woman suffrage in California.
A gala celebration is held for Elizabeth's eightieth birthday.
Elizabeth publishes *The Woman's Bible*, volume 1.

1896    Over Susan's strenuous objections, the NAWSA votes to censor Elizabeth because of *The Woman's Bible*.
Women win the right to vote in Idaho.

1897    Ida Husted Harper works with Susan to write her biography.

1898    Volumes 1 and 2 of *The Life and Work of Susan B. Anthony* are published. Volume 3 will be published in 1908. Elizabeth publishes volume 2 of *The Woman's Bible.*

1900    Susan retires as president of the NAWSA and is made an honorary president. Carrie Chapman Catt is elected president. Susan raises the necessary money to force the University of Rochester to admit women.

1902    Elizabeth writes to President Theodore Roosevelt, asking him to advocate for woman suffrage. A few days later, on October 26, she dies, three weeks before her eighty-seventh birthday.

1903–    Susan attends NAWSA conventions in New Orleans,
1906    Louisiana; Washington, DC; Portland, Oregon; and Baltimore, Maryland. In 1904, at the age of eighty-four, she goes to the ICW meeting in Berlin, Germany.

1906    Susan dies on March 13, at the age of eighty-six.

1920    Women win the right to vote when the Nineteenth Amendment is added to the United States Constitution.

1921    The *Portrait Monument to Lucretia Mott, Elizabeth Cady Stanton, and Susan B. Anthony,* sculpted by Adelaide Johnson, is dedicated in the United States Capitol Rotunda, then placed in the Crypt, a much less visible space.

1997    The *Portrait Monument* is returned to the United States Capitol Rotunda, after a passionate grassroots lobbying and fund-raising effort.

# PLACES TO VISIT

**Adams, Massachusetts**
- Susan B. Anthony Birthplace Museum, 67 East Road
- Quaker Meeting House, Maple Street Cemetery

**Battenville, New York**
- Anthonys' house from 1826 to 1839, 2835 Route 29 (a marker is on view, but the home is not currently open to the public)

**Canandaigua, New York**
- Bust and Painting, site of Susan B. Anthony trial, Ontario County Courthouse, 27 North Main Street

**Johnstown, New York**
- Plaque and Marker, site of Elizabeth Cady's birthplace, 51 West Main Street
- Fulton County Courthouse, where Elizabeth watched her father preside over trials and where, years later, she and Susan held a woman suffrage meeting, 223 West Main Street
- Marker commemorating Elizabeth Cady Stanton, Sir William Johnson Park, between Market and Williams streets
- Marker in front of Mrs. Henry's Boarding House, 9 South William Street
- Memorabilia, including Elizabeth Cady Stanton's piano, Johnstown Historical Society, 17 North William Street
- Mural with a portrait of Elizabeth Cady Stanton on the side of the Water Department building, 27 East Main Street

**New York, New York**
- Bust of Susan B. Anthony, The Hall of Fame for Great Americans, 2183 University Avenue (at West 181st Street), the Bronx

- Carved altar figure of Susan B. Anthony (grouped with Martin Luther King, Jr., Albert Einstein, and Mahatma Gandhi), Cathedral of St. John the Divine, 1047 Amsterdam Avenue
- Place setting representing Susan B. Anthony, *The Dinner Party* by Judy Chicago, Elizabeth A. Sackler Center for Feminist Art, Brooklyn Museum of Art, 200 Eastern Parkway, Brooklyn
- Plaque on the side of the apartment building, recently renamed the Stanton, where Elizabeth Cady Stanton died, 250 West 94th Street
- Burial site of Elizabeth Cady Stanton, Woodlawn Cemetery, Webster Avenue and East 233rd Street, the Bronx

### Rochester, New York
- Plaque of Susan B. Anthony and her sister Mary, lobby, First Unitarian Church of Rochester, 220 Winton Road South
- Stained-glass window of Susan B. Anthony, Memorial African Methodist Episcopal Zion Church, 549 Clarissa Street
- The Susan B. Anthony House, 17 Madison Street, www.susanbanthonyhouse.org
- Susan B. Anthony Square Park, between Madison and King streets, with *Let's Have Tea*, life-size bronze sculptures of Susan B. Anthony and Frederick Douglass by Pepsy Kettavong
- Tree and plaque honoring Susan B. Anthony, Seneca Park, 2222 St. Paul Street
- Susan B. Anthony Center for Women's Leadership, University of Rochester
- Frederick Douglass–Susan B. Anthony Memorial Bridge, Interstate 490 over the Genesee River
- Burial site of Susan B. Anthony, Mount Hope Cemetery, 1133 Mount Hope Avenue (Frederick Douglass is also buried there)

### Seneca Falls, New York
- National Women's Hall of Fame, 76 Fall Street
- Women's Rights National Historical Park, vistors' center at 136 Fall Street; sites include the Wesleyan Chapel (Fall and Water streets) and the Stantons' house from 1847 to 1862 (32 Washington Street)

• Statue, *When Anthony Met Stanton,* by A. E. Ted Aub, beside Van Cleef Lake

• Seneca Falls Historical Society, 55 Cayuga Street

**Tenafly, New Jersey**
• Marker on Elizabeth Cady Stanton's house from 1868 to 1887, 135 Highwood Avenue (now private)

**Washington, DC**
• Embroidered kneeler and stained-glass window honoring Susan B. Anthony, National Cathedral

• Marble busts by Adelaide Johnson of Elizabeth Cady Stanton, Susan B. Anthony, and Lucretia Mott; Elizabeth Cady Stanton's chair; and Susan B. Anthony's desk, Sewall-Belmont House and Museum, 144 Constitution Avenue, NE; www.sewallbelmont.org

• Mahogany table on which Elizabeth Cady Stanton coauthored the Declaration of Sentiments, National Museum of American History, Smithsonian Institution, 14th Street and Constitution Avenue

• *Portrait Monument to Lucretia Mott, Elizabeth Cady, and Susan B. Anthony,* United States Capitol Rotunda

**Waterloo, New York**
• Hunt House, 401 East Main Street (site where first woman's rights convention was planned; part of Women's Rights National Historical Park)

• M'Clintock House, 14 East Williams Street (site where the Declaration of Sentiments was drafted; part of Women's Rights National Historical Park)

# NAMESAKES

The names of Elizabeth Cady Stanton and Susan B. Anthony can be found attached to schools. Their image appeared on United States postage stamps. Susan's likeness appeared on a medallion and a United States dollar coin.

## Elizabeth Cady Stanton
- The Stanton (apartment building where she died), New York, New York
- Elizabeth Cady Stanton Elementary School, Seneca Falls, New York
- Elizabeth Cady Stanton's image, along with Carrie Chapman Catt's and Lucretia Mott's, appears on a three-cent United States postage stamp titled "100 Years of Progress of Women 1848–1948," which was released in 1948

## Susan B. Anthony
- Susan B. Anthony Elementary School, Daly City, California
- Susan B. Anthony Elementary School, Garden Grove, California
- Susan B. Anthony Elementary School, Westminster, California
- Susan B. Anthony School, Intermediate School 238, Hollis, New York
- Susan B. Anthony School, Minneapolis, Minnesota
- Susan B. Anthony School 27, Rochester, New York
- Susan B. Anthony School, Sacramento, California
- Susan B. Anthony Middle School for the Arts, Revere, Massachusetts
- Susan B. Anthony's image appears on a three-cent United States postage stamp titled "Suffrage for Women," which was released in 1936

- Susan B. Anthony's image appears on a fifty-cent United States postage stamp, which was released in 1955
- Susan B. Anthony's picture was featured on First Day of Issue Cover of a six-cent United States postage stamp titled "Woman Suffrage 50th Anniversary," which was released in 1970
- Susan B. Anthony's likeness appeared on a dollar coin minted from 1979 to 1981, and in 1999

**Daniel Cady**: Elizabeth described
her father as "a man of firm character."
[From Stanton, *Eighty Years and More*]

**Margaret Livingston Cady**: Elizabeth
described her mother as "courageous,
self-reliant, and at her ease under all
circumstances and in all places."
[From Stanton, *Eighty Years and More*]

**Daniel Anthony**: Susan's father
encouraged her to be independent
and concerned about social issues.
[From Harper, *The Life and Work of
Susan B. Anthony*, vol. 1]

**Lucy Read Anthony**: Susan never forgot
her mother's "self-sacrificing devotion"
to her family. [From Harper, *The Life and Work
of Susan B. Anthony*, vol. 1]

**Gerrit Smith** was a wealthy landowner who supported many reform movements. [Courtesy of the Library of Congress]

**Elizabeth Cady** at age twenty. [Courtesy of the Brigham Young University Photo Archives, Rexburg, Idaho]

**Angelina** and **Sarah Grimké** were fearless abolitionists and women's rights orators and authors. [Courtesy of the Library of Congress]

The Anthonys lived in this brick house in Battenville, New York, until Daniel went bankrupt. [From Harper, *The Life and Work of Susan B. Anthony*, vol. 1]

**Henry Brewster Stanton:** Elizabeth included this photograph of her husband in her autobiography. [From Stanton, *Eighty Years and More*]

**Lucretia Mott** was one of the most prominent and widely respected people in the nineteenth century. [From Stanton, Anthony, Gage, *History of Woman Suffrage*, vol. 1]

**Wendell Phillips** was a notable reformer who later disagreed with Elizabeth and Susan. [Courtesy of the Library of Congress]

**William Lloyd Garrison** was the most reviled and revered abolitionist of the nineteenth century. [Courtesy of the Library of Congress]

**Frederick Douglass** escaped from slavery and became a famous lecturer and newspaper editor. [Courtesy of Wikimedia Commons]

**Susan** wrote to her family that her dress was made from purple, white, blue, and brown plaid muslin. [From Harper, *The Life and Work of Susan B. Anthony*, vol. 1]

In 1848, **Elizabeth** posed with her sons **Daniel** (known as Neil) and **Henry** (known as Kit). [Courtesy of the Library of Congress]

**Martha Wright** was Lucretia Mott's sister and a close friend of Elizabeth and Susan. [From Stanton, Anthony, Gage, *History of Woman Suffrage*, vol. 1]

**Amy Post** was a well-known reformer and proponent of radical ideas, including spiritualism.
[Courtesy of the Rochester Public Library Local History Division]

**Elizabeth Smith Miller**, Elizabeth's cousin Libby and close friend, is credited with introducing bloomers. [Courtesy of Coline Jenkins, Elizabeth Cady Stanton Trust]

Amelia Bloomer's name got attached to the style because she promoted it in her newspaper, including publishing this woodcut of Elizabeth in bloomers.
[Courtesy of the Library of Congress]

*When Anthony Met Stanton*, a memorial sculpted by Ted Aud in Seneca Falls, New York, shows (from left to right) Susan, Amelia Bloomer, and Elizabeth. [Collection of Penny Colman]

**Elizabeth** in 1854 with **Henry, Jr.**, known as Kit. [From Stanton, *Eighty Years and More*]

74%

**Lucy Stone**, once a close co-worker with Elizabeth and Susan, later formed a rival organization. [Courtesy of the Library of Congress]

24%

**Susan**, in 1852. [Courtesy of the Susan B. Anthony House, Rochester, New York; www.susanbanthonyhouse.org]

**Ernestine Rose**, pictured holding a rolled-up petition, was an unwavering ally of Elizabeth and Susan. [From Stanton, Anthony, Gage, *History of Woman Suffrage*, vol. 1]

ADDRESS
TO THE
Legislature of New-York,
ADOPTED BY THE
STATE WOMAN'S RIGHTS CONVENTION,

HELD AT ALBANY,
Tuesday and Wednesday, February 14 and 15, 1854.

PREPARED BY
ELIZABETH CADY STANTON,
Of Seneca Falls, N. Y.

ALBANY:
WEED, PARSONS AND COMPANY.
1854.

Susan had fifty thousand copies of Elizabeth's speech printed in pamphlet form for distribution. [Courtesy of Coline Jenkins, Elizabeth Cady Stanton Trust]

*Susan B. Anthony*
*1820–Feb. 15–1856*

**Susan** in 1856 at the age of thirty-six. [Courtesy of the Rochester Public Library Local History Division]

**Elizabeth** with **Harriot**, who was born in 1856. [From Stanton, *Eighty Years and More*]

**Sojourner Truth**, a former slave and charismatic speaker, supported universal suffrage. [Courtesy of the Library of Congress]

A petition signed by Elizabeth, Susan, Lucy Stone, Ernestine Rose, and two of Elizabeth's sisters. [Courtesy of the National Archives, Washington, D.C.]

**Horace Greeley**—an influential newspaper owner, editor, and writer. [Courtesy of the Library of Congress]

A sketch of the reform-minded **Hutchinson Family Singers** shows Judson, Abby, John, and Asa. [Courtesy of Wikimedia Commons]

**George Train:** Flamboyant and controversial, his outfits included a pair of lavender kid gloves. [Courtesy of the Library of Congress]

The *Revolution* carried the slogan "Men, their rights and nothing more: Women, their rights and nothing less." [Courtesy of the Library of Congress]

**Isabella Beecher Hooker**, a second-generation activist, aligned herself with Elizabeth and Susan. [From Stanton, Anthony, Gage, *History of Woman Suffrage*, vol. 2]

Elizabeth's house in Tenafly, New Jersey. [Collection of Penny Colman]

An artist's sketch of **Victoria Woodhull** giving her speech to the congressional committee in 1871. [Courtesy of the Library of Congress]

Taken on August 19, 1870, this appears to be the first joint photograph of **Elizabeth** and **Susan**. [Courtesy of the Library of Congress]

The week before Susan's trial began, a newspaper published this cartoon titled "The Woman Who Dared." [From the New York *Daily Graphic*, June 5, 1873]

Sketches of the scandalous trio: **Elizabeth Tilton**, **Henry Ward Beecher**, and **Theodore Tilton**.
[From *Leslie's Monthly Magazine*, August 8, 1874]

Steel engravings of **Elizabeth**, **Susan**, and **Matilda Joslyn Gage** that appeared in *History of Woman Suffrage*. [From Stanton, Anthony, Gage, *History of Woman Suffrage*, vol. 1]

A sketch of **Elizabeth** advocating for the Sixteenth Amendment before a senate committee in 1878.
[From the New York *Daily Graphic*, January 16, 1887]

OPERA HOUSE, MASSILLON.

ELIZABETH CADY STANTON.
Saturday Evening, Feb'y 6, 1875.
LECTURE, "OUR GIRLS."

This poster advertised Elizabeth's speech in Massilon, Ohio.
[Courtesy of the Massilon Museum, East Massilon, Ohio]

Three generations in 1888—**Elizabeth** with **Harriot Stanton Blatch** and five-year-old **Nora**. [From Stanton, *Eighty Years and More*]

**Elizabeth** and **Susan** reviewing material for the *History of Woman Suffrage*.
[Courtesy of the Library of Congress]

Elizabeth and Susan organized the first International Council of Women, where they posed with women from other countries. [Courtesy of the Library of Congress]

Susan with her sister Mary, who was the first woman principal in Rochester, New York. [Courtesy of the Rochester Public Library Local History Division]

Susan and Elizabeth in front of Susan's home in Rochester. [Courtesy of the Susan B. Anthony House, Rochester, New York; www.susanbanthonyhouse.org]

Elizabeth at her eightieth birthday celebration in New York City with her son Robert and daughter Margaret. [From Stanton, *Eighty Years and More*]

The attic where **Susan** and **Ida Husted Harper** wrote her biography, which they dubbed the "bog."
[From Harper, *The Life and Work of Susan B. Anthony*, vol. 2]

This picture of **Elizabeth** appeared in her autobiography. [From Stanton, *Eighty Years and More*]

In August 1899, **Elizabeth** and **Susan** vacationed with **Elizabeth Smith Miller** (Elizabeth's cousin Libby) in Geneva, New York. [Courtesy of Coline Jenkins, Elizabeth Cady Stanton Trust]

Susan at the age of 75 on a tour of Yosemite Valley with suffrage workers and guides. [Courtesy of Henry E. Huntington Library, San Marino, California]

**Susan** in 1897. [Courtesy of the Florida State Archives]

A Chinese newspaper in San Francisco published a sketch of Susan with an article about her campaign. [Courtesy of the Library of Congress]

Sarah Eddy's painting of children giving Susan roses at her eightieth birthday celebration. [Courtesy of the Library of Congress]

The second verse of the poem
Elizabeth wrote for Susan's eightieth
birthday. [Courtesy of the Rochester Public
Library Local History Division]

Elizabeth's flower-covered casket with a picture
of Susan at the head. [Courtesy of the Douglass Library,
Rutgers University, New Brunswick, New Jersey]

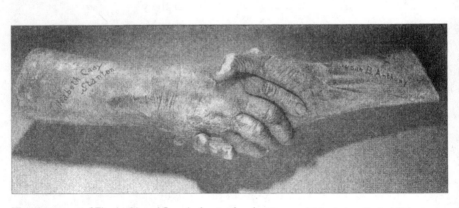

The plaster cast of Elizabeth's and Susan's clasping hands. [Courtesy of Coline Jenkins, Elizabeth Cady
Stanton Trust]

# ACKNOWLEDGMENTS

As with every book I write, there are so many people who played a part. In particular, I want to thank Coline Jenkins, Elizabeth Cady Stanton's great great-granddaughter and president of the Elizabeth Cady Stanton Trust, who continues the matriarchal lineage of "strong-minded" women, for her friendship and generosity. I am grateful for the work of scholars, including Ann D. Gordon, editor of the monumental six-volume series, *The Selected Papers of Elizabeth Cady Stanton & Susan B. Anthony*. Thanks are also due to my graduate students at Queens College, the City University of New York, who read and responded to my manuscript: Denise Gilrane, Debbie Ganeles, Marie Russell, and Christine Schachter. Over the years, I have been stimulated by conversations with my colleague Myra Zarnowski at Queens College. This is my fourth book with my terrific editor, Christy Ottaviano, and the deft designer Meredith Pratt. Thanks to them and to everyone at Henry Holt. Also thank you to Deborah J. Callery, Johnstown Public Library, Johnstown, NY; Kathy Jans-Duffy, Seneca Falls Historical Society, Seneca Falls, NY; Mary Ellen Sweeney and Claire Hawley Zarcone, Susan B. Anthony House, Rochester, NY; Dot Willsey, Gerrit Smith Estate, Peterboro, NY; and Fernanda Perrone, Rutgers University Libraries.

As always, I am forever enriched by my family, in particular my partner, Linda Hickson, who unfailingly and cheerfully supports me; no manuscript leaves my office until "every sentence" passes through her "metaphysical, rhetorical & common sense tweezer," as Elizabeth once advised Susan. While I was writing this book, my granddaughter Sophie Colman de Haën, who was three years old when I started and six when I finished, became ever more interested and engaged in the process of writing a book. She listened with interest and responded to my stories about Elizabeth and Susan, expressed her opinion about various photographs, and said she agreed it would be a good idea for me to dedicate this book to "Everyone who has fought and who is fighting and who will fight for the rights of women everywhere." Thank you, Sophie!

# ELIZABETH

# CADY STANTON

# &

# SUSAN B. ANTHONY

A friendship that
changed the world

## BONUS MATERIALS

# AN INTERVIEW WITH
# PENNY COLMAN

**What did you want to be when you grew up?**

I remember wanting to be a doctor, an unusual choice for a girl growing up in the 1950s. My father, who was a doctor, thought that I should aspire to becoming a stay-at-home wife and mother—the traditional role for women at that time. To thwart my desire to be a doctor, he told me stories about medical school and how male medical students would make my life miserable. They would shun me, mess up my laboratory experiments, and leave a dead rat in my locker.

**When did you realize you wanted to be a writer?**

Both my parents gave me a close-up view of being a writer. I was nine years old when my mother joined the staff of a local newspaper as a journalist and photographer. Occasionally she took me with her when she went off in pursuit of a story. That same year, my father started writing a weekly column, "Everyday Psychology," for several newspapers. Two years later, I published my first article in the first edition of a newsletter I created to announce the start of our neighborhood orchestra, comprised of me, my brothers, and some of our friends.

**What's your most embarrassing childhood memory?**

My most embarrassing childhood memory happened when my tenth-grade English teacher held a tea party for students at her house and I showed up wearing kneesocks. All—yes, all—the other girls were wearing nylon stockings! (Remember: I grew up in the 1950s.) My impulse was to flee, until I imagined what my mother would tell me: "Pen, act like you're wearing the right thing and the others aren't!"

**What's your favorite childhood memory?**

My favorite childhood memory is of the farm we owned when I was in middle school. We had a goat that jumped up on the car hood; six sheep; a flock of exotic chickens (until a fox ate them); and three horses—Rusty for my dad and my oldest brother, Bucky for my two younger brothers, and Gypsy for me and my mother, which was cool because my mother didn't ride.

**As a young person, who did you look up to most?**

My unique artist/musician/journalist mother, an immigrant, who was born in Zagreb, Yugoslavia (now Croatia), and lived in Korycany, a small village in Czechoslovakia (now the Czech Republic). She left in 1938, the year Adolf Hitler ordered the invasion of Czechoslovakia.

**What was your favorite thing about school?**

At school I liked my social studies classes, especially the one taught by Mr. James Johnson, the seventh-grade teacher.

**What were your hobbies as a kid? What are your hobbies now?**

As a kid my hobbies included collecting things: stamps, miniature glass animals, and coins. I played the violin and piano, rode my bike, went canoeing, and played baseball with my brothers. Now you might find me walking along the Hudson River, reading, visiting a museum or historic site, working in my garden, or exploring a cemetery. I love road trips, music, kayaking, bike riding, walking, doing puzzles, playing games, and thinking and talking about ideas.

**What book is on your nightstand now?**

*The Official Scrabble Players Dictionary*, Fifth Edition and *The Secret History of Wonder Woman* by Jill Lepore.

**How did you celebrate publishing your first book?**

I celebrated publishing my first book by immediately starting to write another one. *Corpses, Coffins, and Crypts*, my fifteenth nonfiction book, was published a few months after my mother's death. My sister came from California and my brother came from New York to attend a book party, where I gave a speech that is posted on my website.

**What inspired you to write *Elizabeth Cady Stanton and Susan B. Anthony*?**

I love compelling, significant, and underreported historical stories—especially about women. These are all things I found in the unlikely friendship of two fascinating and inspiring women, Elizabeth Cady Stanton and Susan B. Anthony, who fueled the controversial nineteenth-century fight to improve the social, civil, and economic conditions of women's lives. It is a riveting story of progress and betrayal, with a host of supporting characters that range from admirable to controversial. It is an illuminating account of democracy, citizenship, voting rights, and gender equality. In short, how could I not write this book?

**What was the research like?**

The research was a roller-coaster ride. It started with a sinking feeling when I realized I had to read and digest an Everest-size mountain of primary source material, and evolved to a "whoopee" feeling when I took off on road trips to visit places that were part of Elizabeth Cady Stanton's and Susan B. Anthony's story, including a three-day, 880-mile trip throughout New York state.

**What was the most difficult part about writing the book?**

The most difficult part of writing any book is deciding what descriptions, information, incidents, quotations, anecdotes, etc., to put in or to leave out. I am constantly checking to make sure that the story I am writing is clear, coherent, and compelling. These decisions were particularly challenging with *Elizabeth Cady Stanton and Susan B. Anthony: A Friendship That Changed the World* because I was dealing with two main characters and one of the most profound social movements for equality in American history—whew!

**Who was your favorite—Elizabeth Cady Stanton or Susan B. Anthony?**

Both of them, but for different reasons: Elizabeth Cady Stanton because she was a scintillating thinker, prolifically influential writer, and a fearless orator. And Susan B. Anthony because she was an indefatigable doer, an organizer and planner extraordinaire, and a principled pragmatist. Both of them, for the same reasons: because of their unwavering commitment to the cause, fierce loyalty to each other, and razor-sharp wits. After reading my manuscript, my editor, Christy Ottaviano, wrote in an email that "at first [she] felt partial to Stanton, finding her ability to juggle family life with work quite impressive." As she read on, however, she "became so enamored of Anthony's strength and powerful ethical core [that Christy] ended up loving both women equally."

### What do you find most inspiring about Elizabeth Cady Stanton and Susan B. Anthony?

I find many things inspiring about Elizabeth Cady Stanton and Susan B. Anthony. Mostly, however, I am inspired by their courageous perseverance. Shortly before Elizabeth Cady Stanton died in 1902, Anthony wrote to her: "It is fifty-one years since we first met, and we have been busy through every one of them, stirring up the world to recognize the rights of women." There is still a lot of stirring to do today and much inspiration to be gained from the legacy of Elizabeth Cady Stanton and Susan B. Anthony and their friendship that changed the world.

### Where do you write your books?

Our 105-year-old house has four floors. I've written books on three of them. Currently my office is in the basement, where I wrote *Thanksgiving: The True Story* and *Elizabeth Cady Stanton and Susan B. Anthony: A Friendship That Changed the World*. It has ground-level windows, so it's not gloomy. (There's a short video about it on my blog.) I wrote *Where the Action Was: Women War Correspondents in World War II* in an office on the second floor, which is now used by my partner. The top floor has a bedroom and a small library. That is where I wrote *Corpses, Coffins, and Crypts: A History of Burial*. My computer was set up on a small table in a corner of the bedroom next to two side-by-side windows. The library was where I took breaks, did research, made notes, read what I had written, and revised (my favorite part of writing). I would sit on the floor under the skylight or in my favorite gray barrel chair that twirls around.

### What challenges do you face in the writing process, and how do you overcome them?

I have a long list of challenges, including how to grab a readers' attention, how to keep readers turning the pages, how to write about complicated subjects in a clear, coherent, and compelling way, how to find just the right word and rhythm, how to write a satisfying, meaningful ending. To meet the challenges, I spend a lot of time thinking. I experiment with different solutions (with *Corpses, Coffins, and Crypts* I wrote twenty-three versions of the table of contents until I settled on just the right structure and chapter headings for that book).

**What was your favorite book when you were a kid? Do you have a favorite book now?**
As a kid I loved reading books about real people and historic events. I devoured biographies and social histories in the Signature Books series and Landmark Books series, including *The Story of Helen Keller*, and *To California by Covered Wagon*. I also loved to select a volume from our set of the *Encyclopedia Britannica* and read about whatever caught my attention, such as flowers and horses. If you mean which one of my books is my favorite? (And I do get asked that question a lot.) My answer is that they are all my favorites, although *Corpses, Coffins, Crypts* does have a special place in my heart. If you mean a favorite book by another author, I have several, including *Without Reservations: The Travels of an Independent Woman* by Alice Steinbach and *The Emerald Mile: The Epic Story of the Fastest Ride in History Through the Heart of the Grand Canyon* by Kevin Fedarko.

**Do you ever get writer's block? What do you do to get back on track?**
I never use the term "writer's block." It's too scary, like I've got a terminal disease. Thinking I have "writer's block" distracts me from the real issue, which is that there is a writing problem I need to solve. For example, with *Corpses, Coffins, and Crypts*, I stopped many times to think about what to put in and what to leave out. When I've got a writing problem to solve, I typically do one of two things: take a long walk or work on a jigsaw puzzle, until the solution comes to me. (I always have a puzzle underway in my office.)

**What do you want readers to remember about your books?**
I want readers to remember that literary nonfiction can be a great read!

**What do you consider to be your greatest accomplishment?**
I'm still alive, so perhaps there's more to come. But at this point, I consider my greatest accomplishment to be writing worthwhile books on important subjects that I trust make a difference in readers' lives.

**What would your readers be most surprised to learn about you?**

Readers would probably be surprised that once upon a time ago I hiked the almost-ten-mile Bright Angel Trail, up and out, from the bottom to the top of the almost-a-mile-deep Grand Canyon, past some of the oldest rock on the earth and through different climate zones from desert to pine forest. Awesome every step of the way!

# DISCUSSION QUESTIONS

1. Elizabeth Cady Stanton and Susan B. Anthony used military terms to describe their fight for women's rights. Why do you think that is? What sort of language does the feminist movement use today?

2. What early childhood experiences do you think most influenced Elizabeth's and Susan's decisions to fight against entrenched gender norms of the time? How do you think Elizabeth's and Susan's differing childhoods changed the way they saw the world, and the way they became friends? Do you think their friendship would have been different had they grown up more similarly, or more differently?

3. Four-year-old Elizabeth was puzzled when people said, "What a pity it is she's a girl!" Later, she said she had been confused because she hadn't yet understood "that girls were considered an inferior order of beings" (p. 8). What does she mean by this? What are the ways that society saw her differently because she was a woman? What are some of the things society teaches young girls today?

4. What were Susan and Elizabeth's biggest arguments? How do you think they resolved their disagreements while remaining friends?

5. How was each woman changed by her friendship with the other? How are you changed by your own friendships?

6. Elizabeth wrote that "girls flock round me for a kiss, a curl, an autograph" (p. 161)—many women admired her for her work. What women, either from history or present day, do you admire and look up to?

7. Why did Elizabeth think that it was important to write a history of the women's movement?

8. What did you see as the largest challenges and barriers facing Elizabeth, Susan, and the other women in this book? How did they deal with and overcome these challenges?

9. Did reading this book change your understanding of the woman suffrage or women's rights movement? If so, what changed? Did you find that you recognized many of the influential women mentioned in the book? If not, why do you think you hadn't learned about them before?

10. What do you consider Susan's and Elizabeth's greatest achievements and contributions?

What happens to our bodies when we die? How do
different cultures bury their dead? Learn all about the
biology, history, and rituals of death through the centuries in
*Corpses, Coffins, and Crypts: A History of Burial.*

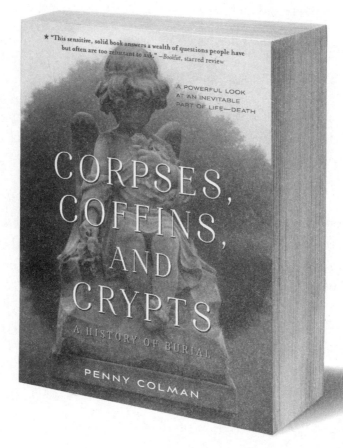

# ·one·

# Dead Is Dead:
# Defining Death

My great-aunt Frieda Matousek called me with the news that her husband, Willi, was "having another attack." I wasn't surprised: Willi was eighty-six years old and he had several health problems, including heart disease.

"Call his doctor," I said. "I'm on my way."

When I arrived, Frieda met me at the door. "He's dead," she said. "Come see him."

I hugged her and kept my arm around her shoulders as we walked down the hallway to their bedroom. The bedroom was bright with sunshine and Willi lay stretched straight out on the double bed. Dressed in blue-and-white-striped pajamas, Willi's body was on top of the blankets, his head and shoulders were propped up by a pile of pillows, and his feet were bare. He looked exactly like Willi except that he was absolutely still and silent.

"Right after I talked to you, he made a noise, sat up a bit, and fell back," Frieda said. Just then the doorbell rang. I answered it.

"I'm the visiting nurse," the woman informed me. "I have an appointment to visit Mr. Willi Matousek."

"He's dead," I said. "He's in the bedroom."

"How do you know he's dead?" the nurse asked as she headed down the hallway.

*This death certificate documents my brother's death. In many countries, including the United States, a death certificate is required in order to dispose of a body, settle an estate, make insurance claims, and get death benefits. The letters DOA mean Dead on Arrival.*

This scene was repeated when the emergency medical technicians (EMTs) arrived at the door with all their equipment.

"He's dead," I said.

"How do you know?" they replied and rushed down the hall.

Then the police arrived.

"He's dead," I said.

"How do you know?" they replied.

At one level their question struck me as funny. "What do you mean, 'How do you know?'" I wanted to say. "He hasn't breathed or moved for at least an hour." But at another level I knew that just because Willi hadn't breathed or moved didn't necessarily mean that he was dead. Throughout history people have been declared dead when they really weren't.

In the late 1500s in England, Matthew Wall was thought to be dead until pallbearers accidentally dropped his coffin and he was revived. In the early 1600s in Scotland, Marjorie Elphinstone was supposedly dead until she groaned when grave robbers broke into her newly buried coffin to steal jewelry from her recently buried body. Forgetting about the jewelry, the robbers fled. Elphinstone climbed out of her coffin and walked home. In

Although this scene titled "Grave Robber Flees from a Corpse That Has Come to Life" was originally published in 1746, grave robbers were common in many times and places. In the case of Margaret Halcrow Erskine, a grave robber unintentionally saved her life. When Erskine appeared to have died in Chirnside, Scotland, in 1674, the sexton buried her in a shallow grave so that he could return at night and steal her jewelry. However, Erskine revived as the sexton was cutting off her finger to remove her ring. Although there's no information about what happened to the sexton, Erskine lived a long and productive life.

the 1860s passersby heard tapping coming from Philomèle Jonetre's grave. On exhuming her body, the director of the morgue in Paris saw her eyelids move. She revived but died the next day, really died. About the same time there was the case of a doctor who cut into a supposedly dead person only to have the person jump up and grab the doctor's throat. The "dead person" survived, but the doctor dropped dead of apoplexy. In the early 1900s a young girl had lain in her open coffin for thirty-six hours when a relative who happened to be a physician decided that she looked alive. He treated her and she recovered.

How can these mistakes happen? Experts have given various explanations for erroneous declarations of death and premature burials, including thanatomimesis, or death feigning; trances; narcotic overdose; concussion; syncope, or fainting; and asphyxia, or lack of oxygen. In 1884 a British medical journal, *Lancet*, offered this explanation: "It is not so much the undue haste as inexcusable carelessness that must be blamed for the premature burying of persons who are not really dead." In 1995 Dr. Kenneth V. Iserson wrote in his book *Death to Dust: What Happens to Dead Bodies?* that the words in *Lancet* "still ring true today," a dreadful thought for those of us still alive. Nevertheless, mistakes are extremely rare today.

The terror of premature burial has prompted people to devise various rituals and devices. Some ancient people waited until the dead body began to decay before they buried or cremated it. The Romans called out a person's name three times before putting the body on the funeral pyre. The ancient Jews stored

**The Viele Memorial, West Point, Highland Falls, New York.** *Egbert Ludovicus Viele, the man who designed this memorial for himself and his wife, was terrified of being buried alive. So he rigged up a buzzer system that would ring inside the cemetery caretaker's house if he found himself alive inside the memorial. The huge memorial is patterned after an ancient Egyptian pyramid, complete with two sphinxes, the symbol of the pharaoh, which was portrayed as a lion with a human head. When Viele died in 1902, his body was placed in a sarcophagus, or stone coffin, inside the memorial. The buzzer never rang, although one caretaker reported being seriously startled until he realized that what he thought was the buzzer was only the telephone. The buzzer is no longer connected.*

dead bodies in caves and open sepulchres and regularly checked on them for a period of time. Some people stuck pins under corpses' nails. One woman instructed her doctor to stick a long metal pin in her heart before she was actually buried. A man wanted a doctor "either to sever my head or extract my heart from my body, so as to prevent any possibility of the return of vitality." In 1896 the Association for the Prevention of Premature Burial was organized in England for people who wanted to have scientific tests performed on their corpses before they were buried.

In St. Helena's Episcopal Churchyard in Beaufort, South Carolina, there's a brick vault with the remains of a Dr. Perry. According to the church history, Dr. Perry was terrified of being buried alive. So he had his friends promise to bury him with a loaf of bread, a jug of water, and a pickax. He had his slaves build a brick vault aboveground with enough room for him to swing his ax. Perry was buried with the bread, water, and pickax. He must have been truly dead because the vault still remains intact.

# SOURCE NOTES

Complete information about the sources is given in the bibliography, page 245

**Abbreviations for frequently used sources are**

Gordon—*The Selected Papers of Elizabeth Cady Stanton & Susan B. Anthony* (5 volumes)

Harper—*Life and Work of Susan B. Anthony* (3 volumes)

Lutz—*Created Equal: A Biography of Elizabeth Cady Stanton*

Stanton, Anthony, Gage—*History of Woman Suffrage* (volumes 1–3)

Stanton—*Eighty Years and More: Reminiscences 1815–1897*

Stanton and Blatch—*Elizabeth Cady Stanton* (2 volumes)

**Author's Note**
The use of war language appears throughout Elizabeth's, Susan's, and their coworkers' speeches, articles, reports, and letters.
"Night after night . . .": Stanton, p. 166.

**Prologue: Imagine a Time**
"Wives, submit . . .": King James Bible, Ephesians 5:22.
"But I suffer . . .": King James Bible, I Timothy 2:12.
"There she stood . . .": Stanton, p. 163.

## PART 1

**Chapter 1: *"Ah, You Should Have Been a Boy!"***
"keenly . . . Alps": Stanton, p. 6.
"a man . . . in all places": Stanton, p. 3.
"heard so many . . . of beings": ibid., p. 4.
"to be all . . . courageous": ibid., p. 21.
"recognize the . . . a boy!": ibid., p. 22.
"I could . . . woman's condition": ibid., p. 32.
"Again I felt . . .": ibid., pp. 33–34.

"swept over . . . of a windmill": ibid., pp. 41–42.
"Returning home . . . more happy": ibid., pp. 43–44.

**Chapter 2: *"An Affectionate Family"***
"Come here . . .": Julia Taft Bayne, *Hadley Ballads*, p. 38.
"the Anthony . . . of Anthonys": Susan B. Anthony, *The Ghost in My Life*, p. 43.
"Although we . . .": Author's conversation with Martin Schub, MD
"very timid . . . devotion": Harper, vol. 1, p. 232.

**Chapter 3: *"Rousing Arguments"***
"The rousing . . . debate": Harper, vol. 1, pp. 53–55.
"I have brought . . . before your arrival": Stanton, pp. 62–64.
"there was not . . . in the work": Otelia Cromwell, *Lucretia Mott*, pp. 51, 130.
"What if . . .": Stanton, Anthony, Gage, vol. 1, p. 335.
"A pretty bold . . .": Mark Perry, *Lift Up Thy Voice*, p. 130.
"intolerably . . .": ibid., p. 153.
"shame and dishonor . . .": ibid., p. 160.
"black and blue . . .": Andrea Moore Kerr, *Lucy Stone*, p. 24.
"indignation at . . .": Perry, p. 133.
"I ask no favors . . .": Pamela R. Durso, *The Power of Woman: The Life and Writings of Sarah Moore Grimké*, p. 123.
"We Abolition Women . . .": Perry, p. 165.
"a passion . . . and astonishment": Stanton and Blatch, vol. 1, pp. 57–58.
"depraved . . . conflict": ibid., p. 71.

**Chapter 4: *"Hardscrabble Times"***
"the pleasure . . . Miracles": Harper, vol. 1, p. 28.

"O, may . . .": ibid., p. 27.

"I have been guilty . . . seems worse": ibid., p. 29.

"2nd mo. . . . twelve": ibid., p. 30.

"baked 21 . . .": ibid., p. 3.

"Be the . . . had seen": ibid., p. 38.

"what a lack . . . is disgraced": ibid., pp. 39–41.

"I have no . . .": Kathleen Barry, *Susan B. Anthony*, p. 36.

### Chapter 5: *"A New World"*

"own . . . rose": Gordon, vol. 1, p. 1.

"months of . . .": Stanton and Blatch, p. 67.

"much . . . blows over": ibid., p. 5.

"did not wish . . .": Stanton, p. 71.

"Yes, no doubt . . .": Wellman, *The Road to Seneca Falls*, p. 33.

"I obstinately . . . relation": Stanton, p. 72.

"Dear Friends . . .": Gordon, vol. 1, p. 10.

"had stood . . . of parting": Stanton, pp. 72–73.

"I soon . . . in this game": ibid, pp. 73–74.

"who believed . . .": ibid., p. 83.

"are constitutionally . . . whites": Dorothy Sterling, *Lucretia Mott*, p. 115.

"No shilly-shallying . . .": Lutz, p.26.

"battling so . . .": Stanton, p. 81.

"Mrs. Stanton . . .": Elisabeth Griffith, *In Her Own Right*, p. 73.

"Nobody doubted . . .": Sterling, p. 114.

"the independence . . .": Alma Lutz, *Susan B. Anthony*, p. 74.

"I sought . . .": Stanton, Anthony, Gage, vol. 1, p. 420.

"felt a new . . .": ibid., p. 422.

"resolved to hold . . .": Stanton, p. 83.

"In all my . . .": Griffith, p. 39.

"Mrs. Stanton . . . woman's rights": ibid., pp. 39–40.

"bright . . . to us": Bonnie S. Anderson, *Joyous Greetings*, p. 127.

"law . . .": Stanton, p. 111.

"The more I think . . .": Griffith, p. 37.

"dose . . . to tears": Wellman, p. 158.

"another lesson . . . earth beneath.": Stanton, p. 18.

"Let me take . . . relieve the pain": ibid., pp. 123–24.

"the Father . . .": Lutz, p. 38.

"I had . . .": Stanton, p. 107.

"did me . . .": Stanton and Blatch, vol. 2., p. 229.

"With a smile . . .": Stanton p. 144.

"solitary . . . protest and discussion": ibid., pp. 147–48.

### Chapter 6: *"Sink or Swim"*

"enjoyed . . .": Harper, vol. 1, p. 44.

"I'd rather . . . both": ibid., pp. 43–44.

"seems . . . Hannah": Barry, pp. 42–43.

"line-boat . . . and home-sick": ibid., pp. 47–48.

"thinking you know it all": ibid., p. 51.

"splendid hats . . . won the victory": ibid., p. 51.

"new pearl . . . stare": ibid., p. 50.

"a fool . . .": ibid., p. 51.

"Well . . .": ibid., p. 47.

"full of . . . paper": Harper, p.38.

### Chapter 7: *"To Do and Dare Anything"*

"earnest . . . rights of women": Stanton, p. 148.

"All men . . . franchise": Wellman, p. 193.

"owing to . . .": Gordon, vol. 4, p. 74.

"as vividly . . .": Wellman, p. 198.

"In due . . .": ibid., p. 203.

"so timely . . . created equal": ibid., pp. 209–10.

"with fear . . .": Stanton, p. 149.

"I have so . . . to do?": Gordon, vol. 1, pp. 123–24.

"The right . . . have begun": Wellman, p. 214.

"start women thinking . . .": Griffith, p. 58.

"a most . . .": Wellman, p. 219.

"stood aloof . . . patience": Stanton and Blatch, vol. 2, p. 39.

"has miscarried . . .": ibid., p. 169.

"What use is . . .": Lutz, p. 58.

"Depend upon it . . .": Gordon, vol. 1, p. 166.

"No men . . ." Stanton, Anthony, Gage, vol. 1, p. 110.

### Chapter 8: *"Out of Sorts with the World"*

"a weariness . . . I could go!": Harper, vol. 1, p. 52.

"printed . . . Canajoharie.": ibid., p. 55.

"It is rather . . .": Gordon, vol. 1, p. 142.

"Sister . . .": Barry, p. 56.

**PART 2**

**Chapter 9:** *"An 'Intense Attraction'"*
"future friend . . .": Stanton, p. 163.
"intense attraction": Barry, p. 64.
"associated with . . .": Harper, vol. 1, p. 70.
"practical difficulties": Stanton, p. 147.
"The sisters . . . disturbers": Harper, vol. 1, p. 65.
"I will gladly . . .": Gordon, vol. 1, pp. 197–98.
"anything     around us": Harper, vol. 1, p. 67.
"a hybrid . . .": ibid., pp. 69–70.
"raised . . . approval": ibid., p. 73.
"nobody who     ": ibid., p. 72.
"the queen . . .": ibid., p. 75.
"brilliant . . . standpoint": ibid., p. 80.
"Rejoice with me . . .": Gordon, vol. 1, p. 212.
"Then you . . .": Stanton and Blatch, vol. 2, p. 36.
"wholly . . . little I have": Stanton, p. 165.
"would modestly . . .": Stanton, Anthony, Gage, vol. 1, p. 494.
"plunged . . . to fry": Stanton and Blatch, vol. 2, pp. 51–52.

**Chapter 10:** *"Do You Not See?"*
"I forbid . . .": Stanton and Blatch, vol. 2, p. 51.
"the Old Fogies . . .": Harper, vol. 1, p. 96.
"grief and . . . make ourselves heard": ibid., pp. 98–99.
"This convention . . . gagged": ibid., p. 102.
"shut-up" . . . be made": ibid., p. 103.
"mob convention": Stanton, Anthony, Gage, vol. 1, p. 570.
"from town . . . of her own": ibid., p. 104.
"I find . . . atrocious": Gordon, vol. 1, p. 237.
"generalize and . . .": Gordon, vol. 1, p. 238.
"story of . . .": Griffith, p. 81.
"a great . . .": ibid., p. 187.
"tears filling . . .": Stanton, p. 188.
"I passed . . .": Griffith, p. 84.
"daughters of . . .": Gordon, vol. 1, p. 241.
"were about . . .": Stanton, p. 190.
"unsex every . . .": Stanton, Anthony, Gage, vol. 1, p. 613.
"Like a captive . . . turn.": Stanton, pp. 201–202.
"resembling . . .": Lutz, p. 78.
"let down . . .": Barry, p. 82.

"My whole soul . . .": Griffith, p. 85.
"My dear daughter . . .": collection of Coline Jenkins.
"She always . . .": Stanton and Blatch, vol. 1, p. xvii.
"Cant . . . uninterrupted": Harper, p. 122.

**Chapter 11:** *"Where Are You?"*
"As soon . . .": Griffith, pp. 87–88.
"the day . . .": Barry, p. 99.
"pleasing . . .": Harper, vol. 1, p. 124.
"strongly continue . . .": ibid., p. 124.
"Husbands are too critical": Griffith, p. 87.
"This is . . . thee": Beverly Wilson Palmer, *Selected Letters of Lucretia Coffin Mott*, p. 233.
"strictly confidential . . . Good night": Griffith, p. 94.
"rapid . . . field": Palmer, p. 233.
"great regret": Harper, vol. 1, p. 126.
"life work . . . thoughts together": ibid., p. 134.
"Height, 5 ft. 5 in . . .": ibid., p. 136.
"very happy . . .": Gordon, vol. 1, p. 316.
"Imagine me . . .": ibid., p. 325.
"So far . . .": ibid., pp. 322–23.
"Come here . . .": ibid., p. 325.
"What an . . .": Griffith, p. 95.
"poor brainless . . .": Gordon, vol. 1, p. 322.
"You must . . .": ibid., p. 325.
"O, the crimes . . .": Harper, vol. 1, p. 160.
"Many a . . . heads.": Harper, p. 154.
"colored . . . social evil": Harper, p. 155.
"I did . . .": Gordon, vol. 1, pp. 351–52.
"in two . . .": Griffith, p. 93.
"How I do . . .": Gordon, vol. 1, pp. 352, 356.
"ah me!!! . . . groans": ibid., pp. 378–79.
"You need . . . see you": ibid., p. 387.
"I am . . . keep well": Lutz, p. 106.
"When you . . . from you": Gordon, vol. 1, p. 391.
"Where are     ": Lutz, p. 109.

**Chapter 12:** *"Nevertheless You Are Right"*
"Mrs. Stanton . . . crossed": Harper, vol. 1, pp. 186–87.
"In thought . . .": Stanton, p. 166.
"sit up far . . .": Harper, vol. 1, p. 187.
"powers . . . sacred right": Gordon, vol. 1, p. 408.
"She'd a great . . .": Harper, vol. 1, p. 193.
"set the . . .": ibid., p. 193.
"face was . . . sustain you": Stanton, p. 219.

"You are . . . slavery": Harper, vol. 1, p. 196.

"Fullest confidence . . .": Gordon, vol. 1, p. 435.

"The desire . . .": Stanton and Blatch, vol. 2, p. 80.

"He has . . .": ibid., p. 82.

"he is a man . . . code": Harper, vol. 1, pp. 195–97.

"the men . . .": Stanton and Blatch, vol. 1, p. 435.

"How can . . .": Gordon, vol. 1, p. 445.

"cautious . . . consequences": Harper, vol. 1, p. 197.

"The child belongs . . . stand by you": ibid., pp. 201–04.

"I think you . . .": Gordon, vol. 1, p. 454.

"a man of courage . . .": Stanton, p. 212.

"new life . . . hesitation": Griffith, p. 106.

"I have not yet . . .": Gordon, vol. 1, p. 468.

**Chapter 13:** *"Put on Your Armour and Go Forth!"*

"We have . . .": Stanton, p. 166.

"Tried to . . .": Harper, p. 216.

"I finished . . . for action": ibid., pp. 216–17.

"public work": ibid., p. 218.

"Any and every . . .": ibid., p. 221.

"While the old . . .": Gordon, vol. 1, p. 97.

"stunned and . . .": ibid., p. 224.

"not simply . . .": ibid., p. 225.

"The country . . . go forth": ibid., p. 226.

"<u>war</u> of <u>ideas</u>": Gordon, vol. 1, p. 500.

"shame on . . .": Harper, vol. 1, p. 227.

"civil and . . .": ibid., p. 229.

"go to the . . .": ibid., p. 230.

"Here's one of . . . of the republic": Stanton and Blatch, vol. 2, pp. 94–95.

"These are terrible . . .": Harper, vol. 1, p. 230.

"These petitions . . .": ibid., p. 235.

"We will have . . .": Lutz, p. 133.

"How I wish . . .": Gordon, vol. 1, p. 535.

"If that word . . .": ibid., p. 569.

"I think such . . . stand alone": Stanton and Blatch, p. 105.

"have their banners . . .": Lutz, p. 137.

"We can no . . . wholly": Gordon, vol. 1, p. 585.

"bore the double . . .": Harper, vol. 1, p. 269.

"extend the right . . . their ancestry": Harper, vol. 1, p. 268.

"emphatically the . . . perilous hour": Anderson, p. 371.

"I would gladly . . .": Gordon, vol. 1, p. 594.

"must buy . . .": Stanton, p. 115.

"two dozen unknown friends": Griffith, p. 126.

"I was convinced . . .": Stanton, p. 254.

**PART 3**

**Chapter 14:** *"Keep the Thing Stirring"*

"There is . . .": Stanton, Anthony, Gage, vol. 2, pp. 193–94.

"Women and colored men . . .": ibid., p. 227.

"With the help . . .": Gordon, vol. 2, p. 69.

"I could . . .": Kerr, p. 125.

"a finger's length": ibid., p. 125.

"The best . . . the constitution": Harper, vol. 1, pp. 278–79.

"most . . . Stanton": Stanton, pp. 117–18.

"so much . . .": Harper, vol. 1, pp. 282–83.

"All were . . . rapidly reduced": ibid., pp. 284–85.

"bushel . . . degree of cheerfulness": Stanton, pp. 246–52.

"come to . . .": Ellen Carol DuBois, *Feminism and Suffrage*, p. 94.

"shut out . . . Democrats": Stanton, Anthony, Gage, vol. 2, p. 264.

"a lunatic . . .": Griffith, p. 130.

"Kansas Suffrage Song": *Hurrah for Woman Suffrage* recording by Miriam Reed, Miriam Reed Productions, www.miriamreed.com.

"narrow policy . . .": Stanton, p. 254.

"first ever . . .": Harper, vol. 1, p. 291.

"I take . . . influence": ibid., p. 293.

"The agitation . . .": Stanton, p. 256.

"solemnly vowed . . .": Stanton, Anthony, Gage, vol. 2, pp. 267–68.

**Chapter 15:** *"Male Versus Female"*

"charged to . . . pretty baby": Harper, vol. 1, pp. 295–97.

"In quite . . .": Stanton, p. 123.

"her usual . . .": Harper, vol. 1, p. 314.

"Woman will . . .": Ellen DuBois, *Feminism & Suffrage*, p. 175.

"The are two . . .": Kerr, p. 140.

"like magic . . .": Lutz, p. 170.

"will be memorable . . .": Gordon, vol. 2, p. 236.

"I wish . . .": DuBois, p. 185.

"Feeling . . .": Harper, vol. 1, p. 319.

"who cannot . . .": Geoffrey C. Ward and Ken Burns, *Not For Ourselves Alone,* p. 123.

"division in . . .": Lutz, p. 180.

"I did my . . .": ibid., pp. 182–83.

"merge their . . .": Palmer, p. 437.

"So, I say . . .": Gordon, vol. 2, p. 284.

"deplored . . . public sentiment": Barry, p. 205.

"You and I . . .": Harper, vol. 1, p. 357.

"My paper . . . business": ibid., 351.

"My Dear Susan . . . mean *ever*": Stanton, pp. 123–25.

"already Free": Gordon, vol. 2, p. 407.

## Chapter 16: *"The Crowning Insult"*

"golden . . . a ribbon": Harper, vol. 1, p. 353.

"It was . . .": ibid., p. 362.

"Our *Revolution* . . .": Stanton and Blatch, vol. 2, p. 126.

"I never . . . my retreat": Gordon, vol. 2, pp. 359–60.

"At a dead lock . . . yoke of bondage": Harper, vol. 1, p. 366.

"Dearest Susan . . . blessed Susan": Stanton and Blatch, vol. 2, pp. 127–28.

"Met Mrs. S . . . tired out": Gordon, vol. 2, pp. 363, 367.

"I send . . . good to eat": ibid., p. 375.

"I loved . . . life's threads": Harper, vol. 1, p. 369.

"I think her . . .": Barbara A. White, *The Beecher Sisters,* p. 163.

"declined to be . . . displaced": Harper, vol. 1, p. 373.

"O, how I have . . . understand": Gordon, vol. 2, pp. 401–02.

"you see . . .": ibid., p. 402.

"on account . . . to races": Stanton, Anthony, Gage, vol. 2, p. 445.

"new, fresh . . . advocating": Harper, vol. 1, p. 367.

"Do not . . . Woodhull": Griffith, p. 148.

"When men . . . chaste": Harper, vol. 1, p. 379.

"I feel . . .": Gordon, vol. 2, p. 407.

"the crowning . . . and friction": Stanton and Blatch, vol. 2, p. 130.

"feeble health, to identify": Palmer, p. 460.

"We mean . . . social principles": Lutz, *Susan B. Anthony,* pp. 184–85.

## Chapter 17: *"I Have Been & Gone & Done It!"*

"We have . . . spirit of love": Harper, vol. 1, p. 388.

"women alone . . .": Stanton and Blatch, vol. 2, pp. 132–33.

"press sneers . . . for it": Harper, vol. 1, p. 387.

"Mrs. Stanton . . .": Stanton and Blatch, vol. 2, p. 134.

"a very pretty . . . children": Stanton, pp. 288–89.

"Never in . . . cut down": Harper, vol. 1, p. 392.

"piled one above another . . .": Stanton, p. 290.

"fat": ibid., p. 393.

"Trust one's . . . jelly": ibid., pp. 292–93.

"grand brave woman": Griffith, p. 151.

"Strong . . . on land again": Harper, vol. 1, p. 395.

"The first fire . . . clear for her": ibid., pp. 396–97.

"seize their . . .": ibid., p. 402.

"Remember that . . . quicksand": Gordon, vol. 2, p. 449.

"Thus closes . . .": Harper, vol. 1, p 407.

"looking over . . .": Gordon, vol. 2, p. 487.

"All our time . . .": Harper, vol. 1, p. 413.

"narrow, bigoted . . .": Ward and Burns, p. 141.

"A sad day . . .": ibid., p. 415.

"oldest and . . .": Barry, p. 247.

"equal rights . . . politicians": Harper, vol. 1, p. 416.

"a splinter . . . nothing": ibid., p. 420.

"dreadfully . . . vocabulary": Stanton and Blatch, p. 141.

"Now register . . .": Harper, vol. 1, p. 423.

"should be . . . right to vote": ibid., pp. 424–26.

## Chapter 18: *"Our Friendship Is Too Long Standing"*

"hardly find . . . the fine is paid": Harper, vol. 1, pp. 436–41.

"my continuous . . .": Stanton and Blatch, vol. 2, p. 143.

"It is as you say . . .": Gordon, vol. 2, p. 592.

"Constitution . . .": Harper, vol. 1, p. 453.

"a great social . . .": Gordon, vol. 3, p. 102.

"free love": ibid., p. 462.

"a friend . . . the subject": Griffith, p. 158.

"Offended, Susan . . .": Stanton and Blatch, p. 145.

"one-half . . .": Harper, vol., p. 475.

"found them . . . her strength": Barry, p. 269.

"We ask . . .": Lutz, *Susan B. Anthony*, p. 228.

"working for . . .": Harper, vol. 1, p. 430.

"wonderful head . . .": Stanton, p. 325.

"*our* children . . . my heart": Harper, vol. 1, pp. 488–89.

"with innumerable . . . people do": Gordon, vol. 4, pp. 560–61.

"I am immersed . . .": Harper, vol. 1, p. 480.

"Do be . . .": Harper, p. 488.

"I sit . . .": Stanton and Blatch, p. 150.

"You would . . .": Lutz, *Susan B. Anthony*, p. 202.

"withered beldames . . . go home": Harper, vol. 2, p. 517.

"newspaper ridicule . . . suffrage": Harper, vol. 1, p. 505.

"Our friendshship . . .": Harper, vol.1, p. 633.


**PART 4**

**Chapter 19: *"We Stood Appalled"***

"the rousingest . . . and lightning": Gordon, vol. 2, p. 527.

"had not . . . neck of woman": ibid., p. 518.

"large room . . . squabbling": Stanton and Blatch, vol. 2, p. 187.

"go down . . . present had": ibid., p. 172.

"bright sunny . . . example": ibid., pp. 177–78.

"stood appalled . . .": Stanton, p. 374.

"I am just sick . . .": Griffith, p. 177.

"We are . . .": Stanton and Blatch, p. 181.

"I welcomed . . .": Stanton, p. 276.

"It is . . .": Harper, vol. 1, p. 535.

"a little . . . the fort": Kerr, p. 208.

"leave these . . .": Gordon, vol. 2, p. 552.

"union of . . . fresh power": Stanton and Blatch, vol. 2, p. 169.

"It is so easy . . .": Harper, vol. 2, p. 537.

"The year . . . for the cause": Harper, vol. 2, p. 539.

"mischief . . . families": Stanton, Anthony, Gage, vol. 3, p. 199.

"thrilled . . . and blest": ibid., p. 228.

"O, how I . . .": Harper, vol. 2, p. 542.

"while the . . .": Kerr, p. 194.

"do credit . . .": Ward and Burns, p. 162.

"tall, dark . . .": Ellen Carol DuBois, *Harriot Stanton Blatch and the Winning of Woman Suffrage*, p. 40.

"one of . . . guard her": Stanton and Blatch, vol. 2, p. 200.

"Only think . . .": Harper, vol. 2, p. 544.

"an extra . . . Anthony": ibid., p. 547.

"stormy periods . . . in the wind": ibid., p. 549.

"the tiptoe . . .": Harper, vol. 2, p. 553.

"Our friends . . .": Stanton and Blatch, vol. 2, p. 208.

"Even the . . .": Harper, vol. 2, p. 265.

"the first . . .": DuBois, *Harriet Stanton Blatch*, p. 58.

"As I sit . . .": Stanton and Blatch, vol. 2, p. 217.

"more worlds . . .": Barry, p. 282.

"I prefer . . . of my own": Harper , vol. 2, p. 667.

"When Hattie and I . . .": Stanton and Blatch, vol. 2, p. 212.


**Chapter 20: *"Brace Up and Get Ready"***

"amalgamation . . . yours": Harper, vol. 2, p. 586.

"number of . . . great world": Stanton and Blatch, vol. 2, pp. 216–17.

"to keep . . . to vote": ibid., p. 219.

"I really think . . .": Harper, vol. 2, p. 600.

"was enough . . . dead standstill": Stanton and Blatch, vol. 2, p. 226.

"week . . . accomplish this": ibid., pp. 228–30.

"As to . . . cisterns": Carol Lasser and Marlene Deahl Merrill, *Friends and Sisters*, p. 250.

"Death . . . beyond": Stanton and Blatch, vol. 2, p. 236.

"I fear . . . no doubt.": Gordon, vol. 2, pp. 263–64.

"our beloved . . . a century": Gordon, vol. 4, p. 550.

"the rights . . .": Harper, vol. 4, p. 617.

"unsex . . .": ibid., p. 620.

"That we . . .": Anthony and Harper, vol. 4, p. 122.

"Oh dear . . .": Barry, p. 285.

"Put every . . .": Gordon, vol. 5, p. 10.

"all the women . . .": Stanton and Blatch, vol. 2, p. 237.

"We have . . . back": Harper, vol. 2, p. 635.

"the faithful . . . must go": Stanton and Blatch, vol. 2, p. 248.

"I am ablaze . . . permitted": Harper, vol. 2, p. 636.

"splendid agitation": Stanton and Blatch, p. 250.

"gay-hearted . . . minutes": ibid., pp. 637–38.

"Even the preamble . . . violence": Anthony and Harper, vol. 4, p. 138.

"up hill . . . weather": Stanton and Blatch, p. 320.

"mission to . . . seventh heaven": Stanton and Blatch, vol. 2, p. 259.

**Chapter 21: *"Under Your Thumb"***

"tempted . . . February": Stanton and Blatch, vol. 2, p. 260.

"Would . . . close of the war": ibid., p. 261.

"I am very . . . at my right hand": Harper, vol. 2, pp. 667–68.

"utmost liberty . . . vote for Mrs. Stanton": Gordon, vol. 5, pp. 246–47.

"greater . . . demonstration": Stanton and Blatch, vol. 2, p. 261.

"showed . . . for me": Gordon, vol. 5, p. 268.

"Saint-Susan . . . meeting": Anthony and Harper, vol. 4, p. 173.

"unalterably . . . without woman suffrage": ibid., pp. 999–1,000.

"I cannot . . . soul": Stanton and Blatch, p. 265.

"very . . . green grapes": Harper, vol. 2, pp. 689, 691.

"My advice . . . desire": Harper, vol. 2, p. 707.

"anchored": ibid., p. 712.

"filled with sadness . . . as possible": Stanton, p. 359.

"they might . . . utterances": Harper, vol. 2, p. 712.

"eyrie": Stanton, p. 433.

'summoned . . . command": ibid., pp. 433–34.

"I felt . . . mittens": Harper, vol. 2, p. 715.

"to think . . . years": Stanton and Blatch, vol. 2, p. 281.

"The point . . .": Estelle B. Freedman, *The Essential Feminist Reader*, p. 123.

"To Elizabeth . . .": Lutz, *Elizabeth Cady Stanton*, p. 290.

"clamber up . . . me": Stanton and Blatch, vol. 2, p. 290.

"general reading . . . into": Lutz, *Elizabeth Cady Stanton*, p. 297.

"Susan is . . . read them": Stanton and Blatch, p. 287.

"whole matter . . .": Harper, vol. 2, p. 729.

"simply overwhelmed": ibid., p. 737.

"She came . . .": Stanton, p. 375.

"he'd learn . . .": Rheta Childe Dorr, *Susan B. Anthony*, p. 306.

"Now we . . . moves": Stanton and Blatch, vol. 2, p. 301.

"the happiest . . .": Harper, vol. 2, p. 753.

""an insurrection . . . judgment": Harper, vol. 2, pp. 769–70.

"I seem . . . other": Stanton and Blatch, p. 304.

"great . . . oligarchy": ibid., p. 307.

"If the . . . South": Harper, vol. 2, p. 815.

"literally buried . . .": ibid., p. 827.

"thinner . . . if dead": ibid., p. 840–41.

"I never . . . the mend": ibid., p. 842.

"Surely . . . dream": ibid., p. 846.

"pioneers . . . Anthony": ibid., p. 848.

"able to . . .": Lutz, p. 293.

"Do all . . . think": Stanton and Blatch, p. 252.

"may feel . . . despair": "Elizabeth Cady Stanton," *The New York Times*, November 13, 1895, p. 1.

"Church and . . . man": Stanton et al., introduction.

"Women have . . .": Lutz, *Susan B. Anthony*, p. 304.

"Get political . . .": Harper, vol. 1, p. 857.

**Chapter 22: *"To Stir You and Others Up"***

"I could cry . . . narrow action": Lutz, *Susan B. Anthony*, pp. 279–80.

"Won't it . . . your help": Harper, vol. 2, p. 879.

"A great loss . . . on one subject": Stanton and Blatch, vol. 2, pp. 320–21.

"It is not . . . successes than any": Harper, vol. 2, p. 903.

"natural and . . .": Stanton, Anthony, Gage, vol. 2, p. 626.

"dimmer and dimmer": Stanton and Blatch, vol. 2, p. 325.

"would she . . . affairs": Harper, vol. 2, p. 914.

"It was a . . .": ibid., p. 917.

"The first . . . its own": Stanton and Blatch, vol. 2, p. 327.

"the prime . . . strong as ever": ibid.,
pp. 328–29.
"You will . . .": Stanton, Anthony, Gage, vol.
4, p. 288.
"Spring is . . . no report": Harper, vol. 3,
p. 1,113.
"her Queenmother . . . subjection": DuBois,
*Harriot Stanton Blatch*, p. 58.
"I really believe . . .": Barry, p. 327.
"I am as . . .": Stanton and Blatch, vol. 2,
p. 337.
"Though she . . .": Barry, p. 330.
"failing . . . planet": Stanton and Blatch,
vol. 2, p. 335.
"a warm . . .": ibid., p. 344.
"She accepted . . . to wait": ibid., p. 337.

Chapter 23: *"Oh, This Awful Hush"*
"ought to be done . . . of the nation": Stanton
and Blatch, vol. 2, p. 346.
"The hardships . . .": Harper, vol. 3, p. 1163.
"seem to know . . .": Stanton and Blatch,
vol. 2, p. 358.
"I am . . . do it well": Harper, vol. 3, p. 1170.
"You have . . . there again": Stanton,
Anthony, Gage, vol. 4, p. 389.
"The friendship . . .": Harper, vol. 3, p. 1186.
"As I was . . .": ibid., p. 1269.
"Give it . . . and Courage": ibid., pp.
1223–26.
"There is no . . . A-MEN!": Barry, p. 337.
"I thought . . . be seen": Harper, vol. 3,
p. 1,228.

"persuaded not . . . always well": Stanton and
Blatch, vol. 2, p. 354.
"But it . . .": ibid., p. 358.
"loyalty . . . convention": Harper, vol. 3,
p. 1232.
"had earned . . .": Stanton and Blatch, p. 358.
"magnificent view . . .": ibid., p. 1241.
"He said . . .": Stanton and Blatch, vol. 2,
p. 358.
"crept along . . .": Harper, vol. 3, p. 1244.
"though Mrs. Stanton . . . still strong": ibid.
p. 1255.
"Shall I . . . know it": ibid., p. 1256.
"sure there . . .": Lutz, *Elizabeth Cady Stanton*,
p. 318.
"It is fifty- one . . .": Ida Husted Harper,
*History of Woman Suffrage*, vol. 5,
pp. 741–42.
"Mother passed . . . who dies!": Harper, vol.
3, pp. 1262–64.
"Dear Mr. Roosevelt . . .": ibid., p. 1275.
"The pioneers . . .": ibid., p. 1289.
"We have . . .": ibid., p. 1308.
"Why not . . .": ibid. , p. 1306.
"because of deeds . . .": ibid., p. 1365.
"The fight . . . endlessly!": ibid., 1397.
"There have been . . . is impossible": ibid.,
p. 1408.
"So dear Susan . . .": ibid., p. 1453.

Epilogue
"Three ladies . . ." Author's conversation
with tour guides.

# SELECTED BIBLIOGRAPHY

Additional sources, a reading guide, and podcasts are at www.pennycolman.com.

Anderson, Bonnie, S. *Joyous Greetings: The First International Women's Movement, 1830–1860* (New York: Oxford University Press, 2000).

Anthony, Susan B. *The Ghost in My Life* (Old Tappan, NJ: Fleming H. Revell, 1971).

Banner, Lois W. *Elizabeth Cady Stanton: A Radical for Woman's Rights* (Boston: Little, Brown, 1980).

Barry, Kathleen. *Susan B. Anthony: A Biography of a Singular Feminist* (New York: Ballantine Books, 1988).

Bayne, Julia Taft. *Hadley Ballads* (Kila, TN: Kessinger Publishing, 2009).

Blatch, Harriot Stanton, and Alma Lutz. *Challenging Years: The Memoirs of Harriot Stanton Blatch* (New York: G. P. Putnam's Sons, 1940).

Buhle, Mari Jo, and Paul Buhle, eds. *The Concise History of Woman Suffrage: Selections from the Classic Work of Stanton, Gage, and Harper* (Urbana, IL: University of Illinois Press, 1978).

Cromwell, Otelia. *Lucretia Mott* (Cambridge, MA: Harvard University Press, 1958).

Dorr, Rheta Childe. *Susan B. Anthony: The Woman Who Changed the Mind of a Nation* (New York: Frederick A. Stokes, 1928).

DuBois, Ellen Carol. *Feminism & Suffrage* (Ithaca, NY: Cornell University Press, 1999).

———. *Harriot Stanton Blatch and the Winning of Woman Suffrage* (New Haven, CT: Yale University Press, 1997).

DuBois, Ellen Carol, ed. *Elizabeth Cady Stanton/Susan B. Anthony: Correspondence, Writings, Speeches* (New York: Schocken Books, 1981).

DuBois, Ellen Carol, and Richard Cándida Smith, eds. *Elizabeth Cady Stanton, Feminist as Thinker: A Reader in Documents and Essays* (New York: New York University Press, 2007).

Flexner, Eleanor, and Ellen Fitzpatrick. *Century of Struggle: The Woman's Rights Movement in the United States*, enlarged edition (Cambridge, MA: Harvard University Press, 1996).

Foner, Philip S., ed. *Frederick Douglass on Women's Rights* (New York: Da Capo Press, 1992).

Freedman, Estelle B., ed. *The Essential Feminist Reader* (New York: The Modern Library, 2007).

Frost, Elizabeth, and Kathryn Cullen-DuPont. *Women's Suffrage in America* (New York: Facts On File, 1992).

Ginzberg, Lori D. *Elizabeth Cady Stanton: An American Life* (New York: Hill and Wang, 2009).

Gordon, Ann D., ed. *The Selected Papers of Elizabeth Cady Stanton & Susan B. Anthony,* volumes *1–5* (New Brunswick, NJ: Rutgers University Press, 1997–2009).

Griffith, Elisabeth. *In Her Own Right: The Life of Elizabeth Cady Stanton* (New York: Oxford University Press, 1984).

Gurko, Miriam. *The Ladies of Seneca Falls: The Birth of the Woman's Rights Movement* (New York: Schocken Books, 1974).

Harper, Ida Husted. *The Life and Work of Susan B. Anthony: Including Public Addresses, Her Own Letters and Many from Her Contemporaries During Fifty Years,* 3 volumes (Indianapolis, IN: The Hollenbeck Press, vols. 1 and 2, 1898; vol. 3, 1908).

Holland, Patricia G., and Ann D. Gordon, eds. *The Papers of Elizabeth Cady Stanton and Susan B. Anthony,* microfilm edition (Wilmington, DE: Scholarly Resources, 1991).

——. *Guide and Index to the Microfilm Edition* (Wilmington, DE: Scholarly Resources, 1992).

Jones, Martha S. *All Bound Up Together: The Woman Question in African American Public Culture, 1830–1900* (Chapel Hill: University of North Carolina Press, 2006).

Kerr, Andrea Moore. *Lucy Stone: Speaking Out for Equality* (New Brunswick, NJ: Rutgers University Press, 1992).

Keyssar, Alexander. *The Right to Vote: The Contested History of Democracy in the United States* (New York: Basic Books, 2000).

Lasser, Carol, and Marlene Deahl Merrill, eds. *Friends and Sisters: Letters Between Lucy Stone and Antoinette Brown Blackwell 1846–93.* (Chicago: University of Illinois Press, 1987.)

Lutz, Alma. *Created Equal: A Biography of Elizabeth Cady Stanton, 1815–1902* (New York: The John Day Company, 1940).

——. *Susan B. Anthony: Rebel, Crusader, Humanitarian* (Boston: Beacon Press, 1959).

Mayer, Henry. *All on Fire: William Lloyd Garrison and the Abolition of Slavery* (New York: St. Martin's Griffin, 1998).

McMillen, Sally G. *Seneca Falls and the Origins of the Women's Rights Movement* (New York: Oxford University Press, 2008).

Painter, Nell Irvin. *Sojourner Truth: A Life, a Symbol* (New York: W. W. Norton, 1996).

Palmer, Beverly Wilson, ed. *Selected Letters of Lucretia Coffin Mott* (Urbana and Chicago: University of Illinois Press, 2002).

Parton, James, et al. *Eminent Women of the Age: Being Narratives of the Lives and Deeds of the Most Prominent Women of the Present Generation* (Hartford, CT: S. M. Betts & Co., 1869).

Penney, Sherry H., and James D. Livingston. *A Very Dangerous Woman: Martha Wright and Women's Rights* (Amherst: University of Massachusetts Press, 2004).

Perry, Mark. *Lift Up Thy Voice: The Grimké Family's Journey from Slaveholders to Civil Rights Leaders* (New York: Penguin Books, 2001).

Russo, Ann, and Cheris Kramarae, eds. *The Radical Women's Press of the 1850s* (New York: Routledge, 1991).

Sherr, Lynn. *Failure Is Impossible: Susan B. Anthony in Her Own Words* (New York: Times Books, 1995).

Sklar, Kathryn Kish. *Women's Rights Emerges Within the Antislavery Movement 1830–1870: A Brief History with Documents* (Boston: Bedford/St. Martin's, 2000).

Stanton, Elizabeth Cady. *Eighty Years and More: Reminiscences 1815–1897* (New York: Shocken Books, 1971; reprinted from T. Fisher Urwin edition, 1898).

———— *The Woman's Bible* (Boston: Northeastern University Press, 1993; first published 1895).

Stanton, Elizabeth Cady, Susan B. Anthony, and Matilda Joslyn Gage, eds. *History of Woman Suffrage*, volumes 1–3 (New York: Fowler and Wells, 1881, 1882; Rochester, NY: Susan B. Anthony, 1886).

Stanton, Theodore, and Harriet Stanton Blatch, eds. *Elizabeth Cady Stanton as Revealed in Her Letters, Diary, and Reminiscences*, 2 volumes (New York: Harper & Brothers, 1922).

Sterling, Dorothy. *Lucretia Mott, Gentle Warrior* (New York: The Feminist Press, 1999).

Ulrich, Laurel Thatcher. *Well-Behaved Women Seldom Make History* (New York: Alfred A. Knopf, 2007).

Ward, Geoffrey C., and Ken Burns. *Not for Ourselves Alone: The Story of Elizabeth Cady Stanton and Susan B. Anthony* (New York: Alfred A. Knopf, 1999)

Wellman, Judith. *The Road to Seneca Falls: Elizabeth Cady Stanton and the First Woman's Rights Convention* (Urbana: University of Illinois Press, 2004).

White, Barbara Anne. *The Beecher Sisters* (New Haven, CT: Yale University Press, 2003).

# WEBLIOGRAPHY

Elizabeth Cady Stanton Trust is online at www.elizabethcadystanton.org.

The Elizabeth Cady Stanton & Susan B. Anthony Papers Project, Rutgers, the State University of New Jersey, and the National Historical Publications and Records Commission, online at http://ecssba.rutgers.edu/.

"George Francis Train and the Woman Suffrage Movement, 1867–70," Patricia G. Holland, from *Books at Iowa* 46 (April 1987) online at www.lib.uiowa.edu/spec-coll/bai/holland.htm.

The Lucretia Coffin Mott Papers Project is online at http://Mott.pomona.edu.

"This Shall be the Land for Women: The Struggle for Western Women's Suffrage, 1860–1920," Women of the West Museum, online at http://theautry.org/explore/exhibits/suffrage.

"Susan B. Anthony: Celebrating 'A Heroic Life,'" includes many images, is online at http://www.lib.rochester.edu/index.cfm?page=4119.

"Susan B. Anthony House Virtual Tour," featuring her home in Rochester, is online at www.susanbanthonyhouse.org/tour0.shtml.

"Susan B. Anthony in Nebraska, late August–October 14, 1882," part of Women on the Rails: Nebraska Suffragists and the Railroad, is online at http://segonku.unl.edu/~lworking/SBA_TourMovie.html.

The Susan B. Anthony Manuscript Collection, including the entire poem Elizabeth wrote for Susan's eightieth birthday celebration, can be read at http://www.libraryweb.org/rochimag/SBA/ephemera.htm.

"Votes for Women: Selections from the National American Woman Suffrage Association Collection, 1848–1921," Library of Congress, is online at http://memory.loc.gov/ammem/naw/nawshome.html.

"Votes for Women: Suffrage Pictures, 1850–1920," Library of Congress, is online at http://memory.loc.gov/ammem/vfwhtml/vfwhome.html.

"Western New York Suffragists: Winning the Vote" online resource at www.winningthevote.org.

The Women's Rights National Historical Park is online at www.nps.gov/wori.

Note: The following books can all be read online at http://books.google.com: *Elizabeth Cady Stanton as Revealed in Her Letters, Diary, and Reminiscences*, edited by Theodore Stanton and Harriot Stanton Blatch; *The History of Woman Suffrage* by Elizabeth Cady Stanton, Susan B. Anthony, and Matilda Joslyn Gage; *The Life and Work of Susan B. Anthony* by Ida Husted Harper; *The Solitude of Self* by Elizabeth Cady Stanton; *The Woman's Bible* by Elizabeth Cady Stanton; and the novel *Adam Bede* by George Eliot, which Elizabeth and Susan discussed.

# INDEX

Abolitionism, 18–21, 23, 24, 31, 43, 55–56, 61, 70, 86, 91, 93–94, 99, 120, 174; debate over women's proper roles in society and, 20, 22–23, 33–34; Lincoln's policies and, 94–95, 100–101; outbreak of Civil War and, 96, 98; Quakers split over, 28; Radical Republicans and, 105; riots against, 20–21; Susan's petition campaign and, 102, 104; World's Anti-Slavery Convention of 1840 and, 31, 33–34

*Adam Bede* (Eliot), 98–99

Albany, N.Y., woman's rights convention in (1854), 72

American Anti-Slavery Society (AASS), 19–20, 23, 83, 106, 108

American Equal Rights Association (AERA), 107, 114, 126, 127

American Woman Suffrage Association (AWSA), 128–29, 156, 169–70, 172, 186, 188

*Anna Karenina* (Tolstoy), 183

Anthony, Anna (sister-in-law), 105

Anthony, Daniel (brother), 15, 27, 104–5

Anthony, Daniel (father), 13, 14, 15, 25, 40, 44, 53, 54, 55, 98; bankruptcy of, 27, 42–43; death of, 100; supportive of Susan's activism, 60, 94, 100, 159

Anthony, Eliza (sister), 15

Anthony, Guelma (sister). *See* McLean, Guelma Anthony

Anthony, Hannah (sister). *See* Mosher, Hannah Anthony

Anthony, Jacob (brother), 15, 27

Anthony, Lucy (mother), 13–16, 27, 29, 42–43, 44, 53, 55, 56, 60, 98, 191

Anthony, Mary (sister), 15, 27, 42–43, 56, 129, 151, 152, 190–91, 203, 215, 216, 220, 222–23

Anthony, Merritt (brother), 15, 42–43

Anthony, Susan B.: abolitionism and, 14, 28, 40, 43, 55, 56, 83, 86, 99, 102, 104, 174; arrest and trial of, 152–55, 162; birth and childhood of, 3, 12–16; death of, 222; education of, 14, 16, 25; eightieth birthday celebration for, 213, 214–15, 218; Elizabeth's collaborative work with, 88–89, 160; Elizabeth's first meeting with, 3, 59–60; European vacation of, 175–76; first public speech of, 54–55; history of woman's movement written by (*see History of Woman Suffrage*); lecture tours of, 83, 121, 133, 134, 135, 142–47, 161; marriage prospects and, 28, 41, 44–45, 53, 79; petition campaign of, for woman's rights, 71–72, 73, 78–79, 81, 89; physical appearance of, 12–13, 107, 117, 174; portraits of, 192, 218, 224; religious upbringing of, 13–15, 60, 201; Rochester home of, 190–91; seventieth birthday of, 188, 190–91; stroke suffered by, 216–17; as teacher, 25, 27, 28, 29, 40, 43–44, 53, 55, 60; temperance and, 14, 54–55, 56, 60, 61–63, 64, 66–67, 68, 70–71; tensions in leadership of woman's movement and, 126–29, 148–49, 169–70, 172, 180, 186, 188; voting rights and (*see* woman suffrage); war effort and, 97, 101–2

Anti-Female Suffrage Committee, 118

"Antis," 197

Anti-Slavery Convention of American Women, 21

Antislavery movement. *See* Abolitionism

*Appeal to the Christian Women of the South, An* (A. Grimké), 21–22

Baptists, 13–14

Bascom, Mary, 48

Bayard, Edward (Elizabeth's brother-in-law), 11, 24, 31, 38, 106

Bayard, Tryphena Cady (Elizabeth's sister), 8, 11, 38, 106, 191

Bayne, Julia Taft, 12

Beecher, Catharine, 22
Beecher, Henry Ward, 127, 128, 132, 156–57
Bible. *See Woman's Bible, The*
Bingham, Anson, 88
Birney, James G., 32, 33
Black Codes, 125
Black male suffrage, 105–6, 107–8, 109, 114, 115, 116, 120, 125, 128
Blackwell, Antoinette Brown, 70, 80, 83, 85, 180
Blackwell, Henry, 80, 114, 115
Blackwell, Samuel, 80
Blatch, Harriot Stanton (known as Hattie, Elizabeth's daughter), 50, 82, 85, 106, 135, 147, 159, 161, 168, 172–73, 175, 179, 180, 181, 187, 189, 191–92, 197, 210, 215, 219, 220
Blatch, Nora (Elizabeth's granddaughter), 176, 210
Blatch, William Henry, Jr. (known as Harry, Elizabeth's son-in-law), 173, 175
Bloomer, Amelia, 51, 59, 62
Bloomers, 59, 65, 66, 74–75, 123
Bradley, Joseph P., 206
Brant, Joseph, 43
Brown, Antoinette. *See* Blackwell, Antoinette Brown
Brown, John, 86, 87
Brown, Rev. Olympia, 115, 135, 201, 218
Browning, Elizabeth Barrett, 98
Bullard, Laura Curtis, 133
Burtis, Sarah Anthony (Susan's cousin), 56
Bush, Abigail, 49

Cabot, Caroline, 211
Cady, Catharine (known as Cate, sister), 8, 35, 106, 178
Cady, Daniel (father), 7, 8–9, 11, 18, 24, 35, 37, 38, 60, 72–73, 86, 87
Cady, Eleazar (brother), 8, 9
Cady, Harriet (sister). *See* Eaton, Harriet Cady
Cady, Margaret (known as Madge, sister), 8, 31–32, 35, 178
Cady, Margaret Livingston (mother), 7–8, 18, 64, 73, 103, 145
Cady, Tryphena (sister). *See* Bayard, Tryphena Cady
California: Susan and Elizabeth's trip to, 142–45; woman suffrage referendum in, 197, 204–5

Canajoharie Academy, 43–44, 53, 55
Canajoharie Daughters of Temperance, 54–55
Capitol Rotunda, U.S., 224
Cary, Mary Ann Shadd, 150
Catt, Carrie Chapman, 196, 214
Centennial Celebration (1876), 157–58, 159
Channing, Rev. William Ellery, 72
Chapman, Maria, 38
Child, Lydia Maria, 38
Children, custody or guardianship of, 9, 72, 92–94, 132–33
*Cincinnati Enquirer,* 122
Citizenship: of freed slaves, 105–6 (*see also* Fourteenth Amendment); gender and, 102, 105–6, 124, 131, 139–40, 181–82, 224; military draft and, 102–3; right to vote and, 114, 125, 131, 138, 153–54, 155 (*see also* Fifteenth Amendment)
Civil War, 94–104, 125; cessation of campaign for woman's rights during, 96, 97, 99–100, 104, 109; draft riots and, 102–4; Elizabeth and Susan's disagreement over, 96, 97; slavery issue and, 94–95, 96, 98, 100–102, 104; woman's organization in support of, 101–2
Claflin, Tennessee, 137, 138
Cleveland, Grover, 194
Cleveland, Ohio, national woman's rights convention in (1853), 71
Cody, William "Buffalo Bill," 195, 196
Coeducation, 82
Colby, Clara Bewick, 173, 201, 202, 211, 219
College education for women, 9–10, 84, 161, 194, 215–16
Colorado, woman suffrage in, 161, 196, 209
Congress, U.S., 125, 208, 214; Elizabeth's candidacy for seat in, 108–9; slavery and, 20, 83, 104, 105; woman suffrage and, 107, 108, 124, 126, 131, 134, 137–38, 139–40, 147, 171–72, 181–82, 184, 185, 187–88, 189–90, 193–94, 210, 211, 221, 222
Constitution, U.S., 86, 101, 104, 107, 153, 155, 185; word "male" first inserted into, 105–6, 124. *See also specific amendments*
Cook, Coralie Franklin, 214
Cooper, Alice, 222
Copperheads (Peace Democrats), 101, 119–20
Correll, Erasmus, 173
Correll, Lucy, 173

Cowles, Betsey Mix, 52
Crittenden, A. P., 144
Crystal Palace (New York City), 70
Cuba, 210–11

Daughters of Temperance, 54–55, 60, 61
Davies, Charles, 69, 70, 84
Davis, Paulina Wright, 47, 64
Declaration of Independence, 49, 153, 158
Declaration of Sentiments, 47, 48, 51, 56,
    209, 213
Democratic Party, 134, 149, 168, 194
*Denver News*, 143
Divorce, 62, 66, 89–91, 123, 136
Douglass, Frederick, 38, 48, 49, 55, 59, 149,
    177–78, 199
Douglass, Joseph, 214
Dress reform, 51, 59, 65, 66, 74–75, 123
*Dublin Weekly Herald*, 34
Duniway, Abigail Scott, 146
"Duty of Church to Women at This Hour,
    The" (Stanton), 218

Eaton, Daniel C. (Elizabeth's brother-in-
    law), 32, 35
Eaton, Harriet Cady (Elizabeth's sister), 8,
    32, 35, 106
Eddy, Eliza Jackson, 171, 218
Eddy, Sarah J., 218
"Educated suffrage," 208, 219
Education: coeducation and, 82; college, for
    women, 9–10, 84, 161, 194, 215–16; race
    segregation and, 84
*Eighty Years & More* (Stanton), 11, 36–37, 73,
    109, 118–19, 168, 191–92; writing of,
    204, 206, 208–9
Eliot, George (Mary Ann Evans), 98–99,
    183
Emancipation Proclamation, 100–101
*Epistle to the Clergy of the Southern States*
    (S. Grimké), 22
Exhibition of Industry of All Nations
    (1853), 70

Fair, Laura D., 144
Federation of Women's Clubs, 212
Ferry, Thomas W., 158
Fifteenth Amendment, 125–26, 127, 128,
    138, 139, 140, 147
Finney, Charles Grandison, 10
First National Woman's Rights Convention
    (1850), 52, 56

Foster, Rachel, 169, 175
Fourteenth Amendment, 105, 108,
    109, 124, 125, 131, 138, 139, 147, 151,
    155
Freedom of speech, 95
"Free love," 138, 140, 156, 157
Fugitive Slave Act (1850), 83, 94
Fuller, Margaret, 47

Gage, Matilda Joslyn, 64, 148, 155, 158,
    159, 169, 201
Gardner, Nanette, 151
Garrison, William Lloyd, 19, 23, 33, 59, 77,
    91, 93–94, 122, 128
Grant, Julia Dent, 139
Grant, Ulysses S., 139, 149, 150
Greeley, Horace, 49, 114, 115–16, 132, 140,
    143, 149, 150
Greenwood, Grace (Sara Jane Lippincott),
    124–25
Grimké, Angelina, 21–23, 31, 36, 65,
    150
Grimké, Sarah, 21–23, 31, 36, 47, 65,
    150

Halstead, Alva, 217
Happersett, Reese, 155
Harper, Ida Husted, 45, 206, 207, 215, 221
Harris, Ira, 92, 93
Hawaii, 210
Hay, William, 72
*Herkimer Freeman*, 49
Hicks, Elias, 28
*History of Woman Suffrage* (Cady, Anthony,
    and Gage), 80, 159–61, 168, 169, 170–71,
    172, 178–80, 215
*Home Journal*, 122–23
Hooker, Isabella Beecher, 127, 128, 130,
    136–37, 138, 148, 149, 157, 170, 181
Hovey, Charles, 38, 91
Hovey Fund, 91, 96
Hunt, Jane, 46
Hunt, Ward, 153–55
Hutchinson, John, 120, 214
Hutchinson Family Singers, 101, 115, 120,
    158

Idaho, woman suffrage referendum in, 204,
    205–6
Immigrants, 54, 125, 208
Inheritance rights, 89
Intermarriage of races, 177–78

# Index

International Council of Women (ICW), 182, 183–85, 211, 221
International Woman Suffrage Conference (1902), 219

Jackson, Francis, 218
Johnson, Adelaide, 192, 224
Johnstown Academy, 8, 9
Julian, George Washington, 126, 159

Kansas, woman suffrage referendums in, 113–15, 116–21, 162, 196
Kansas-Nebraska Act (1854), 83
"Kansas Suffrage Song," 120
Ku Klux Klan, 125

Lapham, Anson (Susan's cousin), 129
*Letters on the Equality of the Sexes and the Condition of Woman* (S. Grimké), 22–23, 47
*Letters to Catharine Beecher* (A. Grimké), 22
*Liberator*, 19, 22, 91
*Lily*, 51, 52, 79
Lincoln, Abraham, 94–95, 100–101, 105
Liquor Dealers' League, 204
Longfellow, Rev. Samuel, 90
Lozier, Clemence, 124, 179

Madison, James, 153
Married women, legal rights of, 9, 24, 47, 60, 71–74, 88–89
Married Women's Property Act of 1848, 47
Married Women's Property Act of 1860, 88–89; repeal of parts of, 99–100; Susan's petition campaign and, 71–72, 73, 78–79, 81, 89
Martineau, Harriet, 162
May, Rev. Samuel J., 47, 62, 95
Mayo, Rev. A. D., 90
McCrummel, James, 20
McFarland, Daniel, 132–33
McLean, Aaron (Susan's brother-in-law), 28–29, 41
McLean, Ann Eliza (Susan's niece), 136
McLean, Guelma Anthony (Susan's sister), 15, 16, 27, 28, 29, 151, 152
McLean, Thomas (Susan's nephew), 136
M'Clintock, Mary Ann, 46, 47, 48, 209
Meeker, Nathan Cook, 143
Meeker, Ralph, 143
Minor, Francis, 131, 138, 155
Minor, Virginia, 131, 138, 155

*Minor v. Happersett*, 155, 162
Missouri Compromise (1820), 83
Moore, Thomas, 30
Morgan, John Tyler, 171
Mosher, Eugene (Susan's brother-in-law), 41–42
Mosher, Hannah Anthony (Susan's sister), 15, 16, 27, 41–42, 55, 151, 152
Mott, Abigail, 40
Mott, James, 33, 34, 46, 108
Mott, Lucretia, 13, 23, 34, 35, 46, 50–51, 64–65, 80, 145, 148, 159, 169, 171, 184, 192, 199, 221; in anti-slavery movement, 20, 21, 28, 33, 34; in woman's rights movement, 34, 46, 47, 48, 49, 64, 76–77, 90, 108, 125, 128, 135, 140, 158, 174
Mott, Lydia, 92, 100
Deborah Moulson's Female Seminary, 25–26
*Myra Bradwell v. Illinois*, 206

National American Woman Suffrage Association (NAWSA), 188–89, 194; annual conventions of, 189, 193, 202–3, 205, 208, 209–10, 213, 214, 217, 219, 221–22; formation of, 186, 188; Susan and Elizabeth's program for future of, 213–14
*National Anti-Slavery Standard*, 108
National Woman's Council, 199
National Woman Suffrage Association (NWSA), 127, 128, 148–49, 158, 167, 170, 186, 188
National Woman Suffrage Conventions, 130–31, 136–37, 138–39, 147, 171, 181, 193; first (1869), 124–25
Neall, Elizabeth, 33, 36
Nebraska, woman suffrage referendum in, 173–74
New Departure, 131, 138, 139, 147, 151, 155
New Woman, 195
New York City: draft riots in, 102–4; Elizabeth as congressional candidate in, 108–9; Elizabeth's homes in, 99, 101, 105, 134, 192, 210; national woman's rights conventions in, 89–91, 107, 135; reform groups' September 1953 conventions in, 70–71; Woman Suffrage Bazaar in (1900), 217; Women's Loyal National League meeting in (1863), 101–2
New York Lyceum Bureau, 128

New York State: battle over woman suffrage in, 113–14, 115–16, 140–41, 162, 178, 196–97; teachers' conventions in, 68–70, 81, 82–83, 84, 98, 100
New York State Constitution, 108, 113, 115–16
New York State Legislature: Elizabeth's address to (1854), 72–74; Married Women's Property acts and, 47, 88–89, 99–100; Susan's petition campaign on behalf of woman's rights and, 71–72, 73, 78–79, 81, 89; woman suffrage and, 113–14, 115–16, 207
*New York Sunday Times*, 123
*New York Times*, 155
*New York Tribune*, 79, 114, 115, 116, 132, 143
Nichols, Clarina Howard, 169
Nineteenth Amendment, 224
 *See also* Sixteenth Amendment
Northrop, Mrs., 70

Ohio Women's Convention (1850), 51–52
Oregon: Susan's lecture tour in, 146; woman suffrage referendum in, 178
Osborne, Eliza Wright, 207, 221

Pacifism, 13, 60, 96
Paine, Thomas, 153
Parker, Theodore, 37–38, 81
Peace Democrats (Copperheads), 101, 119–20
People's League, 66
Phelps, Charles Abner, 92–94
Phelps, Phoebe Harris, 92–94
Philadelphia, Pa., national woman's rights convention in (1854), 76
Philadelphia Female Anti-Slavery Society, 20
Phillips, Ann, 33
Phillips, Wendell, 33, 78, 89–91, 96, 106, 107, 108, 123, 171
Pillsbury, Parker, 38, 122
Pitts, Helen, 177–78
*Portrait Monument to Lucretia Mott, Elizabeth Cady Stanton, and Susan B. Anthony* (Johnson), 224
Post, Amy, 49, 55, 59, 90
Postal Service, U.S., 156
Potter, Helen, 200
Powell, Elisha, 47
Powell, Harriet, 18–19

Property rights of women, 9, 71–74, 88–89
Public speaking, as male vs. female sphere, 22
Pugh, Sarah, 33, 135
Purvis, Robert, 107, 174

Quakers (Society of Friends), 13, 14, 28, 33, 44, 60, 201

Radical Republicans, 105
Read, Joshua (Susan's uncle), 27, 42, 43
Reagan, John, 189
Reconstruction, 105
Religious revivals, 10, 54
"Remonstrants," 197
Republican Party, 75, 94, 105, 114, 118, 119–20, 121, 125, 134, 139, 168, 194; equal rights for women mentioned in platform of, 149–50
*Revolution*, 121, 122–23, 124, 125, 126–27, 129–30, 133–34, 170
Rhode Island, woman suffrage referendum in, 182
Richardson, Albert D., 132
Riddle, Albert Gallatin, 138
Robinson, Charles, 118, 120
Robinson, Harriet, 170
Rochester, N.Y.: New York State Teachers' Convention in (1853), 68–70; temperance convention in (1852), 62; woman's rights convention in (1848), 49, 52, 56
Rogers, Seth (Susan's cousin), 81
Roosevelt, Theodore, 221, 222
Rose, Ernestine, 47, 64

Sacajawea, 222
Sage, Abby, 132
*St. Louis Reveille*, 49
Scott, Dred, 83
Second Great Awakening, 10
Segregation of races, 84
Selden, Henry R., 151–52
Senate, U.S. *See* Congress, U.S.
Seneca Falls, N.Y.: antislavery meeting in (1851), 59–60; woman's rights convention in (1848), 46–49, 50, 51, 52, 56, 80, 183, 190, 208, 209
"Sewing" (Stanton), 51
Shaw, Anna Howard, 194, 198
"Significance and History of the Ballot, The" (Stanton), 208

Sixteenth Amendment (ratified as Nineteenth Amendment), 126, 128, 134, 136, 155–56, 162, 167–68, 181–82, 224

Slavery, 18–21; abolished by Thirteenth Amendment, 104, 125; Brown's raid and, 86, 87; emancipation and, 94, 95, 100–102; legislation of 1850s and, 83; Lincoln's policies and, 94–95. *See also* Abolitionism

Smith, Ann (known as Nancy, Gerrit's wife), 17, 18, 30–31, 103

Smith, Elizabeth (known as Libby, Elizabeth's cousin), 17, 109, 124, 143, 176, 207, 211, 221

Smith, Elizabeth Oakes, 63–64

Smith, Gerrit (Elizabeth's cousin), 17–19, 24, 31, 106, 123, 162

"Solitude of Self, The" (Stanton), 193

*Sonnets from the Portuguese* (Browning), 98

Sons of Temperance, 60, 61, 62–63

South Dakota, woman suffrage referendum in, 190

Southwick, Joseph, 38

Southwick, Thankful, 38

Southworth, Louisa, 199

Spanish-American War (1898), 210

Spencer, Sara, 167

Stanton, Daniel Cady (known as Neil, son), 36, 39, 65, 96, 98, 103, 106, 135, 159, 168, 179, 186, 191

Stanton, Elizabeth Cady, 30–39, 46–52, 56; abolitionism and, 18–19, 23, 24, 34, 86, 95, 104; autobiography of (*see Eighty Years & More*); birth and childhood of, 3, 7–9; Boston years of, 37–38; as candidate for seat in Congress, 108–9; courtship and wedding of, 23–24, 30–31; death and funeral of, 219–21; dress reform and, 51, 59, 65, 66, 74–75; education of, 8, 9–10, 17; eightieth birthday celebration of, 199–201; European sojourns of, 31–35, 172–73, 175–76, 180–81, 183–84, 187, 189, 191–92; history of woman's movement written by (*see History of Woman Suffrage*); illnesses and declining health of, 170, 211–12; inferior status of women experienced by, early in life, 8–10; introduced to reform movements, 17–19, 23; lecture tours of, 121, 130, 142–45, 161; as mother, 36–37, 39, 50–51, 52, 59, 63, 64–66, 68, 72, 74, 75, 78, 80, 82, 84–86, 95, 96, 98, 99, 134, 160; New York City homes of, 99, 101–3, 105, 106, 134, 210; physical appearance of, 106–7, 117; portraits of, 192, 224; religious beliefs of, 10–11; religious institutions critiqued by, 196, 200, 218, 219 (*see also The Woman's Bible*); Seneca Falls home of, 38–39; seventieth birthday celebration of, 179; Susan's collaborative work with, 88–89, 160; Susan's first meeting with, 3, 59–60; temperance and, 36, 37, 51, 61–62, 66–67; Tenafly home of, 134, 135, 159–60, 178–79, 185; tensions in leadership of woman's movement and, 126–29, 148–49, 169–70, 172, 180, 186, 188; vision problems of, 204, 212; voting rights and (*see* Woman suffrage); war effort and, 97, 101–2

Stanton, Elizabeth Cady, II (known as Lizette, granddaughter), 172

Stanton, Gerrit Smith (known as Gat, son), 37, 39, 65, 96, 98, 106, 135, 159, 168, 185, 186

Stanton, Harriot Eaton (known as Hattie, daughter). *See* Blatch, Harriot Stanton

Stanton, Henry (husband), 30–32, 33, 34, 35, 37, 38, 48, 65, 75–76, 86, 95, 96, 99, 101, 106, 134, 135, 159, 168; courtship and wedding of, 23–24, 30–31; death of, 180–81; objections of, to Elizabeth's woman's rights work, 79, 80

Stanton, Henry Brewster, Jr. (known as Kit, son), 37, 39, 65, 96, 98, 106, 135, 159, 168

Stanton, Margaret Livingston (known as Maggie, daughter), 50, 64–65, 75–76, 106, 135, 159, 160, 168, 185–86, 191, 192, 207, 210, 217, 222–23

Stanton, Marguerite Berry (daughter-in-law), 172

Stanton, Robert Livingston (known as Bob, son), 85, 106, 135, 159, 168, 192, 210, 217

Stanton, Theodore Weld (known as Theo, son), 59, 65, 106, 135, 159, 168, 172, 191–92

Starrett, Helen Ekin, 117

Stone, Lucy, 22, 64, 68, 70–71, 80, 83, 114–15, 120, 145, 194; tensions in leadership of woman's movement and, 126, 127, 128, 170, 172, 180, 188

Stowe, Harriet Beecher, 127, 129–30

Suffrage. *See* Black male suffrage; Voting; Woman suffrage

Sumner, Charles, 104
Supreme Court, U.S., 83, 153, 155, 206
Syracuse, N.Y., national woman's rights
    convention in (1852), 63–64

Taylor family (Fort Edward, N.Y.), 40
Temperance, 14, 36, 37, 51, 54–55, 56, 60,
    61–63, 68, 70–71
Tesla, Nikola, 218
Thirteenth Amendment, 104, 125
Thompson, George, 59
Tilton, Elizabeth (known as Lib),
    156–57
Tilton, Theodore, 156–57, 199–200
Tolstoy, Leo, 183
Tompkins, Sarah J. Smith, 135
Train, George Francis, 119, 121, 122, 126,
    127, 139, 170
Troy Female Seminary, 10, 17
Truth, Sojourner, 114, 150
Tubman, Harriet, 98

*Una*, 79
Underground Railroad, 18–19, 40, 46, 52,
    93, 98
Unitarianism, 40
*United States v. Susan B. Anthony*, 152–55, 162
Universal suffrage, 107, 109, 114, 123, 208
University of Rochester, 215–16
Utah, woman suffrage in, 162, 182, 205,
    209

Vail, Moses (cousin), 41
Van Buren, Martin, 29
Vance, Zebulon, 187–88
Vaughn, Hester, 124
Vest, George Graham, 171, 189
Victoria, Queen, 212
Vosburg, Mrs. J. R., 70
Voting: "educated suffrage" and, 208, 219;
    Fifteenth Amendment and, 125–26, 127,
    128, 138, 139, 140; Quakers' refusal of,
    13, 60; universal suffrage and, 107, 109,
    114, 123, 208. *See also* Black male suffrage;
    Woman suffrage

Wages: married women's right to, 9, 71–72,
    89; unequal, of men and women, 27, 40,
    53, 60, 70, 82–83, 123
Washington, Joseph, 189
Washington, woman suffrage in, 176, 182,
    209

Webb, Richard D., 35
Weld, Theodore, 31, 36, 65
Wells, Ida B., 197–98
Whig Party, 40–41
Whittier, John Greenleaf, 37
Willard, Amelia, 65, 95, 98, 159
Willard, Emma, 10, 17
Wollstonecraft, Mary, 47
"Woman" (Stanton), 51
*Woman's Bible, The* (Stanton), 201, 202–3,
    204, 206
Woman's Christian Temperance Union,
    182
"Woman's Declaration of Rights," 158
*Woman's Journal*, 128, 170
Woman's rights conventions, 63, 70, 81,
    85; canceled due to Civil War, 96, 99.
    *See also specific convention sites*
Woman suffrage, 47, 48, 50, 51–52, 64, 73,
    89, 97, 104, 125–29, 134, 140–41,
    167–74, 220, 221; black male suffrage
    and, 105–6, 107–8, 109, 128; Centennial
    Celebration and, 157–58; congressional
    committees and, 131, 137–38, 139–40,
    147, 171–72, 184, 185, 187–88, 193–94,
    210, 221; constitutional amendment and
    (see Sixteenth Amendment); Elizabeth
    and Susan's lecture tours on, 121, 142–47,
    161; in municipal elections or local
    affairs, 162, 178; New Departure and,
    131, 138, 139, 147, 151, 155; petition
    campaign for, 107, 108; state referendums
    on, 113–21, 128, 161, 162, 173–74,
    196–97, 204–6 (*see also specific states*);
    Susan's arrest and trial and, 152–55;
    tensions in leadership of woman's
    movement and, 126–29, 148–49, 162,
    169–70, 172, 180, 186, 188; in territories,
    162, 176, 182, 189–90, 211; women
    running for elected office and, 108–9;
    women showing up at polling places and,
    147, 150–55, 160. *See also* National
    American Woman Suffrage Association;
    National Woman Suffrage Convention
Woman Suffrage Bazaar (1900), 217
Women's Loyal National League, 101–2,
    104
Women's New York State Temperance
    Society, 61–62, 66–67
Wood, Samuel, 113, 114, 117, 120
Woodhull, Victoria, 137–39, 140–41, 142,
    148–49, 156, 157, 170, 173

*Woodhull and Claflin's Weekly*, 137, 148

Worcester, Mass., national woman's rights conventions in (1950 and 1951), 52, 56, 63–64, 135

Worcester Hydropathic Institute, 81

Working Woman's Association, 124

World's Anti-Slavery Convention (1840), 31, 33–34

World's Columbian Exposition (1893), 192, 195–96

World's Temperance Convention (1853), 68, 70–71

Wright, Martha Coffin, 46, 50–51, 88, 96, 116, 136, 137, 140, 162, 199, 221

Wyoming, woman suffrage in, 162, 189–90, 209